Blues For Dummies®

P9-DCX-718

Cheat Sheet

Map of Important Places in Blues History

1. **Baton Rouge:** If you're wondering exactly where and when Louisiana "swamp blues" was born, try Baton Rouge in the 1950s. The Baton Rouge area was home base to Slim Harpo, Lightnin' Slim, and many others. Other blues artists recorded in nearby Crowley, Louisiana.

2. **California:** Both Los Angeles and the San Francisco Bay area have had active blues and R&B scenes since the late 1940s. Notable blues artists from the West Coast include Pee Wee Crayton, Lowell Fulson, James Harman, Wynonie Harris, and Etta James.

3. **Chicago:** Chicago is generally considered to be the modern-day center of the blues. Home of the fabled Chess studio, it's also where Willie Dixon, Howlin' Wolf, Little Walter, Muddy Waters, and others recorded their greatest music and made blues history in the 1950s and 1960s.

4. **Kansas City, MO:** In the 1930s and 1940s, Kansas City was a center for both blues (with Big Joe Turner and the birth of the boogie-woogie piano style) and jazz (Count Basie, Lester Young, and the birthplace of Charlie Parker). Best known in song through the 1960s rock 'n' roll standard, "Kansas City" by Wilbert Harrison.

5. **Memphis:** Home to the famous Beale Street district (where W.C. Handy and many others played at the turn of the century) and the legendary Sun recording studios, where owner Sam Phillips recorded Howlin' Wolf, B.B. King, and Elvis Presley (plus Johnny Cash, Roy Orbison, and others) in the early 1950s.

6. **Mississippi Delta:** The Mississippi Delta is the agricultural region of the state generally considered to be the birthplace of the blues. Artists who were born or worked in this region include Son House, Robert Johnson, Charlie Patton, Muddy Waters, and many others.

7. **New Orleans:** New Orleans, the Crescent City, has a long and rich musical tradition. The city's native musical gumbo includes everything from the blues (Guitar Slim), to jazz (Louis Armstrong, King Oliver), to R&B and soul styles (Professor Longhair, Irma Thomas).

8. **Piedmont Region:** The Piedmont is a region of the country that stretches from the Carolinas down to Georgia. This area is famous for producing great acoustic blues artists during the 1920s and 1930s, including Barbecue Bob, Blind Blake, Reverend Gary Davis, Blind Boy Fuller, Brownie McGhee, Blind Willie McTell, and Ma Rainey.

9. **St. Louis:** A city best known in blues history for being immortalized in song (W.C. Handy's "St. Louis Blues"). Rocker Chuck Berry, R&B artist Ike Turner, and blues artists Albert King and Little Milton all worked there during the 1950s.

10. **Texas:** Dallas, Houston, and Austin all played a major part in the development and history of Texas blues. Famous blues artists who were born or worked in Texas include Clarence "Gatemouth" Brown, Lightnin' Hopkins, Blind Lemon Jefferson, Janis Joplin, Stevie Ray Vaughan, the Fabulous Thunderbirds, Johnny Winter, and T-Bone Walker.

IDG BOOKS WORLDWIDE

...For Dummies: Bestselling Book Series for Beginners

Blues For Dummies®

Cheat Sheet

Big Moments in the Blues

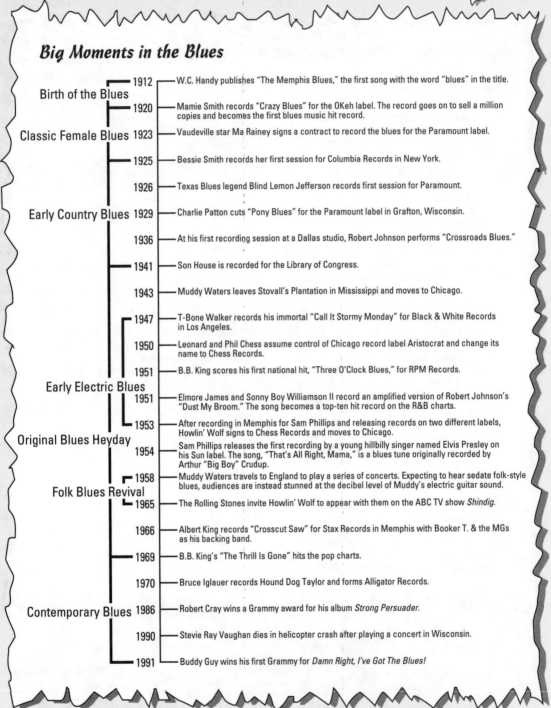

Birth of the Blues

1912 — W.C. Handy publishes "The Memphis Blues," the first song with the word "blues" in the title.

1920 — Mamie Smith records "Crazy Blues" for the OKeh label. The record goes on to sell a million copies and becomes the first blues music hit record.

Classic Female Blues **1923** — Vaudeville star Ma Rainey signs a contract to record the blues for the Paramount label.

1925 — Bessie Smith records her first session for Columbia Records in New York.

1926 — Texas Blues legend Blind Lemon Jefferson records first session for Paramount.

Early Country Blues **1929** — Charlie Patton cuts "Pony Blues" for the Paramount label in Grafton, Wisconsin.

1936 — At his first recording session at a Dallas studio, Robert Johnson performs "Crossroads Blues."

1941 — Son House is recorded for the Library of Congress.

1943 — Muddy Waters leaves Stovall's Plantation in Mississippi and moves to Chicago.

1947 — T-Bone Walker records his immortal "Call It Stormy Monday" for Black & White Records in Los Angeles.

1950 — Leonard and Phil Chess assume control of Chicago record label Aristocrat and change its name to Chess Records.

1951 — B.B. King scores his first national hit, "Three O'Clock Blues," for RPM Records.

Early Electric Blues

1951 — Elmore James and Sonny Boy Williamson II record an amplified version of Robert Johnson's "Dust My Broom." The song becomes a top-ten hit record on the R&B charts.

1953 — After recording in Memphis for Sam Phillips and releasing records on two different labels, Howlin' Wolf signs to Chess Records and moves to Chicago.

Original Blues Heyday **1954** — Sam Phillips releases the first recording by a young hillbilly singer named Elvis Presley on his Sun label. The song, "That's All Right, Mama," is a blues tune originally recorded by Arthur "Big Boy" Crudup.

1958 — Muddy Waters travels to England to play a series of concerts. Expecting to hear sedate folk-style blues, audiences are instead stunned at the decibel level of Muddy's electric guitar sound.

Folk Blues Revival

1965 — The Rolling Stones invite Howlin' Wolf to appear with them on the ABC TV show *Shindig*.

1966 — Albert King records "Crosscut Saw" for Stax Records in Memphis with Booker T. & the MGs as his backing band.

1969 — B.B. King's "The Thrill Is Gone" hits the pop charts.

1970 — Bruce Iglauer records Hound Dog Taylor and forms Alligator Records.

Contemporary Blues **1986** — Robert Cray wins a Grammy award for his album *Strong Persuader*.

1990 — Stevie Ray Vaughan dies in helicopter crash after playing a concert in Wisconsin.

1991 — Buddy Guy wins his first Grammy for *Damn Right, I've Got The Blues!*

...For Dummies: Bestselling Book Series for Beginners

 ™

References for the Rest of Us!™

BUSINESS AND GENERAL REFERENCE BOOK SERIES FROM IDG

Do you find that traditional reference books are overloaded with technical details and advice you'll never use? Do you postpone important life decisions because you just don't want to deal with them? Then our *...For Dummies*™ business and general reference book series is for you.

...For Dummies business and general reference books are written for those frustrated and hard-working souls who know they aren't dumb, but find that the myriad of personal and business issues and the accompanying horror stories make them feel helpless. *...For Dummies* books use a lighthearted approach, a down-to-earth style, and even cartoons and humorous icons to diffuse fears and build confidence. Lighthearted but not lightweight, these books are perfect survival guides to solve your everyday personal and business problems.

> *"More than a publishing phenomenon, 'Dummies' is a sign of the times."*
> — The New York Times

> *"...you won't go wrong buying them."*
> — Walter Mossberg, Wall Street Journal, on IDG's ...For Dummies™ books

> *"A world of detailed and authoritative information is packed into them..."*
> — U.S. News and World Report

Already, millions of satisfied readers agree. They have made *...For Dummies* the #1 introductory level computer book series and a best-selling business book series. They have written asking for more. So, if you're looking for the best and easiest way to learn about business and other general reference topics, look to *...For Dummies* to give you a helping hand.

IDG BOOKS WORLDWIDE ™

5/97

BLUES FOR DUMMIES®

by Lonnie Brooks, Cub Koda,
and Wayne Baker Brooks

Foreword by Dan Aykroyd

Afterword by B.B. King

IDG Books Worldwide, Inc.
An International Data Group Company

Foster City, CA ♦ Chicago, IL ♦ Indianapolis, IN ♦ New York, NY

Blues For Dummies®

Published by
IDG Books Worldwide, Inc.
An International Data Group Company
919 E. Hillsdale Blvd.
Suite 400
Foster City, CA 94404
www.idgbooks.com (IDG Books Worldwide Web site)
www.dummies.com (Dummies Press Web site)

Library of Congress Catalog Card No.: 98-85428

ISBN: 0-7645-5080-2

Printed in the United States of America

10 9 8 7 6 5 4 3 2 1

1E/RZ/QV/ZY/IN

Distributed in the United States by IDG Books Worldwide, Inc.

Distributed by Macmillan Canada for Canada; by Transworld Publishers Limited in the United Kingdom; by IDG Norge Books for Norway; by IDG Sweden Books for Sweden; by Woodslane Pty. Ltd. for Australia; by Woodslane Enterprises Ltd. for New Zealand; by Longman Singapore Publishers Ltd. for Singapore, Malaysia, Thailand, and Indonesia; by Simron Pty. Ltd. for South Africa; by Toppan Company Ltd. for Japan; by Distribuidora Cuspide for Argentina; by Livraria Cultura for Brazil; by Ediciencia S.A. for Ecuador; by Addison-Wesley Publishing Company for Korea; by Ediciones ZETA S.C.R. Ltda. for Peru; by WS Computer Publishing Corporation, Inc., for the Philippines; by Unalis Corporation for Taiwan; by Contemporanea de Ediciones for Venezuela; by Computer Book & Magazine Store for Puerto Rico; by Express Computer Distributors for the Caribbean and West Indies. Authorized Sales Agent: Anthony Rudkin Associates for the Middle East and North Africa.

For general information on IDG Books Worldwide's books in the U.S., please call our Consumer Customer Service department at 800-762-2974. For reseller information, including discounts and premium sales, please call our Reseller Customer Service department at 800-434-3422.

For information on where to purchase IDG Books Worldwide's books outside the U.S., please contact our International Sales department at 650-655-3200 or fax 650-655-3295.

For information on foreign language translations, please contact our Foreign & Subsidiary Rights department at 650-655-3021 or fax 650-655-3281.

For sales inquiries and special prices for bulk quantities, please contact our Sales department at 650-655-3200 or write to the address above.

For information on using IDG Books Worldwide's books in the classroom or for ordering examination copies, please contact our Educational Sales department at 800-434-2086 or fax 817-251-8174.

For press review copies, author interviews, or other publicity information, please contact our Public Relations department at 650-655-3000 or fax 650-655-3299.

For authorization to photocopy items for corporate, personal, or educational use, please contact Copyright Clearance Center, 222 Rosewood Drive, Danvers, MA 01923, or fax 978-750-4470.

is a trademark under exclusive license to IDG Books Worldwide, Inc., from International Data Group, Inc.

About the Authors

Lonnie Brooks is one of the true modern-day legends of the blues. His soulful blues style and engaging stage presence have made him one of the most popular performers on the blues scene.

His career dates back in the early 1950s when zydeco great Clifton Chenier "discovered" Lonnie (who was known as Guitar Junior then) and invited him to join Chenier's famous Red Hot Louisiana Band. In the mid-1950s, Lonnie cut a series of Gulf Coast proto-rock 'n' roll hits, including "Family Rules" and "The Crawl," which were later recorded by Johnny Winters and The Fabulous Thunderbirds and are now considered swamp-rock classics. In 1960, while working in Sam Cooke's touring caravan, Guitar Junior fell hard for the Chicago blues, changed his name to Lonnie Brooks, joined bluesman Jimmy Reed's touring band, and recorded for the Mercury, Chess, and Capitol labels.

Lonnie's unique sound — a melding of hard Chicago blues, rock 'n' roll, rhythm and blues, funky Cajun boogie, and country twang — snagged him a contract with Chicago's famed Alligator Records. Lonnie went on to become one of Alligator's biggest stars, recording seven albums loaded with his signature guitar playing and rich vocals. In 1980 his album *Bayou Lightning* won a Grand Prix Award (Europe's equivalent of the Grammy) and in 1988 his album *Live From Chicago* was nominated for a Grammy Award.

Current releases from Lonnie include the CDs *Roadhouse Rule* and *Deluxe Edition,* a compilation of Lonnie's greatest hits. Lonnie currently keeps up an international touring schedule, playing more than 200 shows each year, and can be seen in the *Blues Brothers* movie sequel, *Blues Brothers 2000.*

Cub Koda is a multifaceted performer with a long history in both rock 'n' roll and the blues. Koda is best known for his multimillion-selling hit "Smokin' In The Boys' Room" (one of two gold records Cub has earned) and the solo roots-rock and blues records he's made since 1980. Cub has also recorded and toured with Hound Dog Taylor's backing group, the Houserockers, and contributed a track to the *Hound Dog Taylor — A Tribute* CD on Alligator Records.

Koda began writing his "Vinyl Junkie" column in 1979, which now appears monthly in *Discoveries,* a magazine devoted to record collecting and music history. Cub's also compiled and written liner notes for more than 50 compact discs of vintage music for various labels, including releases of 1950s rockabilly on the legendary Sun label, a Spike Jones retrospective, and a series of rare blues material on the Excello label that won Cub the Living Blues Critic's Award for Best Reissue Liner Notes in 1996. Koda is also a contributing editor to the *All Music Guide to the Blues.* With a dual-edged career going full blast, Cub continues to write, compose, record, and tour with seemingly little sign of slowing down.

Wayne Baker Brooks made his musical debut at the age of 5 playing percussion on a drum kit made out of boxes and spoons for one of his father Lonnie's home recordings. Since 1991, Wayne has played rhythm and lead guitar with the Lonnie Brooks band, in which he shares the stage with his brother Ronnie and other members of the band.

Wayne considers himself lucky to have grown up around blues legends such as Muddy Waters, Willie Dixon, and Albert Collins. Listening to them and learning from them, Wayne gained appreciation for the roots of the blues. Today, as part of a new generation of blues musicians, Wayne honors his classic Chicago blues roots while adding elements of Memphis soul and Texas rock to his brand of "power blues." Wayne has jammed with Luther Allison, Buddy Guy, Jonny Lang, John Mayall, Chris Robinson of the Black Crowes, Otis Rush, Slash of Guns 'N' Roses, Koko Taylor, and Junior Wells. He toured internationally with bluesman Kenny Neal during the Alligator Records 25th Anniversary Tour.

Wayne also performs with his own band, runs a Blues in the Schools educational program in Chicago, and is founder and president of the Blues Island Production Company, for which he produces blues music, books artists for Blues in the School events, promotes shows, and plans blues-themed parties. In his spare time, Wayne writes music and loves to jam at Chicago blues clubs.

ABOUT IDG BOOKS WORLDWIDE

Welcome to the world of IDG Books Worldwide.

IDG Books Worldwide, Inc., is a subsidiary of International Data Group, the world's largest publisher of computer-related information and the leading global provider of information services on information technology. IDG was founded more than 25 years ago and now employs more than 8,500 people worldwide. IDG publishes more than 275 computer publications in over 75 countries (see listing below). More than 60 million people read one or more IDG publications each month.

Launched in 1990, IDG Books Worldwide is today the #1 publisher of best-selling computer books in the United States. We are proud to have received eight awards from the Computer Press Association in recognition of editorial excellence and three from *Computer Currents'* First Annual Readers' Choice Awards. Our best-selling ...*For Dummies*® series has more than 30 million copies in print with translations in 30 languages. IDG Books Worldwide, through a joint venture with IDG's Hi-Tech Beijing, became the first U.S. publisher to publish a computer book in the People's Republic of China. In record time, IDG Books Worldwide has become the first choice for millions of readers around the world who want to learn how to better manage their businesses.

Our mission is simple: Every one of our books is designed to bring extra value and skill-building instructions to the reader. Our books are written by experts who understand and care about our readers. The knowledge base of our editorial staff comes from years of experience in publishing, education, and journalism — experience we use to produce books for the '90s. In short, we care about books, so we attract the best people. We devote special attention to details such as audience, interior design, use of icons, and illustrations. And because we use an efficient process of authoring, editing, and desktop publishing our books electronically, we can spend more time ensuring superior content and spend less time on the technicalities of making books.

You can count on our commitment to deliver high-quality books at competitive prices on topics you want to read about. At IDG Books Worldwide, we continue in the IDG tradition of delivering quality for more than 25 years. You'll find no better book on a subject than one from IDG Books Worldwide.

IDG
BOOKS
WORLDWIDE

John Kilcullen
CEO
IDG Books Worldwide, Inc.

Steven Berkowitz
President and Publisher
IDG Books Worldwide, Inc.

*Eighth Annual
Computer Press
Awards ≧1992*

*Ninth Annual
Computer Press
Awards ≧1993*

*Tenth Annual
Computer Press
Awards ≧1994*

*Eleventh Annual
Computer Press
Awards ≧1995*

Author's Acknowledgments

From Lonnie Brooks:

I would like to thank the following people for their support, especially Nancy DelFavero, Mark Butler, Kathy Welton, and the rest of the staff at IDG Books; Peter Strand, John Orosz, Carol Lockett, Bruce Iglauer, Nora Clarke, Buddy Guy, The House of Blues, Dick Shurman, *Living Blues* magazine, Buzz Kilman, Mr. A, Pervis Spann, Jim Gaines, Marty Salzman, Koko Taylor, Cookie, Jerry Coltro, Raymond J. Pohl, Mary Smith, Agnes Copeland, Lorraine Owens, Betty Miller, Shure Brothers, Jim Allen, Jim Kilough, Gibson Guitars, Hamer Guitars, and Shelly and Coco. Thanks also to the members of The Lonnie Brooks Band, David Miller, Patrick Doody, Steve Utting, Jesse Hutson, Clay Taylor, and George Laskarin. A special thanks to my wife, Jeannine, and to my kids Linda and Lee, Denise and Russell, Jackie and Bobby, and my baby girl Gina, and a very special thanks to my sons Wayne and Ronnie.

From Cub Koda:

The Cubmaster wishes to thank the following people for making this book possible: My lovely wife, Lady J, for putting up with my kicking out the backs of chairs and acting irascible for six months while I labored over the manuscript; my friend and manager Doc Cavalier for keeping the business part of it straight; the project editor, Nancy DelFavero, for keeping this book clearly focused and on course; Michael Erlewine at Matrix Software for steering me to this project in the first place; and the acquisitions editor, Mark Butler, for keeping a good thought throughout.

From Wayne Baker Brooks:

I would like to thank IDG Books, Nancy DelFavero, and Mark Butler (both of you were awesome), Heather Albright, Nickole Harris, Kevin Thorton, and Kathy Welton. Thanks go out to these people who do a great job at Keeping The Blues Alive — Bruce Iglauer, Ron Kaplan, Garry Buck, Nora Clarke, Mike Kappus, Scott Cameron, Jerry Del Giudice, Howard Stovall, Pat Mitchell, The Blues Foundation, Sid Sedenberg, Dan Aykroyd, Lisa Pastrana, *Living Blues* magazine, Marty Salzman, Eric Maxen, Bill Dahl, John Gabersiak, Shirley Dixon, John Boncimino, Becky Mussell, and Tina France.

Special thanks to my mom Jeannine Baker; my kids Sharonda, Jonathon, Keira, and Shekeila; my brothers Ronnie, Russell, Bobby, and Lee; my sisters Linda, Jackie, Denise, and Gina; Laura Johnston for her help; my friends Timothy Turner, Peter Strand, Jason Blakenship, Frank and Lilly Blinkal, Geoff Rodgers, Beverly Howell, Sheila Casserly, Buddy Guy, Koko Taylor, Bernard Allison, and James Solberg. And, a very big thanks to Sharon Hughes and Sarah Kennedy for the great time we had during the Chicago Blues Fest which led to the writing of this book.

Dedication

This book is dedicated to the friends we lost recently — Luther Allison, Johnny Copeland, and the great Junior Wells.

Publisher's Acknowledgments

We're proud of this book; please register your comments through our IDG Books Worldwide Online Registration Form located at http://my2cents.dummies.com.

Some of the people who helped bring this book to market include the following:

Acquisitions, Editorial, and Media Developent

Project Editor: Nancy DelFavero

Acquisitions Editor: Mark Butler

Copy Editor: Constance Carlisle

Technical Editor: Bill Dahl

Editorial Manager: Mary C. Corder

Editorial Assistants: Paul E. Kuzmic, Donna Love, Michael D. Sullivan

Production

Project Coordinator: E. Shawn Aylsworth

Layout and Graphics: Lou Boudreau, J. Tyler Connor, Angela F. Hunckler, Todd Klemme, Drew R. Moore, Anna Rohrer, Brent Savage, Janet Seib, Kate Snell

Proofreaders: Christine Berman, Kelli Botta, Chris Collins, Rachel Garvey, Nancy Price, Rebecca Senninger, Janet M. Withers

Indexer: Steve Rath

Special Help

Maureen F. Kelly, Paula Lowell, Patricia Yuu Pan, Allison Solomon, Kevin Thornton, Karen Young

General and Administrative

IDG Books Worldwide, Inc.: John Kilcullen, CEO; Steven Berkowitz, President and Publisher

IDG Books Technology Publishing: Brenda McLaughlin, Senior Vice President and Group Publisher

Dummies Technology Press and Dummies Editorial: Diane Graves Steele, Vice President and Associate Publisher; Mary Bednarek, Director of Acquisitions and Product Development; Kristin A. Cocks, Editorial Director

Dummies Trade Press: Kathleen A. Welton, Vice President and Publisher; Kevin Thornton, Acquisitions Manager

IDG Books Production for Dummies Press: Michael R. Britton, Vice President of Production and Creative Services; Beth Jenkins Roberts, Production Director; Cindy L. Phipps, Manager of Project Coordination, Production Proofreading, and Indexing; Kathie S. Schutte, Supervisor of Page Layout; Shelley Lea, Supervisor of Graphics and Design; Debbie J. Gates, Production Systems Specialist; Robert Springer, Supervisor of Proofreading; Debbie Stailey, Special Projects Coordinator; Tony Augsburger, Supervisor of Reprints and Bluelines

Dummies Packaging and Book Design: Robin Seaman, Creative Director; Jocelyn Keleita, Product Packaging Coordinator; Kavish + Kavish, Cover Design

◆

The publisher would like to give special thanks to Patrick J. McGovern, without whom this book would not have been possible.

◆

Contents at a Glance

Cartoons at a Glance

By Rich Tennant

page 319

page 337

page 43

page 5

page 231

page 271

Fax: 978-546-7747 • E-mail: the5wave@tiac.net

Table of Contents

Foreword

· ·

*T*he blues . . . a journey that takes you from sad to glad with stops along the way at despair, loss, heartache, and uncertainty, and then ultimately hope and joy.

The seeds of what would become the blues, and later rock 'n' roll, were first heard in Sunday morning church services in small towns like Panther Burn and Sunflower, Mississippi. The gospel choirs soaked up the burble of the organ and the boom of the piano, and those tunes were taken home to clapboard porches. Add a pluck on a National steel guitar here, a suck on a Chinaboy wood reed harmonica there, throw in a goat string attached to a wash bucket, and the Delta blues sound was born.

When the blues went electric, legends such as Son House, John Lee Hooker, Howlin' Wolf, James Cotton, Little Walter, and Big Walter embraced the tube amps alongside Roosevelt Sykes and Otis Spann at the keyboards, taking blues to a higher and more powerful level.

The blues can claim some of the absolute great artists in music — Ma Rainey, Bessie Smith, T-Bone Walker, the Kings B.B., Albert, and Freddie, Muddy Waters, Albert Collins, Clarence "Gatemouth" Brown, Etta James, Koko Taylor, and even some of the rock crossover stars such as Elvis, Jimi Hendrix, and Janis Joplin. Rock legends including the Rolling Stones, Led Zeppelin, The Animals, and even The Beatles all have the blues to thank for their rhythm, soul, and spirit.

A rare few artists qualify as 24-hour blues devotees, a select membership that includes Lonnie Brooks, who interprets blues with his precision guitar and honey vocals; Cub Koda, who's played, recorded, and written about the blues for more than 30 years; and Lonnie's son Wayne, with his inspired musical talents and love of the blues. These gentlemen are full-time players and lovers of the blues and have prepared a book to help all blues fans to better appreciate the subject. *Blues For Dummies* lays it all out, all the basics for us simple folks who can never know enough about this shining and awe-inspiring part of American culture.

Dan Aykroyd

Introduction

· ·

*H*ave you noticed that blues music (and blues musicians) seem to be everywhere lately? Turn on the TV and you can hear the blues used to sell everything from soft drinks and pantyhose to sport utility vehicles and bran muffins. Blues music clubs are springing up all over the place and a number of blues legends have even hung out their own shingles. (Plus, that nationwide chain of blues clubs may just be coming to your town soon.) What was once a fringe musical scene with a small but intensely devoted following has now gone mainstream in a big way.

We like to think that we're experiencing a new blues renaissance to rival the early blues wave of the 1920s and the blues explosion of the 1960s. We also think that without the blues there would have been no rock 'n' roll, no soul or funk, no rap or hip-hop, and jazz would have turned out a whole lot different. *Blues For Dummies* is more than a one-stop-shopping reference on the blues, it's also a celebration of one of the most important art forms of this century (and beyond).

Why This Book Is for You

One of the myths about the blues, which we're downright happy to eradicate, is that it belongs to some insider's club of music know-it-alls — the type who insist on calling Muddy Waters by his real name (it's McKinley Morganfield, by the way). We say nuts to that.

We figure that you bought this book because you listen to the blues and enjoy it. We also figure that you may not know a whole lot about the blues and you just want to be better informed so that you can more fully appreciate everything about the music. We also think that you'd appreciate hearing the whole blues story, which consists of far more than three guitar chords and woeful stories of love gone bad.

We intend for this book to introduce you to the rich musical stew that is the blues, without any stuffy lectures and heavy-duty music theory. *Blues For Dummies* tells you about the artists who have made the biggest impact on the blues and who have created the best blues music ever. This book also delves into the nitty-gritty of the music itself — where it came from, how it's played, and where you can get some of it yourself, because the best cure for the blues is a healthy dose of blues music.

How to Read (And Listen to) This Book

We broke this book into six separate chunks to keep all the similar stuff together and to make it easier for you to digest it all.

Part I: What Are the Blues and How Do I Know I Have Them?

The first part of the book tells you how to recognize the blues when you hear it, alerts you to the key elements of the blues sound, and fills you in on the blues music's connection to jazz, rock, country, and other types of music.

Part II: Who's Who in the Blues

This biggest, juiciest part of the book provides biographies of many of the most-famous and influential artists in the blues and lists recommended recordings made by each of the artists.

Part III: Listening to the Blues

This part of the book is designed for the true blues consumer. We give you suggestions for building a collection of quality blues music and directions on where to go to hear real, live blues.

Part IV: Playing the Blues

In this part we provide expert advice about playing the blues at both the amateur and professional level (and a real-life peek into a blues musician's life on the road).

Part V: The Blues Community

In case you're wondering if anyone else has the same thirst for the blues that you do, we introduce you to the worldwide blues community — organizations, foundations, societies that promote the blues, the online blues network, and blues-oriented Web sites — and we even offer suggestions for throwing a blues-themed party.

Part VI: The Part of Tens

The final part of the book includes quick bits of information that may come in handy sometime, such as who's doing what to spread the word about the blues and how much that old and scratchy blues 78 record is *really* worth.

The music CD

Another cool thing about this book is the CD that comes with it (you can find it glued inside the back cover). We've collected a dozen of the all-time great blues recordings by some of the real legends. So while you're reading about the famous names in the blues, you can also listen to some of their best work.

And, one tip about this book's set-up: It's designed so you can just jump in and start reading anywhere. Or, if linear motion is your style, you can begin at page one and just keep going. If you're looking for a particular subject or artist, a quick glance at the Table of Contents or Index can steer you in the right direction.

Icons Used in This Book

To make this book as user-friendly as possible, we've sprinkled helpful graphic icons here and there in the left-hand margins of the pages. These icons point out information you may want to home in on, or that you may want to skip right over (for now).

Stop here for words of wisdom from one of the great blues artists of all time and some juicy tidbits on other blues stars he knows and admires.

This icon points out what we think is the best recording ever made by a particular artist (that's readily available, of course) or the best recorded sampling of a certain style of blues.

You already have a great book on the blues right here, but you may want to do more in-depth reading on a particular artist or topic. Just in case, this icon alerts you to other printed titles worth checking out.

If we delve into an advanced topic or high-end terminology, we give you plenty of advance notice with this icon.

Whenever we wander into subject matter that's typically the province of blues snobs, we warn you with this icon.

This icon tips you off to a suggestion (or a heads-up) to help you get more enjoyment out of your blues experience.

The CD that comes with this book is loaded with great blues songs and recorded performances. When we mention one of them in the book, this icon magically appears nearby.

Part I

What Are the Blues and How Do I Know I Have Them?

THOUGH HEAVILY DISGUISED, CERTAIN LYRICAL TRADEMARKS WOULD SOON GIVE AWAY BARRY MANILOW'S NEW IDENTITY

I got a woman, who kicks me around,
She hurts me so good, I smile when I frown.
If she ever left me, I'd be so empty
I'd fling open the window, and cry for...

MAAAANDY!

In this part . . .

*L*ike the road sign for the juke joint up ahead says, "When you're near it, you'll hear it." In this part, we fill you in on the blues basics — the major components of the blues sound, the various strains of blues music, and how the blues has influenced other musical forms (and vice versa).

Chapter 1

Recognizing the Blues Sound and Style

*B*lues music is the original cross-over star. Everyone from hard rockers to country warblers to lounge singers have taken a stab at it and said with a straight face that they're playing the blues. (To prove it, one of the authors of this book has an album entitled *The 101 Strings Play the Blues* hidden away in his record collection, but we won't bring it up again if you don't.)

As a character in one of our favorite B-movies says, "There's all kinds of critters in Farmer Vincent's fritters." When you take a bite of the blues, you can taste all sorts of musical and lyrical ingredients mixed into the batter, but how do you know it's really the blues you're sampling and not something else? For help in fine-tuning your blues-music taste buds, just read on.

Tossing Away Some Old Notions

To understand what the blues *is,* you first have to understand what the blues *isn't,* and perhaps lose some preconceived notions along the way. Over the years, the blues has been portrayed as slow, mournful music rife with bleak images of personal despair ("my baby left me, I'm feelin' low, and my mojo's in the shop") — in short, the ultimate bummer music. However, just the opposite is true.

The blues is a means of self-expression, a *catharsis,* if you will. (You don't mind if we toss around some five-dollar words, do you?) It provides the artist and, in turn, the listener with some relief from the pain of life's woes. It's the ultimate Saturday night music.

The Story Of The Blues by Paul Oliver (Chilton). One of the very first comprehensive books on the history of blues music and still one of the very best. Invaluable as a resource on the history of the blues from plantation times up to the golden blues age of the 1960s. Loaded with great photos, illustrations, and pictures of record company ads and labels, this is one coffee table book that deserves to be out on display.

Deep Blues by Robert Palmer (Penguin Books). This musical and cultural history of the blues was written by the late Robert Palmer, former chief music critic for *The New York Times.* Palmer displays enormous insight into the development of the blues, and it's a darned good read, to boot.

Listening for the Key Ingredients

Getting back to the question, "So how do I know it's the blues when I hear it?", the answer is in zeroing in on some of its key elements.

- ✔ One of the major ingredients of the blues sound is the *beat.* Even in acoustic (as opposed to electrically amplified) variants of the blues, a pronounced rhythm is in everything that's played. The reason for this is simple — the blues has always been a sort of *dance* music, whether the tempo is a shuffling boogie or a slow blues grind.

- ✔ The second key ingredient to the blues is the *singing.* Strongly rooted in the gospel tradition, blues vocals are full of raw emotion and heartfelt expression, performed in a direct and honest manner.

  How the voice should be used to sing the blues is not so easy to pin down. Blues singing can be as smooth as Bobby "Blue" Bland's or as nasty as Howlin' Wolf's, and it's still the blues. Blues singing isn't about perfect pear-shaped tones and hitting every note precisely on pitch, but rather about projecting genuine emotion (from mournful to jubilant and all points in between) directly into the music.

- ✔ Another element of the blues is the *instrumentation.* Like the old saw about the walking and quacking duck, if a blues band *looks* and *sounds* like a blues band, it probably *is* a blues band. You won't find cellos, oboes, or a timpani on the bandstand at your local blues club. What you will see are guitars, drums, a harmonica, and maybe a washboard or two if you're in Louisiana. (You can find more information on musical instruments later in this chapter and in Chapter 10.)

Various Artists — *Blues Masters, Volume 10: African Roots* (Rhino). A 16-track compilation that features work songs, African music, hymns, and other early examples of blues music. An illuminating history of the origin of the blues, and you don't have to pick through a big boxed set to hear some really good stuff.

Checking Out the Instrumental Lineup

One way to define a particular kind of music is to examine the instruments that are used to play it. Most blues musicians make use of the following musical apparatus:

Guitar

Although it didn't come into common usage until the 1920s when it replaced the banjo as the instrument of choice in Southern rural music, the guitar is now *the* common denominator of the blues. An electric guitar's sound (once it's put through an amplifier) has enormous range — from silky smooth to raw and distorted. (For in-depth information on the various types of blues guitars, turn to Chapter 10.)

Guitars in the blues come in two basic varieties, electric and acoustic. The acoustic guitar is most often used as vocal accompaniment — usually the singer and the instrumentalist are one and the same person — or as a solo instrument with a musical voice all its own. Electric guitars are almost always employed in a small band format in the blues.

Harmonica

The harmonica is the second great solo voice of the blues. Certainly the most portable instrument of the blues, the harmonica — also known as a *harp* — came to be used prominently in the blues at about the same time as the guitar. (For you virtuosos, the harmonica is considered a *reed* instrument, played by forcing air over metal and wooden reeds.)

Warm and expressive, the harmonica's broad tones can range from piercing acoustic wails to the full-bodied sounds of the electric Chicago style of harp playing. Played acoustically, the harmonica's sound is shaped (or altered, depending how you look at it) by the way the player cups and moves his hands around the instrument. What comes out are vocal-like nuances that resemble a warble.

When played in the electrically amplified style, the harp is placed directly against a cheap microphone (yes, in this case, cheaper is better) to emit a "dirty" distorted tone that's the hallmark of the modern Chicago style.

Piano

The piano was perhaps the first musical instrument — besides the human voice — to be heard on a blues record. Nowadays, the piano most often shows up only in *classic* blues band lineups, but for many years the piano reigned as blues music's premier solo instrument.

Like the guitar, the piano is capable of playing both rhythm chords and solo passages simultaneously. Perhaps the piano's greatest contribution to the blues was the *boogie-woogie figure* played with the left hand. Adapted to the bass strings of the guitar, this is a mainstay musical figure in the blues and one of its strongest rhythms.

Boogie-woogie is primarily a piano blues style in which the left hand does most of the work, rolling out repetitive bass *figures* (or melodic *motifs*). The left hand keeps the steady rhythm, while the right hand improvises. And, depending on the player, the right hand *does* know what the left hand is doing.

Drums

Although the history of drums in African-American music can be traced back several centuries, the modern-day drum set was introduced to the blues right after World War II. By the early 1950s after the formation of the first electric blues combos, a set of drums on a blues bandstand was a regular sight.

Unlike the massive drum setups used by rock groups, the drum kit you'll see in a blues band is much more basic. The blues drum setup is largely modeled after the standard four- to five-piece sets used by jazz players.

In the blues, the drummers rarely solo out, but instead concentrate on keeping a steady beat that locks the group into a solid rhythm.

Bass

The other member of the rhythm section, the bass guitar, first started appearing in blues bands in the late 1940s. Back then, it was the standard acoustic upright bass that was used exclusively. It produced deep, sonorous tones that held the musical foundation of the rhythm. In addition, the strings of the upright bass could be slapped to produce a percussive effect.

By the early 1950s, the upright bass was replaced by electric solid-body models that featured an elongated neck similar to a six-string guitar's. Many musicians switched from the bulky upright to the smaller electric, which has been a staple of the blues rhythm section ever since.

Horns and woodwinds

Trumpets, trombones, saxophones, and clarinets were used to play the blues in early jazz combos. With the exception of jump-blues groups and R&B-soul bands, which feature a full horn section including saxophones, trumpets, and the occasional trombone, horns are rarely seen in modern blues combos.

The tenor saxophone is the most commonly heard horn instrument in the blues. Although some blues artists have employed a sax section in their groups — typically two tenors and, in New Orleans blues, a baritone sax as well — it's usually a lone tenor saxophonist you'll find in modern blues bands.

A Word on Blues Lyrics

One of the most wrong-headed notions about the blues is that the lyrics *always* deal with depressing topics. If you want to blow holes through that stereotype real quick, just listen to Louis Jordan for example. A list of his greatest hits — "Let The Good Times Roll," "Choo-Choo Ch'Boogie," "Caldonia," and "Saturday Night Fish Fry" — reads like a roll call of everything worth celebrating in life.

Nevertheless, the blues does contain some downright disturbing subject matter that wouldn't surface in your average pop song. When Lightnin' Slim sings about a herd of bedbugs eating holes in his hands and feet in "Bed Bug Blues," he isn't complaining about the condition of his hotel room, folks.

Blues music dealt with the harsh realities of life long before pop musicians decided to make their lyrics "relevant." With subject matter that included insect plagues and floods, grinding poverty, and abusive treatment at the hands of the plantation boss, blues tackled these topics fearlessly. Even with the universal themes of love longed for and lost, the blues addresses them in a far more direct and down-to-earth way than pop music ever did (or could). You won't find a recording of Peggy Lee warbling "hellhound on my trail" anymore than you'd find one with Muddy Waters reminiscing about "chestnuts roasting on an open fire." (While there *is* such a thing as Christmas Blues music, *that* isn't it.)

"*Everybody* has the blues, no matter how rich you are. Sometimes a rich person can have the blues worse than a poor person, but in a totally different way. Blues comes from the heart; that's what you hear in those songs. When I write a song, I try to put that blues feeling into it, no matter what I'm singing about. You can be in love and sing the blues about it, even if you're happy! As a matter of fact, a lot of blues lyrics could be put to a rock tune or a country song. It's the *feeling* and having that blues thing in them that really makes them the blues."

It's Not a Club Circuit: Examining 12-Bar Blues

If you've ever spent any time around a serious blues musician or music aficionado, you've probably heard the phrase "12 bar blues" tossed about. A *bar* is a musical phrase, a way of measuring the music against its rhythm, and blues songs are structured in a 12-bar format, which we explain in the following few sections.

Defining bars and measures

The rhythm — not the *tempo* or relative speed of the music — is measured in a *time signature*. Ninety-nine percent of all blues music is played to a 4/4 time signature. If you can count to four (go ahead, 1-2-3-4 — hey, nice work!), you've just counted out exactly one *bar* of blues music.

The term "bar" is derived from each of the vertical lines that are drawn through a musical staff. (The *staff* is the set of horizontal lines on which musical notes are written.) The bar lines mark off metered units of a piece of music, which are called *measures*.

To hear where the *backbeat* falls, just stress the *2* and *4* of a four-beat count (1-**2**-3-**4**, 1-**2**-3-**4**) and you've got your basic rhythm together. Now take that rhythm, speed it up or slow it down according to the tempo you want, and you've got the blues beat.

A standard blues progression generally consists of three chords that are usually, but not always, played in a major and rather than a minor key. In a 12-bar progression, each of those chords is assigned four bars of the progression (and that number may change depending on the song's structure).

Where does the number 12 figure in?

In basic, bare-bones blues, the main musical *theme* is expressed in the first four-bar line, then repeated again in bars five through eight. The closing four bars usually cap the original theme line by putting a twist on it or summing up the original statement. And that adds up to 12 bars (or measures).

A musical *theme* is simply the melody that distinguishes one tune from another. The lyrical theme is the story line. And thyme is an herb.

To get an idea of how this works, take a look at the following example, a typical bar count for a standard 12-bar blues verse. (This 12-bar "chunk" is a *stanza* of the song lyric.) To hear the rhythm, count each number out loud. Below each metered line are the lyrics, which state a basic theme that's repeated in the second line, and then wrapped up in the closer.

1-2-3-4, 2-2-3-4, 3-2-3-4, 4-2-3-4

I woke up this morning, feeling oh so bad . . .

5-2-3-4, 6-2-3-4, 7-2-3-4, 8-2-3-4

I woke up this morning, feeling oh so bad . . .

9-2-3-4, 10-2-3-4, 11-2-3-4, 12-2-3-4

Thinking about my baby and it makes me oh so sad.

Turnarounds and stop time

In a 12-bar blues song, the final four bars are used as a musical *resolve* to finish off the verse. This four-bar figure typically either ends the song or sets up another 12-bar stanza. When it does the latter, it's referred to as a *turnaround*.

Mastering musical turnarounds that resolve on the third chord of a three-chord progression is an art form in and of itself. To hear resolves done to their best and most creative effect in a two-guitar format, check out the recordings of Muddy Waters or Jimmy Reed (see Chapters 5 and 7 for some suggested recordings by these two artists).

Another structural variant in 12-bar blues is something loosely referred to as *stop time.* The first four bars of a verse are extended to eight bars, and "breaks" or "stop time" figures are inserted to chop up the verse line. That eight-bar line is then appended to the remaining eight bars of a standard

12-bar blues progression. A perfect example of stop time is found in the Willie Dixon composition "I'm Your Hoochie Coochie Man," made famous by Muddy Waters.

Keeping the Beat

Several rhythms are used to anchor the blues, with almost all of them grounded in a 4/4 beat. The three most commonly used rhythms in blues music are the *shuffle,* the *slow blues,* and what's generically described as the *rock beat.* Although it is possible to create such a thing as a blues waltz or a blues rumba, virtually all of the blues you hear — both live and on record — use the three big beats.

The shuffle

Shuffles come in many varieties. The Chicago variant has a strong back beat stressing the two-count and four-count of a four-beat measure. The *Texas shuffle* is generally more lilting and easy-going, and puts greater accentuation on the first and third beats of a measure. A *boogie* is another variant of the shuffle, which is played to an incessant rhythm that's designed for dancing. Boogie's stylistic cousin is the *cut shuffle,* a sprightly two-beat rhythm that also shows up in Dixieland jazz and country music.

When a Texas shuffle is played at a rapid to hyper-paced tempo, it's usually dubbed a *Vegas shuffle,* so called because its most avid practitioner was Las Vegas lounge entertainer Louis Prima.

Slow blues

Although the term "slow blues" is fairly self-explanatory, there's no hard and fast rule as to which tempo makes the blues *slow.* Generally speaking, slow blues is any blues played at the same tempo that a ballad or folk song would be played. While mood and ambiance can enrich slower numbers, a tempo that is too slow sometimes causes musicians to overplay to fill in the aural "holes." (If you've ever heard a guitarist playing a million miles an hour while the rest of the band is just creeping along in the background, you already know what that sounds like.)

The rock beat

The rock beat didn't really show up in the blues until the mid- to late-1960s, but now it's used regularly by most contemporary artists. A rock beat takes your standard blues progression and applies it to a 4/4 rock 'n' roll beat (or a funk or soul variant of rock). A good example of the blues-rock beat is found in Junior Wells's "Messin' With The Kid" or Albert Collins's "Mastercharge."

Tunes with all three beats

To help you "put a face with a name" for the various blues beats, the following table lists some classic blues tunes and the various rhythms they employ. Also included is the best-known version by artist and record label. (By the way: A number of these tunes are on the *Blues For Dummies* CD — "Killing Floor," "Juke," "The First Time I Met the Blues," "Okie Dokie Stomp," and "Frosty.")

	Counting Out the Beat with 25 Blues Tunes	
The Rhythm	*The Tune*	*The Best-Known Version*
Cut Shuffle	"Got My Mojo Working"	Muddy Waters (MCA-Chess)
Cut Shuffle	"Hi-Heel Sneakers"	Tommy Tucker (MCA-Chess)
Cut Shuffle	"Feelin' Good"	Little Junior's Blue Flames (Rhino)
Cut Shuffle	"Just Like I Treat You"	Howlin' Wolf (MCA-Chess)
Cut Shuffle	"Big Boss Man"	Jimmy Reed (Vee-Jay)
Rock Beat	"The Thrill Is Gone"	B.B. King (MCA)
Rock Beat	"Born Under A Bad Sign"	Albert King (Mobile Fidelity)
Rock Beat	"Baby Scratch My Back"	Slim Harpo (Excello/Hip-O)
Rock Beat	"Killing Floor"	Howlin' Wolf (MCA-Chess)
Rock Beat	"Messin' With The Kid"	Junior Wells (Paula)
Shuffle	"Baby What You Want Me To Do"	Jimmy Reed (Vee-Jay)
Shuffle	"Mama Talk To Your Daughter"	J.B. Lenoir (Relic)
Shuffle	"Juke"	Little Walter (MCA-Chess)
Shuffle	"Walking By Myself"	Jimmy Rogers (MCA-Chess)
Shuffle	"Sweet Home Chicago"	Robert Johnson (Columbia/ Legacy)

(continued)

Counting Out the Beat with 25 Blues Tunes *(continued)*

The Rhythm	The Tune	The Best-Known Version
Slow Blues	"The Sky Is Crying"	Elmore James (Capricorn)
Slow Blues	"The First Time I Met The Blues"	Buddy Guy (MCA-Chess)
Slow Blues	"Double Trouble"	Otis Rush (Paula)
Slow Blues	"Nine Below Zero"	Sonny Boy Williamson II (Arhoolie)
Slow Blues	"Long Distance Call"	Muddy Waters (MCA-Chess)
Texas Shuffle	"Farther Up The Road"	Bobby "Blue" Bland (MCA)
Texas Shuffle	"Okie Dokie Stomp"	Clarence "Gatemouth" Brown (Rounder)
Texas Shuffle	"Everyday I Have The Blues"	B.B. King (MCA)
Texas Shuffle	"Reconsider Baby"	Lowell Fulson (MCA-Chess)
Texas Shuffle	"Frosty"	Albert Collins (MCA)

Chapter 2

The Many Shades of Blues

- -

In This Chapter

▶ Getting the lowdown on the major blues styles

▶ Finding out who the best-known players are

▶ Discovering related reading and listening

- -

*T*he title says it all — the musical world is colored with more than just one shade of blues music and more than just one way of playing the music. In this chapter, you discover the different blues movements and the people who made those styles popular.

Some of the various blues styles — jump blues and piano blues, for instance (which we also call *subgenres* for you virtuosos) — are related to each other and we point that out along the way. We also list those artists who are the leading practitioners of a particular style. We did this to help you identify the acknowledged masters of a particular strain of blues when you go shopping for some blues music.

We also tell you about other suggested reading that you can find at your local bookstore or library, just in case you want more information about a particular style or artist. And, to keep all the bases covered, we even recommend a recording or two you may want to add to your collection.

Classic Female Blues

The word "classic" gets tossed about nowadays with increasing frequency. The term is used to describe everything from 1960s automobiles, to 1970s rock music, to 1980s video games. But *classic female blues* is a term that's been used for decades to describe a particular style of the blues.

Every style is the best style

Some blues critics think that history and chronology determine the superiority of one blues style over another. They'll tell you that that the older blues music, such as the Delta sound, is superior to the newer stuff simply because it came first. In their minds, anything more complicated than just one singer strumming one acoustic guitar on the front porch of his house is just way too over-produced and commercially oriented to be taken seriously.

Some blues fans raised on rock 'n' roll and pop music like their blues loud and electric, something that conforms to what *they* think of as the blues. Other blues aficionados champion the 1950s to mid-1960s period of Chicago blues, citing the wealth of talented musicians and great recordings that came out of that relatively short period of time.

Some folks want to hear their blues all dressed up with horns and a big band sound. Others like their blues sprinkled with liberal doses of jazz inflections, while still others want the blues as down-home and simple as it can possibly get. Some blues fans soak up doom-filled and introspective lyrics, while other blues consumers don't listen to the words at all and are content to simply savor the blues for the sheer musicianship involved. Others just want a party-hearty sound that rolls on full tilt.

The bottom line is this: No one style of blues is better than another; they're just different. All kinds of blues music are alive and well for you to investigate, and you'd be doing yourself a great disservice if you didn't sample as many flavors from the blues menu as possible. But, before you place your order, discover the various blues stew recipes that can fill your musical plate. Then you can decide which sounds best suit your listening tastes.

In the early 1920s when blues music first made it onto records, the recordings were dominated by female singers and musicians. For the most part, male blues singers weren't recorded until the later part of that decade. Most of those first female artists started out in vaudeville, or performed in *tent shows* or *medicine shows* (low-budget road shows, usually set up in circus tents outside of city limits, which were peopled with traveling salesmen hawking some form of cure-all elixir).

The early female blues artists possessed both a strong command of popular musical forms and a jazz sensibility, and were equipped with voices loud enough to be heard without the help of amplification. While some worked with only piano accompaniment, several were backed with full jazz bands that included a clarinet, trumpet, trombone, saxophone, and drums.

As the dominant form of blues music, the classic female style flourished only until the mid-1930s. But every powerhouse female blues singer who followed in later decades drew her inspiration from the early classic female performers. Notable artists who performed in the Classic Female Blues style include the following women (more information on them can be found in Chapter 4):

- ✔ Ma Rainey
- ✔ Bessie Smith
- ✔ Mamie Smith
- ✔ Victoria Spivey

Various Artists — *Blues Masters, Volume 11: Classic Blues Women* (Rhino). This 18-song compilation makes an excellent entry-level disc to some of the best classic female artists. This CD features ground-breaking tunes by Mamie Smith (including the first blues hit, "Crazy Blues," in 1920), Trixie Smith, Bessie Smith, Ida Cox, Victoria Spivey, Sippie Wallace, and the ever sublime Ma Rainey. Start digging in to early female blues music right here.

Jump Blues

If you cross up-tempo blues with big-band era jazz, and add stabbing horn lines darting around boogie-woogie rhythms, you'd have *jump blues* — a swingy amalgam of styles that occupies a unique slot in the blues sound.

Jump blues grew out of the boogie-woogie piano craze of the 1940s. It typically features a quick beat, big-band era jazz influences (primarily in the horn lines used by the trumpets, trombones, and saxophones), a powerful lead vocalist fronting a combo with at least six players, plus a horn section ranging from a couple of saxophones to a full nine pieces.

Jump blues may lack modern accouterments, such as flashy electric guitar work, but that doesn't prevent it from being party music of the first order. (It isn't called "jump" blues for nothing.) A full-scale jump blues revival seems to be going on, with bands such as Roomful of Blues attracting enthusiastic crowds with happy feet.

Some artists who made jump blues popular include the following (for more information on Louis Jordan and Big Joe Turner, see Chapter 4):

- ✔ Nappy Brown
- ✔ Roy Brown
- ✔ Wynonie Harris
- ✔ Louis Jordan
- ✔ Jimmy Liggins

- Amos Milburn
- Roy Milton
- Big Jay McNeely
- Johnny Otis
- Louis Prima
- Red Prysock
- Big Joe Turner
- Jimmy Witherspoon

Various Artists — *Blues Masters, Volume 5: Jump Blues Classics* (Rhino). This wonderful CD collection contains classic tracks by the genre's most avid practitioners, including Louis Prima, Wynonie Harris, Tiny Bradshaw, Red Prysock, Roy Brown, and Big Joe Turner.

Country Blues

Country blues is really a catch-all phrase that describes all the various forms of acoustic blues. Country blues covers all the regional styles, including Mississippi Delta (Son House, Robert Johnson, and others), Piedmont (Brownie McGhee and Sonny Terry), early Chicago (Big Bill Broonzy), pre-electric Louisiana (Smoky Babe), and Atlanta (Barbecue Bob).

Country blues also embraces all the stylistic variants of early guitar-based blues music, including folk and *songster* blues (a style performed by blues artists such as Mance Lipscomb and Leadbelly, who sang older non-blues and folk-based material) and ragtime (Blind Blake).

Like the Delta blues, the *Piedmont blues* refers to a style of playing that came out of a particular region of the country, in this case the southeastern U.S. between Richmond and Atlanta. The Piedmont blues style was distinguished by lively finger picking on the guitar. Early practitioners included Blind Blake, Blind Willie McTell, Barbecue Bob, and Brownie McGhee.

Although some country blues practitioners switched over to electric guitars after World War II (with little or no noticeable change to their basic playing style), country blues is, by and large, acoustic music. Country blues is alive and thriving. In fact, many newer artists such as Rory Block and John Hammond, Jr. consider themselves country blues practitioners.

Notable artists who performed in the country blues style include the following individuals (for more information on many of these artists see Chapters 4 and 5):

- ✔ Blind Blake
- ✔ Mississippi John Hurt
- ✔ Skip James
- ✔ Leadbelly
- ✔ Mance Lipscomb
- ✔ Bukka White

Mississippi John Hurt — *Avalon Blues* (Columbia/Legacy). This 13-track CD compilation brings together all of Hurt's 1928 recordings for the Okeh label, a remarkable collection of early country blues at its finest.

The Life & Legend of Leadbelly by Charles Wolfe and Kip Lornell (Harper Collins). Extensively researched and well-written, this is one of the best biographies available on the life and times of this major folk and blues musician. Nobody working in popular music before the rock 'n' roll era had a more tumultuous life than Leadbelly, who spent several stretches in prison before being discovered and recorded by folk music researchers.

Blind Blake — *Ragtime Guitar's Most Foremost Picker* (Yazoo). Blake was such a mysterious bluesman that no one knows exactly which year he was born or even when he died. But during the late 1920s and early 1930s, he left behind a substantial body of good-time music filled with astounding finger-picking guitar work. This 23-track compilation samples some of his very best.

Piano Blues

While the guitar wasn't introduced to the blues until the 1920s, the piano had been part of the blues music mix since the turn of the century, decades before the blues was recorded.

Piano blues encompasses myriad blues offshoots, including turn-of-the-century *ragtime* style (similar to the piano music heard in the movie *The Sting*), *boogie-woogie* (an up-tempo style played mostly with the left hand and having a pronounced eight-beats-to-the-bar figure), New Orleans *second line* (a hip-shaking blues piano style combining heavily syncopated bass notes laced with Caribbean rhythms), *barrelhouse blues* (a hard-pounding form of boogie-woogie), West Coast jazz stylings (what we call "supper club" blues), and Chicago blues (which is covered later in this chapter).

Both the lead (or solo) and rhythm parts can be simultaneously played on a piano, which make it an almost self-contained combo. The piano can, however, also fit perfectly into most any blues band configuration. Current practitioners of piano blues include Ron Levy, Dave Alexander, Pinetop Perkins, and Patrick Hazell.

Some of the well-known artists who were masters at "radiating the 88s" include the following:

- Albert Ammons
- Leroy Carr
- Professor Longhair
- Big Maceo Merriweather
- Sunnyland Slim
- Otis Spann
- Roosevelt Sykes

Chess Blues Piano Greats (MCA-Chess). This two-CD sampling contains great Chicago-based piano blues from Otis Spann, Lafayette Leake, Eddie Boyd, and Willie Mabon. A nice reminder that Chicago blues music is made with more than just guitars and harmonicas.

British Blues

The distinction between British blues and other styles is more than just a matter of geography; British blues could almost be called a "school" of popular music. In the late 1950s to early 1960s (when British blues was being born) musicians across the Atlantic put their heart and soul into replicating American blues styles. Working largely off the music of electric Chicago blues artists and acoustic folk-blues players (with jazz music influences tossed in), British blues was performed with enormous admiration for the early blues artists (bordering on elevating them to sainthood).

By the mid-1960s, British blues had been filtered through the post-Beatles rock sound and evolved into a musical form that most critics say epitomizes the blues-rock style. Many of the early British "pub blues" bands (the British equivalent to an American bar band) became chart-topping rock groups, among them the Rolling Stones, the Animals, the Yardbirds, and the original lineup of Fleetwood Mac.

Some notable artists who plied their trade playing British blues include these people (and you can find out more about Eric Clapton in Chapter 6):

- The Animals
- Jeff Beck
- Duster Bennett
- Eric Clapton
- Fleetwood Mac (early recordings)
- Rory Gallagher
- Alexis Korner
- John Mayall
- Gary Moore
- Rolling Stones (early recordings)
- The Yardbirds

If you want proof of the influence of the blues on a generation of British rockers, just check out the following releases:

John Mayall's Bluesbreakers with Eric Clapton (Mobile Fidelity). This is Eric Clapton's shining moment on lead guitar and the album that introduced the British blues scene to an American audience.

The Rolling Stones — *England's Newest Hitmakers* (ABKCO). The Stones' debut album is loaded with solid blues performances.

The Yardbirds — *Five Live Yardbirds* (Rhino). Clapton appears on lead guitar with the legendary Yardbirds, recorded live in a club setting.

Fleetwood Mac — *Black Magic Woman* (Epic). The best of their early blues recordings made before Fleetwood Mac became California pop-rock superstars.

Jeff Beck — *Truth* (Epic). Call it a rock album, or call it a blues-rock album, this record has scorching versions of B.B. King's "Rock Me Baby" and Howlin' Wolf's "I Ain't Superstitious."

Blues: The British Connection by Bob Brunning (Blanford Press). Brunning was in the original Fleetwood Mac lineup before John McVie joined their ranks. Brunning went on to serve time in Savoy Brown and other British blues bands. Brunning brings first-hand knowledge of British blues-era bands and the music they played exactly as it went down. With great chapters on John Mayall, the Yardbirds, the Pretty Things, and Rory Gallagher, this book concentrates on the mid- to late-1960s period when British blues hit its peak and hot guitar players seemed to be playing on every street corner.

Modern Electric Blues

Modern electric blues musicians replicate older styles of blues playing — mostly from the 1950s and 1960s — and interject it with more contemporary influences. In fact, you could say a little bit of everything is mixed into modern electric blues, including rock, soul, and funk.

Modern electric practitioners include those playing a blues-rock hybrid (replete with flashy guitar solos and plenty of feedback and distortion), bands faithfully reinterpreting older-style Chicago and country blues artists (such as Muddy Waters and Robert Johnson), and artists taking the blues into the future by combining the traditional styles of blues with funk, hip-hop, and electronic music.

Some contemporary artists who have been at the forefront of modern electric blues music include the following (for more information on many of these folks, turn to Chapter 6):

- Luther Allison
- William Clarke
- Deborah Coleman
- Robert Cray
- Debbie Davies
- Jonny Lang
- Bonnie Raitt
- Roomful of Blues
- Kenny Wayne Shepherd
- George Thorogood
- The Fabulous Thunderbirds
- Stevie Ray Vaughan
- Joe Louis Walker

Stevie Ray Vaughan — *Greatest Hits* (Epic). Stevie Ray was the most popular performer of the modern era and this sampling is a perfect introduction to his sound and style.

Luther Allison — *Reckless* (Alligator). Luther's final album before his death in 1997 was not only one of his best, but a great example of what the modern blues should sound like.

Modern Acoustic Blues

The modern version of acoustic blues is steeped in tradition, with contemporary artists reviving and replicating the older, country-style blues playing of artists such as Son House, Blind Blake, Brownie McGhee, Robert Johnson, and others who worked in the 1920s and 1930s.

Performing largely in a solo format (although some modern acoustic artists prefer full-band backing), these performers revive old classics and write new material that captures the flavor of the original music. Modern acoustic is primarily a guitar-based format with the harmonica also used as a solo or a supplemental instrument.

Some notable artists who have revived the traditional acoustic blues sound (while putting their own stamp on it) include the following (some of whom you can also read about in Chapter 6):

- Rory Block
- John Cephas
- Guy Davis
- John Hammond, Jr.
- Corey Harris
- Alvin Youngblood Hart
- Taj Mahal
- Keb' Mo
- John Mooney
- Bonnie Raitt (early recordings)
- Roy Rogers
- Kenny Sultan
- Harmonica Phil Wiggins

Introduction to Acoustic Blues by Kenny Sultan (Centerstream Publications). Sultan is one of the finest modern players in acoustic blues. This instruction package includes a book and cassette. Aspiring guitarists are introduced to the fundamentals of acoustic guitar playing. You can also find useful information on basic rhythms, techniques of famous players, finger-style playing techniques, open tunings, and slide guitar playing.

John Hammond, Jr. — *The Best Of John Hammond* (Vanguard). Sample the music of one of the first — and best — modern acoustic blues players in this fine collection.

Rhythm & Blues and Soul Blues

Perhaps the most modern of all the blues styles we talk about in this chapter of the book, R&B-soul blues combines 1950s rhythm-and-blues styles (such as that of Big Joe Turner, LaVern Baker, and Clyde McPhatter) with mid-1960s Southern soul music (such as that of Otis Redding, James Carr, and O.V. Wright) to create a distinctive hybrid with a strong blues flavor to it.

Some R&B-soul artists work within a small-combo format, but the majority of R&B-soul performers use a horn section (even if it's a small one) to flesh out their sound, not unlike the lineup of the famous Memphis Horns.

Notable singers and musicians who have played or are playing in the R&B-soul blues style include the following artists (for more on Bobby "Blue" Bland, see Chapter 5):

- Johnny Adams
- Kip Anderson
- Bobby "Blue" Bland
- Otis Clay
- Vernon Garrett
- Denise LaSalle
- Latimore
- Little Milton
- Bobby Rush
- Johnnie Taylor
- Artie "Blues Boy" White

Denise LaSalle — *Smokin' In Bed* (Malaco). For a solid collection of tunes that will appeal to fans of blues, soul, and R&B, add this one to your shopping list.

Regional Blues Styles

Regionalism flourished throughout the early development of the blues. Within a particular geographic area — Chicago, Texas, or the Mississippi Delta, for instance — blues musicians worked and performed in proximity to each other, thereby sharing influences and developing their own way of playing that was different from the way blues music was played and sung in other parts of the country.

Soon after phonograph records and radio broadcasts began spreading blues music across the country, the Chicago style of Jimmy Reed and Muddy Waters was influencing Louisiana blues artists such as Slim Harpo and Lightnin' Slim, who in turn inspired a young Ray Charles. Regional influences still exist in blues music to this day.

Chicago blues

Probably the most popular and widely heard style of blues, Chicago blues is what most people think of when you mention live blues played in a night-club setting. The popular image of a tiny bandstand in a smoky bistro crowded with musicians jamming away on electric guitars, amplified harp (or harmonica to you classical fans), piano, bass, and drums can be traced directly to the early Chicago style.

Chicago grew to be a blues music center during the 1930s and 1940s when thousands of Mississippians (including blues players from the Delta) left the fields and headed north for factory work. Chicago blues is really a hybrid — it captures the rawness of the Delta style, then it pumps it up with a fully amplified sound packed into a small-combo format.

The early electric Chicago blues of the 1950s featured highly amplified harmonica, slide guitar, and piano as its lead instruments. Use of this instrumental lineup was pioneered by the original Muddy Waters band. By the late 1950s, the Chicago blues style continued to evolve with a new breed of guitarists taking their inspiration from B.B. King, whose style of single-string playing (as opposed to strumming) helped shape the sound of the modern blues guitar.

Some of the notable artists associated with the Chicago blues style of playing include the following (you can find out more about these artists in Chapters 4 and 5):

- Lonnie Brooks
- Big Bill Broonzy
- Willie Dixon

- Buddy Guy

- Elmore James

- Big Walter Horton

- Tampa Red

- Jimmy Reed

- Jimmy Rogers

- Otis Rush

- Magic Sam

- Hound Dog Taylor

- Little Walter

- Muddy Waters

- Junior Wells

- Howlin' Wolf

Chicago Blues by Mike Rowe (DaCapo). Rowe covers the days of the pre-War Chicago style and its stars (Tampa Red, John Lee "Sonny Boy" Williamson, and Big Bill Broonzy), the blues heyday (Muddy Waters and Howlin' Wolf), and the 1960s Chicago blues revival (Buddy Guy and Magic Sam). This book is jam-packed with great photos, record label shots from old 78 singles, trade advertisements from *Billboard* and *Cash Box* magazines, and show posters.

I Am The Blues by Willie Dixon and Don Snowden (DaCapo). Nobody had a bigger role in shaping the sound of modern electric Chicago blues than Willie Dixon. As a songwriter, producer, arranger, and bass player, he made major contributions throughout blues music's original heyday in the 1950s and 1960s. Dixon tells his story in a way that makes you want to hear more, especially how he wrote all those songs that became blues classics. Fascinating stories told by one of the all-time great movers and shakers in the blues.

The Chess Blues-Rock Songbook (MCA-Chess). This two-disc collection features the original versions of blues songs found on the play lists of rockers the world over. Ten of the 36 tunes were penned by Willie Dixon and are considered blues-rock classics. Although you'll find a few rock 'n' roll selections (including five classics by Chuck Berry), this collection of blues singles answers the question, "Who did that song first?"

Delta blues

Delta blues also goes by the moniker *Mississippi blues,* but either term refers to the blues style of playing that came out of the Delta region of Mississippi, the fertile cotton-producing area of the state (not to be confused with the Mississippi River delta). Most Delta blues is played *acoustically,* in the manner of the original recordings of the 1920s and 1930s, with hollow-bodied guitars that were made before the electric guitar was introduced to the blues in the late 1940s. This brand of blues stands as the first guitar-based blues to be recorded.

In the Delta style, performers typically work solo, and are usually self-accompanied on an acoustic six-string guitar. In the Delta style, you can also hear the first flowerings of the small-combo format — sometimes called a *string band* combo — that would reach its zenith with the Chicago and modern electric blues styles.

The Delta blues style features plenty of great guitar playing with elaborate finger-picking, slashing slide work, and deep boogie rhythms, and all of it delivered with an emotional depth that oozes from each recording.

In the *slide guitar* style of playing, the guitarist depresses the strings of the guitar with a cylindrical slider worn over a finger of the left hand, rather than using his or her fingertips. This style is also called *bottleneck* guitar because early sliders were fashioned from glass bottlenecks that were fired to create a smooth surface. Slider material has included everything from bones to knives to various metals, such as brass.

Notable early blues artists who played in the Delta style include some of the very greatest (for more information on these artists, see Chapter 4):

- Son House
- Robert Johnson
- Mississippi Fred McDowell
- Charlie Patton

Various Artists — *Deep Blues* (Atlantic). This collection contains modern-day Delta blues (recorded in 1992) played with a passion that's seldom heard on today's records. Features great performances by R.L. Burnside, Junior Kimbrough, Big Jack Johnson, Booba Barnes, and others.

Various Artists — *The Friends of Charlie Patton* (Yazoo). This superb collection contains original Delta-Mississippi blues recordings by some of the all-time greats, including performances by Tommy Johnson, Son House, Willie Brown, Kid Bailey, Bukka White, and Ishmon Bracey.

Searching For Robert Johnson by Peter Guralnick (E.P. Dutton). A small (83 pages) biography of the life, times, and music of the most famous (and mysterious) Delta bluesman of all time. While hard-and-fast facts about Robert Johnson are in short supply, Guralnick assembles as many of them as possible, and his quotes from legendary blues players Johnny Shines and Robert Jr. Lockwood are so provocative that they alone are worth the cover price. Guralnick carefully speculates — and sheds new light — on how Johnson created the timeless music he did during his short and tragic life.

King of the Delta Blues: The Life and Music of Charlie Patton by Stephen Calt and Gayle Wardlow (Rock Chapel Press). Patton ruled the Delta blues circuit during the 1920s and early 1930s, packing the barrelhouses and selling loads of records to prove it. An essential read in finding out about the early history of the Delta blues, it includes an appendix featuring examples of Patton's songs and a glossary of expressions used in his lyrics.

Texas blues

Texas blues has been around for most of the 20th century and blossomed during two historical periods. Its first flowering occurred during the 1920s when it embraced both country-blues and songster traditions associated with the Southwest. The next creative phase introduced the post-War electric Texas blues style — notable for its jazz-influenced, single-string guitar soloing made famous by T-Bone Walker, who later influenced B.B. King and others. In electric Texas blues, guitarists usually play in front of a backing combo featuring a sizable horn section of four or more pieces.

Stylistic hallmarks of the Texas blues (sometimes referred to as *Texas shuffle* blues) include its relaxed, laid-back playing style (that moves just a little bit behind the beat), and a pronounced swing to the rhythm, not unlike that heard in a 1930s- or 1940s-era jazz group.

Artists who helped shape the Texas blues sound include the following (for more information on these blues players, see Chapters 4 through 6):

- ✔ Clarence "Gatemouth" Brown
- ✔ Albert Collins
- ✔ Johnny Copeland
- ✔ Lightnin' Hopkins
- ✔ Blind Lemon Jefferson
- ✔ T-Bone Walker

Those guitar tricks have names

Single-string soloing is a common guitar-playing technique in which instrumental solos or melodies are picked out one string at a time on the instrument, rather than strummed. (Think of B.B. King's playing.)

When a guitarist pushes against a string to produce a different note without otherwise changing the position of his hand, it's called *string bending*. If a *trill* (a rapid change in pitch) is produced when the string is bent, that's called a *finger vibrato*.

Blues guitar solos usually incorporate elements of single-string soloing, string bending, and finger vibrato. Add a snappy suit, an amplifier, and a sound check and what more do you need?

Various Artists — *Blues Masters, Volume 3: Texas Blues* (Rhino). An excellent 18-track CD collection that covers the lengthy history of Texas blues, it features outstanding tracks by Blind Lemon Jefferson, Lightnin' Hopkins, T-Bone Walker, Clarence "Gatemouth" Brown, the Fabulous Thunderbirds, and Stevie Ray Vaughan.

Memphis blues

When blues aficionados discuss Memphis blues, they could be talking about either of two completely different strains of the music — the brand from the 1920s or that from the 1950s. The Memphis blues of the 1920s developed during the era of tent and medicine shows, which featured traveling bands of musicians and other entertainers who played the small-time vaudeville venues that dotted the rural landscape. Later, *jug bands* (also called *spasm bands* for reasons completely unknown) appeared on the scene.

Jug bands played a humorous, almost novelty, type of blues for tips or for their own amusement. Jug bands took the basic string-band lineup and fleshed it out with makeshift "instruments" that imitated the brass and woodwind sounds of a jazz combo. Usually added to the mix was someone blowing into an empty jug in order to imitate the sound of a tuba (thus the name *jug band*). These outfits introduced the now-standard practice of assigning song parts for lead and rhythm guitar, something all modern-day blues bands still do.

By the early 1950s, Memphis blues had plugged in and gone electric. Fans of electric Chicago blues probably found late-period Memphis blues equally appealing. Featuring highly amplified (and sometimes extremely distorted) guitar work, Memphis blues from that period was played with loads of aggressive and thunderous drumming. The passionate vocals made the music even more dramatic.

Notable artists who have played the blues Memphis-style include the following people (you can find more on B. B. King and Howlin' Wolf in Chapter 5):

- Gus Cannon
- Memphis Jug Band
- B.B. King (early recordings)
- Furry Lewis
- Howlin' Wolf (early recordings)

Memphis Masters (Yazoo). Subtitled "Early American Blues Classics, 1927–1934," this collection of 20 original, rare-as-hens'-teeth 78s provides an excellent overview of the early Memphis acoustic style. It features important tracks by the Memphis Jug Band, Furry Lewis, and Gus Cannon.

Sun Records Harmonica Classics (Rounder). This disk features 14 tracks by Memphis harmonica wizards Big Walter Horton, Joe Hill Louis, Hot Shot Love, Sammy Lewis, and Doctor Ross. You get a healthy dose of the amplified post-War style that took Memphis by storm in the early 1950s, plus a glimpse into the kind of records Sam Phillips was making before Elvis walked into his Sun Records building.

Good Rockin' Tonight: Sun Records and the Birth of Rock 'n' Roll by Colin Escott with Martin Hawkins (St. Martin's Press). Sam Phillips discovered Elvis, Jerry Lee Lewis, Carl Perkins, Roy Orbison, Charlie Rich, and Johnny Cash. With that stable of talent, Phillips almost single-handedly launched the 1950s rock 'n' roll movement. But before all of that happened, Phillips recorded and released some of the best blues music Memphis had to offer. This book is loaded with great photos and a complete discography for all of Phillips's record labels.

West Coast blues

West Coast blues borrows a large part of its swing tempo and rhythmic lilt from post-War Texas blues, which stands to reason. Many of the most avid practitioners of the West Coast blues were transplanted Texans who began playing in the West Coast style in the late 1940s (see the "Texas blues" section earlier in this chapter).

Although you can find plenty of great West Coast blues guitar players, this style is primarily piano-based (and boasts a number of jump blues artists as well). West Coast blues guitar solos tend to be very fluid and feature jazzy improvisational playing. Artists of note who played in the West Coast blues style include these musicians (for more on Lowell Fulson, see Chapter 5):

- ✔ Charles Brown
- ✔ Pee Wee Crayton
- ✔ Floyd Dixon
- ✔ Lowell Fulson
- ✔ Percy Mayfield
- ✔ Jimmy McCracklin

Lowell Fulson — *The Complete Chess Masters* (MCA-Chess). A two-CD set chronicling Fulson's stay at Chicago's Chess label — full of nonstop, ultra-smooth West Coast blues.

Louisiana blues

Louisiana is a state rich in many native musical styles including jazz, *second-line New Orleans* (a blues piano variant heavy in island rhythms), *Cajun* (a type of folk music played by French Acadians who live in Louisiana), *zydeco* (an African-American variant of the Cajun sound laced with R&B and blues sounds), and *swamp pop* (rock 'n' roll played by Louisiana natives who add their own distinctive touches). In addition, Louisiana blues owes much of its overall sound to post-War Chicago electric blues.

Although heavily influenced by Chicago blues players Muddy Waters and Jimmy Reed (especially), the Louisiana version of Chicago blues is much looser and less emotionally charged than its Windy City counterpart. *Bayou blues* (or *swamp blues*) recordings from this region feature lazy beats and doom-laden reverb that makes the music sound like it was recorded in the thick of the bayou.

Louisiana blues was the stock in trade of several musicians, including these artists (you can find more information on Lightin' Slim and Lazy Lester in Chapter 5):

- ✔ Slim Harpo
- ✔ Silas Hogan
- ✔ Lazy Lester

✔ Lightnin' Slim

✔ Lonesome Sundown

Slim Harpo — *The Best Of Slim Harpo* (Excello-Hip-O). Harpo is the best known of all the Louisiana blues performers, and this is a scintillating collection of his biggest hits.

New Orleans blues

New Orleans is a town best known for throwing the ultimate party come Mardi Gras time. So it's not surprising that the New Orleans brand of blues sounds like a celebration set to music. Heavy on rollicking piano rhythms and energetic horn sections, New Orleans blues counts many jump blues practitioners among its ranks, all of them with a distinct Crescent City flavor to their music.

The New Orleans style is also distinguished by its strong Caribbean rhythms (the rumba beat in particular) and the *second-line strut* derived from the Dixieland style of jazz. New Orleans blues combines a wide range of different styles that coexist happily in one musical stew. Notable artists who cooked up the New Orleans style of blues playing include the following folks (turn to Chapter 5 for more on Guitar Slim):

✔ Dave Bartholomew

✔ Fats Domino (early recordings)

✔ Snooks Eaglin

✔ Smiley Lewis

✔ Professor Longhair

✔ Guitar Slim

I Hear You Knockin' by Jeff Hannusch (Swallow). Hannusch does an admirable job of providing 31 solidly researched portraits of various New Orleans rhythm-and-blues performers, both famous and obscure. This book makes a great reference. It's chock-full of chart listings and features a discography of every important New Orleans blues recording.

Professor Longhair — *Fess: The Professor Longhair Anthology* (Rhino). This two-CD set defines virtually everything that's great about New Orleans style R&B.

Chapter 3

The Blues Connection to Other Music

In This Chapter

▶ Discovering blues music's link to jazz, R&B, rock, gospel, and country

▶ Checking out examples of each musical style

*L*isten close enough and you can hear traces of the blues in virtually every other kind of American music. Sometimes, the connection is inescapable, such as the very direct link between the blues and its musical offspring rock 'n' roll.

In this chapter, we examine five musical forms that all demonstrate strong elements of the blues. In addition, we suggest some representative recordings and other reading that make the connections even clearer.

Jazz: The Chicken or the Egg?

Of all American musical forms, jazz is the one with the strongest — and longest — historical connection to the blues. But trying to figure which genre influenced the other (that is, which came first) is tough to say.

The best historical bet is that both strains of music evolved and influenced each other simultaneously. Bandleader and songwriter W.C. Handy recalled hearing blues street singers and string bands around the turn of the century, which coincided with his first hearing African-American bands playing brass and reed instruments — standard jazz band components.

Legend has it that in 1903 Handy "discovered" the blues while waiting for a train in a Mississippi depot. While trying to catch some shut-eye in the train station, he heard a plaintive sound similar to a Hawaiian steel guitar. The man playing was actually pressing a knife on the strings — more or less playing "slide" guitar. (See the sidebar later in this chapter, "W.C. Handy: The first blues music promoter?")

Jazz bands were the first to feature and record classic female blues singers such as Ma Rainey and Bessie Smith. Jazz bands, including cornetist Buddy Bolden's band in New Orleans, reportedly played almost nothing except blues and blues-derived music at the turn of the century.

After jazz musicians began improvising on pop tunes, jazz music headed in new directions that are still being explored. But even after big band outfits such as the Count Basie and Duke Ellington orchestras became the musical rage, the blues remained a musical touchstone that jazz players turned to as a source of inspiration.

Various Artists — *Masters of Jazz, Volume 1: Traditional Jazz Classics* (Rhino). Tap into this CD and you'll find a nice sampling of early jazz classics with strong blues overtones. Highlights include the New Orleans Rhythm Kings doing "Tin Roof Blues," Bessie Smith's "St. Louis Blues," Frankie Trumbauer with Bix Beiderbecke doing "Singin' The Blues," and Louis Armstrong's "Struttin' With Some Barbecue."

Louis Armstrong and King Oliver — *Louis Armstrong and King Oliver* (Milestone). Long before he was singing and grinning his way through pop material such as "Hello, Dolly" and "What a Wonderful World," Louis Armstrong was the hottest cornet player in New Orleans. Working alongside his mentor, King Oliver, Armstrong made jazz history with these 1923 recordings with Oliver's Creole Jazz Band. This is real New Orleans jazz with a strong blues base to it.

A Pictorial History of Jazz by Orrin Keepnews and Bill Grauer, Jr. (Crown). This 300-page hard-bound book traces jazz history from its earliest beginnings into the 1950s modern era. The early photos are the highlights here and feature some of the early jazz greats, including the only known photo of the legendary Buddy Bolden, leader of New Orleans's first jazz band.

R&B: Putting Some Rhythm in the Blues

Whether you call it rhythm and blues, soul music, jump 'n' jive, or boogie-woogie, music with a big beat has always been one of the strongest elements of the blues. And, as blues musicians moved from their rural homes to settle in the big city, the beat became more pronounced. As time went on, other musical elements meshed with and transmuted this dance-friendly blues offshoot.

The seeds of rhythm and blues were sown by the post–World War II *jump bands.* Spearheaded by artists such as Louis Jordan, jump players took the big band jazz style, slimmed it down to a smaller-combo format, and infused it with a heavy beat.

Figure 3-1:
The jump blues sound was epitomized by Louis Jordan and his combo, shown here in a movie still from *Swing Time of 1946* (photo courtesy of the Everett Collection).

Eventually, the *jump blues* style of the 1940s evolved out of the jump band movement. Laced with a strong boogie-woogie rhythm made for dancing, jump blues featured blasting horn sections and a more urban and jazzier sound than the country blues or string band version being played in Chicago at that time. Big-voiced vocalists were eventually added to the mix, and after that, the music developed into *rhythm and blues,* combining many of the same elements of jump blues but with a stronger emphasis on vocal leads.

The influence of gospel singers on rhythm and blues added a new slant to the music and soon it was simply called R&B. Its mid-'60s incarnation added the label *soul music,* and from then on, it was called R&B-soul by those in the know. R&B-soul combines the best of soul music, gospel, and the blues into a heady mixture of its own.

Unsung Heroes of Rock 'n' Roll by Nick Tosches (Harmony Books). Tosches has an incisive wit (and an R-rated vocabulary). One of the best reads that you'll ever come across on several of the R&B pioneers.

Sweet Soul Music by Peter Guralnick (Harper & Row). Nobody tackles a subject with as much verve and flair as Guralnick does, and this book evokes the times of the soul music movement of the 1960s like no other. Highly recommended.

W.C. Handy: The first blues music promoter?

W.C. Handy was a bandleader and composer who is often referred to as "The Father of the Blues." A statue of him was erected in the Memphis Park that bears his name, he's been honored with his own United States postage stamp, and the annual Handy awards are the most prestigious music awards in the blues.

Born in Muscle Shoals, Alabama, in 1873, W.C. (which stood for William Christopher) was a schooled musician who performed with various tent and minstrel shows throughout the South. In his travels, Handy heard early versions of what later became the blues. Handy claims to have discovered the blues in 1903 when he heard a street musician playing his guitar with a slide, rather than picking the strings with his fingers.

Handy was far from a blues purist. His nine-piece dance band produced upscale entertainment for the African-American community. The early blues music he heard may have been compelling, but he considered it too crude for mass consumption. He changed his mind when a combo consisting of a guitar, mandolin, and string bass played during an intermission at one of his dances. After playing one number, the trio earned more in tips than what Handy's entire band made for the evening.

In 1912, Handy published his first blues composition, "Memphis Blues." The success of this song led to more hits for Handy, including "St. Louis Blues," "Ole Miss," "Beale Street Blues," and "Yellow Dog Blues."

W.C. Handy didn't invent the now standard three-line blues verse, but he was enormously influential in popularizing it. Handy encouraged other composers and music publishers to investigate this new form of music. One of those young composers was Perry Bradford, whose "Crazy Blues" was the first blues song to be recorded when it was covered in 1920 by Mamie Smith. The song was a hit. By the late 1920s, blues and hillbilly music — another previously untapped market — accounted for almost 45 percent of all record sales.

Various Artists — *Jump Blues Classics* (Rhino). This disc is packed with 18 classics of the highest order featuring artists such as Big Joe Turner, Big Mama Thornton, Louis Prima, Ruth Brown, and Wynonie Harris. Not every artist is a household name, but their songs shouldn't be missed for a second. Includes Ann Cole's original "Got My Mojo Working" and Tiny Bradshaw's "Train Kept A-Rollin'."

Various Artists — *Beg, Scream & Shout! The Big Ol' Box of '60s Soul* (Rhino). This six-CD set supplies all the great soul tunes, both well-known and obscure, in a package that justifies its healthy price tag. If you like soul music, this is the one to add to your collection.

Rock 'n' Roll: The Blues Had a Baby . . .

If any form of American music is descended directly from the blues, it's that 20th century phenomenon called rock 'n' roll. From Bill Haley's "Rock Around The Clock" to Chuck Berry's "Johnny B. Goode" to the Rolling Stones' "Honky Tonk Woman," the blues resonates throughout all of rock music.

The phrase "rock 'n' roll" itself can be traced back to the practitioners of up-tempo jazz music of the 1920s. However, rock is by and large unadulterated blues wearing a big beat. For proof of that, listen to Chuck Berry's vocals on "Maybellene," Gene Vincent's "Be-Bop-A-Lula," Carl Perkins's "Blue Suede Shoes," or Wilbert Harrison's rendition of "Kansas City."

The earliest rock 'n' roll tunes were not unlike the 1940s-era jump blues numbers. Consider "Shake, Rattle & Roll" — a highly rhythmic, three-chord blues progression set to a hard driving beat. But rock 'n' roll will be forever cited as the first popular music form to be embraced by the youth culture of *all* races.

As rock 'n' roll has evolved and fragmented itself into a zillion little hyphenate subgenres (it even spawned its own version of blues called blues-rock), rock can always be traced back to its blues roots.

The Sound of The City — The Rise of Rock 'n' Roll by Charlie Gillett (Souvenir Press). This is one of the first great books to tell the tale of early R&B, how it blossomed into rock, and the connections between the two musical styles. It's loaded with information, including a historical discography and a tale that's as big as a stack of Marshall amps.

Chuck Berry — *His Best, Volume 1 and 2* (MCA-Chess). This two-CD set contains 40 classics that helped define the sound of early rock 'n' roll. Berry's inventive wordplay and guitar work are superlative, and his songwriting and playing all have strong, undeniable blues roots.

"Rock 'n' roll is nothing but the blues speeded up; you can call it 'rhythm and blues' or whatever, but it's still *the blues*. When the R&B singers came along in the '40s, they just updated the sound of older singers like Lightnin' Hopkins and John Lee Hooker. Listen to those horns, man! It was a bigger sound with a bigger beat to it. Then rock 'n' roll came along, took that sound, shrunk it down to a small combo format, and put that big beat to it. But it's still *the blues*."

Gospel: Blues with Religion

Once upon a time, blues music and gospel music were compared to the fork in a spiritual road — one path lead to sin, the other to salvation. However, "sacred" gospel music and "profane" blues music cross musical paths more often than you may think.

Many early blues performers, including Son House and Charlie Patton, played both blues and gospel tunes in their live performances. Patton even recorded in both styles, and issued his spiritual recordings under the name of "Elder J.J. Hadley."

Blues vocalizing is derived directly from gospel music. The *trills* (a rapid "shaking" of the voice), the flattening of certain notes, the use of *melisma* (stretching a single syllable across several notes), and the emotional fervor found in the best blues performances have deep roots in church music. Many blues singers got their early vocal training singing in church, and several soul singers — Sam Cooke and Johnnie Taylor among them — made good use of their gospel training and became exceptional rhythm-and-blues vocalists.

Various Artists — *Sacred Steel* (Arhoolie). Although gospel music's connection to the blues is primarily a vocal one, this collection focuses on the steel slide guitar playing heard in the Dominion sect churches of Florida. Recorded live at several church services, the music is wild and unrestrained, a revelation for those who think all church music is stuffy.

Various Artists — *None But The Righteous* (MCA-Chess). This is a wonderful 18-track collection of various gospel artists who recorded for Chicago's Chess Records. The artists range from the famous (Aretha Franklin and her father, C. L. Franklin, the Five Blind Boys of Alabama, and the Soul Stirrers) to the more obscure (the Bells of Joy, the Evangelist Singers of Alabama, and Cleo Jackson Randle). The music is heartfelt and soulful throughout.

Country: Blues with a Twang

On the surface, country music may seem far removed from the blues, but just a quick view of American music history shows that the two musical forms have been keeping steady company for a number of decades.

The fellow we like to think of as the "Father of Country Music," Jimmie Rodgers's, ascended to stardom in the 1920s by singing endless variations of his "Blue Yodel" theme, which was nothing more than a series of blues verses with a cowboy yodel tacked onto the end of every other verse.

Other cowboy singers, including Gene Autry and Jimmie Davis, followed Rodgers's lead in the 1930s and 1940s by constructing country songs with a strong blues-based sound to them. The person most successful at making this musical hybrid into a true art form was the legendary Hank Williams, Sr., whose hits "Move It On Over" and "Mind Your Own Business" display elements of traditional blues lyrics and blues musical structure (sung with Williams's distinctive twang).

The emotionalism in the song lyrics is perhaps the strongest link between country and blues music. Whether the song is about love longed for, love lost, cheating and mistreating, or getting ready for a big Saturday night, both blues and country treat their subject matter with unvarnished honesty.

As country music gains a larger mainstream audience and the median age of country music buyers drops, modern country is beginning to sound more and more like rock 'n' roll, which makes its connection to the blues even stronger.

Country — The Twisted Roots of Rock'n'Roll by Nick Tosches (DaCapo). Check out the updated edition of Tosches's book that examines blues, country, rockabilly, and how they all relate. An entertaining read packed full of insider information of the most obscure sort.

"Country music has got so much of the blues in it, it'll surprise you. Listen to those old Hank Williams songs. Listen to what he's singing about. You think *he* didn't have the blues when he wrote them or was singing them? A lot of us black people listened to white singers on the Grand Ole Opry on our little radios when we were kids. I know I did."

Part II

Who's Who in the Blues

In this part . . .

A century's worth of blues has produced some of the most influential and innovative artists in the history of recorded music. To introduce you to these blues music greats, we profiled as many notable singers, songwriters, and musicians as we could fit in the pages of this book. After reading about these folks you'll probably want to hear some of their music, so we also include our recommended picks for each artist's best recording.

Chapter 4

Early Blues Legends (1900 to 1945)

• •

• •

*T*his chapter of the book examines the lives of those legendary artists who put the blues on the musical map. The singers, songwriters, and musicians featured in these pages were the originators of the blues, and their seminal influence defines much of the blues sound to this day. They were also the first to record blues music, which became a best-selling enterprise as early as the 1920s. The impact these men and women had on the music was enormous, even if many of them didn't live long enough to reap huge financial rewards or enjoy the spoils of worldwide fame.

We included as many important artists as we could who rose to prominence and recorded their best-known work during the first half of this century. Even the early blues scene had its own star system and, when the music was young, these were the folks who glittered most brightly.

Big Bill Broonzy

Big Bill Broonzy (1893–1958) was the most important figure of pre–World War II Chicago blues. Before Muddy Waters came to town and changed the whole blues scene forever, Big Bill was the king of the Chicago blues singers. He recorded and composed songs prolifically, and like other Chicago blues stars of the period, he combined raw country blues with an edgy urban sound to create an exciting new musical mix.

Ragtime roots

Broonzy was born June 26, 1893, in Scott, Mississippi, to sharecropping parents. He played the violin as a youngster and didn't start playing the guitar until 1920 when his family moved to Chicago. Getting pointers from local guitarist Papa Charlie Jackson, Broonzy was soon making some noise around the Windy City and cut his first records by the mid-1920s. On those early sides, he played ragtime, but Big Bill soon developed his own style that combined smooth vocals and polished lyrics set to fluid guitar playing.

By the 1930s, Broonzy was well-established on the Chicago scene, recording and working with the likes of Tampa Red, John Lee "Sonny Boy" Williamson, Jazz Gillum, and Washboard Sam. At that time, they all recorded for Bluebird Records and their collective sound came to be known as "The Bluebird Beat" which mixed older vaudeville styles with new swinging rhythms. Broonzy broadened his horizons and tapped into a whole new audience when he participated in John Hammond's *Spirituals To Swing* concerts at New York's Carnegie Hall in 1938 and 1939.

Bringing live folk blues to Europe

After Muddy Waters and the Chicago electric guitar sound took off in the late 1940s, Big Bill's music was considered somewhat passé in the blues community. So Broonzy simply reinvented himself as an acoustic folk blues artist. He toured Europe in 1951 and 1952, one of the very first, if not *the* first blues artist to do so. Performing a set of blues tunes, folk songs, and spirituals, Big Bill won over an international audience and opened the door for other blues artists to head overseas to perform.

Broonzy worked with Yannick Bruynoghe on his autobiography, *Big Bill's Blues*, which was published in London in 1955. In 1957, Broonzy was diagnosed with throat cancer, and died from the disease a year later. A blues pioneer and one-time patriarch of the Chicago blues scene, Big Bill Broonzy was elected into the Blues Foundation's Hall of Fame in 1980.

Good Time Tonight (Columbia/Legacy). This CD features 20 tracks from the height of Big Bill Broozy's career. This is the perfect place to begin appreciating this seminal blues artist.

Son House

Before the 1960s, only a handful of blues enthusiasts were chronicling the early history of the blues and most of them were white record collectors. The big record labels reissued little if any older material, cassettes hadn't appeared yet, and home taping was limited to those who could afford expensive and bulky reel-to-reel tape recorders.

In their search for original blues 78s, record collectors scoured thrift stores and garage sales and canvassed neighborhoods where blues players had once lived. Rare records were passed from one collector to another to be savored as if they were precious and almost priceless commodities (which they pretty much were). Among the most coveted of those early recordings were those made on the Paramount label by Son House (1902–1988).

The blues, plain and simple

Son House was one of the original practitioners of the Mississippi-Delta style of blues playing that blossomed in the South during the 1920s. Although Son was a contemporary of legendary Delta blues artist Charlie Patton, his influence was more wide ranging. He had an impact on Robert Johnson, Muddy Waters, and later a whole new generation of blues and folk musicians who rediscovered Son House in the mid-1960s.

What made Son House so fascinating was his complete emotional commitment to his music. In the 1960s, many older blues artists were being rediscovered by the folk-music community and invited to play for enthusiastic audiences at festivals and coffeehouses in the U.S. and Europe. Many of these artists managed to give performances that only suggested at their former greatness, but that wasn't the case with Son House. He may have lost some dexterity with age, but the fire and passion he brought to the music still burned bright.

When Son hit a lick on his old National steel-bodied dobro and began shouting the blues, audiences had little doubt that they were experiencing the blues — plain, simple, and emotionally real. A typical House performance was peppered with rambling monologues about what the blues was, and wasn't, and even the occasional *a cappella* spiritual.

The preacher plays the "devil's music"

Son House was born Eddie James House, Jr., on March 21, 1902, in Riverton, Mississippi. His family moved frequently during his childhood and was strongly devout in their religion. By his early teens, House was preaching in several Baptist churches in the area and preparing for a life in the ministry while working the fields on the various plantations where he settled.

By all accounts, at first he didn't care for the sound of a guitar and considered the blues "devil's music." While unwinding at a party one night (with the help of a little moonshine whiskey), House launched into an impromptu blues solo. The 25-year-old was showered with tips for his unexpected performance and suddenly he had an interest in the blues. He continued to preach the gospel, but there was *always* more money to be made singing and playing the blues.

The newfound good life turned ugly for House after he shot and killed a man at a house frolic in Lyon, Mississippi, in the late 1920s. After a swift trial he was sentenced to Parchman Farm, one of the roughest prisons in the area. His life sentence was commuted after two years largely due to the intercession of his parents who insisted the shooting was in self-defense. After his release (and after the local judge urged him to leave town), House decided to devote himself to playing the blues when he wasn't preaching the gospel.

The Son House–Charlie Patton partnership

After his release from prison, Son House subsisted by hitching rides on freight trains and hunting for churches that would pay him for doing a guest sermon. His travels led him to Lula, Mississippi, where he ran into local blues legend Charlie Patton, who was building a considerable reputation throughout the Mississippi Delta as a big-voiced singer, virtuoso guitarist, and house-rocker extraordinaire.

Patton was a true showman from the word go. He was the polar opposite of House, a subdued performer who forever felt remorse over leaving the church to play blues music. Nevertheless, Son House poured his heart and soul into the blues and could mesmerize a crowd without having to resort to any showbiz antics.

An unlikely twosome, House and Patton became close friends and playing partners. The basis of their friendship (outside of music) seemed to revolve around a fondness for bootleg whiskey and arguing over just about any subject that came up. In fact, it was Patton who introduced House to the record business. Patton had been recording for the Paramount label and one day in 1930 he brought Son along to one of his sessions, and the rest is history.

Any of the recordings from the Paramount blues series of the 1920s and early 1930s sells for staggeringly large sums of money even though many of them are made of inferior material and have suffered decades' worth of damage. But no matter how many hisses, pops, and scratches you hear on Son's old 78s (including "Dry Spell Blues," "My Black Mama," and "Preachin' The Blues"), they can't disguise the voice of a superlative blues performer.

Recording for the Library of Congress

Although House's Paramount singles were poor sellers at the time of their release, his music had an enormous effect on folklorist Alan Lomax. While compiling folk music for the Library of Congress (lugging along a primitive, 300-pound "portable" recording machine), Lomax headed to Mississippi in 1941 in the hope of recording Son House and other blues artists.

Lomax asked Son to record some solo numbers backed only by his guitar. House turned in performances every bit the equal of his old Paramount sides done 11 years earlier. But the real surprise came when Son asked some of his old buddies to join in. With Fiddlin' Joe Martin on mandolin, and Leroy Williams and Willie Brown on guitar, Son laid down tracks that were primal Delta blues played in a band format, providing a blueprint for the amplified Chicago blues style played a decade later.

Instead of capitalizing on the new interest in his music, House left the Delta and disappeared to Rochester, New York, until he was tracked down by blues researchers Nick Perls, Phil Spiro, and Dick Waterman in 1964. Son hadn't touched a guitar since his old pal Willie Brown died in 1952, so the trio introduced fellow blues scholar and guitarist Al Wilson to House. Wilson (who would later become a founding member of the blues-rock group Canned Heat) re-taught House all of his old licks and pretty soon the old fire and passion was rekindled.

On the folk festival circuit

Waterman became Son's manager and immediately started booking him on the folk festival and coffeehouse circuit. In 1965, House recorded for Columbia Records with John Hammond, Sr. producing. Those sessions were released on the album *Father of Folk Blues* and introduced Son's music to its widest audience yet. That same year, he appeared at Carnegie Hall.

Son House's appearances in film documentaries from the 1960s delighted and confounded his new fans. He wavered between being cordial and cantankerous. In his mind, his opinions about the blues were the only ones that mattered, and he was highly critical of up-tempo blues and electric blues players.

House neared the end of the road in the early 1970s. He had difficulty remembering the lyrics to songs he had played hundreds of times, and his hands shook so violently he could barely hold a guitar. Although years of heavy drinking were first thought to be the cause, he was later diagnosed with both Parkinson's disease and advanced Alzheimer's.

Son gave up live performing in 1976. He was inducted into the Blues Foundation's Hall of Fame in 1980. He moved to Detroit and died there on October 19, 1988, at the age of 86. Although his known recordings are scarce, the quality of his work is so great and his influence so enormous that Son House remains one of the true pivotal artists in the development of blues history.

Masters Of The Delta Blues: The Friends of Charlie Patton (Yazoo). This features all six of House's original 1930 singles for the Paramount label plus a previously unissued take of "Walkin' Blues." Indispensable.

Blind Lemon Jefferson

Blind Lemon Jefferson (1897–1929) was blues music's first great guitar star. He was one of the earliest country blues artists to record and certainly one of the most popular. In a three-year span between 1926 to 1929, he recorded more than a hundred different titles, the majority of which sold briskly.

Jefferson (see Figure 4-1) was also the first great Texas blues guitar player (influencing both Lightnin' Hopkins and T-Bone Walker) and his success encouraged other male blues artists to record during an era that was dominated by female singers.

Supporting his family by playing on Dallas street corners

Not much is known of Lemon's early life (Lemon was his real name, incidentally). He was born blind into a family of seven children in Couchman, Texas, in July 1897 and evidently taught himself to play guitar and sing as a means of supporting himself. He quickly became a popular fixture on the streets of Dallas, making enough in tips to support a wife and child. Despite his blindness he traveled extensively — to the Mississippi Delta region, Oklahoma, Georgia, and the Carolinas.

Jefferson's career took off in 1925 when Dallas music store owner Sammy Price steered him to Paramount Records, which invited the singer to Chicago to record. Aside from a brief affiliation in 1927 with OKeh Records (which produced the classics "Matchbox Blues" and "That Black Snake Moan"), Lemon recorded exclusively for Paramount for the next four years.

The recordings he left behind were full of marvelous guitar work. He used the instrument as a second voice to finish phrases and his single-string flourishes extended the meter in odd places. His voice, an equally powerful instrument, had a two-octave range. Jefferson was versatile enough to work in the company of other musicians, but his best recordings were his solo efforts. He recorded spirituals under the name Deacon L.J. Bates, as well as the blues.

A life story full of contradictions

Records such as "Jack O'Diamonds," "Easy Rider Blues," and "See That My Grave Is Kept Clean" sold well throughout the 1920s but information about

Jefferson during this period of success is sketchy and contradictory. Some of his associates painted him as a hard-drinking womanizer who was paid with prostitutes and whiskey, while others recall a singer who wouldn't play on Sundays because his mother told him that was the Lord's day.

Even the details of his death in 1929 are somewhat speculative. The most widely repeated story tells of his freezing to death outdoors in the middle of a Chicago snowstorm. No death certificate for Lemon Jefferson has ever been found.

But Blind Lemon Jefferson's music has lasted, influencing countless other musicians and providing an archetype for all the blues guitar players who followed him. If you're stacking up the building blocks of modern-day blues, Blind Lemon Jefferson is right there at the foundation.

Blind Lemon Jefferson (Milestone). This collection makes for a solid introduction to this Texas legend, and includes the numbers "See That My Grave Is Kept Clean" and "Matchbox Blues."

Figure 4-1:
Blind
Lemon
Jefferson
(CD booklet
photo
courtesy of
Fantasy,
Inc.).

Lonnie Johnson

A major influence on Robert Johnson, T-Bone Walker, and B.B. King, Lonnie Johnson (1889–1970) was the first great modern blues guitarist and was one of the first blues recording stars. With his amazing control over his guitar, he recorded everything from low-down and dirty blues to sprightly jazz duets with fellow guitarist Eddie Lang.

Johnson's ideas were technically advanced and his versatility on the instrument allowed him to embrace blues, jazz, and pop and dress them up in his own style. He even invented a playing style that combined rhythmic stretches with solo passages, all performed on one instrument. His discography spans more than 40 years and includes hundreds of recordings made under his own name and as an accompanist to other artists.

A departure from the Delta blues sound

Johnson was born in New Orleans on February 8, 1889, into a musical family. He first studied the violin, but the guitar quickly became an all-consuming passion. After a flu epidemic in 1919 claimed almost his entire family, Johnson moved to St. Louis and started playing in local jazz bands. When he won a blues contest at a local theater in 1925, he was offered a recording contract with OKeh Records.

Lonnie recorded on his own and in a number of groups and worked with jazz legends Louis Armstrong and Duke Ellington. Johnson's style was something other than the country blues of the Mississippi Delta or the Texas sound of Blind Lemon Jefferson. Lonnie's music was clean, intricate, and carefully constructed. With guitarist Eddie Lang, Johnson recorded some duets that set the stage for the development of jazz guitarists including Charlie Christian, reportedly a Lonnie disciple.

Johnson's recording career was hit hard by the Depression and he didn't resume recording until 1939 when he moved to Chicago and signed with Bluebird Records. He had one big hit with the label ("He's A Jelly Roll Baker") before moving on to King Records in 1947. There he enjoyed the biggest hit of his career with the ballad, "Tomorrow Night," later to be recorded by both Elvis Presley and Jerry Lee Lewis at Sun Records.

Rediscovered in his seventies

More hits followed, but the rise of rock 'n' roll in the mid-1950s temporarily forced Lonnie out of music. While working as a hotel janitor in Philadelphia in the early 1960s, he was rediscovered by folk-blues enthusiasts and lured back into recording. Taking advantage of renewed interest in the blues and a whole new blues audience, Lonnie recast himself as a folk-blues guitarist.

But his new career wasn't to last long. In 1969 at the age of 80, he was hit by a car and died a year later from the injuries. It's safe to say the history of blues guitar would be written much differently without the pioneering work of Lonnie Johnson.

Steppin' On The Blues (Columbia/Legacy). These 19 tracks serve as the perfect introduction to this absolutely amazing guitarist. Check out the ballad "She's Making Whoopee In Hell Tonight."

Robert Johnson

If you ask just about any blues aficionado to name the most important artist who ever recorded, it's a lead-pipe cinch you'll hear the name Robert Johnson (1911–1938). His compositions "Sweet Home Chicago," "Love In Vain," "Crossroads," "Rambling On My Mind," and "Stop Breakin' Down" are certified blues classics of the highest order that were turned into hits decades after he wrote them by the Rolling Stones, Eric Clapton, Led Zeppelin, and other rockers who long admired this almost mythological figure.

Johnson himself was a total enigma. Only two known photographs of him exist and the story of how he came to acquire his spectacular talent is the stuff of legend. The Johnson myth paints him as a cursed and haunted genius, whose muse was largely the product of the inner demons that possessed him. His lyrics do seem to suggest a tortured soul: All his love was in vain; Satan came knocking at his door and the next thing you know he and the Devil were walkin' side by side; hellhounds were forever on his trail; he longed to be buried by the side of the road so the evil spirits within him could catch the next bus out of town. Of all the poetry in the blues, Johnson's was by far the most harrowing.

"The Crossroads Story," as it's usually told

Two versions of the Robert Johnson life story exist: the fable and the more prosaic (and much more likely) version. First up is "the crossroads story," which follows along these general lines:

As a youngster living on Dockery's plantation, Robert made up his mind to become a blues musician and pursued that goal relentlessly. Having been instructed to take his guitar to a nearby crossroads at midnight, Johnson was met there by the Devil himself, who grabbed Johnson's guitar, tuned the instrument, and handed it right back. From that day on, Johnson's supernatural powers enabled him able to play and sing better than any blues musician ever heard.

Producer John Hammond wanted Johnson to perform at a Carnegie Hall *Spirituals To Swing* program in 1938 and sent out scouts to track him down and bring him up to New York. Unfortunately, word came back from Mississippi that Johnson was dead, poisoned at a juke joint by a girlfriend's jealous husband. Legend has it that he was last seen alive foaming at the mouth and down on all fours snapping at people like a mad dog. His dying words supposedly were, "I pray that my Redeemer will come and take me from my grave."

The same story in a 38 Regular

The somewhat more factual version of the Robert Johnson story (or what we know of it) is definitely lacking some of the superstition and mystery of the Johnson fable. Johnson was born on May 8, 1911, in Hazlehurst, Mississippi, to the wife of a successful furniture maker (who was forced to flee Mississippi and move to Memphis) and a local man, not her husband, named Noah Johnson. (Robert went by the last name of Spencer until he learned the identify of this real father when he was in his teens.) He taught himself how to play the harmonica in his spare time, and learned the rudiments of the guitar by watching others play.

The Mississippi Delta plantation area where Johnson spent his youth boasted the best blues guitar players for miles around and young Robert would see them play at every opportunity. The older blues players including Son House, Charlie Patton, and Willie Brown had no inclination to tutor this overeager youngster. According to Son House, Johnson's guitar playing at the time amounted to no more than an unmusical racket.

Johnson married in 1929 and was set to settle down to family life. A year later, both his wife and son died in childbirth. After that, Robert furtively traveled from town to town around the Delta playing the blues. He was forever on the move, practicing constantly to hone his craft, and performing at every possible opportunity.

When he returned home a few years later, he ran into Son House and Willie Brown at a juke joint dance in Banks, Mississippi. During a break, Johnson was asked to sit in. When he was done, House and Brown had only one explanation for this revelatory talent — Robert Johnson must have sold his soul to the Devil. (Johnson probably did little to discourage such rumors.)

Johnson's expertise on slide guitar can be traced directly to the time he spent absorbing the techniques of Son House and Charlie Patton while sitting at their feet in countless music joints. Johnson's other big influences included Kokomo Arnold, Scrapper Blackwell, Skip James, and especially the blues star Lonnie Johnson. Robert used many of Lonnie's guitar licks to write new tunes of his own, examples of which are "Malted Milk" and "Drunken Hearted Man." But, by all accounts, Johnson's biggest influence was a mysterious blues artist from Hazelhurst named Ike Zinneman.

Practice sessions at the local cemetery

Johnson made a habit of following Zinneman to the local graveyard where Ike liked to practice at night. What Johnson learned while sitting in the dark leaning against a gravestone is purely speculative, but after a year under Zinneman's tutelage, Johnson returned home a musical giant. Johnson was able to not only play and sing anything from country tunes to hit pop songs to polkas, but was also writing songs, as well.

Robert loved to travel and hoboed freights to Chicago, Detroit, New York, St. Louis, and Canada, with stops in between. He recorded for the Vocalion label in 1936 and his first release, "Terraplane Blues," sold three or four thousand copies, a hit for its day. He recorded a dozen singles in his lifetime and all of those recordings are now considered prize collectibles of that era.

A Saturday night dance and the fatal jug of whiskey

Johnson resumed his nomadic existence until one August Saturday night. He was working a dance in Three Forks, Mississippi, with guitarist Honeyboy Edwards and harmonica ace Sonny Boy Williamson II. The story goes that Robert was flirting with a woman at the dance, and her jealous husband or boyfriend decided to get even by serving the singer a jug of moonshine whiskey with a cake of lye floating in it. Johnson kept drinking and playing until he was too sick to continue. He was taken to nearby Greenwood where, after an excruciating few days, he died of pneumonia on August 16, 1938. He was 27.

In addition to his considerable gifts as a singer and songwriter, Johnson's major contribution to the blues was his innovative boogie-woogie bass line played on the bottom strings of his guitar. Boogie-woogie had been by and large piano music since the late 1920s. Once Johnson introduced guitar boogie-woogie, it spread quickly throughout the Delta blues community and was exported north to Chicago and used as a main component of the electric Chicago blues style practiced by Elmore James, Jimmy Reed, Eddie Taylor, and Hound Dog Taylor.

In 1961, a compilation of Johnson's old 78 singles was released on Columbia Records as part of their *Thesaurus of Classic Jazz* series. The album, *King Of The Delta Blues Singers,* introduced his music to a worldwide audience for the first time. It sold well enough to warrant a second volume of additional Johnson material, which was released in the 1970s.

Finally, the complete recordings

In 1990, Columbia Records released *The Complete Recordings* — every piece of recorded Robert Johnson music known to exist. It was packaged in a double-record boxed set with extensive liner notes, complete lyrics, and rare photos of blues stars of the day. At the time of its release, Columbia was hoping to move 10,000 units. Instead, more than a half-million copies of the boxed set were sold and it ended up winning a Grammy award. The Robert Johnson renaissance was officially in progress. In 1986, he was inducted into the Rock and Roll Hall of Fame.

Today Robert Johnson's likeness decorates everything from calendars to posters to T-shirts, and his signature is found on guitar straps, guitar picks, and polishing cloths. But the commercialized Robert Johnson does nothing to diminish the blues legend whose music is more influential than ever.

"In every generation of the blues, there's always somebody who's the best. These are the people that everybody follows because their sound is new and different. Just like T-Bone Walker was the tops for his day and B.B. King is today, well, Robert Johnson was the greatest for his day."

The Complete Recordings (Columbia/Legacy). This two-disc set of Robert Johnson's best-known tunes should be one of your very first purchases in assembling the perfect blues collection. The booklet containing the lyrics to his songs is alone worth the sticker price.

Louis Jordan

Louis Jordan (1908–1975) was the clown prince of the rhythm-and-blues scene in the late 1940s and one of the top practitioners of the musical style called jump blues. Saxophonist, singer, bandleader, songwriter, and show-man extraordinaire, Jordan (see Figure 4-2) helped to tear down racial barriers in popular music while blending the blues with the pop sounds of his time.

With his band, the Tympany Five, Jordan sold millions of records, toured extensively, and was a name on movie house marquees. The sound he created was frequently imitated and his song writing had an enormous influence on the young Chuck Berry, among others.

Jordan was born on July 8, 1908, in Brinkley, Arkansas. His father was a musician and Louis received early musical training as a member of the Rabbit Foot Minstrels and formal education in music theory when he attended Arkansas Baptist College.

"Caldonia" and 56 other hits

When his family moved to Philadelphia, Jordan landed a job with bandleader Chick Webb and worked numerous dates with bandleader Cab Calloway, whose musical and performing style made its way into Jordan's act. Louis stayed with Webb until 1938 before going out on his own, first recording under the name Elk's Club Rendezvous Band, then a year later under Louis Jordan and his Tympany Five.

After signing with Decca Records, Jordan racked up 57 R&B charts hits between 1942 and 1951, beginning with the classic, "I'm Gonna Move To The Outskirts Of Town." Hits such as "Caldonia" and "Beware" were big enough that Hollywood film producers hired Jordan to appear in single-reel shorts based on those songs.

Figure 4-2:
Louis Jordan, shown with Bing Crosby during a recording session for Decca Records (photo courtesy of the Everett Collection, Inc.).

Starring roles in movie musicals

After the success of the movie shorts, Jordan was cast as the lead in the full-length movie musicals *Swing Parade of 1946, Reet, Petite and Gone, Look Out, Sister* and *Meet Miss Bobby Socks.* Other songs from this fertile period include the classics "Let The Good Times Roll" (which is on the *Blues For Dummies* CD), "Five Guys Named Moe," "Choo Choo Ch'Boogie," and "Saturday Night Fish Fry." Louis Jordan seldom sang a sad tune; his specialty was good-time party music of the dance variety.

But the party started winding down for Jordan during the 1950s when rock 'n' roll blasted onto the scene. Jordan made an ill-fated attempt at fronting a big band in 1951. In 1954, he signed with the Aladdin label, then moved over to Vik, X, and Mercury, all before 1958. Despite pressing a spate of fine singles (that influenced the likes of Ray Charles), and continuing to make records right into the 1970s, Louis Jordan's recording career was like the title of one of his earlier hits, "Stone Cold Dead In The Marketplace."

In the fall of 1974, Jordan suffered a heart attack while on the road. He recovered and announced his plans to tour Europe the following spring. But a second attack proved fatal and he died at his home in Los Angeles on February 4, 1975. His music would eventually reach a new appreciative audience through the acclaimed Broadway musical *Five Guys Named Moe*.

The Best Of Louis Jordan (MCA). If 1940s-era jump blues is what you like, check out this collection of hits that made Louis Jordan famous.

Leadbelly

Leadbelly's music was an engaging throwback to the *songster* era, when musicians in the rural South filled their repertoire with country tunes, folk songs, ragtime numbers, popular standards, and a smattering of the blues. More than any other folk-blues artist of his time, Leadbelly (1888–1949) exposed white America to the musical riches of traditional African-American music. His music embraced field songs, spirituals, dance numbers, prison songs, pop tunes, folk ballads, and of course, the blues.

Leadbelly was born Huddie Ledbetter on January 20, 1988, in Mooringsport, Louisiana. Little is know about Leadbelly's early life, but it's generally assumed he met and began working with Blind Lemon Jefferson around 1915. The two briefly played together while Ledbetter improved his skills on his new instrument of choice, the 12-string guitar.

Singing for (and winning) a prison release

Leadbelly was a huge man with an even bigger temper, and his first 40 years were largely spent in one scrap after another with the law. In 1917, he killed a man in Texas and was sentenced to 30 years at the Huntsville Prison Farm, with another six years tacked on when he tried to escape. But Leadbelly was smart enough to make use of his musical talents to escape hard prison work and eventually prison itself.

In 1925, Leadbelly won his freedom when he composed and sang a song for Texas governor Pat Neff asking for his release. But five years later, Leadbelly was arrested again and convicted, and sentenced to the Angola Prison Farm in Louisiana.

When historians John and Alan Lomax were collecting folk and blues songs for the Library of Congress in 1933, they visited prisons as part of their search for authentic folk music. The knowledgeable and talented Huddie Ledbetter made a distinct impression on the Lomaxes. Because they regarded Leadbelly as a human repository of African-American folk songs, the Lomaxes petitioned Louisiana governor O.K. Allen for the singer's release. Freed in 1934, the singer went to work for the Lomaxes as a chauffeur and occasionally performed and recorded.

A hit on the New York coffeehouse scene

In 1935, Leadbelly moved to New York and became the toast of the town and a fixture in folk music circles. He worked with folk singers Pete Seeger and Woody Guthrie, performing in union halls and often supporting political causes. He recorded prolifically during this time for the Library of Congress, Folkways, Capitol, and other labels. Leadbelly's recordings of "Goodnight, Irene," "The Midnight Special," "Cotton Fields," and "Rock Island Line" have since become folk music standards.

In 1949, Leadbelly left for Europe hoping to build a following there. After his return, he was diagnosed with Lou Gehrig's disease and died on December 6 of that year. The next year, in 1950, the folk group the Weavers, led by Pete Seeger, made a number-one hit out of "Goodnight Irene." Since Leadbelly's death, an eponymously titled movie of his life was produced, he was inducted into the Blues Foundation's Hall of Fame in 1986, and inducted into the Rock and Roll Hall of Fame in 1988.

Midnight Special (Rounder). Leadbelly's earliest Library of Congress recordings make a great introduction to this complex and compelling artist, and blues music pioneer.

Memphis Minnie

Sometime in the 1930s, the public's taste in blues music and the blues scene in general made a major shift. The "classic" female blues singers who dominated the business (and who were making and selling the vast majority of blues records) were suddenly out of fashion. It was the male artists who were then pressing the records and getting the radio play, and almost all of them played the guitar.

The few women who were still making blues records and could wield a mean guitar made for a really select group. Those women who dared to gain entry into the exclusive boy's club that the blues had become were performers such as Sister Rosetta Tharpe, who was primarily a gospel artist. But one lady held her own when it came time to strap on a guitar and show everyone how the blues was played. Her name was Memphis Minnie (1897–1973).

Beating the guitar competition (including the guys)

Memphis Minnie was more than just a pretty face who could strum a few chords. True, she was gorgeous, but she could also sing with authority and could eliminate almost any male guitarist in any "headcutting" competition she was in. That Minnie accomplished what she did, at the time she did it, while earning the respect of both blues audiences and her peers, still seems amazing.

Minnie was born Lizzie Douglas on June 3, 1897, in Algiers, Louisiana, and at 10 moved with her family to a Mississippi border town just south of Memphis. She was playing guitar and banjo by her early teens, working under the name Kid Douglas and playing the Memphis streets for spare change. By the 1920s, Douglas was well-established on the Beale Street blues scene.

In 1929, she was discovered by Columbia Records who released "Bumble Bee," her first record as Memphis Minnie. She recorded the number with her second husband Kansas Joe McCoy on guitar (all three of her husbands were guitar players). It was a big enough hit that the two moved to Chicago in 1930 to tap into the blossoming blues scene there. Minnie made the Windy City her home base for the next quarter of a century.

Wielding an electric axe in designer dresses

After Minnie beat both Big Bill Broonzy and Tampa Red in a guitar battle, she and her husband Joe started getting some attention. Minnie also established a reputation as a woman not to be fooled with, her toughness a byproduct of her years playing in Southern juke joints. Even while elegantly dressed in her beaded sheaths and silver bracelets, Minnie, when provoked, had been known to wield a guitar, pistol, or any other object that was handy.

In 1939, Minnie teamed up with her third guitar-playing husband, Ernest Lawlers, who worked as Little Son Joe. By this time, her music was edging closer to the urban blues sounds that were popular in Chicago. Minnie continued to record prolifically for Decca, Vocalion, and Bluebird into the early 1950s. By this time, she was playing an electric guitar and recording for Regal, Checker, and JOB Records with limited success.

When her health began to fail in the mid-1950s, Minnie gave up recording and performing and returned to Memphis. She spent her final years in a nursing home confined to a wheelchair, where she passed away from a stroke on August 6, 1973. This pioneer of both the blues and the entire music industry was inducted into the Blues Foundation's Hall of Fame in 1980.

Queen Of The Blues (Columbia-Legacy). These 18 stellar selections show what a potent musical force Memphis Minnie was. Includes the original version of "When The Levee Breaks," later recorded and (wrongly) credited to Led Zeppelin.

Mississippi Fred McDowell

Mississippi Fred McDowell (1902–1972) didn't turn professional until the mid-1960s, and today it seems incredible that his music was never recorded during the 1920s and early 1930s when so many other of the early blues greats were making records.

When he was "discovered" by folk researcher Alan Lomax in 1959, McDowell played his guitar bottleneck style using a hollowed-out steer bone for a slide. His personal style, the intensity of his playing, and his gritty vocals reminded Lomax of the early work of Son House and Charlie Patton, both important influences on McDowell.

By the end of his career, McDowell had upgraded to an electric hollow-body guitar, but he played it no differently than the cheap, pawn shop acoustic model he used when Lomax first recorded him. Fred declared at the time that he didn't play rock 'n' roll, only the "straight and natural blues" (which became the title of one of his albums).

A small-town farmer and part-time blues man

McDowell was born January 12, 1904, in Rossville, Tennessee, and was an accomplished guitarist by his early teens. After the death of his parents, McDowell split his time between playing live blues and farming to make a living. By the 1920s, the traveling bug hit McDowell and he spent time in Memphis, playing on the streets for spare change and hitchhiking from town to town.

He eventually settled in Como, Mississippi, his home base for the rest of his life. McDowell would farm during the week, and then play music on the weekends at local fish fries, picnics, house parties, and outdoor dances. In 1959, his placid 30-year-long routine was interrupted when Alan Lomax recorded McDowell for a series of albums of blues and folk songs to be produced by Atlantic Records.

McDowell stirred up a lot of excitement. A performer of his caliber was considered a major find, but Fred took it in stride. He was delighted to hear his voice and guitar played back from Lomax's portable tape recorder and hear the record that was eventually made from the tape, but after that, not much changed. Fred still worked the farm during the week and played outside the local candy store in town for tips on weekends.

The Arhoolie recordings that made him a star at the age of 60

Things started happening for McDowell in a big way when he was approached by Chris Strachwitz, a folk music and blues fan who owned the tiny Arhoolie label in California. Strachwitz made a point of seeking out McDowell and getting him studio time. After the recordings were released on Arhoolie in the mid-1960s, McDowell's life was never the same again.

Titled simply *Fred McDowell, Volume 1,* and *Fred McDowell, Volume 2,* these albums set the folk music community abuzz. Where had this guy been all this time? How could a blues artist with so much emotional depth, and a seemingly unlimited repertoire of material, not have been recorded decades earlier?

The success of the two Arhoolie albums (largely by word of mouth) allowed Fred to play professionally full time. The audiences at folk festivals and coffeehouses quickly took to McDowell, and the folk circuit became his new home for performing. McDowell's quiet good nature and almost self-effacing manner endeared audiences to him all the more.

McDowell worked his way over to Europe as a member of the American Folk Blues Festival touring troupe in the mid-1960s. He recorded with Big Mama Thornton and played the Newport Folk Festival where he passed on some of his slide guitar secrets to a young Bonnie Raitt.

A regular face in documentary films

Like other rediscovered blues artists of the 1960s (including Skip James, Son House, and Bukka White), McDowell turned up in a number of film documentaries about the blues. He appeared in *The Blues Maker* (1968), *Fred McDowell* (1969), and *Roots of American Music: Country and Urban Music* (1970).

The 1960s started out with Fred playing his music for his own enjoyment or for a few friends. The decade ended with his being signed to Capitol Records, which released his album *I Do Not Play No Rock 'n' Roll* and having his songs covered by Bonnie Raitt and the Rolling Stones.

While out on tour in 1971, Mississippi Fred McDowell was diagnosed with cancer. He retired from playing and headed back to the farm community of Como, Mississippi, where he died in July 1972 at age 68.

The First Recordings (Rounder). Just as the title says, what you'll find here are simple recordings that ooze with great good blues feeling.

Charlie Patton

Charlie Patton (1887–1934) was the first great star of the brand of blues born and nurtured in the Mississippi Delta region. During the 1920s and early 1930s, Patton was *the* man to beat in any contest between Delta region guitarists. He was possessed of a guitar playing style that made everybody want to get up and dance, and a rough and booming voice that filled even the noisiest juke joint.

Live on stage, Patton performed everything from ballads, to ragtime, to spirituals, but he was best known as a consummate blues artist. At the height of his fame, his records (especially his first and biggest hit, "Pony Blues") were huge sellers throughout the South.

Living the romantic bluesman's life

In many ways, Patton's lifestyle exemplified many of the romantic (and stereotypical) notions that persist to this day about early blues artists.

He was a loud and boisterous lover of good times who found intimate company in nearly every town he played. He had an appetite for greasy food, a big thirst for whiskey, and a penchant for gambling. Patton was married a reported eight times and didn't live to see 50, but he sure made the most of life while he was here.

The exact date of Charlie Patton's birth is unknown; some historians say 1881, some say 1887, and some say April 1891. He was born in the Mississippi Hill country in the town of Edwards, but his family later moved to the Delta to work the Dockery plantation. By the 1920s, Charlie was a local star who had fans all up and down the Mississippi. After playing a dance, he'd linger for a few days around the local plantation just long enough to stir up some action.

Patton's voice was enormous, even by Delta blues standards. One of the great legends about Charlie is that he once sang so loud at an outdoor plantation dance that he could be heard a quarter-mile away. Mississippi blues artist Sleepy John Estes insisted that no blues singer he ever heard was louder than Charlie Patton, who stood only five-foot-five and weighed a mere 135 pounds.

The original master of guitar gymnastics

Patton was fond of flashy on-stage guitar tricks. He'd throw his expensive guitar into the air and narrowly miss catching it, he played the guitar behind his neck, behind his back, with one leg draped over the neck, or with only one hand. The guitar showmanship that became the trademark of Guitar Slim, Jimi Hendrix, T-Bone Walker, and Stevie Ray Vaughan can be traced back to the fun-loving Charlie Patton.

Patton would pound and slap the top of his guitar to make it sound like a drum, while snapping the bass strings against the guitar's fingerboard. He had funk-guitar moves down cold 40 or 50 years before Parliament/Funkadelic came along. Charlie tuned his guitar a step or two above concert pitch in order to be heard over the noise in juke joints and at outdoor dances. And, to make sure the crowd heard the dance rhythms loud and clear, Patton attached metal cleats to his shoes and stomped out the beat while he played.

Patton's slide guitar playing was masterful and his habit of finishing off his vocal phrases with a slide riff influenced Son House, Robert Johnson, and Muddy Waters. As for Patton's singing style, it was closer to a vaudeville routine than classic blues vocalizing. He mumbled and carried on conversations with himself, changing his voice in order to sound like two different people.

Those rare and very collectible original recordings

Like Blind Lemon Jefferson, Son House, and others, Patton recorded for the Paramount label. His first recording session was in 1929 and it produced "Pony Blues," a hit by early blues standards (several thousand copies sold, as opposed to millions). Paramount brought him back for session after session and soon Charlie was not only the biggest-selling artist on the label, but also its most prolific.

Even though several of his titles sold well when they were released, Patton's Paramount sides are among the rarest of all early blues recordings and sell today for a very tidy sum. And, good luck if you can find one of those recordings that hasn't been ground to a pulp by those huge steel phonograph needles.

In addition, no *masters* (clean, original recordings that are used to press copies) of any kind exist for the 60 or so tracks he cut in the days before the invention of magnetic tape. Charlie Patton CDs have been compiled from what survives of the best-quality original 78s. (The performances themselves are great, but are obscured by a nasty blizzard of surface noise.)

Patton eventually left Paramount and his final session was for the small ARC label, done only a couple of months before his death in 1934 of heart failure. Patton's physical condition had deteriorated by the time of those final sessions, which produced recordings with only marginally better fidelity than that of the Paramount sides.

Warnings and disclaimers aside about the quality of the audio, Charlie Patton's music is well worth investigating, surface noise and all. He brought passion and intensity to every one of his performances that makes it easy to dismiss the pops, crackles, and hisses of a well-worn record.

Founder Of The Delta Blues (Yazoo). This is a solid collection of this seminal artist's best work — it's noisy as all get out, but definitely worth adding to your collection.

Ma Rainey

Ma Rainey (1886–1939) was celebrated as the "Mother of the Blues." Although she wasn't the first blues artist to cut a record, she was performing and popularizing blues music for almost 20 years before she made her first record. Her success paved the way for many other female blues artists, including her protégé Bessie Smith.

As a live performer, Ma Rainey was nothing less than electrifying. She made her stage entrances emerging from a giant replica of a Victrola, extravagantly draped in a beaded gown, rhinestone jewelry, and feathered boa, wearing a horse hair wig topped with a jeweled tiara, and dripping with chains made from 20-dollar gold pieces.

Once onstage, she would strut, stop, pose for the crowd, laugh, moan, scream, and generally carry on. Audiences would get so swept up in her performance that they moaned right along with her. She sang with an earthiness and down-home purity that captivated her listeners. To say Ma Rainey had a strong voice is understating the case. The only time she used a microphone was in the recording studio and even that's doubtful given the crude equipment of those days.

The Ma and Pa Rainey traveling minstrel show

Ma Rainey (see Figure 4-3) was born Gertrude Malissa Pridgett on April 26, 1886. Her gifts as a singer were evident from an early age. At 12, she made her musical debut at a talent show in her home town of Columbus, Georgia. She married minstrel show manager William "Pa" Rainey in 1904 and changed her professional name to "Ma," an odd choice for an 18-year-old girl but one that nevertheless seemed to suit her. Ma and Pa Rainey put together an act and played circuses, tent shows, and the minstrel circuit, billing themselves as "Rainey and Rainey, the Assassinators of the Blues."

Ma began gathering songs from the black minstrel tradition — rural folk music considered bizarre to most listeners — and started weaving them into her stage show. By 1905, the songs had a special place in her act, first as encores then as part of her main act.

A squat woman with a kind face and a mouthful of gold dental work, she was affectionately dubbed by her contemporaries "the ugliest woman in show business." Nevertheless, Ma Rainey had many admirers. She was elegant, gracious, direct, and honest, and always able to put everyone around her at ease. Blues pianist Champion Jack Dupree said about Rainey, "When she opened her mouth, that was it. She knew how to sing those blues and she got right into your heart. What a personality she had!"

"C.C. Rider" and the first touring bus

Ma eventually left Pa behind and went out as a headliner with her Georgia Jazz Band. By this time she was known as "Madame Rainey." She started recording for the Paramount label in 1923 when she was 37. For the next five

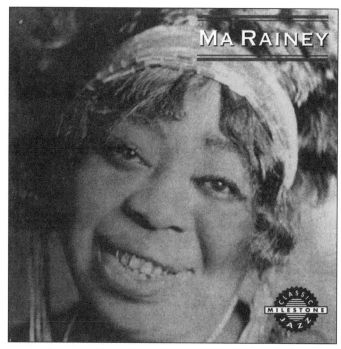

Figure 4-3:
Ma Rainey
(CD booklet
photo
courtesy of
Fantasy,
Inc.).

years, she recorded between 90 and 100 songs, including her versions of "See See Rider Blues" (better known to modern audiences as "C.C. Rider") and "Bo Weevil Blues," both considered blues classics. These records were marketed primarily through mail-order catalogs and sold extremely well in the deep South, Rainey's stronghold.

Rainey became a featured performer on the T.O.B.A. circuit (the Theater Owners Booking Association). She traveled from Chicago to Texas oil camps and through the deep South in what can be described as the first "touring bus" — a rickety wooden house trailer perched precariously on top of her automobile. She was fond of young musicians, and her romantic zeal didn't diminish a bit in middle age. She had a reputation as a demanding bandleader and tough-minded businessperson who wasn't to be messed with.

Wherever she played, crowds came from miles around to hear her, and the bond with her audience was stronger than ever. She identified equally with young women ("Trust No Man") and men working hard labor ("Levee Camp Moan"). When she performed in Northern cities, her act was considered somewhat exotic or just downright weird, but the number of encore calls kept climbing. Rainey almost defiantly insisted in keeping her music close to its country roots while her contemporaries flirted with cabaret and pop styles.

Surviving through savvy business sense

In the early 1930s, the Depression and shift in popularity from female blues singers to male country blues players forced Ma to retire from recording and touring. While many of her contemporaries drifted into relative obscurity and fell on financial hard times, the indomitable Ma Rainey prospered.

She had socked away considerable earnings from her time in the limelight and purchased a lavish home for her family in Columbus. In her "retirement" years, she owned and operated two vaudeville theaters in nearby Rome, Georgia. She was a member of the Columbus Friendship Baptist Church, where her brother presided over the congregation. Ma Rainey died in 1939 at the age of 54 with a life well-spent in show business and blues music. She was inducted into the Blues Foundation Hall of Fame in 1983 and the Rock and Roll Hall of Fame in 1990.

Ma Rainey (Milestone). Nobody could belt out a blues tune like Ma Rainey and here's a great collection that proves it. An essential buy for collectors of classic female blues.

Bessie Smith

Of all the blues singers who recorded during the height of the classic female blues period from the early 1920s through the early 1930s, none was a greater talent or more famous than Bessie Smith (1894–1937), who was dubbed "The Empress of the Blues." The depth of emotion she brought to her songs and her impeccable timing and sense of rhythm made Bessie Smith the standard against which many female blues (and jazz) singers were measured.

In her heyday, Smith sold more records and made more money than any other blues artist, male or female. Her influence can be heard in the singing of Billie Holiday, Janis Joplin, and even today in the music of rap-soul singer and bass player Me'Shell Ndege'Ocello.

A pioneering statement of female independence

Bessie Smith (see Figure 4-4) was a pioneering woman who became a cultural hero because of her no-nonsense assertiveness and liberated lifestyle that broke with many social conventions. She was an emancipated woman who had little patience for anyone who attempted to exploit her. One of her earliest records, "'Tain't Nobody's Bizness If I Do," was a declaration of female independence sung by someone who obviously had the experience to back it up. Decades before Madonna brazenly addressed sexual themes in her music, Bessie Smith was celebrating them in hers.

Born in Chattanooga on April 15, 1894, Bessie was introduced to show business by her brother Clarence, who later left town with a traveling vaudeville show. With his encouragement, Bessie learned to sing and dance, and when Clarence and the Moses Stokes Company returned to Chattanooga, Bessie was ready for show business. She began her professional career in 1912 as a dancer with the Rabbit Foot Minstrels, featuring Ma Rainey at the top of the bill. Stories differ on whether Rainey taught Bessie how to sing the blues, but the two were great friends and admirers of each other's styles.

Record-breaking sales figures

Bessie spent the remainder of the decade working in various road shows and theaters in the South and building up a large following along the way. She didn't start recording until 1923, but her first release, "Down Hearted Blues," sold more than 750,000 copies, an unheard of sales figure for those days. For the next ten years, Smith recorded nearly 160 songs for Columbia.

Smith worked with jazz greats including Louis Armstrong and needed nothing more than a piano behind her to sound powerful. She forbid the use of drums, claiming her voice was the timekeeper in her music (and her recordings substantiate her claim).

Bessie became a genuine star, crossing racial barriers to play in theaters and nightclubs, forming her own road shows, and recording one hit after another. Dressed in elegant gowns, she delivered jazz and pop numbers, but the blues remained her show-stopping specialty. In 1929, she filmed a movie short based on her hit version of "St. Louis Blues," the only footage that exists of her. That same year she also recorded the Depression-era classic, "Nobody Knows You When You're Down And Out" (a title that in some ways foretold her future).

A short-lived comeback

As the public's taste for blues music began to change, the best of the female singers, including Bessie, suddenly found that their time in the limelight was over. She was dropped by Columbia in 1931 and began drinking heavily. Broke and down on her luck, she was back singing in small clubs when producer John Hammond, Sr. tracked her down to record her.

Figure 4-4:
Bessie
Smith
(photo
courtesy of
the Everett
Collection,
Inc.).

In 1933, Hammond arranged for a return session with Columbia that featured Benny Goodman and Jack Teagarden. After that, Bessie eased herself back into performing. While driving through Mississippi during a 1937 tour, her car smashed into an oncoming truck. The crash nearly severed one of her arms and she bled to death. A great voice was stilled forever, but the recorded legacy remains. Bessie Smith was inducted into the Blues Foundation's Hall of Fame in 1980 and the Rock and Roll Hall of Fame in 1989.

The Essential Bessie Smith (Columbia/Legacy). This two-disc set features some of the greatest blues singing of all time and trims Bessie's large discography down to a fine introductory package. Essential listening.

Tampa Red

"The Guitar Wizard," Tampa Red (1904–1981), was Chicago's first big guitar star and one of the city's most influential blues players. His single-string solo stylings and creamy-smooth slide techniques turned up later in the music of Robert Nighthawk, Earl Hooker, Chuck Berry, and Duane Allman.

Tampa Red was also a great blues composer, and several of his songs were recast into hits by other blues artists. His "Anna Lou Blues" became Robert Nighthawk's "Anna Lee," his "Black Angel Blues" became "Sweet Little Angel" for B.B. King, and "It Hurts Me Too" was a hit later on for Elmore James.

Creating a bawdy brand of blues called "hokum"

Hudson Whitaker was born in Smithville, Georgia, on January 8, 1904. (He was dubbed Tampa Red because of his Florida upbringing and bright red hair.) When Tampa moved to Chicago in the mid-1920s, he teamed with pianist-composer "Georgia" Tom Dorsey. The two recorded a bawdy blues number, "It's Tight Like That," that became a huge hit. Follow-up recordings started the whole trend of *hokum blues* — light and bouncy numbers with double-entendre-filled lyrics. The two singers kept recording as the Hokum Boys until 1930 when Dorsey turned to gospel music.

Tampa became a mainstay of producer Lester Melrose's Bluebird label house band, while recording on his own and with others for Bluebird. With pianist Big Maceo Merriweather, Tampa helped to create what became known as "The Bluebird beat," which melded older sounds with bass and drum beats. He spent most of the 1930s and 1940s ruling the pre–World War II Chicago scene with his great friend and drinking buddy, Big Bill Broonzy.

Opening his home to the blues community

During his years as the unofficial goodwill ambassador for Chicago's blues community, Tampa Red literally opened his home to fans, foreign visitors, struggling young musicians, and down-on-their-luck older ones. His house became Chicago's "blues central" — part rehearsal hall, booking agency, and rooming house.

Tampa continued to record into the early 1950s, but the blues was changing, and the louder, amplified sound had taken over. He recorded two albums for Prestige-Bluesville in 1960, but retired from music shortly after that. Tampa Red died on March 19, 1981, in a nursing home. That same year he was inducted into the Blues Foundation's Hall of Fame.

It Hurts Me Too: The Essential Recordings (Indigo). This great introduction to Red's music includes his early "hokum" recordings and the original versions of "It Hurts Me Too," "Don't You Lie To Me," and "Love Her With A Feeling."

Big Joe Turner

No singer in the history of the blues possessed a voice that rumbled as deeply or made the floor boards shake as much as Big Joe Turner's (1911–1985). Over the course of his lengthy career, Turner was labeled a boogie-woogie singer, a jazz singer, a rhythm-and-blues singer, and a rock 'n' roll singer. But Big Joe Turner never really changed his style — he was always first and foremost a blues singer.

Playing that trendy boogie-woogie piano

Big Joe Turner was born May 18, 1911, in Kansas City, Missouri, where he grew up. He built his vocal style by singing in church choirs and on street corners. By the 1930s, he was bartending and singing in various clubs around town and had formed a partnership with pianist Pete Johnson. The two began experimenting with that new musical trend, boogie-woogie, for all it was worth.

Traveling to New York, Turner and Johnson performed on Benny Goodman's Camel Caravan radio show in 1936 and in 1938 made a landmark appearance at Hammond's Spirituals To Swing concert at Carnegie Hall. Their performance of "Roll 'Em Pete" helped to kick off the boogie-woogie craze that engulfed popular music during the 1940s.

Shake, rattle, and a rock 'n' roll hit

Turner made his first records in 1938 and began recording in earnest by the 1940s, cutting tracks for Decca, OKeh, Vocalion, Varsity, National, Stag, Excelsior, MGM, Swing Time, Modern, and Coral before the decade ended. After cutting stray singles for Freedom, Imperial, and Aladdin, Big Joe signed up with the fledgling Atlantic label in 1951, producing the hit "Chains Of Love" at his first session. By 1953, Turner was ruling the R&B charts with "Honey Hush," "TV Mama," and his biggest hit, "Shake, Rattle and Roll," which, reinterpreted by Bill Haley and the Comets, ushered in the rock 'n' roll era.

Big Joe continued to record for Atlantic until 1961, but the market for his brash brand of blues started to shrink. He continued to record into the 1980s for smaller jazz labels, including Pablo, and continued to perform at clubs such as Tramps in New York. Even when he was in his 70s, Big Joe's voice could still fill a room while he banged the butt of his cane on the floor in time to the music. He sang right up to the end when he died of kidney failure at age 74 on November 24, 1985. He was inducted into the Blues Foundation's Hall of Fame in 1983 and the Rock and Roll Hall of Fame in 1987.

Big, Bad & Blue (Rhino). This great three-disc set features a satisfying cross-section of the best from Big Joe's lengthy career in the blues.

John Lee "Sonny Boy" Williamson I

Two famous figures in the blues were named Sonny Boy Williamson. If you skim through Chapter 5, you may spot the name Sonny Boy Williamson II (real name, Aleck "Rice" Miller). In this chapter, we tell you about the original Sonny Boy Williamson (1914–1948).

But first, we'll take a moment to tell you about Sonny Boy's younger namesake. Rice Miller was urged to assume the identity of Sonny Boy the First in the late 1940s while hosting a radio show in Helena, Arkansas. The commercial sponsor thought the show would draw more listeners if Miller pretended to be the original Sonny Boy. There was marquee value in the Sonny Boy name because John Lee "Sonny Boy" Williamson was already a well-established blues star. Both men, as it turned out, were harmonica players with highly individual and influential styles who wrote and sang some of the best blues ever committed to phonograph records.

The harmonica gets some respect

John Lee "Sonny Boy" Williamson I (the subject of this section of the book) forever changed how the harmonica was perceived and how it was played and used in the blues. In his hands, the humble "mouth organ" became an expressive instrument capable of solo flourishes and octave-spanning fills. If anyone "citified" the harmonica and gave it a solo voice, it was Sonny Boy.

Born in Jackson, Tennessee, on March 30, 1914, Williamson taught himself the harmonica and was later influenced by Memphis harp players Will Shade, Hammie Nixon, and Noah Lewis. Sonny Boy traveled during the Depression and polished his craft by playing with Robert Nighthawk, Yank Rachell, and Sleepy John Estes. By the time he arrived in Chicago in 1934, Sonny Boy had a fully matured playing style.

His classics reinterpreted

He began recording for Bluebird Records in 1937 under the direction of producer Lester Melrose. (Sonny Boy had a unique vocal style that owed to a slight speech impediment.) His first single, the classic "Good Morning Little Schoolgirl," made Williamson an instant star, and the hits continued into the next decade. Sonny Boy's material would be reinterpreted the following decade by other blues artists — "My Little Machine" (Lightnin' Slim and Driftin' Slim), "Bluebird Blues" and "Decoration Blues" (Howlin' Wolf), "Sloppy Drunk" (Jimmy Rogers), and "Better Cut That Out" (Junior Wells).

Sonny Boy was a true star and a big-hearted member of Chicago's blues community with friends on every corner. He was always willing to help out young players with advice and encouragement. Tragically, in 1948 when he was at the height of his fame, Sonny Boy Williamson I was stabbed to death in the doorway of his home after returning from a club engagement. His induction into the Blues Foundation's Hall of Fame in 1980 was long in coming and much deserved.

Sugar Mama (Indigo). This solid 24-track collection serves as a primer for 1940s Chicago blues and some of the most influential harmonica playing of all time.

Other Notable Artists

Although they never reached household-name status, sold millions of records, or were cited as major influences as often as the big names of the blues, the following folks made important work that's definitely worth your time and attention.

Barbecue Bob

Recording for Columbia Records from 1927 to 1930, Barbecue Bob Hicks (1902–1931) was the label's best-selling blues guitarist of the time. Barbecue Bob was one of Atlanta's best-known players in the late 1920s and early 1930s. His specialty was the 12-string guitar, which he often played with the finger slide. Barbecue Bob had a percussive guitar style and a strong voice with a keening falsetto wail he used to great effect. He was taught the blues by his brother, Charley Hicks (also known as Charley Lincoln).

Discovered by a Columbia Records scout while playing at a local barbecue pit, Bob's lone publicity photo shows him playing his 12-string in a chef's outfit while standing over a steaming pit of ribs and chicken. Barbecue Bob sold a fair amount of records in his short career, and recorded close to 70 sides in a three-year flurry of activity that ended with his death from pneumonia in 1931 at the age of 28.

Chocolate To The Bone (Yazoo). These 20 tracks include two songs with Barbecue Bob as part of the Georgia Cotton Pickers and one backing up vocalist Nellie Florence on "Jacksonville Blues." He's clearly enjoying himself on these cuts, which make for a sample of some of his best work.

Blind Blake

Blind Blake (early 1890s–1933) is one of the great mystery men of the blues (so mysterious, in fact, no one knows what year he was born). He was a blues artist who enjoyed respectable record sales and left behind 81 solo recordings, yet virtually every detail of his life history is open to speculation. He was born Arthur Blake or Arthur Phelps sometime in the last decade of the 1890s, either in Jacksonville, Florida, or in the Georgia Sea Islands.

The details of his childhood, most of his adulthood, and even what influenced his astounding guitar technique is a matter of guesswork. He moved to Chicago in the mid-1920s and secured a recording contract with Paramount Records, releasing his first single, "West Coast Blues," in 1926. He recorded prolifically for the next six years and worked with the vaudeville show Happy-Go-Lucky in 1930 and 1931.

In 1932, when the bottom temporarily fell out of the recording industry, Blind Blake stopped making records and just as quickly disappeared, never to be seen or heard from again. Details surrounding his death remain unsubstantiated to this day.

Ragtime Guitar's Most Foremost Picker (Yazoo). Blake may have been a total mystery man, but he left behind a solid body of work filled to the brim with astounding finger-picked guitar work and good-time sounds. This 23-track compilation samples some of his very best.

Leroy Carr

Smooth-singing piano player Leroy Carr (1905–1935) was the first person to play what later was called "urban blues." Carr's playing style was simple and direct, but it carried none of the emotional intensity of the rural Delta singers. After teaming with guitarist Scrapper Blackwell in the late 1920s, Leroy quickly became one of the top blues stars of his day.

Carr recorded some 200 sides in his brief career, writing his own material, including the all-time classics "How Long, How Long Blues" and "Blues For Sunrise." Born in Nashville, Carr moved to Indianapolis as a child. He taught himself how to play the piano and, after spending his youth working a variety of odd jobs, returned in Indianapolis in 1928 where he met Blackwell. The two formed a partnership and were recording by year's end.

For the next seven years, Leroy Carr was one of the most successful blues artists in America. But Carr was also drinking heavily during this period and it eventually caught up with him. He died of the effects of alcoholism a month after his 30th birthday.

Naptown Blues (Yazoo). A collection of some of Leroy Carr and Scrapper Blackwell's best duet work from 1929 to 1934. This single-disc compilation demonstrates that the roots of urban blues go way back to the landmark recordings of this splendid partnership.

Ida Cox

If they were giving out posthumous awards to the classic female blues singers of the 1920s, Ida Cox (1896–1967) would definitely win for "Best All-Around Singer." Not a powerful shouter like Ma Rainey or Bessie Smith, Cox had a straightforward style that made her popular both as a live performer and recording star. But Ida Cox was no shrinking violet when it came to taking charge of her own career.

Given the social and professional standards of the times, her career moves were unprecedented — she wrote many of her own songs, hired all of her own musicians, produced her own stage shows, and managed her own touring company, Raising Cain. Cox also epitomized the newly liberated woman in modern society with her lavish wardrobe, up-to-the-minute urban attitudes, and savvy business sense. She didn't do much recording in the 1930s after the demand for female blues singers withered, but kept on performing nonetheless.

Ida caught a break performing at John Hammond's 1939 Spirituals To Swing concert at Carnegie Hall, which led to new recordings in the 1940s. She suffered a stroke in 1944 which forced her retirement, but rallied back to cut one more session in 1961 with jazz great Coleman Hawkins. Ida Cox died of cancer in 1967 at the age of 71.

Blues For Rampart Street (Riverside). This is Ida's final session in 1961 with tenor sax great Coleman Hawkins. Although a recording from later in her career, this finds her in excellent form and features several of her best-known songs.

Alberta Hunter

To call her a blues singer only partly describes the talents of Alberta Hunter (see Figure 4-5) (1895–1984). Over the years, Hunter reinvented herself as a supper club singer, jazz singer, and interpreter of ballads, all the while perfecting her song-writing craft.

Born in Memphis, by 1912 (while still in her teens), Hunter was already singing in clubs. In 1921, she moved to New York where she began her recording career. Two years later, one of Hunter's tunes, "Downhearted Blues," became Bessie Smith's first hit. Hunter continued to write and record under various pseudonyms for different labels using jazz legends Louis Armstrong, Fats Waller, Sidney Bechet, and Eubie Blake on her sessions. A tough-minded individual, Hunter kept working her way up the show business ladder, eventually starring in a London production of *Showboat* with Paul Robeson in the late 1920s.

Alberta worked the USO tours during both World War II and the Korean War, then decided to become a nurse at the age of 61! She continued with her nursing career until she was forced to retire in 1977. The following year, at the age of 83, she made a comeback as a jazz singer, working regularly around New York City, recording for Columbia, and writing the music for the movie *Remember My Name* in 1978. She continued performing right up until her death in 1984 at age 89.

Young Alberta Hunter (Vintage Jazz). This 23-track compilation captures Hunter at the top of her game. These recordings, from 1921 to 1940, showcase Alberta backed by both small combos and large bands, and includes her work with bandleader and jazz great Fletcher Henderson.

Figure 4-5: Alberta Hunter, shown during the first phase of her career and during the time of her 1970s comeback (photo courtesy of the Everett Collection, Inc.).

Skip James

If you're in the mood for highly dramatic Mississippi Delta blues, then take a listen to the original recordings of Nehemiah "Skip" James (1902–1969). He filled his lyrics with dark and creepy images, and his otherworldly moaning and eerie guitar tones were downright bone-chilling. (Skip played with an open-D minor tuning that was down two whole steps from concert pitch.) He played in minor keys (a rarity in the blues) with a complicated three-finger picking style more common to bluegrass or country musicians than blues players.

James recorded 26 sides for the Paramount label in 1931. One of those numbers, "Devil Got My Woman," become the blueprint for the Robert Johnson composition, "Hellhound On My Trail." Skip spent the next 15 years playing in various gospel groups and did not record again for another three decades. He had been away from the music business for 20 years when he was discovered in 1964 by folk music researchers Bill Barth, John Fahey, and Henry Vestine, who was a member of the blues-rock group Canned Heat.

Skip was a huge hit at the 1964 Newport Folk Festival and started playing full time again, recording new material for the Vanguard label. He never achieved the measure of success that other rediscovered country blues artists enjoyed at the time, but did achieve some celebrity status when Eric Clapton and Cream recorded his tune "I'm So Glad" on their debut album. Skip James died of cancer in November 1969. He was inducted into the Blues Foundation's Hall of Fame in 1992.

Complete Early Recordings (Yazoo). This 18-track compilation brings together all the early sides that made Skip a blues legend, including the original versions of "I'm So Glad" and "Devil Got My Woman" — an important addition to anyone's Delta blues collection.

Cripple Clarence Lofton

Boogie-woogie piano man and entertainer supreme Cripple Clarence Lofton (1896–1957) was the 1930s blues version of Jerry Lee Lewis. Owing to his background working the tent show circuit, Lofton used every trick in the book to win over a crowd. Despite Lofton's nickname (his limp stemmed from a birth defect), he was by all accounts a fine dancer and, in fact, got his start in show business as a tap dancer.

Banging out the most rudimentary boogie-rhythms while standing up at the piano, Lofton danced, sang, whistled, and generally created a racket to keep an audience's attention. His early recordings indicate that hitting every note spot on, or making chord changes at exactly the right time, were not major priorities with him, nor was finesse his strong suit. Nevertheless, Clarence was one of the first popular boogie-woogie piano players and his performances, both live and on record, did much to promote piano blues, especially in Chicago.

He recorded for six different labels into the late 1940s when the boogie-woogie craze dwindled, forcing Clarence into early retirement. At the age of 69, Cripple Clarence Lofton died in 1957 of a brain aneurysm.

Cripple Clarence Lofton and Walter Davis (Yazoo). A selection of some of Lofton's best work done in his noisy and boogie-heavy style, this CD also features equally fine sides by his piano-playing contemporary Walter Davis.

The Memphis Jug Band

No group epitomized the 1920s jug band sound and style better than the Memphis Jug Band. Only fellow Memphis residents, Gus Cannon's Jug Stompers, rivaled the Jug Band in popularity. Formed by guitarist Will Shade right on Beale Street in the mid-1920s, this noisy little group played a variety of blues, ragtime, and vaudeville numbers, all delivered with a large dollop of good humor.

Shade and his group were signed to Victor Records in 1927 and for the next seven years recorded close to 60 songs for the label. The group was also a proving ground for up-and-coming Memphis talent, including Casey Bill Weldon, Furry Lewis, Charley Polk, and a very young Walter Horton, all of whom were in the band's ranks at one time or another. Shade maintained various configurations of the Memphis Jug Band until his death in 1966.

Memphis Jug Band (Yazoo). This single-disc, 28-track collection spans the group's heyday from 1927 to 1934. It includes the original version of "He's In The Jailhouse Now," later to become a country music standard.

Mamie Smith

In 1920, African-American composer Perry Bradford convinced the executives at OKeh Records that an entire record market was left completely untapped. As a bold experiment, OKeh agreed to issue one single, "Crazy Blues," by a young singer named Mamie Smith (1883–1946) aimed exclusively at an African-American audience. OKeh hoped to make a slim profit on the deal.

Instead, the record sold almost a million copies and suddenly record executives in America were stumbling over themselves to record this strange new music. So, it can be argued that Mamie Smith (see Figure 4-6) was the first recorded blues singer, the first blues artist to score a major hit, the singer who ushered in the "classic female" blues era, and the person whose success marked the beginnings of recorded blues history.

Although Mamie's career was by and large over by 1923, her pioneering efforts made the recording careers of Ma Rainey, Bessie Smith, and all other blues singers (male and female) who followed her possible. Mamie Smith died in obscurity in 1946.

Blues Masters, Volume 11: Classic Blues Women (Rhino). If you want to hear the song ("Crazy Blues") and the lady (Mamie Smith) that started the whole blues recording business, this 18-track compilation is the place to go. It features other ground-breaking tunes by Trixie Smith, Bessie Smith, Ida Cox, Victoria Spivey, Sippie Wallace, and the always sublime Ma Rainey.

Figure 4-6:
Mamie Smith (photo courtesy of the Everett Collection, Inc.).

Victoria Spivey

Victoria Spivey (1906–1976) was part of the first wave of classic female blues singers that took the recording industry by storm in the 1920s. Born in Houston, she started singing early and often worked locally with guitarist Blind Lemon Jefferson. She had a hit with her first recording in 1926, "Black Snake Blues," and three years later made her movie debut, appearing in the all African-American MGM musical *Hallelujah*.

When the vogue for female blues singers ended in the mid-1930s, Victoria kept working in vaudeville and in various road shows, including a tour in the 1940s with the Hellzapoppin' road show. In addition to her vibrant stage performances and wonderful recorded work, Spivey was also a top-notch songwriter and shrewd businesswoman. This business acumen kept her in good stead in the early 1960s when she launched her own label, Spivey Records, which was devoted to the blues.

Spivey recorded the Muddy Waters band, Big Joe Williams, and a young Bob Dylan, among others. Her timing was always perfect and the label's releases earned good reviews from the folk community who was just discovering blues. A true survivor, she continued to sing, record, and perform until her death in 1976, 12 days shy of her 70th birthday.

Victoria Spivey: 1926–1931 (Document). This compilation features Victoria in top form during her peak period. It includes the classics "Steady Grind," "Blood Thirsty Blues," and her first hit, "Black Snake Blues."

Sippie Wallace

"The Texas Nightingale" Sippie Wallace (1898–1986) was the daughter of a Baptist deacon and a big-voiced veteran of the tent show circuit by the time she was in her teens.

Settling in Chicago, Wallace (see Figure 4-7) made her first records for the OKeh label in 1923, scoring hits with "Up The Country Blues" and "Shorty George." For the next four years, Sippie recorded more than 40 songs for OKeh and was backed on many of them by jazz legends King Oliver, Louis Armstrong, and her brothers Hersal and George Thomas. Sippie wrote much of her own material or cowrote it with her brothers. Moving to Detroit in 1936, Wallace joined the Leland Baptist Church and for the next 30 years stayed away from show business.

In 1966, Sippie's old friend Victoria Spivey encouraged her to record again and the resulting duet album with Spivey announced to the blues world that Sippie Wallace was back. She also befriended a young Bonnie Raitt, who produced her 1983 Atlantic album, *Sippie*. Wallace died in 1986 at the age of 88.

Figure 4-7:
Sippie
Wallace
(photo
courtesy of
the Everett
Collection,
Inc.).

Women Be Wise (Alligator). Recorded by Sippie on Halloween night 1966 in Copenhagen, this is one of the few "blues rediscovery" albums of the 1960s that's really outstanding. With Little Brother Montgomery and Roosevelt Sykes sharing the piano chores, Sippie belts out one great song after another, making this a perfect introduction to her sound and style.

Big Joe Williams

The cantankerous and idiosyncratic Delta blues guitarist Big Joe Williams (1903–1982) had a career in the blues that lasted nearly 50 years. He made records and performed anytime and anywhere the mood struck him, that is, when he wasn't in transit hoboing around the country.

Big Joe (See Figure 4-8) truly led the life of the wandering blues minstrel, playing the streets for food and spare change, sleeping in railroad cars, and maintaining a fiercely independent spirit. He also left the blues with more than a couple of classics, most notably the often-recorded "Baby, Please Don't Go."

Figure 4-8:
Big Joe
Williams
(photo
courtesy of
Burton
Wilson,
Austin, TX).

Playing a homemade *nine-string* guitar, sometimes amplified through crudely constructed rigs, he used a picking technique that turned the guitar into a sort of percussion instrument. His booming voice sliced through every recording he made. In short, Big Joe had a style that was all his own. His recording career began in 1935 for Bluebird Records and despite his raw, solo-artist style (he never felt comfortable playing with a band), Williams continued to record into the late 1960s for small labels and maintained a touring schedule until the late 1970s. Big Joe Williams died in 1982 at the age of 79 and was inducted into the Blues Foundation's Hall of Fame ten years later.

Shake Your Boogie (Arhoolie). This single-disc collection contains two of Big Joe's 1960s albums — *Tough Times* and *Thinking Of What They Did*. This makes a wonderful introduction to the music of this idiosyncratic blues artist. All at once brutal and graceful, Big Joe never bowed to fashion and these wonderful recordings prove it.

On The Side: Sidemen of Note

While front men (and women) typically garner most of the fame and acclaim, without instrumentalists, live and recorded music would have only a fraction of its impact. All of the following artists recorded under their own names, but their major contribution to the blues was their work as instrumental sidemen.

Scrapper Blackwell

Scrapper Blackwell (1903–1962) was best known as pianist Leroy Carr's partner. Blackwell's guitar-playing talents can be heard on more than 100 sides he made with Carr. Blackwell also recorded under his own name and left a legacy of his own for you to discover. Born in North Carolina, Francis Hillman Blackwell started out playing piano and then taught himself guitar on a variety of homemade instruments.

After moving to Indianapolis in the mid-1920s, he hooked up with Carr, and the two enjoyed a solid recording career until Carr's early death in 1935. (Scrapper also recorded under his own name and with singers Georgia Tom Dorsey and Black Bottom McPhail.)

By all accounts a withdrawn and difficult man to work with, Blackwell dropped out of music after Carr died and was back in Indianapolis at the end of the 1930s working as a manual laborer. Coaxed out of retirement in the late 1950s, Blackwell made an album for the Prestige/Bluesville label. He seemed poised to join other blues artists in reaping some of the rewards of the 1960s blues revival. It wasn't to be, however. In 1962, Scrapper Blackwell was shot to death after being mugged in an alley in Indianapolis.

Virtuoso Guitar, 1925–1934 (Yazoo). The 14 tracks in this collection feature Scrapper working with Leroy Carr, Black Bottom McPhail, Tommy Bradley, and on his own. The guitar playing throughout is impeccable and Blackwell's solo sides are every bit as interesting as his work as a sideman.

Jazz Gillum

Next to John Lee "Sonny Boy" Williamson, no harmonica player was as much in demand for recording session work in the 1930s than Jazz Gillum (1904–1966). A linchpin of the Bluebird label house band, Gillum recorded extensively in the company of Big Bill Broonzy and others as well as recording numerous tracks under his own name.

Somewhat of a child prodigy, Jazz (real name William McKinley Gillum) taught himself harmonica at the age of 6. He ran away from home a year later and spent his teenage years living with relatives in Charleston, Mississippi, honing his craft while working the streets for tips on weekends.

He went to Chicago in 1923 where he met Broonzy and other blues players. Gillum first recorded for ARC and later Bluebird. When Bluebird wound down to a halt in the early 1950s, Gillum's recording career seemed to also slow to a stop. A 1961 session with Memphis Slim would be his last recorded work. On March 29, 1966, while in the middle of an argument, Jazz Gillum was shot and killed.

Roll Dem Bones, 1938–1949 (Wolf). A solid compilation of Gillum's best Bluebird material from his prime years. This import is tough to get but serves as the best available Jazz Gillum collection until something is issued domestically.

Big Maceo Merriweather

Big Maceo Merriweather (1905–1953) was a piano-playing contemporary of Leroy Carr, Little Brother Montgomery, and Roosevelt Sykes. His career spans the period between the early blues piano era and the era of Chicago blues pianists such as Otis Spann and Johnnie Jones.

Major Maceo Merriweather was born in Georgia, learned to play the piano as a child, and moved to Detroit while still in his teens. His solid piano work coupled with his dusky vocals proved an irresistible combination, and Big Maceo enjoyed much success as both a sideman and as a solo artist. His biggest hit was the blues standard "Worried Life Blues" recorded in 1941.

In the late 1940s, a stroke paralyzed his right side, but Big Maceo gamely continued recording with other pianists sitting in for him until 1949 when he retired from playing. Big Maceo Merriweather died in 1953.

The Bluebird Recordings, 1941–1942 (RCA). The 16 tracks on this disc are from Big Maceo's first studio sessions for the Bluebird label and include his big hit, "Worried Life Blues." Merriweather's keyboard work pointed the way for future Chicago blues piano players.

Washboard Sam

Washboard Sam (1910–1966) was a popular blues artist of the 1930s and 1940s and one of the principal purveyors of *hokum blues,* a musical style with strong ties to the vaudeville novelty song tradition. His highly energetic work spiced the recordings of Big Bill Broonzy, Jazz Gillum, Memphis Slim, and Bukka White. In addition to his distinctive washboard playing (in which he took the laundry device and turned it into a percussion instrument), Sam (real name Robert Brown) also had considerable talents as a songwriter.

Washboard Sam was a strong vocalist with a dead-on sense of how to put a song across. While the washboard may not be the most expressive solo instrument in the blues, he certainly knew how to work it for all it was worth.

Sam played on literally hundreds of recordings between 1935 and 1953 until the new electric Chicago style of blues made his style of playing outmoded. He came out of retirement and made one last recording (for Victoria Spivey's record label) in 1964 before his health declined. Washboard Sam passed away from heart disease in 1966.

Washboard Sam, Volume 1 (Document). This single-disc import collection brings together 18 sides from the heyday of Bluebird Records and features rock-solid support from Big Bill Broonzy and pianists Blind John Davis and Black Bob.

Chapter 5

Artists from the Original Blues Heyday (1946 to 1969)

. . . .

. . . .

*F*or almost a quarter of a century between the mid-1940s and the late 1960s, the blues experienced a musical renaissance of such richness and ground-breaking creativity that it probably could be compared to the bebop period in jazz, or the flowering of rock in the 1960s. This period in the blues produced some of the absolute greats who literally and figuratively electrified the blues and continue to influence a younger generation of artists.

And unlike the previous blues generation, these artists had the ready means to create a permanent record of their music (and sell it to mass audiences). After World War II and the rise of small, locally owned, independent record labels, blues artists didn't have to travel all the way to Chicago or New York to record their music.

The invention of magnetic tape made it possible for anyone with a tape recorder and a microphone to produce at least a bare-bones recording. By the late-1940s, record labels that were independent (the so-called *indies*) from the major labels spread like kudzu across the American musical landscape (for more information on independent record labels, see Chapter 7).

Quickly discovering that there were specialized markets that the major labels were ignoring, the upstart independents zeroed in on the blues (as well as folk and jazz). Blues started selling, and seemingly every artist with a couple of solid songs made at least one record of his or her music. Other performers with greater talent or opportunities went on to press a library of great music.

We list (in alphabetical order) as many important artists who rose to prominence during this blues music period as we could fit in these pages.

Various Artists — *Southern Journey: Voices From The American South, Volume 1* (Rounder). Folklorist Alan Lomax captured these raw, unvarnished performances in 1959 and 1960. Filled with 24 tracks of blues, ballads, hymns, reels, shouts, chants, and work songs, this is a collection loaded to the brim with authentic Southern rural music.

Bobby "Blue" Bland

John Lennon once said that if you were going to give rock 'n' roll another name, you'd call it "Chuck Berry." In that case, if you gave R&B-soul blues another name, you'd call it "Bobby 'Blue' Bland." Along with Ray Charles, Sam Cooke, and Junior Parker, Bobby "Blue" Bland (born 1930) was one of the principal architects of what eventually became the modern soul sound.

Bland possesses one of the great voices in the rhythm-and-blues soul style. His vocals glide almost effortlessly from an unearthly growl to a shrieking falsetto, sometimes in mid-song. (His trademark vocal "squall" was borrowed from gospel singer C. L. Franklin, father of Aretha.)

During the 1950s and early 1960s, Bland developed a style that mixed gospel fervor, uptown blues, and R&B flavorings to develop a sound that was distinctly his own. With records that were heavy on brass arrangements, Bland was such a regular fixture on the R&B charts for more than two decades that he ranks with the top dozen best-selling R&B artists of all time.

Somewhat surprising is the fact that Bland doesn't play any musical instruments or write any of his own material. But, he does have that voice and a charismatic onstage presence that has made him a sex symbol to a legion of female fans.

Hanging with the Beale Streeters

Robert Calvin Bland was born in the small town of Rosemark, Tennessee, on January 27, 1930. When he was 17, his family moved to Memphis and there Bobby started singing gospel with various groups, including one called The Miniatures. His first professional job came with a loose musical aggregation called the Beale Streeters, a small combo that included future blues stars B.B. King, Junior Parker, Johnny Ace, and Rosco Gordon. It was with the Beale Streeters in 1952 that Bland made the record "Lovin' Blues" — the first of many for his long-time label, Duke Records.

Bland's career was interrupted by a two-year stretch in the Army. When he returned to Memphis in 1955, he discovered that the entire Duke Records label, including its master tapes and all of its artists' contracts (Bland's included), had been bought by Houston impresario/club owner/record label president Don Robey.

One of Robey's first tasks was to record Bobby in Houston, with Bill Harvey's Orchestra providing the horn-laden backing. The Bland legend began with those sessions because it was there Bobby created his signature style — a conversational form of blues singing with meaningful lyrics that went well beyond the standard rhyming blues couplets.

The stellar guitar playing on those tracks with Bill Harvey's Orchestra were courtesy of Pat Hare, Clarence Holliman, Roy Gaines, and Bland's long-time six-string partner, Wayne Bennett. When Bill Harvey's trumpet man Joe Scott took over the band, he wrote crystalline chart arrangements that perfectly framed Bobby's vocals. Scott worked with Bland, improving his diction, phrasing, and timing. No one was more important in developing Bland's talents than Joe Scott, who by 1957 had become his bandleader, arranger, and personal mentor.

Turning on that love light

The hits started coming regularly in the late 1950s beginning with the number-one R&B hit, "Farther Up The Road." Bland hit the touring circuit with Junior Parker, doing triple duty as Parker's valet, tour bus driver, and opening act for the Blues Consolidated show. Bland stayed with Parker's revue before striking out on his own (with Joe Scott in tow) in 1961. The 1960s brought Bland many more more hits — "I Pity The Fool" (which is on the *Blues For Dummies* CD), "Turn On Your Love Light," and "That's The Way Love Is," his third number-one record.

Recording at every possible opportunity, Bland and Scott kept the hits coming, but the real money was to be made on the road. Bobby kept up a punishing schedule, playing 300 dates a year while sandwiching in new recordings wherever and whenever he could.

After years of heavy touring, Joe Scott and Wayne Bennett moved on, and Bobby's band broke up in 1968. Bland stayed with Duke Records until Don Robey sold the label to ABC in 1973. The albums he cut on the new label showed how much Scott and Bennett were missed. When ABC was swallowed up by MCA, Bland switched labels again, recording albums with B.B. King as well as on his own.

Since the mid-1980s, Bobby's recorded for the Jackson, Mississippi, Malaco label (for more information on Malaco, turn to Chapter 9). Still in demand as a live performer and recording artist, Bobby Bland remains among the greatest of the soul-tinged blues singers. In 1992, he was inducted into the Rock and Roll Hall of Fame.

I Pity The Fool: The Duke Recordings, Volume 1 (MCA). A fine two-disc collection of Bland's early recordings, featuring great songs, solid arrangements, and a voice that made blues — and R&B — history.

Michael Bloomfield

Michael Bloomfield (1943–1981) was the first true blues-rock guitar hero. In the mid-1960s, Bloomfield was America's number-one electric guitar hotshot, single-handedly fighting off the British-invasion guitar gods with a machine gun attack, pumped-up volume, and limitless energy. Whether it was playing on Bob Dylan's *Highway 61 Revisited* or burning up the fretboard with the original Paul Butterfield Blues Band, Bloomfield played his instrument like he was skinning rattlesnakes.

He was an ace rock 'n' roll and rockabilly player, but his first love was the blues, and his knowledge of the music was encyclopedic in its scope. His style was clearly indebted to all three Kings — B.B., Albert, and Freddie — and the Chicago blues triumvirate of Buddy Guy, Otis Rush, and Magic Sam. But Bloomfield's inventive riffs and blistering guitar attack made him a true original who had an immediate and profound influence on blues-rock.

Bloomfield was born in Chicago on July 28, 1943. He got his first guitar at 13, and immediately gravitated toward the rock 'n' roll style of Chuck Berry, Elvis Presley, and Presley's guitarist Scotty Moore. Within a year's time, Bloomfield got real good, real fast, and began searching out broader musical horizons and seeking wilder musical sounds. He found it in his home town's burgeoning blues scene.

Conquering Chicago's South Side blues scene

The underage Butterfield sneaked into clubs to hear Muddy Waters, Magic Sam, and Howlin' Wolf. Exhibiting brazen teenage behavior, Butterfield would jump onstage and ask to sit in, not waiting for an answer while he plugged in his guitar and whipped off a few hot licks. His sheer bravado — coupled with the novelty of a young white Jewish teenager playing the blues in all-black clubs — quickly endeared him to the South Side blues community.

Bloomfield spent the next few years immersing himself in blues music, going out of his way to look up old blues singers and emulating their playing styles *and* their personalities. He wrote a brilliant short story during this period, "Me and Big Joe," about his exploits with old-time blues artist Big Joe Williams. Michael acted as musical advisor in Mike Shea's documentary about Chicago's Maxwell Street open air market, "And This Is Free," and also managed a folk music club, the Fickle Pickle, where he regularly booked local blues artists.

In 1965, Bloomfield was invited to join the Paul Butterfield Blues Band. With Butterfield's harmonica wizardry and Bloomfield's guitar prowess, the two made excellent musical foils, drawing the best out in each other. Their music extended past traditional Chicago blues to embrace free-form jazz and music from the Far East (just listen to Bloomfield's psychedelic composition "East-West").

Bloomfield and Butterfield part ways

The alliance between Butterfield and Bloomfield was nevertheless an uneasy one, and after much recording and touring — including backing Bob Dylan when he "went electric" at the Newport Folk Festival in 1966 — Michael left the band in 1967.

Anxious to move in new musical directions, he quickly formed his next band, The Electric Flag, with old friends Nick Gravenites, keyboardist Barry Goldberg, bassist Harvey Brooks, and Wilson Pickett's drummer, Buddy Miles. The band was initially well-received and recorded a promising debut album, but just as quickly fell apart in a morass of egos, mismanagement, and drug problems.

Bloomfield had grown weary of the road and guitar stardom and retreated to San Francisco. There, he scored films and played at studio sessions. One of those studio assignments involved Al Kooper, who played the distinctive Hammond organ fills on Dylan's *Highway 61 Revisited* album. The two old friends jammed all day and the results were later released as the hit album *Super Session.* The best-selling record of his brief career, Bloomfield later called it a "scam," but it nonetheless perfectly captured his wild tone and searing style in a handful of extended performances in which he could just stretch out and be himself.

Retreating from fame

Bloomfield shunned the spotlight after the success of the *Super Session* release. He retreated to San Francisco, kept an even lower profile, and essentially retired from performing. Aside from being lured into cutting an

Electric Flag reunion album, an abbreviated tour in 1974, and some lackluster super-session side projects (such as the group KGB and the *Triumvirate* album with John Hammond, Jr. and Dr. John), Bloomfield mostly stuck around San Francisco in virtual seclusion.

Crippled by chronic drug problems, Bloomfield would play and record only when the muse struck or if he needed some quick cash to survive. As the '70s wore on, his reputation for erratic behavior and missing shows eventually cost him both personal and professional relationships.

A charismatic guitar player with a big heart and loads of friends, he willingly passed his guitar hero title on to Eric Clapton and others. Mike Bloomfield died alone in his car of a drug overdose on February 15, 1981.

Don't Say That I Ain't Your Man (Sony). This 15-track compilation contains highlights from Bloomfield's recordings during the 1960s when he was at the peak of his creativity.

Clarence "Gatemouth" Brown

Clarence "Gatemouth" Brown (born 1924) expanded the definition of single-string solo guitar work with a batch of brilliant recordings done in the early 1950s for Don Robey's Peacock label in Houston (see the entry on Bobby "Blue" Bland for more on Robey).

Gatemouth is more than a bluesman. He's a true American artist adept at playing the guitar, violin, harmonica, bass, drums, and mandolin. He's a versatile master of many styles of American music, from jazz to country to Cajun, as well as the blues.

Brown was born April 18, 1924, in Vinton, Louisiana. His penchant for working in a variety of musical styles started when Gatemouth was a youngster growing up in Orange, Texas. His father was a local musician who himself played country, bluegrass, and Cajun music. The big band sounds of Duke Ellington, Count Basie, and others provided another seminal influence for Brown. At the age of 10, Gatemouth was playing the violin, and was accomplished on the guitar and four other instruments by the time he was drafted into the service during World War II.

The big break at the Bronze Peacock

Shortly after the end of his military stint, Brown got his big break one night in Houston. Filling in for an ailing T-Bone Walker at the Bronze Peacock nightclub, Gatemouth wowed the crowd. The overwhelming response to his music caught the attention of the club's owner, Don Robey, who became Brown's mentor, manager, and booking agent. Robey bagged a two-record deal with Aladdin Records for Gatemouth, but when those singles went nowhere saleswise, Robey started his own label, Peacock Records, in 1949 specifically to promote his new artist.

Brown stayed with Robey and Peacock through 1960, recording and touring at a fairly steady clip. Although he had only one R&B chart record to show for his stay at Peacock — 1949's "Mary Is Fine" — he scored several regional hits. His classic instrumental "Okie Dokie Stomp" (which is on the *Blues For Dummies* CD) still serves as a litmus test of a guitar player's talent. During the 1960s, Gatemouth's career went into a bit of a slump. He moved to Nashville, cut some country singles that had lackluster sales, and for a brief while in 1966 was the house band leader for the syndicated television show *The Beat.*

Gatemouth, Rounder, and a Grammy

During the 1970s, Brown worked hard to rebuild his career. He was discovered by European audiences and crossed over to reach new ones with his duet album with country artist Roy Clark, *Makin' Music.* That album led to a recording deal with Rounder Records, which released Brown's *Alright Again!* in 1982 to great acclaim, including a Grammy award for best blues recording.

Clarence "Gatemouth" Brown hasn't looked back since, touring around the globe doing 200 to 300 dates a year, while recording for Rounder, Alligator, and Verve. When he isn't on the road, he's at home in Slidell, Lousiana, on the north shore of Lake Pontchartrain, where he's a reserve deputy sheriff. His latest release, *Gate Swings,* marks his 50th year as a recording artist.

The Original Peacock Recordings (Rounder). This disc features the recordings that made Brown a household name among Texas guitarists and includes the classics "Dirty Work At The Crossroads" and "Okie Dokie Stomp."

Paul Butterfield

Along with his bandmate Michael Bloomfield, no one did more to spread the word about (and stretch the boundaries of) electric Chicago blues in the mid-1960s than Paul Butterfield (1942–1987). The Paul Butterfield Blues Band weren't just a bunch of white rockers trying to play the blues — they were the real deal. They were also the first popular racially integrated blues-rock band. Among their members was Howlin' Wolf's old rhythm section — drummer Sam Lay and bassist Jerome Arnold — deftly underpinning a band boasting no less than four able soloists.

Butterfield and his cohorts weren't the first white men to play the blues, but they were the first blues band to tap a mainstream white audience (and they did so during the turbulent time of the '60s Civil Rights movement). They convinced countless white rock musicians to do more than just mindlessly mimic African-American music styles and, instead, play and sing blues music from the heart.

The attorney's son turns blues harpist

Butterfield grew up in Chicago, the son of a prominent attorney father and artist mother, and studied flute with a member of the Chicago Symphony Orchestra. But it was the blues sound that captivated Butterfield and soon he was ducking classes to go "club hopping" (being underage, he'd stand outside the taverns listening to the music).

Butterfield started out playing guitar, but it was the harmonica that became his all-consuming passion. He would head out to the lakefront in Chicago's Hyde Park and practice by himself for hours on end. Around this time, he met Elvin Bishop, who was then attending the University of Illinois. Elvin played guitar and loved playing the blues and the two formed a partnership, playing the neighborhood as an acoustic duo.

Building the core of the Butterfield Blues Band

By 1963, Butterfield and Bishop were well-known and respected by other Chicago blues artists for their sincerity and their playing ability, and frequently sat in with most of the greats, including Muddy Waters, Howlin' Wolf, Little Walter, Magic Sam, and others. An offer to play at a club called Big John's on the city's predominately white North Side gave Paul (with Bishop on guitar) an opportunity to put his first band together.

Butterfield lured both Lay and Arnold away from Howlin' Wolf's band with an offer of more money. The four musicians became the core of the original Paul Butterfield Blues Band and their successful debut at Big John's was the first step in exposing white America to the traditional blues sound.

By early 1965, the band was anxious to record, and Butterfield wanted to beef up their sound. With the back-to-back additions of guitarist Michael Bloomfield and keyboardist Mark Naftalin bolstering the original lineup, the group recorded its debut album for Elektra Records. In the summer of '65, the band made its famous appearance at the Newport Folk Festival where Bloomfield, Arnold, and Lay formed the core of the band backing Bob Dylan's legendary "electric performance."

East-West and beyond

For their second album, *East-West*, drummer Billy Davenport replaced Sam Lay and the Butterfield Blues Band moved away from straight Chicago blues to explore jazz and rock themes. Although *East-West* was highly regarded and proved to be a big influence on other musicians, it signaled the beginning of the end. Bloomfield left the band in 1967 to form his own group, the Electric Flag. Butterfield responded by enlarging the band to include a horn section — one of whom was saxophonist David Sanborn — and drifting toward an R&B sound. Naftalin left the band after its third album, and by the time the Butterfield band played at Woodstock, their glory days were behind them.

Butterfield disbanded the group in 1972 but soldiered on for the rest of the decade, putting together a new group (Better Days) and continuing to record. He appeared with The Band in their documentary *The Last Waltz*, directed by Martin Scorcese in 1976, and released two more albums before drugs and alcohol got the better of him. He spent his remaining years battling personal demons and struggling to get his career back on track. Paul Butterfield died of a drug-related heart attack on May 3, 1987, at the age of 44.

The Paul Butterfield Blues Band (Elektra). The debut album from this band is definitely the place to start. Butterfield blows great harp and sings with conviction, the rhythm section swings, and Michael Bloomfield sprays wild guitar licks all over the place.

Clifton Chenier

Clifton Chenier (1925–1987) was the absolute monarch and the king of his domain — the American musical art form known as *zydeco*. He ruled his kingdom wearing a crown on his head (literally) and an accordion strapped to his chest. He had an unquenchable desire to turn every place he played into a gigantic party. As the years rolled by, he watched his crowd of loyal subjects expand from Louisianians and Texans to musical fans from around the world.

First, we'll fill you in a bit on zydeco. It's a unique musical genre that has its roots in the folk music played by the French Acadians who migrated to Louisiana from Canada. The Acadians spoke a French dialect called Cajun, and their music (called Cajun music, of course) was largely of the dance variety — waltzes and two-steps featuring an accordion as the lead instrument.

Zydeco is the African-American version of Cajun music, originally played in a manner quite similar to the older French Acadian style of playing. It consisted of the usual two-steps, waltzes, and fiddle-accordion arrangements, that is, until Clifton Chenier came along.

The zydeco formula: Cajun plus R&B plus a driving beat

What Chenier did was infuse Cajun music with hard-driving blues, rock 'n' roll instrumentals, modern R&B melodies, and even country-and-western themes. He played like a wild man on the accordion, an instrument not commonly equated with soulfulness, and hot-wired Cajun dance music by making the beat more pronounced and heavier.

Chenier (see Figure 5-1) brought excitement and energy with him everywhere he went. There was virtually no difference between a Clifton Chenier "concert" and an all-night dance featuring Chenier in some lone parish in Louisiana. The music was the same and so was the feeling, packed with good-time exuberance galore. One of Clifton's signature tunes was "Bon Ton Roulet," his French adaptation of the Louis Jordan number, "Let The Good Times Roll." And, he meant every word of it.

The once and forever "King of Zydeco" was born on June 25, 1925, in Opelousas, Louisiana. His family was large and musically gifted and included several semi-professional musicians in their ranks. Clifton's parents were sharecroppers, but played their music on weekends at local parties and picnics.

Amedee Ardion and French la-la's

Clifton's father, John, an accordion player, provided early musical inspiration. His uncle, Maurice "Big" Chenier, played violin and guitar, further prompting the youngster to pursue music. Another local musician, Izeb Laza, also did his part by giving young Clifton his very first accordion. But Chenier's biggest influence came from the music of Amedee Ardoin.

Ardoin was the biggest local name in Louisiana zydeco music and his reputation extended all the way back to the late 1920s when the music was known as *French la-la's.* Amedee, by all accounts, appears to be the first African-American Creole musician to play the blues on an accordion.

The records Ardoin left behind as his legacy made the biggest impression on Clifton. In zydeco, he found a template on which to build his new musical vision. Here was music that could be played in a traditional way yet was as modern and up-to-date as tomorrow. Chenier found he could play waltzes and two-steps right along with the big R&B hits of the day and it would all fit together.

Figure 5-1: Clifton Chenier (photo courtesy of Burton Wilson, Austin, TX).

Let the good times roll

As a teenager, Clifton worked side by side with his brother Cleveland, laboring in the oil fields during the week and playing on weekends around the Lake Charles, Louisiana, area. (Cleveland played the *rub board,* a metal washboard-like contraption worn like a vest and played with metal scrapers.)

The duo made a lot of good-sounding music together, but what made it unique and enhanced their reputation was that it wasn't the traditional Cajun or zydeco music. The two Cheniers were playing R&B material such as Joe

Liggins's "The Honeydripper," but filtered through the zydeco style, right down to the vocals translated into Cajun French.

But Clifton had an even bigger sound in mind, and by his mid-20s, put together his first full-size band. They were alternately known as the Hot Sizzling Band or the Hot Sizzlers and featured an instrumental lineup that included Clifton's accordion, Cleveland's rub board, an electric guitar (or sometimes two), tenor saxophone, piano, bass, and drums. Up until then, zydeco was performed in back yards and on front porches. That was about to change.

Auditioning over the telephone lines

The Hot Sizzling Band was making a name for itself on a circuit that found Clifton and company playing clubs and outdoor dances in Louisiana and Texas. One of Clifton's frequent ports of call was Clarence Garlow's Bon Ton Drive-In in Beaumont, Texas. Clifton had been packing them in for three years at the Drive-In and Garlow certainly knew a good thing when he saw it.

In 1954, Garlow called record producer J.R. Fullbright and told him about this accordion-playing phenomenon. When Fullbright told Garlow he'd think about auditioning Clifton, Garlow simply dragged the telephone over to the stage and set the receiver down next to Chenier's amplifier while the band was playing. When Garlow picked up the phone to ask J.R. what he thought, Fullbright said he was on his way over.

After Fullbright arrived, he sped Clifton and the Hot Sizzling Band to a radio station in Lake Charles, Louisiana, for a swift recording session. In one day, they recorded seven tracks that would constitute Clifton's first singles on the Elko and Post labels. Those three singles sold well enough to net Fullbright and Chenier a recording contract with Specialty Records in Los Angeles. It was those 1955 sessions that Clifton recorded for the Los Angeles-based R&B label that would forever change the history — and direction — of zydeco music. Fullbright's role in the studio was then reassigned by the label to producer Bumps Blackwell, who later worked with Little Richard, producing several of his biggest hits.

A sound shaped by legendary record producer Bumps Blackwell

Blackwell heard too much ornamentation, and just too much *music* surrounding Clifton's accordion playing in the Hot Sizzling Band. In the first studio session, he methodically stripped away one competing instrument after another until he had Chenier up front in the mix.

Whatever studio magic Blackwell concocted must have worked, because Clifton's first single for the label became an R&B hit record. Both sides of the single, "Ay-Tete Fee" and "Boppin' The Rock," were up-tempo and rocking enough to make Chenier and band an added attraction on many R&B package shows, where he shared the bill with Jimmy Reed and a very young Etta James.

Unfortunately, Clifton's R&B chart success was short lived. Little Richard's success with rock 'n' roll convinced Specialty to trim their artist roster to concentrate fully on new artists performing this new brand of music (who were selling lots of records). Clifton was released from the label, but just as quickly rebounded with a pair of singles for the Chess label in Chicago. By 1958, Clifton had signed up with the Zynn label in Crowley, Louisiana, where he would record for the next two years.

The prolific Arhoolie label years

Back in his native environment and the well-traveled circuit of Texas and Louisiana, Clifton just kept on working and making more records. By 1960, the work in Texas was plentiful enough that he relocated to the Frenchtown quarter of Houston.

Chris Strachwitz, a young folk and blues music historian from California was in Houston at that time. None other than Lightnin' Hopkins introduced Strachwitz to Clifton and his brand of neo-zydeco. He saw plenty of potential in Chenier's repertoire and started recording him for his own Arhoolie label. Clifton recorded a number of albums for Arhoolie (into the 1980s), and his recorded legacy displays a wide range of musical approaches and material. Strachwitz recorded Clifton doing everything from traditional French la-la duo work with his brother to full-blown live performances of Chenier and the band at a Saturday night dance.

But as many records as Chenier cranked out for Arhoolie, he also spent a great amount of time label hopping. During his tenure at Strachwitz's label, he also cut records for the Bayou label in Ville Platte, Louisiana, and before he stopped recording in 1982, Clifton released records on the Alligator, Bell, Blue Star, Blue Thumb, Caillier, Crazy Cajun, GNP Crescendo, Jin, and Maison de Soul labels.

Taking zydeco around the world

The albums Clifton recorded for Arhoolie in the 1960s gained him an international audience for the first time. In 1969, he appeared as a member of the American Folk Blues Festival touring troupe, bringing zydeco music to Europe for the first time. Clifton was an immediate hit and stayed on after the tour finished to do more shows throughout Europe. The following decade he continued touring the globe.

The hectic pace finally caught up with Chenier. In the early 1980s, he was diagnosed with diabetes and his doctors told him to take some time off. The advice went only partially heeded. Clifton managed to arrange his medical needs around his back-breaking road schedule. He eventually had to have a foot partially amputated and required regular kidney dialysis treatments. Nevertheless, Chenier still kept on playing, until he passed away on December 12, 1987.

Zydeco Dynamite: The Clifton Chenier Anthology (Rhino). This two-disc, 40-track anthology not only makes a perfect introduction to Chenier's music, but it also serves as an equally fine starting point for listeners turning on to zydeco music for the first time.

Willie Dixon

With the possible exception of Muddy Waters, no one helped shaped the sound and style of Chicago blues more than Willie Dixon (1915–1992). He was the ultimate behind-the-scenes man with estimable talents. He could write you a hit song, arrange it, pull together all the key players to record it, and produce the session, while contributing the best string bass playing you'd ever want to hear. Willie Dixon was definitely the embodiment of the blues renaissance man.

He wrote some of the most enduring songs in the Chicago blues canon, and listing just some of them sounds like the history of blues music itself: "Spoonful," "Back Door Man," "I Ain't Superstitious," "Little Red Rooster," and "Evil" (for Howlin' Wolf); "My Babe" and "Mellow Down Easy" (for Little Walter); "I'm Your Hoochie Coochie Man," "I Just Want To Make Love To You," and "You Shook Me" (for Muddy Waters); "I Can't Quit You Baby" (for Otis Rush); "Bring It On Home" (for Sonny Boy Williamson); and "Wang Dang Doodle" (for both Koko Taylor and Howlin' Wolf).

A Golden Gloves champ

Dixon was born July 1, 1915, in Vicksburg, Mississippi. His mother wrote and recited religious poetry, which instilled in the youngster a strong sense of meter and rhyme, a skill that would serve him well as a professional musician. Willie naturally gravitated toward gospel music and sang with the Union Jubilee Singers on local radio station WQBC.

For a brief while, Dixon was a professional boxer. His boxing career took him to Chicago in 1936 and within a year's time he won the Illinois State Golden Gloves heavyweight championship. He even worked as Joe Louis's sparring partner. Willie had only four fights to show for his professional boxing career before hanging up his gloves to play music full time.

The Five Breezes, Four Jumps of Jive, and The Big Three

Dixon (see Figure 5-2) started playing the string bass in 1939 and formed his first group, The Five Breezes, with guitarist Leonard "Baby Doo" Caston. They worked Chicago clubs and recorded for Bluebird until 1941. When the U.S. entered World War II, Willie declared himself a conscientious objector. He was then arrested and sent to prison for refusing to be drafted into the armed services.

After his release from prison, Dixon put together a new group, the Four Jumps of Jive, who recorded for Mercury Records in 1945. When Caston returned from a USO club tour, the two reformed their partnership and put together the Big Three Trio with guitarist Bernardo Dennis, who was later replaced by Ollie Crawford. With a wide-ranging repertoire of blues, pop, novelty tunes, and boogie-woogie, the group was a hit with supper club audiences and recorded for both the Bullet and Columbia labels.

Talent-scouting for Chess Records

While still a member of the Big Three Trio, Dixon also spent his spare time jamming in various Chicago blues clubs. This led to a friendship with Muddy Waters and, through him, an association with Leonard and Phil Chess (for more on the Chess brothers see Chapter 7). In 1948, the two brothers were just starting up their first record label and offered Willie a part-time job with the company as a talent scout. He accepted, and when the Big Three Trio broke up, he went to work for Chess Records full time.

Dixon came into his own in the early 1950s, writing songs for Chess artists Eddie Boyd ("Third Degree"), Willie Mabon ("The Seventh Son"), Muddy Waters ("I'm Your Hoochie Coochie Man"), and Howlin' Wolf ("Evil"), as well as releasing a few singles under his own name. Willie was never much of a singer, but as a session bass player he was incomparable and a major driving force of the Chess house band, recording with Muddy Waters, Little Walter, Chuck Berry, and Bo Diddley.

In 1957, Dixon moved over to rival Cobra Records, writing and producing songs for Otis Rush, Magic Sam, Buddy Guy, and other artists before the label went bankrupt two years later. Both Rush and Guy moved over to Chess after Dixon returned to the Chess fold in 1960.

Dixon was a virtual human Rolodex who had contacts to almost every blues artist working in Chicago, and was tapped to help organize the Chicago wing of the American Folk Blues Festivals in the mid-'60s. In the late '60s, he organized the Chicago Blues All Stars (which included Johnny Shines and Big Walter Horton), a loose touring group that also recorded. Suddenly, for the first time in his long career, Willie Dixon himself was in demand as a live performer.

Figure 5-2:
Willie Dixon
(photo
courtesy of
MCA-Chess).

Finally getting his (financial) due

Although Willie had written numerous blues standards over the decades, he hadn't seen much in the way of royalties. With the proliferation of rock groups recording his old songs (including Cream's rendition of "Spoonful"), Dixon began to suspect that a lot more money should have come his way.

After an out-of-court settlement with Led Zeppelin over their copyright infringement of "You Need Love" (recast by them as "Whole Lotta Love") and a second lawsuit against his former music publisher, the ownership of these valuable song copyrights reverted back to Dixon along with some sizeable royalty checks that were long overdue.

To give something back to the blues community and other musicians in his situation, Willie organized the Blues Heaven Foundation, and spent the rest of his life helping other blues artists recover back royalties due to them. He also got involved with movie soundtrack work, producing old Chess label mate Bo Diddley for the soundtrack of *La Bamba*. In 1989, he published his autobiography, *I Am The Blues*. He remained active as a performer into the 1990s when ill health forced him to curtail live shows. He passed away in his sleep on January 29, 1992, after a life well spent playing the blues. He was honored with induction into the Rock and Roll Hall of Fame in 1994.

The Chess Box (MCA-Chess). This box set features Dixon's best known songs as interpreted by the likes of Muddy Waters, Howlin' Wolf, Koko Taylor, Bo Diddley, and others. As such, it functions doubly as a Chess Records Greatest Hits package.

Lowell Fulson

Few blues artists have stretched the boundaries of the genre as much as Lowell Fulson (born 1921). An integral part of the blues community for more than 50 years, he boasts a voluminous recorded legacy of everything from slick, urban blues, to soulful grooves, to folksy guitar duets.

With his smooth vocals and edgy single-note guitar lines considered by many the epitome of the cool West Coast blues style, Fulson was a seminal influence on a young B.B. King, Lonnie Brooks, and many others.

Fulson (see Figure 5-3) was born March 31, 1921, to African-American and Native-American parents on a Choctaw reservation just outside of Tulsa, Oklahoma. Music was always a part of the Fulson household; his grandfather played violin and his two uncles and younger brother Martin all played guitar. In his formative years, Lowell was exposed to everything from blues and gospel to the Western swing music of Bob Wills. By the time he was 18, he started working as a rhythm guitarist in a large string band that traveled the Southwest.

California, there he goes

After working briefly with Texas Alexander, Lowell served in the Army during World War II. After his discharge, he relocated to Oakland, California. Hooking up with Bob Geddins's Big Town Records, Lowell made his first recording in 1946 with his brother Martin on second guitar. Soon after his entry into the recording world, Fulson began writing songs, formed his first band (with a young Ray Charles on piano), and started touring.

Lowell charted R&B hits during the early 1950s on the Swing Time label. Two of these hits — "Everyday I Have The Blues" and "Three O'Clock In The Morning" — caught the ear of Memphis disc jockey B.B. King and would, in time, become staples of his repertoire. In 1954, Fulson moved to Chess Records and scored the biggest hit of his career with the classic "Reconsider Baby," which peaked at Number Three on the R&B charts.

It's Fulson, not Fulsom

Lowell stayed with Chess Records until 1964. But he tired of traveling all the way to Chicago to record, so he switched to the Kent label in Los Angeles. The company listed his last name as "Fulsom," rather than Fulson, and the error appears on all of his releases for Kent (although "fulsome" may be a word used to describe his far-ranging musical style). Lowell's biggest record for the label was also one of his oddest, the soul-inspired "Tramp," which charted in 1966. The song would become an even bigger hit in a duet version for Otis Redding and Carla Thomas the following year.

Lowell moved to the Jewel label in the 1970s, expanding his musical reper-toire even further by recording blues-rock covers of Beatles tunes! The '80s saw him backing off from recording and touring, but in the '90s, he returned as strong as ever with a spate of interesting albums for the Rounder and Bullseye Blues labels.

Fulson was inducted into the Rhythm & Blues Hall of Fame in 1993 and in the same year was honored with induction into the Blues Hall of Fame, in recogni-tion of his work as a blues artist and writer of the classic "Reconsider Baby."

The Complete Chess Masters (MCA-Chess). This two-disc set features Lowell Fulson's biggest hit, "Reconsider Baby," along with 44 other examples of his smooth and supple style.

Buddy Guy

When most blues artists would be happy with one period in their careers that would put them in the history books, Buddy Guy (born 1936) has enjoyed two stretches at the forefront of the business. First, in the late 1950s and early 1960s, along with fellow guitarists Magic Sam and Otis Rush, Buddy helped carry blues guitar playing into the modern musical era. And now, in his current position as the elder statesman of Chicago blues, he has Grammy awards and a popular nightclub in the Windy City to show for his long dedication to the blues.

Developing a style worthy of imitation

Guy (see Figure 5-4) combines the stinging, single-string guitar stylings of B.B. King with the outrageous pyrotechnics and loudness of Guitar Slim (both of whom were early influences) into an edgy, intense style all his own. His amazing ability to improvise on one chorus after another makes few experiences in the blues as exciting as a Buddy Guy guitar solo. As a live performer *par excellence,* his emotional fervor and his arsenal of virtuoso tricks have made him a crowd-pleasing entertainer for more than 40 years.

Figure 5-4:
Buddy Guy
(photo
courtesy of
MCA-Chess).

Guy's influence on younger blues and rock players is incalculable. Eric Clapton calls him the greatest blues guitar player ever, and Jimi Hendrix and Stevie Ray Vaughan drew heavily from his wailing guitar attack. Both Hendrix and Vaughan cribbed from Buddy's stage performances; Jimi played the guitar with his teeth and Stevie Ray played with his guitar behind his back, but the guy they learned it from was Buddy.

Lightnin' Slim, Boogie Chillen, and a blues epiphany

Buddy was born George Guy on July 30, 1936, in Lettsworth, Louisiana, to the sharecropping family of Sam and Isabell Guy. Like many blues artists before him, he picked cotton in the fields along with the rest of his family, including his brother Phil who also played professionally. In 1949, when electricity was fed into the Guy household for the first time, Sam Guy immediately went out and bought a radio and a used record player.

Buddy soaked up the blues music radio broadcasts and saved enough money to travel to nearby Baton Rouge to buy his first record, John Lee Hooker's "Boogie Chillen." The youngster went crazy for the boogie rhythm on the 78 record, strumming along to it daily on the screen door with such ferocity that his father finally relented and purchased Buddy a second-hand guitar — to be played outdoors only. The teenage Buddy thought he had everything he needed to play the blues the way he heard it on the radio and on records, until he went into Baton Rouge one Sunday afternoon.

In *CD Review Magazine* in 1993, Buddy said, "The first electric guitar I ever saw was Lightnin' Slim's. I'd had my allowance — which was 30 cents — and he had a little amplifier and a guitar playing 'Boogie Chillen.' I couldn't believe that was a guitar. I didn't know what an electric guitar was back then! I ended up giving him my allowance that Sunday evening and we became the best of friends. I had the opportunity to play with him a lot as a youngster. I would get in his way a lot, because I was trying to steal licks from him, but that's something I'll cherish and carry to my grave."

Another formidable influence for Guy was the flamboyant guitarist and showman Eddie Jones, known throughout the South as Guitar Slim, who had a hit with "The Things I Used To Do." In his show, Guitar Slim would mount the stage in a cherry red suit and white shoes, dragging behind him a 200-foot-long guitar cord that allowed to walk all around, and outside, almost any size club he worked in. As Buddy stated in his biography, *Damn Right I've Got The Blues,* "When I saw him . . . I'd made up my mind. I wanted to play like B.B. (King) but act like Guitar Slim."

Leaving Baton Rouge for the Windy City

Guy first started playing small engagements in and around Baton Rouge under the tutelage of "Big Poppa" Tilley (who got the young teen over his stage fright by fortifying him with wine laced with "patent" medicine). Buddy developed an act that was knocking them dead on the Louisiana club circuit, but he wanted a bigger audience than what his local celebrity would provide him. Buddy recorded a demo tape at radio station WXOK with an eye on getting signed to Chicago's Chess Records. Toting a suitcase full of fried chicken and salami sandwiches, Buddy took a train up to Chicago, never looking back.

But when Guy arrived at the doorstep of Chess Records, he found that his demo tape had never arrived and that the label wasn't really interested in auditioning new talent fresh off the street. He scuffled around the city for a while until he got his break the night he sat in with Otis Rush's band at the 708 Club. He ignited the crowd with his rendition of "The Things I Used To Do." Later, Muddy Waters took an almost paternal interest in Buddy, encouraging him to stay in Chicago while introducing him to the local club scene.

Soon, Guy was regularly featured in "head cutting" player-elimination contests at various Chicago blues clubs, taking on established players such as B.B. King, Freddie King, Otis Rush, Magic Sam, and Earl Hooker. Buddy would pull out every one of Guitar Slim's stage tricks — walking on top of the bar trailing a 150-foot-long cord, dropping to his knees during his solos, and cranking his amp as loud as it would go — and emerge victorious from these guitar battles. The word was soon out on the street about some new guitar hotshot in town, whose name was Buddy Guy.

Clocking time as a session musician

His growing reputation secured Guy his first recording deal — on Eli Toscano's Cobra label in 1958. His two singles on Toscano's Artistic subsidiary raised enough noise about Buddy that he was eventually signed to Chess Records in 1960. From the time he cut his first session for the label, Buddy was pressed into regular service as a session musician. He fullfilled his childhood dreams of recording and backing Howlin' Wolf, Sonny Boy Williamson, Muddy Waters, Little Walter, Koko Taylor, and Willie Dixon on many a legendary Chess recording session. Staying with the label through 1967, Buddy created a body of material that stood as the foundation of his style and, for some, the apex of his recorded work.

Guy formed a bond with white rock audiences in the early 1960s during his successful tours of Europe. With Eric Clapton and Jeff Beck singing his praises in rock circles, Guy earned critical high marks and a newfound market of his own. Guy left Chess in 1967 to sign with Vanguard Records, producing his first albums for a more mainstream American audience.

Partnering with Junior Wells

In the 1970s, Buddy formed a partnership with harmonica player and singer Junior Wells that lasted the entire decade. The two men had been "running buddies" for some time (Guy had played on Junior's *Hoodoo Man Blues* album in 1965). Both were brilliant musicians but also mercurial personalities — both onstage and in the recording studio — which resulted in unpredictable performances that ranged from absolutely scintillating to completely scattered.

Unable to secure an American record deal throughout the 1980s, Guy turned out a spate of highly erratic albums for various foreign labels. With slipshod production and less-than-inspired playing, those albums provided only a glimmer of his true talent. He returned to the American blues club circuit and did tours of Europe to make ends meet, largely ignored by the rock audience that had embraced him in the late 1960s.

Opening Chicago's top live blues spot

The lackluster '80s made way for a whole new beginning in the '90s for Guy. In 1989, Buddy opened up his own nightclub, Buddy Guy's Legends, which quickly became the number-one blues venue in Chicago. In 1991, Eric Clapton invited Guy to play with him in a series of shows at the Royal Albert Hall in London. Buddy's performances with Clapton led to a record deal with the British label Silvertone.

The first album Guy released after the Silvertone pact was signed, *Damn Right, I've Got The Blues,* won him his first Grammy award in 1991. Buddy followed its success with *Feels Like Rain, Slippin' In,* and *Live! The Real Deal,* which added more Grammy awards to his mantle shelf. Nowadays, he sells out auditoriums and makes television appearances with Jay Leno and David Letterman. And if they ever had a Mayor of Chicago Blues they can skip the election — the certain winner is Buddy Guy.

"Buddy Guy is a master. He's the bravest guitar player I've ever seen on a bandstand. He'll pull you into his trap and just kill you. He *owns* that bandstand and everybody knows it when Buddy's up there. He's great with dynamics; he'll take the volume down to a whisper, then turn it around and just slam it back to you, cranking it up as loud as he can get it!"

The Very Best Of Buddy Guy (Rhino). What you'll find here is a nice single-disc summary of Buddy's career up to his mainstream breakthrough. Loads of great guitar playing and impassioned singing make this one a must-have.

Slim Harpo

Most of the great swamp-blues recordings were produced by a man from Crowley, Louisiana, named J.D. Miller. He leased his finished product on the Excello label in Nashville and enjoyed his biggest success in the blues field — and later in the pop field — with the recordings of harp player and guitarist extraordinaire Slim Harpo (1924–1970).

Electric Louisiana blues is sometimes called *swamp blues* because of its lazy, laid-back rhythm and heaping amounts of echo effect and reverb that give the overall sound a dark and doom-laden texture. Much of the popularity of the electric Louisiana style can be traced to Chicago blues artist Jimmy Reed. His languid vocals, use of boogie rhythms, and uncomplicated harmonica solos was a blueprint almost any blues artist could follow and have success with. Reed's hit-making formula was successful enough that he frequently crossed over onto the pop charts.

Slim Harpo mined turf similar to Reed's but with some notable differences. They both blew harmonica and played guitar, but Harpo was the better player of the two on both instruments. While Reed's music followed the same basic pattern (played at mid-tempo or as slow blues), Harpo was far more adventurous, trying different beats ranging from soul accents to hillbilly hoe-down grooves.

Putting his own stamp on the swamp blues sound

Harpo's singing was high-pitched, nasal, and full of vocal inflections straight out of country-and-western music. He elongated the pronunciation of certain words and stressed odd syllables for added effect. His music lacked the aggression heard in the music of many of his contemporaries, and that's partly what earned him a mainstream audience. Back when Harpo's first singles were on the radio and jukeboxes all over the South, pop musicians figured they could sing and play the blues, too. You didn't have to sound menacing like Howlin' Wolf to sing the blues, they said, just listen to this Slim Harpo guy.

Older white Southerners weren't the only folks who adopted the Slim Harpo style. His music would eventually be recorded by blues-rockers and country-rockers including Dave Edmunds with Love Sculpture, the Fabulous Thunderbirds, the Kinks, the Rolling Stones, the Yardbirds, Hank Williams, Jr., and a long list of others.

No more James Moore — introducing Slim

Slim Harpo was born James Moore in Lobdell, Louisiana, on January 11, 1924. Moore lost both his parents at an early age and dropped out of school to become a full-time musician. Moore worked the private party and juke joint circuit under the stage name Harmonica Slim. He had his mind set on making records, so he enlisted the aid of local blues kingpin Lightnin' Slim, who promptly directed him to record producer J.D. Miller. Miller had been producing records for Lightnin' Slim and others and started using Moore as a backup player on various sessions.

In 1957, Moore cut his first singles for Miller — "I'm A King Bee" and "Got Love If You Want It" — which were all ready to lease to the Excello label, but there was one small problem. A blues artist on the West Coast was already using the name Harmonica Slim. Moore's wife, Lovelle, more or less transposed the name Harmonica Slim and came up with Slim Harpo — and yet another colorful stage name entered the annals of blues history.

"I'm A King Bee" and "Got Love If You Want It" became a two-sided hit on the R&B charts, even inspiring a cover version medley of both songs on Sun Records by rockabilly singer Warren Smith that same year. More tunes in the "King Bee" formula followed, but Harpo's next big record would find him crossing over onto the pop charts.

The record was a simple but effective ballad in the blues vein entitled "Rainin' In My Heart." Released in 1961, it crossed over and was a Top 40 hit on the *Billboard* pop charts. Everyone from country to rock 'n' roll musicians started playing it and, once again, Slim Harpo's music was finding new audiences.

Scoring pop and R&B hits

Harpo's music hit the pop charts a couple more times. First, the Rolling Stones recorded "I'm A King Bee" on their debut album. Then, in 1966, Slim himself made the pop chart Top 20 with "Baby, Scratch My Back," later recorded by the Fabulous Thunderbirds on their first album. Follow-ups to his biggest hit included "Tee-Ni-Nee-Ni-Nu" and "Tip On In," both of which made the R&B charts.

Slim's chart success earned him bookings in cities such as New York and Los Angeles for the first time. He then contacted his old friend and mentor Lightnin' Slim; the two men added a drummer and toured around the country as a blues trio that just happened to feature the two biggest names in Louisiana swamp blues.

This musical alliance between the two Slims lasted until the end of the 1960s. The year 1970 started off strongly for Harpo, who had first-time offers for a European tour and recording session in London to kick it all off. But Slim never did make it to Europe. He died of a heart attack on January 31, 1970.

The Best Of Slim Harpo (Excello/Hip-O). Slim's laid-back Louisiana sound is well represented on this 16-track collection. It features the hits "I'm A King Bee," "Got Love If You Want It," "Rainin' In My Heart," and "Baby, Scratch My Back."

Jimi Hendrix

If anybody tries to tell you that Jimi Hendrix (1942–1970) doesn't belong in a book on blues music because he's really a psychedelic rock guitarist, don't believe it. Jimi Hendrix bridged traditional blues and modern blues-rock such as no other artist. His influence is heard not only in the music of contemporary blues artists including Stevie Ray Vaughan, Kenny Wayne Shepherd, and Jonny Lang, but also in the music of an earlier generation of blues standard bearers that included Buddy Guy and Luther Allison.

Jimi Hendrix worked his musical magic at a time when rock 'n' roll was experiencing galvanic changes. Hendrix became rock's greatest guitar hero, yet everything he played (and the way he played it) was steeped in traditional blues.

Cutting his teeth in the chitlin circuit

Jimi got his early show business training by performing for many years in the R&B *chitlin circuit* — low-paying clubs, roadhouses, and dance halls that booked African-American blues and R&B artists almost exclusively. The circuit was a highly competitive one and showmanship was prized as much as musical talent. In fact, many of the tricks Hendrix used onstage — playing the guitar behind his head, behind his back, and with his teeth — were crowd-pleasers first employed by blues performers going back to Charlie Patton and later, T-Bone Walker, Guitar Slim, Buddy Guy, and others.

Another hallmark of the chitlin circuit style that Hendrix brought to rock was the competitive nature of his performances. Rock 'n' roll has always been a gigantic battle of the bands, and Jimi brought a no-holds-barred sense of showmanship that automatically made everyone around him want to play and perform better. They *had* to, otherwise Hendrix would cut them to musical ribbons. Just ask any survivor of a jam session with Jimi.

Hoping for a break at Seattle teen clubs

James Marshall Hendrix was born in Seattle on November 24, 1942. He picked up the guitar at an early age, playing it left-handed with the strings reversed. By the time he was 11, he taught himself Chuck Berry tunes and hoped to land a spot in a local rock 'n' roll band. During his early teen years, Hendrix was a regular audience member at the Seattle teen nightclub The Spanish Castle. Many nights he would leave his guitar and amp by the stage, hoping to get called up by one of the local bands to sit in for a song or two.

In 1959, Jimi dropped out of high school and enlisted in the Army. His two-year stretch included time in the 101st Airborne division, where he met future bass player Billy Cox, who would later record and tour with Hendrix as a member of the *Band of Gypsies* project. After the Army, Hendrix found work outside of Seattle on the chitlin circuit. Working every R&B music venue along the way, Hendrix served in road bands large and small and had notable stints with the Isley Brothers and Little Richard.

In 1964, Hendrix moved to New York City. Scraping along with a blues cover band he had put together, he was drawn to the blues and folk scene in Greenwich Village. By the end of 1965, he was playing lead guitar at the Cafe Wha? behind singer-guitarist John Hammond, Jr. and creating a buzz around the Village about his wild new blues guitar sound.

Getting discovered in Greenwich Village

On one of those nights in the Village, Chas Chandler, the bass player for the British blues-rock group the Animals, heard Hendrix and Hammond playing together. Jimi's playing and stage presence impressed Chandler, who was hoping to get into producing and managing artists. Chandler convinced Hendrix into following him to England to start up his own band.

After auditioning players around London, Jimi and Chas tapped bass player Noel Redding and drummer Mitch Mitchell, and the Jimi Hendrix Experience was born. By the close of 1966, the buzz on Hendrix and his band was all over London, and the young guitarist was already being ranked with Britain's best.

Blazing away on the festival and ballroom circuit

The Jimi Hendrix Experience stormed the British charts in 1967 with hit singles and a debut album *(Are You Experienced?)* that upped the musical ante for every artist that followed. Jimi became an established star in the U.S. after his legendary performance at the Monterey Pop Festival where he set his guitar on fire as the finale to his show.

The following two years found Hendrix churning out excellent albums and staging equally inventive live performances. He worked every hippie ballroom and festival in America and took his music around the world to appreciative audiences. His influence was wide ranging, particularly in the R&B market that he supposedly was no longer a part of because of his rock star status. (The Jimi Hendrix Experience was inducted into the Rock and Roll Hall of Fame in 1992.)

Stories concerning his future plans and personal life at the time of his accidental death in 1970 (he choked to death in his sleep, allegedly after an overdose of barbiturates) were as numerous (and as incredible) as any you'd hear about any famous performer who leaves the party way too early. Hendrix left behind a large body of unfinished and unreleased music and, as all those recordings become available, Hendrix's status as a blues music innovator will become more and more obvious. Although Jimi went on several flights of musical fancy in his short career, he was always packing the blues.

The Ultimate Experience (MCA). Get yourself experienced with this 20-track collection that hits all the high points of Hendrix's much-too-brief career.

Earl Hooker

Back in the early '60s, you could walk into any small blues club in Chicago and hear Muddy Waters, Howlin' Wolf, Buddy Guy, Otis Rush, or Magic Sam playing their music for the hometown crowd. But if you had asked any of those legends to name the place where the best guitarist in the Windy City was performing, they'd all tell you it's wherever Earl Hooker (1930–1970) was playing that night.

What couldn't he play?

Hooker could play it all — any style of blues, R&B, or rock 'n' roll you could name — all night long. Adept at a multitude of styles, including hillbilly, jazz, and seemingly every flavor of blues imaginable, Hooker worked as both a sideman and front man in more bands than probably any other modern blues artist. His lead guitar work graced the recordings of Junior Wells, G.L. Crockett, Muddy Waters ("You Shook Me" was the only time Muddy gave up his slide guitar chair to someone else), and others. But, Earl's solo career didn't blossom until the late 1960s.

Earl never rose much higher than "a player's player" status for a couple of reasons — he wasn't much of a vocalist because of the tuberculosis that eventually killed him in 1970, and his all-over-the-musical-map approach made him a hard act to market in the blues field. But that same well-rounded style made him the perfect session player, and his tenure as bandleader-sideman supreme for Mel London's Age, Chief, and Profile labels, as well as his small batch of solo albums from the late 1960s, is what much of his reputation rests on.

Soaking up Nighthawk's slide guitar secrets

Hooker (see Figure 5-5) brought a modern flavor to his music while never straying far from his Clarksdale, Mississippi, roots. He was born into the blues cradle of Mississippi as Earl Zebedee Hooker on January 15, 1930. (Until the end of his life, most Chicago blues people who knew him called him Zeb rather than Earl.) A cousin to John Lee Hooker, Earl taught himself the rudiments of blues guitar while still a youngster living in Mississippi.

Earl's family moved up to Chicago in the early 1940s and he enrolled at the Lyon & Healy Music School. Soon, Hooker extended his stringed instrument knowledge to include the banjo and mandolin, and he became proficient on piano and drums. But Earl also played the blues on the streets of Chicago to pick up some spare change. Around that time, he developed a friendship with slide guitar master Robert Nighthawk. It was Nighthawk who sparked Hooker's interest in playing slide, and no one could have had a better teacher. By the time Robert had passed down his secrets, Earl's slide guitar work was the most technically advanced of all bluesmen.

On the road with Ike Turner

In 1949, Earl moved to Memphis and fell in with the area's blues community, which lead to an appearance on Sonny Boy Williamson's King Biscuit Time radio program. Earl then joined Ike Turner's Kings Of Rhythm band and toured extensively throughout the South. By 1952, he started recording some tunes for the Miami-based Rockin' label, some others for King Records in 1953, and some tracks for Sun Records that remained unissued for the better part of two decades.

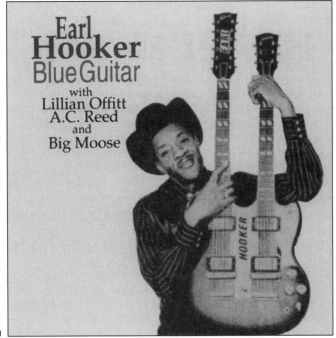

Figure 5-5:
Earl Hooker
(CD booklet
photo
courtesy of
Jewel
Paula Ronn
Records, A
Division of
Sue
Records,
Inc.).

By the mid-1950s, Hooker was back in Chicago putting his first band together and hitting the road for the better part of the decade, recording a
one-off single for Bea & Baby in 1959. The 1960s saw him sticking more and
more around Chicago, becoming an in-demand session player for Mel
London's cache of labels (often working with Junior Wells) and recording
singles under his own name for C.J., Age, and the Checker labels.

Introducing wah-wah pedals and double-neck guitars

Hooker headed to Europe in 1965 as part of the American Folk Blues Festival,
topping off the European tour dates with an appearance on the TV show
Ready Steady Go! with the Beatles on the same bill. Earl had long been
obsessed with having the newest model guitars, amplifiers, and electronic
attachments. In the mid-1960s, Earl was the first blues guitarist to incorporate
the revolutionary *wah-wah pedal* into his bag of tonal tricks and brandished
double-neck guitars years before rock musicians caught onto them.

Earl continued to record throughout the rest of the '60s, releasing singles on Cuca and albums for ABC-Bluesway, Blue Thumb, and Arhoolie, the latter introducing him to a new audience. Earl certainly seem poised on the verge of bigger rewards, but the chronic tuberculosis that weakened him all his days finally took his life on April 21, 1970. He was 40 years old.

Blue Guitar (Paula). Earl Hooker's immense guitar talents are on fine display in this 21-cut collection that features him in both solo and sideman roles.

John Lee Hooker

John Lee Hooker (born 1917) is firmly established as one of the true giants of the blues, along with Muddy Waters, B.B. King, and Howlin' Wolf. Hooker is often called the "King of the Boogie" and his driving, rhythmic approach to guitar playing has become an integral element of the blues sound and style.

When he made his recording debut in 1948, scoring a nationwide hit with "Boogie Chillen," John Lee Hooker was considered something of an anachronism. Except for his thunderous electric guitar, Hooker's one-chord and two-chord modal stylings sounded very much like those of a Delta blues artist from the 1920s. But Hooker's music is altogether more fierce and rhythmic than old Delta blues. Early in his career, he played solo for the most part — his dark, hypnotic voice and relentless foot-stomping his only accompaniment.

John Lee has cut records for seemingly every large and small blues label that's ever existed (and doing so without having to vary his approach). Hooker's music is raw, riveting, and almost doom-struck Mississippi blues that demands much of a listener. His music provides one of the great emotional listening experiences in the blues. John Lee Hooker stands alone as a true creative original, often imitated, but never equaled.

From Clarksdale to the Motor City

Born on August 17, 1920, in Clarksdale, Mississippi, John Lee grew up surrounded by the blues, having been taught the guitar by his stepfather, Will Moore. In childhood, Hooker's main musical influence had been his church spiritual singing, that is, until the blues took over.

When he was 15, John Lee ran away from home and moved to Memphis to make his mark in the blues scene. He was caught and sent back home, but eventually returned to Memphis. To make ends meet, he worked as an usher at the New Daisy Theatre movie house. He later moved to Cincinnati, singing with various gospel groups including the Big Six and the Fairfield Four. Enticed by the prospect of regular work in the automobile industry, Hooker moved to Detroit in 1943.

After becoming a fixture on the Detroit blues club and house party scene, John Lee began recording in 1948, hitting pay dirt on his first try with his recording of "Boogie Chillen." Sounding like absolutely nothing else that was on the radio or the jukeboxes at that time, its pounding rhythm helped carry that record all the way to Number One on the R&B charts in 1949.

What's in a name?

Hooker (see Figure 5-6) spent the next six years cutting records for just about every label that offered him a deal, recording under a number of fake names, nicknames, or names that were a variation of his own. Starting with Modern (under his real name), he went on to record for Staff (as Johnny Williams), Gotham (as John Lee), Regent (as Delta John), Savoy (as Birmingham Sam and his Magic Guitar), Regal, Gone (as John Lee Booker), Sensation, Danceland (as Little Pork Chops), Fortune (as Sir John Lee Hooker), King (as Texas Slim and John Lee Cooker), Swing Time, Acorn (as The Boogie Man), Deluxe (as Johnny Lee), Chart, JVB, Specialty, Chance (as John L Booker), and Chess, before moving over to Vee-Jay under his real name in 1955. It was at Vee-Jay Records where he had his longest affiliation with a single label, recording for them into the early 1960s and scoring hits with "Dimples" and "Boom Boom."

With his solo acoustic blues sound, Hooker gained an appreciative new audience among followers of the folk scene. He performed and recorded extensively throughout the '60s, and his first-ever tour of Europe in 1962 had an enormous impact on the emerging British blues scene. By the end of the decade, John Lee was playing his blues in the hippest rock clubs and biggest festivals around the country.

Pulling up stakes to head to California

In 1970, Hooker moved from Detroit to Oakland. Once there, he recorded the *Hooker 'n' Heat* album with blues-rockers Canned Heat. John Lee Hooker issued new albums by the truckload in the 1970s, with the occasional misguided attempt to update his sound by pairing him with rock musicians who had little sensitivity for his spontaneous changes in timing and his unconventional modal approach to song.

Highlights for Hooker in the 1980s were his being inducted into the Blues Foundation's Hall of Fame and a flurry of reissues of his early recordings on a variety of foreign and domestic labels. He also made a cameo appearance in the movie *The Blues Brothers,* stomping out his trademark boogie patterns on the tune "Boom Boom."

Figure 5-6:
John Lee
Hooker,
at the
microphone,
and his
band (photo
courtesy of
Burton
Wilson,
Austin, TX).

Bigger than ever

John Lee's career took a major upswing with the 1989 release of *The Healer,* featuring newly recorded material and guest appearances by Bonnie Raitt, Carlos Santana, Robert Cray, and others. The album was nominated for a Grammy award for best blues recording, and Hooker won a Grammy for "I'm In The Mood," a duet recorded with Raitt.

In 1990, Hooker was inducted into the Rock and Roll Hall of Fame, and in the years following, he was honored at a star-studded tribute concert at Madison Square Garden, played dates with the Rolling Stones, and even appeared in a Pepsi commercial. In 1997, he opened his own blues club in California — John Lee Hooker's Boom Boom Room — and continues to this day to record and perform after almost a half a century in the business.

The Ultimate Collection (Rhino). This two-disc set covers Hooker's best known numbers from 1948 to 1990. Blues doesn't sound any deeper or is played with more intensity than when it's done by John Lee.

Lightnin' Hopkins

Lightnin' Hopkins (1912–1982) could be labeled in any number of ways, depending on which blues historian you talk to and which part of Hopkins's career you examine. You have the early Lightnin' of the traditional blues style. Then there's the lonesome-sounding Texas songster Lightnin' who carried on the tradition of Blind Lemon Jefferson. You also have the folk-singing, coffeehouse-entertainer Lightnin' Hopkins. And, of course, there's the electric-boogie-playing Lightnin' who dragged rhythm sections around by the scruff of the neck while altering time and meter so much his sidemen perpetually scurried to keep up with him.

Reaching back to his songster roots

In the history of great Texas blues singers, Lightnin' Hopkins (see Figure 5-7) is the yardstick by which all others are measured. From the time he started out as a seeing guide for Blind Lemon Jefferson to his final days on the concert stages of the world, Hopkins had the longest career and recorded more music than any other blues player with the possible exception of John Lee Hooker (and even that point is debatable).

Figure 5-7: Lightnin' Hopkins (photo courtesy of Burton Wilson, Austin, TX).

With more than a hundred albums to his credit and several hundred single recordings for labels large, small, and microscopic, Hopkins's easygoing style worked well in every conceivable setting. His guitar playing was seamless and fluid, combining lead and rhythm passages simultaneously. His lyrical themes had strong roots in the tradition of Texas *songsters* (the genre-crossing singers and musicians who played in a rustic old-fashioned style), and some of his playing reached back to slavery days for its inspiration.

Finding the Lightnin' to go with the Thunder

Born Sam Hopkins in Centerville, Texas, on March 15, 1912, Lightnin' learned the rudiments of guitar from his older brother Joel, whom Lightnin' recorded with in the 1960s. At the age of 8, Lightin' met and performed with Blind Lemon Jefferson who befriended the youngster. After spending his teenage years working as a field hand picking cotton, Hopkins reconnected with Jefferson. Acting as his mentor's eyes, Hopkins chauffeured the unsighted Jefferson from engagement to engagement.

Hopkins's next blues lessons came when he hooked up with his cousin, Texas Alexander, a singer who had been recording during the 1920s. The two men spent the 1920s and most of the 1930s working the bars in Houston and playing across East Texas. This partnership came to an abrupt end in the mid-1930s, when Lightnin' was sent to the Houston County Prison Farm for some alleged offense.

Sometime in the early 1940s, Hopkins married his first wife and tried settling down as a sharecropper, working the soil for landowner Tom Moore, a man with a mean reputation that Lightnin' later cemented in song. Drifting back to work again with Alexander on the streets of Houston, Hopkins was discovered by a talent scout for Aladdin Records, who teamed Hopkins with pianist Thunder Smith. Sam was renamed Lightnin' Hopkins (to create the duo of "Thunder and Lightnin'") and after recording some demos in Houston, the two were invited out to Los Angeles to record.

The pay-per-tune days

Hopkins' stepped into the studio for the first time on November 4, 1946, and his first vocal from that session — "Katie Mae Blues" — became a hit in the Southwest. More sessions followed and soon Lightnin' was recording as a solo act. He then fell in with Houston studio owner Bill Quinn, recording at Quinn's Gold Star Studios.

Creating tunes off the top of his head, Lightnin' would cut a quick session and settle for a cash-per-tune payment with no royalty interest of any kind. The Gold Star masters ended up being released on several different labels, including Aladdin, Modern, Imperial, Jax, Harlem, and Quinn's own Gold Star imprint.

Hopkins's music was an aural antidote to the smooth supper club blues dominating radio play at the time, and by 1950, Hopkins was an established hit-making commodity. When Gold Star went of business in 1951, Lightnin' went on to record prolifically for the labels Decca, Mercury, Jax, Sittin' In With, Herald, "77" LA, Chart, and Ace throughout the rest of the 1950s.

Lightnin' Hopkins, folk singer

Success never sat well with Lightnin' Hopkins. He had hit records despite the fact he didn't like to travel to promote his career. He preferred to stick around Houston, playing outside the area only when he had to go out of town to record. As Chicago-styled blues began its ascendancy in the early 1950s, Hopkins's recording career ran out of gas, and after 1954 he didn't record again for several years. Unfazed by it all, Lightnin' simply went back to playing the Houston ghetto bars that were his haven.

In 1959, Hopkins was rediscovered by blues historians Mack McCormack and Samuel Charters. With McCormack and Charters both producing separate sessions, Hopkins revived his career with a spate of recordings made for Folkways, Prestige/Bluesville, and other labels in the early 1960s. Thus began the second career of Lightnin' Hopkins. Although he continued to play around Houston, he quickly became a mainstay of the folk-blues festival and coffeehouse circuit, introducing a new, young college audience to his music. In 1964, he played England and Europe with the American Folk Blues Festival touring troupe to wide acclaim.

The Blues according to Lightnin'

By the end of the 1960s, Hopkins's music also caught on with young rock audiences and he headlined bills featuring bands including the Jefferson Airplane and Grateful Dead. He stayed just as busy into the 1970s, appearing in three short films for documentary director Les Blank, *The Blues According To Lightnin' Hopkins, The Sun's Gonna Shine,* and *Blues Like Showers In The Rain.* Hopkins's music was also featured in the soundtrack to the movie *Sounder.*

Lightnin' appeared at Carnegie Hall 10 years after his debut there, toured Europe, and kept cranking out records for any label that offered him cash up front. In one of his last filmed performances for the TV show *Austin City Limits,* Hopkins turned in a bravura set. Resplendent in a powder blue rhinestone suit and matching hat, he played a Fender Stratocaster fed through a wah-wah pedal and spit out a steady stream of nasty solo guitar licks.

In July 1981, Hopkins underwent surgery for cancer of the esophagus at a Houston hospital. He was back in again at the end of the year, and on January 30, 1982, he died from complications due to pneumonia. A quote from Lightnin' in *The Blues According To Lightnin' Hopkins* sums it all up: "When I play a guitar, I play it from my heart and soul and I play my own, *own* music."

"I heard a lot of guitar players growing up; my grandfather was a musician, but when I heard Lightnin' playing electric guitar, it was like, '*Now,* I want to play guitar!' To me, Lightnin' Hopkins was the ultimate; the blues doesn't get any more low down than that."

Mojo Hand: The Lightnin' Hopkins Anthology (Rhino). This two-disc set provides the healthiest sampling you can find of Hopkins' voluminous recorded output.

Walter Horton

Big Walter Horton (1917–1981) was the sad-eyed harmonica genius of the blues. An introverted man who seldom spoke, Big Walter seemed to do all of his talking through his harp. Although one of the all-time greatest blues harmonica players, Walter's recording career was highly erratic. He recorded only a handful of full-length albums, most of them done at the twilight of his career, and an equally small number of singles.

But anyone who doesn't list Big Walter Horton among the greatest blues harmonica players of all time is in serious need of a blues history lesson. Big Walter ranks with Little Walter and Sonny Boy Williamson II (Rice Miller) as one of the most innovative harmonica players ever.

As a sideman on other artists' records, Big Walter laid down legendary harmonica solos that were simply astonishing. He was one of the most widely recorded harp players in Chicago blues history, equally adept at playing acoustic or amplified harp with a tone that was fat and warm. His playing style was full of melodic invention and lyricism, ranging from a whisper to a sledgehammer-heavy blast.

The harmonica child prodigy

Horton was born in Horn Lake, Mississippi, on April 6, 1917. He was playing harmonica by the time he was 5 years old, and the child prodigy gained some notoriety working house parties and country dances.

The Horton family moved to Memphis and young Walter was soon playing on the streets for tips and hanging out with the Memphis Jug Band, who brought the 10-year-old wunderkind out on tour with them playing theaters and shows throughout the Midwest. The band also featured young Walter on a pair of Victor 78s recorded in 1927. Horton spent much of the 1930s working around the Memphis area with Honeyboy Edwards, Homesick James, Eddie Taylor, and others, eventually moving to Chicago in 1940.

Heading into the studio with Sam Phillips

By all accounts, Walter moved back and forth between Chicago and Memphis sporadically until 1951, when he began his recording career after being heard by Memphis engineer-producer Sam Phillips, who recorded Walter frequently over the next three years.

Phillips found willing buyers for the masters Horton cut at Phillips's Memphis Recording Service. Consequently, the harmonica player's first singles were released on a number of labels — Modern, RPM (where he was listed as "Mumbles"), and Chess. On Phillips' own Sun label, he recorded the classic harmonica showcase instrumental "Easy," as part of the duo "Jimmy and Walter" with old playing buddy Jimmy DeBerry.

Walter finally made Chicago his permanent home in 1953 when he joined up with Eddie Taylor, who was then replacing Junior Wells in the Muddy Waters band. After playing on a couple of sessions with Muddy, Horton attracted the attention of songwriter-producer Willie Dixon. Dixon produced two Horton singles — "Hard Hearted Woman" for the States label in 1954 and "Need My Baby" for Cobra Records in 1956 — but their poor sales kept the harmonica ace from getting another recording deal under his own name for another six years.

After contributing fiery solos on recordings by Jimmy Rogers, Sunnyland Slim and others, Big Walter finally got to record his first full-length album for the Chess label's Argo subsidiary in 1964. Around this time, he toured Europe with the American Folk Blues Festival troupe, scoring a hit with audiences everywhere he played.

Joining the Chicago Blues All Stars

Throughout the rest of the 1960s and into the early 1970s, Horton popped up as a sideman on several recordings behind Johnny Young, Johnny Shines, and others, and recorded a duet album with fellow harpist Carey Bell for Alligator Records. He was also tapped to be a member of Willie Dixon's Chicago Blues All Stars.

In the mid-1970s, Horton put his own band together and recorded the album *Fine Cuts* for the Blind Pig label and made successful showings at various blues festivals and clubs across the United States. Big Walter died on December 8, 1981, leaving behind many fellow musicians and music fans the world over who knew he was truly one of the all-time best on his instrument.

Chicago/The Blues/Today! Volume 3 (Vanguard). Whether he's supporting guitarists Johnny Young and Johnny Shines, dueting with Charlie Musselwhite, or soloing his lungs out, Big Walter's playing is a stand-out.

Howlin' Wolf

Howlin' Wolf (1910–1976) is one of the most important artists in the history of Chicago blues and in all of blues music, period. He was a major influence on a number of rock groups who copied his music and rock singers who attempted to mimic his one-of-kind vocal style. The Rolling Stones may have sounded a lot more like the Dick Clark Five were it not for the music of Howlin' Wolf.

The centerpiece of the Howlin' Wolf sound was his voice — a huge, almost terrifying instrument he employed to shout, moan, and howl the blues at a deafening volume. His singing was completely unlike anyone else's in the history of blues music. Howlin' Wolf didn't just sing the blues; he screamed it at you while waving a finger right in your face.

His guitar playing was somewhat crude and he blew a harmonica with a bit of a rough edge, but few people went at their music with the same sort of primal ferocity. The Wolf stood six-foot-three and weighed close to 300 pounds. He looked big, he sounded big, and man, could he scare the pants off an audience.

Picking up tricks of the trade from Charlie Patton and Sonny Boy II

Wolf grew up on his parent's farm near West Point, Mississippi. He was born there on June 10, 1910, and christened Chester Arthur Burnett (he got the nickname "Wolf" as a child). He worked on the farm during his teenage years under the watchful eye of his father, Dock Burnett.

When Wolf turned 18, he met up with a traveling entertainer and blues musician named Charlie Patton. Patton's exuberant performing style and loud, shouted vocals made an indelible impression on the teen who would later use them as building blocks for his own style.

Wolf started teaching himself Patton's tunes, starting with Patton's big hit, "Pony Blues," which he would later record himself. But Wolf also wanted to play the harmonica in addition to learning the rudiments of playing guitar. Fortunately for Wolf, harmonica ace Rice Miller — later known as Sonny Boy Williamson II — was married to Wolf's half-sister, and Miller was coaxed into teaching the young blues player harmonica basics.

Hitting the radio waves with his own show

Wolf started performing publicly in the early 1930s, working anyplace that would have him. He quickly discovered that the noisier, rougher, and wilder his show and music were, the more the people liked it. Wolf went into the Army for four years during World War II, then decided to farm in West Memphis, Arkansas, after he got out. His playing was restricted to weekends, but it wouldn't stay that way for long. In 1948, Wolf began a broadcasting career of sorts on a local radio station. He had his own 15-minute radio show on a West Memphis radio station, singing blues and giving farm reports, while plugging his own club appearances and the wares of local merchants.

Wolf was joined on these broadcasts by his first band, The House Rockers. The combo featured a young James Cotton on second harmonica, Willie Steele on drums, a piano player who called himself "Destruction," and Willie Johnson on electric guitar. Johnson favored a raw, nasty, distorted tone that was every bit the equal of Wolf's voice.

Memphis record man Sam Phillips heard Wolf's morning show on KWEM and in 1951 invited Wolf and his band to his Memphis Recording Service for an audition. For the next two years, Wolf recorded sides for Phillips that captured the blues in its most primal state.

Scoring two hits and touching off a label war

Sam Phillips hadn't started his Sun Records label yet and was still leasing out material to various labels to make ends meet. He ended up losing two of his biggest accounts when he leased out Howlin' Wolf masters to Chess Records in Chicago and RPM Records in Los Angeles at the same time.

When Wolf's records started selling, Chess and RPM began a bidding war for his services. Leonard Chess doggedly pursued Wolf and finally emerged victorious, signing Wolf to an exclusive contract. In 1953, Howlin' Wolf moved up to Chicago and started recording for Chess in 1954.

The sessions at Sam Phillips's tiny studio in Memphis were a thing of the past. Phillips merely turned the tape recorder on and Wolf began moaning the blues with little regard to arrangement or other musical niceties. After he was in the Chess studios, Howlin' Wolf's songs were recorded over and over again until a satisfactory version was ready for release.

Willie Johnson left the band to head back to Memphis, and Wolf began casting about for a new guitar player to replace him. As it turned out, the next permanent lead guitarist would rise out of the ranks of the band itself; the guitarist's name was Hubert Sumlin. A fan of Wolf ever since he was a young boy, Hubert started out as Wolf's rhythm guitarist in the early 1950s, but by 1958 had taken over permanently as the band's lead guitarist. Sumlin stayed with Wolf right up until the end of the singer's life and longer than any musician who ever worked with him.

Sumlin's guitar style became one of the most unique in all of blues and one of the most influential. He rarely, if ever, played chords and often would just solo right through an entire song, playing wild stuff that would later influence guitar superstars including Eric Clapton, Jimmy Page, Robert Cray, and Stevie Ray Vaughan.

The Willie Dixon touch

Up until the mid-1950s, Wolf had been writing and recording all his own songs. He hit the R&B charts again with one of them, "Smokestack Lightnin'," but by the late 1950s, he was getting more attention as a live attraction than as a recording artist. Chess decided to remedy that situation in 1960 by assigning him to its staff writer and producer Willie Dixon.

Dixon had written hits for Muddy Waters and had already provided Wolf with 1956's "Evil," but from 1960 to 1964, Wolf recorded almost nothing but Willie Dixon tunes. Those songs also happened to turn out to be some of the most famous blues tunes of all time — "Back Door Man," "I Ain't Superstitious," "Shake For Me," "Spoonful," "The Red Rooster" and "Wang Dang Doodle."

The 1960s found Wolf and Hubert heading to Europe as part of the American Folk Blues Festival package. Howlin' Wolf's single "Smokestack Lightnin'" become a surprise hit in England in 1964. Suddenly, rock bands the world over were getting hip to Howlin' Wolf's music. When the Rolling Stones appeared on ABC-TV's *Shindig*, the group demanded that their special guest be Howlin' Wolf. Wolf performed his first R&B hit, "How Many More Years," with the Rolling Stones seated at his feet.

Supplying hits (and inspiration) for British rockers

The end of the 1960s saw Wolf's music gaining more ground with main-stream rock audiences. His songs, and those he had recorded that were written by Willie Dixon, were covered by Jeff Beck, the Blues Project, Cream, the Doors, and the Electric Flag, among others. In 1970, Wolf headed to England to record *The London Howlin' Wolf Sessions* with Eric Clapton, members of the Rolling Stones, and Beatles drummer Ringo Starr.

But Howlin' Wolf's health started to fail him. He had survived everything from automobile accidents to kidney damage to heart trouble, but still he persisted in playing live as often as possible. By rationing his energy, he kept performing until the final months of his life. He died on January 10, 1976.

Since Howlin' Wolf's death, the honors have kept coming his way. Statues of him were erected in parks in Chicago and his birthplace of West Point, Mississippi. In 1980, he was inducted into the Blues Foundation's Hall Of Fame and, in 1991, was inducted into the Rock and Roll Hall of Fame. In 1993, he was honored by the United States Post Office with his own postage stamp. Not bad for a one-time farmer from West Memphis, Arkansas.

Howlin' Wolf — His Best (MCA-Chess). This 20-track collection boasts superior sound and makes the perfect introduction to the Howlin' Wolf brand of blues music.

"I didn't really get Wolf's music until after he died. I saw him many nights, but I always kept my distance, because I was *scared* of him, you understand? But when he passed away, they played his music all day long on the radio, and I sat and listened and it finally made sense to me. Now I knew why all those rock groups were playing his music; this guy had a sound that was different. He just didn't play straight blues; it had a different flavor to it. To me, he was very ahead of his time. He was almost playing rock 'n' roll with heavy blues vocals. If he were alive today, with that style he had back then, he would just *kill* people with that sound."

Elmore James

When it comes to slide guitar, everybody has their favorites. But if you're going to ask who *really* put the slide guitar style on the blues map, the answer is Elmore James, no contest.

Elmore played the coolest licks, he had the baddest guitar tone *ever,* and he put as much feeling into his blues singing as anyone who ever stepped up to a microphone. As a role model to his contemporaries (Joe Carter, Boyd Gilmore, Homesick James, J.B. Hutto, Johnny Littlejohn, and Hound Dog Taylor) and the generations of musicians that followed (Duane Allman, Eric Clapton, Jeremy Spencer of Fleetwood Mac, George Thorogood, and others), Elmore stands out as one of the most influential guitarist in blues history.

Hands down, the King of the Slide Guitar

Elmore built his unique slide style around a guitar lick that Robert Johnson played on his composition, "I'll Believe I'll Dust My Broom." Elmore took the lick, simplified it, amplified it beyond belief, and adapted the song's framework to create his biggest hit and a record number of variations of it over the course of his recording career.

Elmore's guitar tone was unusual, and a precursor to the sounds favored by today's heavy metal and rock players. James rebuilt his amplifiers in his radio repair shop to get more volume and distortion out of his guitars than any other blues artist recording at the time. Although his later recordings demonstrate a cleaner overall sound, Elmore always played a loud and powerful guitar.

Elmore James's singing voice was an instrument capable of filling a room without the aid of a p.a. system. It helped that Elmore had a strong band behind his vocals and slide guitar. They were called the Broomdusters and their outings as the Elmore James band made them one of the top blues acts in Chicago.

Playing juke joints with Robert Johnson and Sonny Boy

Elmore was born in Canton, Mississippi, on January 27, 1918. As a child, he would play "slide guitar" with a lard can and broom handle. By his teenage years, he was playing around the local juke joints with future blues legends Robert Johnson and Sonny Boy Williamson II, who was known back then as Rice Miller.

James put a band together in Mississippi, but World War II broke up that act. Elmore joined the Navy for three years, but got back into music right after his discharge. He started broadcasting on the radio, both on shows of his own and as a guest on Sonny Boy's *King Biscuit Time* on KFFA in Helena, Arkansas.

Despite all this activity, Elmore still didn't have much interest in recording. Then one day in 1951, he accompanied Sonny Boy to a recording session for the Trumpet label in Jackson, Mississippi. While the band was warming up, the tape machine was running and a version of Elmore singing and playing "Dust My Broom" was recorded for posterity.

The recording was crude and sounded real "down-home," but it struck a responsive chord in record buyers, making the Top 10 on the R&B charts in 1952. Suddenly Elmore was in demand, both as a live attraction and as a recording artist, while he jumped from one label to another, including Checker, Meteor, and Flair.

From Mississippi to Chicago and back again

In the 1950s, Elmore made Chicago his new base of operations, although he would frequently move back to Canton when the mood struck him. After a long-standing contract with the Bihari brothers' Modern-Meteor-Flair label group ended in 1957, James moved on to Mel London's Chief label, recording his first version of "It Hurts Me Too."

The late 1950s found Elmore moving back to Canton when problems with his heart and other ailments forced him to put his career on hold. He did manage to cut a one-off session for Chess Records in Chicago in 1960, turning in the classics "I Can't Hold Out" and "Madison Blues."

Elmore got back into full-time playing and recording when he signed a deal with Bobby Robinson's Fire label out of New York. He got another hit on his first release with "The Sky Is Crying" — a classic slow blues tune — and kept recording over the next few years while touring with the Broomdusters.

James ran into trouble with the musician's union in Chicago for unpaid dues and moved back down south, hoping a local Chicago disc jockey could get things untangled for him. Once the problem was sorted out, James returned to Chicago, ready to start again with the club work that was waiting for him. But his return to Chicago was a brief one. He suffered a heart attack and died on May 24, 1963. Elmore James was elected to the Blues Foundation's Hall of Fame in 1980 and in 1992 was elected to the Rock and Roll Hall of Fame.

The Sky Is Crying: The History Of Elmore James (Rhino). The place to start for digging Elmore's legacy, and absolutely essential slide guitar listening.

Janis Joplin

Janis Joplin (1943–1970) will forever be the subject of wistful "What if she had lived?" discussions that seem to dog many musical artists who die much too young. But one thing is certain: Janis was, quite simply, the greatest white female blues singer of her time or any time.

Although she was decidedly part of the San Francisco rock scene, what she sang was the *blues* with unabashed verve, abandon, and energy. Janis (see Figure 5-8) always cited Bessie Smith, the greatest female blues singer of her generation, as her principal inspiration.

Figure 5-8:
Janis Joplin (photo courtesy of Burton Wilson, Austin, TX).

Leaving the Texas coffeehouse scene

Joplin was born in Port Arthur, Texas, on January 19, 1943. She showed an early aptitude for singing and by the early 1960s was working the folk and coffeehouse circuits in Houston and Austin, playing bluegrass and hillbilly music, before moving to California in 1965. It was there that she hooked up with the rock group Big Brother and the Holding Company. She quickly established herself and the band as linchpins of the '60s San Francisco music scene.

With her beads, bangles, feathers, and velvets, the insecure ugly duckling from small-town Texas turned into a glamorous trend-setting swan. (One of the highlights of the Rock and Roll Hall of Fame and Museum is the Porsche convertible with the psychedelic paint job that Janis tooled around town in. Janis and her band are painted on the left-front fender.)

Setting off an industry buzz at Monterey

After she established herself on the local music scene, stardom came quickly for Joplin. Big Brother's debut album was released in 1967, followed by a legendary appearance that summer at the Monterey Pop Festival — an event filled with legendary appearances, including the American debut of the Jimi Hendrix Experience.

Janis's performance at the Monterey festival was the talk of the industry (audiences were startled that a white singer could sound like she did). Columbia Records came calling, contract in hand, and rushed the band into the studio and recorded them live in San Francisco. The band's first album for a major label, *Cheap Thrills,* was a hit (greatly aided by the signature single, "Piece Of My Heart") and made Joplin a household word.

Reforming with a new group

Enticed by the prospect of solo stardom, Janis left Big Brother and formed her own Kozmic Blues Band. Featuring a full horn section and a much slicker sound than Big Brother and the Holding Company, the release of the band's *I Got Dem Ol' Kozmic Blues Again Mama!* was a 1969 hit and included the single "Try (Just A Little Bit Harder)." But Joplin and the band didn't quite mesh stylistically, so Janis broke up the group and formed the Full Tilt Boogie Band. Buoyed by the elastic musicality of her new group, she began recording her next album, to be titled *Pearl,* Janis's nickname among close friends.

Although her career had been sidetracked by drink and drugs, Joplin finished recording *Pearl* and looked poised to get her career going again. But sadly, Janis died of a heroin overdose in October 1970, three months shy of her 27th birthday. *Pearl* was released posthumously to rave reviews and brisk sales, spawning a number-one single, "Me and Bobby McGee," the biggest hit of her career. In 1995, Janis was inducted into the Rock and Roll Hall of Fame.

Janis Joplin's Greatest Hits (Columbia). This collection displays the powerhouse vocals and raw emotional delivery that made Joplin unparalleled among female blues-rock singers.

Albert King

Of all the single-string blues guitar soloists who came to fame in the wake of the success of T-Bone Walker and B.B. King, the most distinctive, versatile, and downright influential of them all was Albert King (1923–1992). Playing his trademark Gibson Flying V guitar upside down and left-handed, King fashioned a lean and mean approach to his playing in which intensity and massive tone took precedence over flash and bombast.

Not that Albert was a shrinking violet when it came to engaging in "head cutting contests" with other blues or rock artists. He made mincemeat out of nearly anyone challenging his turf, giving notice to anyone attempting to dethrone him just exactly who was the King of the Hill. No one could produce more screaming, tormented sounds out of a guitar by bending just one string than Albert King. He was a true original and his influence can be heard in the playing of Jimi Hendrix, Michael Bloomfield, Eric Clapton, and Jimmie and Stevie Ray Vaughan, all of whom incorporated much of King's style into theirs.

Same birthplace, but no relation to B.B.

Although Albert King was born in Indianola, Mississippi, the same town that B.B. King was born in, the two blues artists are not related. To confuse matters a little, King isn't even Albert's real last name. He was born Albert Nelson on April 25, 1923.

The details of his youth are a little blurry, but young Albert was definitely inspired by Blind Lemon Jefferson enough to teach himself how to play guitar. Working his way up through a succession of homemade cigar box guitars, Albert finally got his first real guitar in 1942.

A southpaw, Albert played the guitar left-handed without restringing it from a right-handed setup. He simply flipped the guitar around and played it upside down (he also developed his own tuning for the instrument). After watching one guitar pick after another sail out of his hand while he played, he also further developed his devastating attack by using just the meat of his bare thumb to pluck the strings.

In 1950, Albert moved to Osceola, Arkansas, and played professionally, working the T-99 Club as a member of the weekend house band, the In The Groove Boys. He purchased his first electric guitar with the money he earned driving a trailer truck during the week.

Acquiring his trademark Flying V

In 1953, Albert ventured North, landing in Gary, Indiana. He took the sur-name King after B.B.'s success and was keen on landing a recording session of his own. Through Willie Dixon's help, Albert auditioned for Chicago disc jockey Al Benson, who ran Parrot Records. Benson asked King to sing and play unplugged in the hall outside of his office, then told him to be in the studio that night. Albert King's recording career commenced with the release of his first, and only, single for Parrot, "Be On Your Merry Way." He wouldn't record again for five years.

In 1956, Albert moved to St. Louis to take advantage of its burgeoning blues club scene. Within a couple of years, he was a popular attraction on the local blues circuit and purchased a new guitar — the model with which he's forever associated — the Gibson Flying V.

King generated enough noise around the St. Louis area to get signed to the local Bobbin label in 1959. It was there that King found, and perfected, his modern style — stinging solo guitar work over a solid rhythm backing and a complement of at least two horn players. He scored an R&B hit with 1961's "Don't Throw Your Love On Me So Strong" and for the next few years pressed releases for the Bobbin, King, and the Coun-Tree labels.

Opening night at Fillmore West

Albert King's career went nationwide when he was signed to the Memphis-based Stax label in 1966. Recording with the label's house band, Booker T. and the MGs, Albert's music immediately changed — for the better. His hard-wrought blues style melded perfectly with the Memphis soul groove provided by the band and the various horn sections used on his sessions. Hit recordings such as "Laundromat Blues" and "Born Under A Bad Sign" won him new audiences in both the soul and rock markets.

King was the first blues artist to appear at the rock venue Fillmore West, in 1968 on opening night with Jimi Hendrix, no less. Later that same year, he recorded his album *Live Wire/Blues Power* there, the first time a live blues album had been recorded in front of a rock audience. In 1969, he performed with the St. Louis Symphony Orchestra, making him one of the first blues artist to record in a classical setting.

In the 1970s, Albert King and his music reached a worldwide audience. He continued to churn out albums for Stax and toured around the world, playing for both rock and R&B audiences. When Stax went bankrupt in 1975, King recorded for the Utopia, Tomato, and Fantasy labels into the 1980s. Albert continued to perform throughout the rest of the decade, befriending and encouraging the young Stevie Ray Vaughan along the way.

Although he announced his retirement from music in the mid-1980s, King continued to add concert dates to his calendar into the 1990s. After a concert in Los Angeles on December 19, 1992, Albert flew home to Memphis and suffered a fatal heart attack two days later. With his passing, the blues lost one of its true distinctive stylists.

The Ultimate Collection (Rhino). This two-disc set provides a nice overview of Albert's lengthy career. It surveys the big hits he cut for Stax during the mid- to late 1960s, and collects rarities and great late-period material.

B.B. King

If there's one name in blues music that just about *everyone* knows, it has to be B.B. King (born 1925). With an enormously successful career spanning 50 years, no blues artist has reached more people in more different settings than B.B. King (see Figure 5-9). Who else sells out concert halls, pitches fast food on prime-time TV commercials, turns up on a sitcom with Bill Cosby, and cuts a hit with Irish superstar rockers U2? B.B. King has done more to bring a face to the blues than just about anyone.

It also happens that B.B. has been the most-emulated electric guitarist over the past five decades of popular music. His innovative finger vibrato has become the accepted means by which all modern blues and rock guitarists bend a guitar string. In blues, jazz, rock, and even country, B.B.'s influence is part of the musical fabric.

As a singer, he brought gospel influences to blues belting and made it sound new. B.B. took blues music uptown and eventually brought it to a mainstream audience. As a human being, he has made it his life's work to keep the blues alive and has been the recipient of more awards and honorary degrees than any other blues artist ever. And, all of this success lies on the shoulders of one of the most humble superstars in show business.

Figure 5-9:
B.B. King
and
"Lucille."
(photo
courtesy of
MCA
Records).

Learning slide guitar from cousin Bukka White

B.B. was born Riley B. King on September 16, 1925, in Indianola, Mississippi. He first started singing in church where the minister taught him a few chords on a guitar, sparking the youngster's interest in the instrument. He started listening to blues guitar players, including his principal inspiration, T-Bone Walker, and was enthralled with jazz guitarist Charlie Christian.

But the biggest influence on young Riley was his cousin, slide guitarist Bukka White. King moved to Memphis in the mid-1940s and lived with his cousin for a while, trying to emulate the sound of Bukka's slide by using his bare fingers. It was then that B.B. developed his famous *finger vibrato,* in which he uses his thumb to move the string back and forth rapidly, creating fluctuations in pitch. After moving back to Indianola to try his hand at farming, B.B. moved back to Memphis with his wife Martha, determined this time to become a full-time blues artist.

The Beale Street Blues Boy

Early in his career, B.B. landed himself a radio gig. Broadcasting live on station WDIA for 15 minutes every day at the end of another deejay's shift, King played his music and hawked an alcohol-loaded "health elixir," which lead to his being tagged "The Peptikon Boy." By 1949, he had his own show, singing live and spinning records with a new radio name, "The Beale Street Blues Boy," later shortened to "Blues Boy," and then just plain "B.B." He also began his recording career, first issuing singles on the Bullet label, but quickly moving over to the Los Angeles label RPM Records.

His first chart-topping R&B hit, "Three O'Clock Blues," was cut in a Memphis YMCA in 1951 and B.B. never looked back. In 1952, he scored another hit with "You Know I Love You" and the following year had three more hits with "Please Hurry Home," "Woke Up This Morning," and the highly influential "Please Love Me," in which B.B.'s soloing was at its most distorted and aggressive. He gave up his shift on WDIA and took to the road, touring as much as he could, and recording in Los Angeles whenever possible.

The hits continued throughout the 1950s, and B.B. King's name became synonymous with the best the blues had to offer. Nobody had bigger hits, played meaner a guitar, or sang like he did, and with a full band behind him, nobody had a classier show. His influence extended to the next generation of emerging Chicago players. The careers of Buddy Guy, Otis Rush, Magic Sam, and others may not have been possible without King's trail-blazing efforts of the early 1950s.

The thrill was just beginning

B.B. became an even bigger act in the 1960s when he moved over to the larger ABC-Paramount label, reaching an audience outside of blues circles for the first time with his *Live At The Regal* album. ("Sweet Little Angel" from that album is on the *Blues For Dummies* CD). His breakthrough came in 1970 with the crossover hit, "The Thrill Is Gone." Suddenly, B.B. King and his guitar Lucille were on *The Ed Sullivan Show* and *American Bandstand*. B.B. King was on his way to becoming the most famous blues artist in the world.

He went out on tour with the Rolling Stones, played every rock ballroom and festival that could afford his asking price, and kept scoring hits throughout the 1970s and into the 1980s, making the blues better known and better loved everywhere he went.

B.B. continually updated his music to stay current with musical trends. He did duet albums with Bobby Bland, recorded with the Philadelphia International rhythm section (the sound behind the Spinners and others), and even tried out funk on an album with the Crusaders. His 1993 album, *Blues Summit*, found him working with Buddy Guy, Koko Taylor, John Lee Hooker, and Etta James, and producing his finest album in years.

While the days of his keeping a road schedule of 300 play dates a year are behind him, B.B. continues to play and sing the blues anyplace music fans want to hear it. He remains blues music's ultimate success story, the most innovative force of the post-war era, and its finest goodwill ambassador.

Live At The Regal (MCA). This represents perhaps B.B.'s finest moment and is certainly one of the greatest live blues albums of all time.

Freddy (Freddie) King

You can usually find Freddie King (1934–1976) cited in blues history books as one of the "Three Kings," along with B.B. and Albert (none of whom are related to each other, by the way). But Freddie was not a B.B. (or Albert) imitator. He had a distinctive style of his own and came to national prominence with a clutch of R&B charting instrumentals and vocals. This King played a modern brand of Chicago blues that always made room for some rock 'n' roll.

Freddie's approach to playing was a lot funkier than B.B.'s or Albert's. He played wearing thumb picks and finger picks, like the old country bluesmen once did. Freddie was able to squeeze a single note out of his guitar using his massive hands and make it sustain forever. He could also play in a bluesy single-string style like B.B. or T-Bone Walker if he felt like it, or play in a country blues mode reminiscent of Lightnin' Hopkins.

The Christian who would be (Freddie) King

King was born Freddie (spelled Freddy in the early days of his career) Christian in Gilmer, Texas, on September 3, 1934. Early on, King played in a Lightnin' Hopkins acoustic style, having learned the rudiments of guitar playing and old-time blues standards from his mother and uncle.

When the Christian family moved to Chicago in 1950, Freddie (see Figure 5-10) fell in love with the blues being played in his new hometown and vowed to become part of the scene. Influenced by Robert Jr. Lockwood, Jimmy Rogers, and Eddie Taylor, he formed his first band, the Every Hour Blues Boys, and began working his way into the highly competitive club circuit.

By the mid-1950s, Freddie had adopted the surname King (because of B.B.'s success, just as Albert King had done) and got his first shot at recording in 1957 when he cut "Country Boy" for the microscopically small El-Bee label. But the record flopped, and Freddie wouldn't record again for another three years.

Figure 5-10:
Freddie
King (photo
courtesy of
Burton
Wilson,
Austin, TX).

A breakout hit with "Hide Away"

His next chance to make records came in 1960 when Freddie signed with Federal Records, part of King Records in Cincinnati. His first release for the label, "You've Got To Love Her With A Feeling," actually made the pop charts, a rarity for any blues artist. But his next release in 1961, the instrumental "Hide Away," not only became his biggest hit, but quickly became one of the most widely played tunes on bandstands across the country.

"Hide Away" was based on a song that Magic Sam and Freddie had heard Hound Dog Taylor playing. The song later became a rite of passage of sorts for all aspiring blues and rock 'n' roll guitarists. If you could negotiate all of Freddie's licks on "Hide Away," you were considered a real guitar player.

Although King continued to record strong vocal efforts, it was the instrumentals that caught the public's fancy, with "San-Ho-Zay" and "The Stumble" being particularly good sellers. He continued to record for King Records into the mid-1960s, by which time his songs were being covered by everyone from Magic Sam to Eric Clapton.

Sales went up with "Going Down"

Two albums for Atlantic's Cotillion label in the late 1960s produced no big hits, but a deal with Leon Russell's Shelter Records proved more successful. Freddie recorded three albums for the label and found his new style, wedding blistering guitar to modern rock beats, and scored a hit with Don Nix's "Going Down." In 1974, he left Shelter and signed with RSO Records, releasing *Burglar*, which featured Eric Clapton producing and guesting on the album, followed by *Larger Than Life* in 1975.

Freddie was at the height of his success, but his punishing road schedule, which sometimes had Freddie driving the touring bus himself, was starting to take its toll. He died of heart failure on December 29, 1976, at the age of 42. But in the music of those who he influenced — Clapton, Lonnie Mack, Stevie Ray Vaughan, and loads of others — Freddie King is very much alive and well.

Hide Away: The Best Of Freddie King (Rhino). The wide selection on this set includes all of Freddie's King's best material.

Lightnin' Slim

If you were looking for the most low-down alley cat of a blues singer in Louisiana in the 1950s and early 1960s, your search would have led you straight to a fellow called Lightnin' Slim (1913–1974). Lightnin' had a singing voice that sounded as dry as a desert, which he set against guitar patterns so simple and infectious that they stuck in your brain forever.

Lightnin's records were spartan affairs. His backing "orchestra" usually consisted of somebody beating on a cardboard box (or sometimes a real drum set) and somebody else playing harmonica. This stripped-down formula worked well for Lightnin' Slim. After three regional hits on the Feature label, he scored several more for the Excello label in Nashville, including 1959's "Rooster Blues," which made the national R&B charts (and is on the *Blues For Dummies* CD).

Dark lyrics and a snappy catch phrase

Nobody had it tougher than Lightnin' Slim, and when he had the blues, believe us, he *had* the blues. Lightnin's lyrics were rife with dark images that enhanced his gloomy persona. His first record was also his first hit, a number-one single called "Bad Luck," which introduced the catch phrase "blow your harmonica, son" that turned up on almost every one of his subsequent records.

Lightnin' Slim was born Otis Hicks in St. Louis on March 15, 1913. He was taught to play the guitar by his father and his older brother, Layfield. After the Hicks family moved to St. Francisville, Louisiana, Otis was already starting to play publicly at the picnics and social affairs that dotted the local landscape. By the mid-1940s, he was making his reputation on the Baton Rouge club circuit.

By the 1950s, Lightnin' was doing live radio broadcasts on various shows and working with a harmonica player named Schoolboy Cleve. One of the disc jockeys who heard potential in Lightnin's sound was Ray "Diggy Do" Meaders. He talked local record producer J.D. Miller into recording Lightnin' for a new label he was starting up, Feature Records.

And the DJ played rhythm (on a cardboard box)

With "Diggy Do" beating out a rhythm on a cardboard box, Schoolboy Cleve blowing riffs on his harp, and Lightnin' taking licks on his guitar, the trio recorded Lightin's first single and first local hit, "Bad Luck." After two more singles on Feature, Miller set up a leasing deal with Excello Records in Nashville. For the next 12 years, Lightnin' Slim's singles were released on the Excello label and enjoyed enough regional success to spawn two albums, a rarity for a blues artist back then.

After Lightnin' Slim and Miller parted company in the mid-1960s, Lightnin' moved north to Detroit and took a day job. But tours of Europe, and offers to record while over there, got him back into playing again. He formed an act with Slim Harpo, working with assorted drummers to create a trio. Their prospects looked good until Harpo died in early 1970. Lightnin' Slim continued to play and record until his death in 1974.

Rooster Blues (AVI/Excello). Lightnin's original album is still the best place to start appreciating this down-home Louisiana blues artist.

Little Walter

Little Walter Jacobs (1930–1968) stands as the most influential harmonica player of all time, in the blues or elsewhere. The popular image of a harmonica player hunched over a cheap microphone and blowing for all its worth could be the portrait of Little Walter (see Figure 5-11). His playing was endlessly inventive (not unlike that of an improvisational jazz saxophonist), and he forever changed the sound of the blues and the status of that humble instrument, the harmonica.

Figure 5-11:
Little Walter
(photo
courtesy of
MCA-Chess).

Playing the Maxwell Street "stage"

Walter was born Marion Walter Jacobs in Marksville, Louisiana, on May 1, 1930. A talented youngster, Walter took off for New Orleans at age 12 and made stops in Helena, Arkansas, Memphis, and St. Louis before heading to Chicago in 1946. Playing for spare change on Maxwell Street, he soon attracted the attention of Big Bill Broonzy and Tampa Red. He also cut his first record for the Ora-Nelle label, "I Just Keep Lovin' Her," showing a strong stylistic debt to John Lee "Sonny Boy" Williamson.

Little Walter began working with Muddy Waters in 1948 in a loosely collected group called the Headhunters that included guitarists Jimmy Rogers and Baby Face Leroy Foster. Hitting club after club, the group carved up the competition, securing new work for themselves on the competitive Chicago club circuit.

A cheap mike, a guitar amp, and a new harmonica sound is born

Walter was recording with Muddy by early 1950, and their collaboration resulted in many classic blues recordings that helped shape and define the sound of electric Chicago blues. In order to be heard over the crowds in the noisy clubs where he played, Walter started blowing his harmonica into a cheap microphone plugged into a guitar amplifier. In doing so, he created a new sound that all aspiring electric harp players continue to strive for. This sound was heard nationwide when Walter cut his first big hit, the instrumental "Juke," at the tail end of a Muddy Waters session in 1952. "Juke" is on the *Blues For Dummies* CD.)

Going out on his own, Walter formed his first band (later to be called the Jukes) and took his music in a far more jazzy direction than he had as a member of Muddy Waters's band. He was now using a *chromatic harp* (a larger instrument built with a lever used to change the musical key) in addition to his standard-sized model.

Little Walter racked up 14 Top 10 R&B hits between 1952 and 1958. For all his instrumental virtuosity, the majority of these hits were primarily vocal items. In fact, John Lee Hooker says Little Walter is one of his favorite blues *singers* of all time.

A tragic early death

Little Walter seemed to have difficulty handling the success that came his way. His tough, combative nature cost him many a fine sideman and, as the hits dried up, he turned to alcohol and drugs. He toured England with the Rolling Stones in the mid-1960s, but his once effortless blowing had become a thing of the past.

In his final sessions for Chess Records, he played with a collapsed lung. Little Walter died of head injuries sustained in a street fight, three months short of his 38th birthday. But his influence in the blues and especially on other harmonica players resonates to this day. Little Walter was the ruler of modern-day blues harp.

Little Walter—His Best (MCA-Chess). This 20-track compilation should be your first stop in assembling a definitive blues harmonica collection. These are the sides that defined amplified Chicago blues harp.

Magic Sam

As part of the blues-guitar triumvirate from Chicago's West Side that also included Buddy Guy and Otis Rush, no one better represented the wide-ranging sound and style of the Chicago blues than Magic Sam (1937–1969). With a whiplash singing voice and guitar repertoire that incorporated everything from John Lee Hooker-style boogie to vibrato-filled slow blues to the latest soul music stylings, Magic Sam covered it all and mixed it into a heady concoction.

Sam gets the Magic touch

Born in Grenada, Mississippi, on Valentine's Day 1937, Sam Maghett moved to Chicago in 1950. He soon picked up musical and business pointers from his neighbor Syl Johnson and his "uncle" Shakey Jake Harris. By the age of 20, Sam was working the local club circuit as Good Rockin' Sam with Syl's brother Mack Thompson playing bass in his band.

Sam (see Figure 5-12) made his first records in 1957 for Eli Toscano's Cobra Records label. Toscano wanted to change Sam's stage name, suggesting well-worn monikers such as Singing Sam or Sad Sam, all of which the new blues artist rejected. Legend has it that Thompson suggested that Sam take his last name Maghett and corrupt it to become "Magic." The young singer had a new stage name and Magic Sam was born.

His first single for the label, "All Your Love," was an immediate local hit. (Its catchy minor key guitar riffing was recycled again and again on Sam's early records.) He quickly became a star on the Chicago club circuit and continued recording for Cobra until the label went bankrupt in 1959. After a hitch in the Army, Sam signed with Mel London's Chief Records and released several fine singles into the early 1960s.

Figure 5-12:
Magic Sam (CD booklet photo courtesy of Jewel Paula Ronn Records, A Division of Sue Records, Inc.).

A slice of West Side soul

Sam was still playing regularly on the West Side, but his recording opportunities had grown thin by the mid-1960s until he hooked up with Bob Koester's Delmark label. The two albums that resulted from this pairing — 1967's *West Side Soul* and 1968's *Black Magic* — were the records that introduced Magic Sam to a larger white audience. *West Side Soul* set new standards for the modern day blues album and Sam was enthusiastically received on the blues festival circuit.

The soul label Stax Records was reportedly negotiating for his recording contract and the guitarist seemed poised at the cusp of a new career breakthrough. Sadly, his health inexplicably began to fail him and he dropped dead of a heart attack on December 1, 1969, at the age of 32.

West Side Soul (Delmark). A combination of great songs, inspired playing and singing, and a solid backing band make this Magic Sam session his most inspired ever and one of the definitive Chicago blues albums of the 1960s.

Brownie McGhee and Sonny Terry

When we think of the great partnerships in the blues, several collaborations come to mind — Muddy Waters and Little Walter, Jimmy Reed and Eddie Taylor, and Leroy Carr and Scrapper Blackwell. But right at the top of the list would have to be the acoustic duo Brownie McGhee (1915–1996) and Sonny Terry (1911–1986). It's next to impossible to think of Brownie and Sonny as separate artists with a recording history of their own simply because they worked so tightly as a duo act for more than 30 years.

Overcoming physical challenges

Neither of these great blues partners was blessed with excellent health as children. Brownie was born Walter Brown McGhee in Knoxville in 1915. He contracted polio as a boy and spent most of his bedridden days learning to play the guitar. Sonny Terry was born Saunders Terrell in Greensboro, Georgia, in 1911. Sonny lost his sight in one eye when he was 8 and lost his sight in the other eye when he was 18.

When most of Brownie's mobility was restored after an operation, he began traveling and playing throughout the Southeast, often in the company of washboard player Bull City Red. Sonny started playing on the streets by his teens, eventually hooking up and recording with guitarist Blind Boy Fuller in 1937.

Brownie began recording for Columbia in 1940. After Fuller's death in 1941, his early records were issued under the name Blind Boy Fuller Number 2. By the time of McGhee's third recording session in 1941, he was teamed with Terry who, by then, had his whooping harmonica style perfected. They complemented each other perfectly, and a partnership was formed.

Riding the crest of the folk-blues revival

The duo relocated to New York City in 1942 and quickly became fixtures on the local folk music circuit. By 1946, McGhee was recording for a variety of labels in an early R&B mode while Terry worked on Broadway and was featured in the play *Finian's Rainbow* for two years. They recorded as solo artists with full amplified backing into the mid-1950s, and recorded together with Brownie sitting in on Sonny's sessions.

The folk music revival of the late 1950s cemented their partnership and Brownie and Sonny moved into the folk scene as its premier acoustic blues duo. The two recorded extensively, issuing album after album for Folkways, Fantasy, World Pacific, and other labels. They also started making regular tours throughout Europe, becoming favorites with blues lovers around the world.

Going their separate ways in the end

The duo's partnership lasted into the 1970s, but finally dissolved by mid-decade due to personal squabbles. Terry went on to work in commercials and write an instructional book on the harmonica while McGhee continued as a solo artist and pursued acting work.

Terry recorded a fine album with Johnny Winter for Alligator, *Whoopin'*, in 1984 before his death in 1986. At that time, McGhee was mostly retired, and made his final concert appearance at the Chicago Blues Festival a year before his death in 1996. In 1998, Sonny Terry was honored by the United States Post Office with his own postage stamp. Hopefully, his long-time partner Brownie McGhee will someday be similarly honored.

At The Second Fret (Bluesville). This live set captures the acoustic duo Brownie McGhee and Sonny Terry at the peak of their combined powers.

Robert Nighthawk

Of all the pivotal figures in blues history, certainly one of the most important was Robert Nighthawk (1909–1967). His playing bridged the gap between Delta and Chicago blues. Borrowing slide guitar chops from Tampa Red, he laced them with a rural Mississippi edge learned firsthand from his cousin, Houston Stackhouse.

He recorded from the 1930s to the early 1940s under a variety of names (Robert Lee McCoy, Rambling Bob, Peetie's Boy), finally taking the permanent name Robert Nighthawk from the title of his first record, "Prowling Night Hawk."

The restless Nighthawk

Born Robert McCollum in Helena, Arkansas, on November 30, 1909, Robert rambled far and wide as a youth, picking up guitar from his cousin Houston Stackhouse, and teaming with him to play the numerous country dances and parties. In the mid-1930s, after a shooting incident in which Robert was implicated, he fled to St. Louis and changed his name to Robert McCoy. He recorded for Bluebird Records in 1937, switching over to Decca by 1940.

Robert then headed back to Helena and began broadcasting as Robert Nighthawk on station KFFA during the 1940s. During a trip to Chicago, he met Muddy Waters, who in 1949 arranged a recording session for him at Leonard and Phil Chess's fledgling Aristocrat label (later called Chess Records).

It was then that Robert recorded a pair of his signature tunes, "Anna Lee" and "Black Angel Blues," which B.B. King would later turn into his "Sweet Little Angel." But no hits came out of his alliance with the Chess Brothers, and Nighthawk moved over to United Records for a pair of singles in 1951. When that didn't pan out either, Robert stopped recording until 1964 when he cut sides for Chess and Testament Records.

Happy just playing the one-nighters

It should be noted that the huge lapses in Nighthawk's discography are direct results of his restless nature and seeming disinterest in making records. Nevertheless, once he got into a studio, the results were almost always uniformly excellent (even if it was two or more years between sessions).

Nighthawk never achieved the success of his more celebrated pupils, Muddy Waters and Earl Hooker, and was happiest working one-nighters in taverns and playing the Maxwell Street open market on Sundays.

He eventually left Chicago to return to his hometown in Arkansas, where he briefly took over the *King Biscuit Time* radio show after Sonny Boy Williamson died. After that, Nighthawk worked every small juke joint that dotted the land until his death from congestive heart failure in 1967.

Robert Nighthawk is not a name that usually gets tossed about when discussing the all-time blues greats, and that's a shame. His resonant voice and creamy-smooth slide guitar playing would influence players for generations to come, and many of his songs became blues standards.

Live On Maxwell Street (Rounder). Rough, loose, and informal, Nighthawk's silky slide work is something not to be missed. One of the best live blues albums ever.

Elvis Presley

The real skinny on Elvis Presley is this: He may have been crowned the King of Rock 'n' Roll in the 1950s, a bigger celebrity than any pop star before or since, but he ascended to that throne by being first and foremost a blues singer.

In the beginning of his career, Elvis wasn't even marketed as a pop or rock vocalist. He was sold as a country-western singer, albeit the strangest one anyone had ever seen. His onstage movements were almost spasmodic, his clothes were oddly elegant, and the music he sang was even stranger. Those early Elvis records for Sam Phillips's Sun label in Memphis included one hopped-up blues tune after another, not exactly C&W chart fodder.

A star is born in the Sun Studios

In his first five singles for Sun, Elvis recorded and reconstructed Arthur Crudup's "That's All Right," Roy Brown's "Good Rockin' Tonight," Kokomo Arnold's "Milkcow Blues (Boogie)," Arthur Gunter's "Baby, Let's Play House," and Junior Parker's "Mystery Train." Although hillbilly singers had dabbled with the blues in recent years, the Elvis Presley sound was something completely different.

Most Elvis fans know his biographical facts by heart. Born Elvis Aron Presley on January 8, 1935, in Tupelo, Mississippi, he was a pampered only child whose twin brother, Jesse Garon, died at birth. Raised in the Pentecostal church, Elvis heard gospel music from the time he was very young and at age 11 began playing the guitar.

Not country, not exactly R&B, it was just Elvis

A number of elements made Presley's brand of blues unique. He didn't resort to roughening up his voice in an attempt to sound African-American. You'd never hear phony shrieking or rasping on an Elvis record to make it sound more like "authentic" blues. The rhythm he employed was an attempt to assimilate R&B grooves into the music he played with a little hillbilly duo. But, it wasn't R&B, it wasn't country, it was just *different*. And perhaps most important of all was that Elvis truly *felt* the music he was playing and could express it in a way without having to resort to cheap imitation.

Elvis returned to the blues throughout his incredibly successful career. A down-and-dirty blues performance would unexpectedly turn up in the midst of a Christmas album or a movie soundtrack. You just never knew when the blues muse would strike the King. His 1968 TV special spotlighted extended workouts on Jimmy Reed's "Baby, What You Want Me To Do" and Rufus Thomas's "Tiger Man (King Of The Jungle)," both featuring Elvis in a rare appearance on electric guitar.

Presley's place in the history books as a rock 'n' roll icon is more than assured (hysterical public mourning following his death in 1977), but his commitment to the blues was certainly what started it all. Elvis as a blues singer? You bet.

Last Train To Memphis by Peter Guralnick (Little, Brown). You can find a million books (or so it seems) about Elvis' early rise to fame and fortune, but this is the one worth reading. Exhaustively researched and written in Guralnick's usual impeccable fashion, this is the first installment of the author's multi-volume chronicle of Presley's life and times. If you want to read up on Elvis's early days without the tabloid sleaze, here's where to go.

The Sun Sessions CD (RCA Victor). A hillbilly lad starts singing the blues and the whole world sits up and takes notice.

Jimmy Reed

The brand of blues that Jimmy Reed (1925–1976) played may be likened to a cheeseburger served up at the local diner — definitely nothing fancy, but if you've got a craving for it, it sure hits the spot. Reed (see Figure 5-13) enjoyed more hits on the pop charts than any blues artist *ever,* with a series of records built on the most rudimentary blues formula imaginable.

Figure 5-13:
Jimmy Reed
(photo
courtesy of
Burton
Wilson,
Austin, TX).

Reed's blues playing was about as simple and unassuming as it could possibly be. Not loud and intimidating like the music of Howlin' Wolf (or even Muddy Waters), just smooth and easy. Jimmy not only didn't shout the lyrics in your face, he mumbled them out of the side of his mouth.

Reed's secret: Never leave home without Eddie Taylor

The secret weapon in the Jimmy Reed arsenal was the guitar work of his partner and childhood friend, Eddie Taylor. Playing a muted boogie pattern on the bass strings of his guitar, Taylor created a sound and style that has since become an integral part of blues guitar playing and a basic component of blues music itself.

It wasn't Reed's abilities as a singer and multi-instrumentalist that garnered him hit records on the pop and R&B charts. It was that incessant groove and boogie beat of Taylor's guitar coupled with Reed's simple charm that made the music accessible to both black and white audiences. He may not have won any critic's awards in his lifetime, but the people *loved* Jimmy Reed.

Because his music was so simple and easy to play, songs such as "Baby, What You Want Me To Do," "Big Boss Man," "Bright Lights, Big City," and "Going To New York" were found on the play lists of rock 'n' roll bands, country bands, and any other group that wanted to have a go at playing the blues. Years before the '60s blues revival, Jimmy Reed tunes were played on bandstands everywhere.

Marrying his collaborator "Mama Reed"

James Mathis Reed was born in Dunleith, Mississippi, on September 6, 1925. He spent his teenage years learning harmonica and guitar basics from his childhood friend, guitarist Eddie Taylor. Jimmy moved north to Chicago when he turned 18, and was drafted for a two-year stretch in the Navy.

Jimmy moved back to Mississippi after his discharge just long enough to wed his future collaborator, Mary (always referred to by Jimmy as "Mama Reed"). The Reeds moved to Gary, Indiana, where Jimmy worked in a meat packing plant. He then played with blues singer-guitarist John Brim, and was a member of John's Gary Kings, who played on Brim's biggest record "Tough Times," for the Parrot label.

An unprecedented run on the record charts

But Reed wanted to make records of his own. Chess Records had turned him down, but he found a home with a brand-new label, Vee-Jay Records. Jimmy's recording career began in 1953 with the label's very first release, "High & Lonesome." His third single, "You Don't Have To Go," made the Top Five on the R&B charts. The success of that simple tune signaled the beginning of Reed's amazing run on the charts. Before it was all over, Jimmy had landed 12 songs on the *Billboard* Hot 100 pop charts and 19 entries on their R&B charts, figures topped by no other blues artist before or since. With artists big and small singing and playing his songs, Jimmy Reed was well on his way to becoming the most influential blues artist of all.

But success was not something Jimmy Reed handled well. By all accounts a heavy drinker, Jimmy regularly showed up for live performances in no condition to perform. This was a big problem for everyone concerned with his career because Jimmy was in demand *everywhere*. He worked all the major R&B package shows, including the Apollo theater, with recording sessions sandwiched in whenever possible. But Reed's behavior while intoxicated tarnished his image among his show business contemporaries.

A struggle to regain his health

Reed's condition worsened. He was barely able to get through a recording session, and Vee-Jay went out of business in the mid-1960s. But Jimmy wasn't through recording. His manager, Al Smith, secured a multi-album contract for him with ABC-Bluesway Records. The albums that followed into the 1970s seemed to be recorded quickly and cheaply, with Jimmy sounding tired and confused on most of them.

After years in seclusion and retirement from active playing, Jimmy got long overdue medical treatment for his epilepsy and alcoholism. He gained control over both conditions, regaining enough of his health to start playing live again. He was welcomed warmly everywhere he played. He passed away while on tour in August 1976. In 1991, Reed was inducted into the Rock and Roll Hall of Fame.

Speak The Lyrics To Me, Mama Reed (Vee-Jay). Reed's languid style is filled with easygoing charm, and this collection is loaded with tunes that have become enduring blues classics.

Otis Rush

One-third of Chicago's celebrated West Side school of blues guitarists (the other two notables being Buddy Guy and Magic Sam), Otis Rush (born 1934) quickly distanced himself from the rest by developing a guitar style that was more intense and introspective than that of the other two members of the West Side triumvirate.

Otis's early recordings combined Robert Johnson–style anguished vocals with sweet, stinging guitar solos done in the B.B. King mode with his right-handed guitar played upside-down and left-handed. An influence on countless younger guitarists (Jimmy Page, Eric Clapton, and Stevie Ray Vaughan among them), Rush continues to record and tour to this day, still occasionally connecting with the private demons that make his brand of blues so compelling.

Born in Philadelphia, Mississippi, on April 29, 1934, Otis (see Figure 5-14) moved to Chicago at age 14. After he met Muddy Waters, he decided to start playing the blues right then and there. Entirely self-taught, left-handed Rush took a right-handed guitar and simply flipped it around to the other side without reversing the strings (a "backwards" style of playing made famous by Albert King).

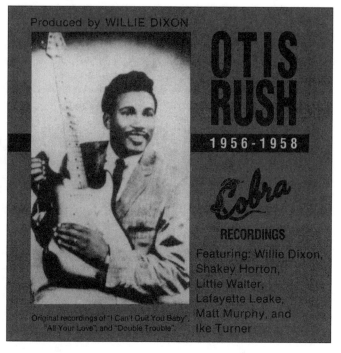

A career push from Willie Dixon

By the mid-1950s, Rush was busy making a name for himself on the Chicago club circuit when he caught the attention of Willie Dixon. Willie got him signed to Cobra Records, produced Otis's first session, and gave Otis a classic song to sing, "I Can't Quit You, Baby." The debut single made Number Six on the R&B charts in 1956 and for the next two years Otis Rush made records for Cobra that have been consistently hailed as the peak of his art. Songs such as "All Your Love (I Miss Loving)" and "Double Trouble" were high watermarks of this, or any other, period in the blues.

Otis's career after leaving Cobra in 1959 seemed to consist of one bad break after another. He moved over to Chess and released another classic, "So Many Roads (So Many Trains)," but just as quickly made a disastrous deal with the Duke label that netted only a single release over several years.

Righteous records, but wrong timing

By the mid-1960s, Rush's name started reaching rock audiences via new recordings for Vanguard and Cotillion. Seemingly poised for breakthrough stardom, Rush signed with Capitol and cut a new album, but the label decided not to release it. That album, *Right Place, Wrong Time,* eventually came out years later on a smaller label, but too late to save Otis's sagging career.

Rush spent the rest of the 1970s and 1980s recording for various labels in the United States and Europe, where he toured frequently. Those recordings alternated between brilliant (*So Many Roads—Live In Japan*) to erratic. Otis's recording fortunes took an upward turn with the brilliant *Ain't Enough Comin' In* released in 1994. He continues to tour and record, having recently signed with the House Of Blues label.

"When right-handed players bend a guitar string, they push it *up* and toward them. But what makes lefties so strong is that they pull *down* on the string. That's where all the strength comes from, when they close their hands to pull that string down. That's what makes Otis Rush so special. He has that left-hander's control over his notes."

1956–1958 Cobra Recordings (Paula). This CD contains the recordings that made Otis Rush's considerable reputation. It includes the original versions of "Double Trouble" and "I Can't Quit You, Baby."

Roosevelt Sykes

Roosevelt Sykes (1906–1983) remains one of the most important piano stylists of the pre–World War II blues era. His musical outlook was as upbeat as the man himself, and Sykes certainly wasn't above peppering his rowdy barrelhouse stylings with lyrical double entendres. His contributions to the blues include such timeless classics as "Driving Wheel," "44 Blues," and "Night Time Is The Right Time."

"44 Blues" and a few different names

Roosevelt Sykes was born on January 31, 1906, in Elmar, Arkansas. He grew up in St. Louis, learning keyboard rudiments by playing the organ in church. He moved over to the piano and started working in various barrelhouses and juke joints around Helena, Arkansas.

Using St. Louis as his base of operations, Sykes started making regular trips to Chicago and Memphis in the late 1920s. His first opportunity to record came in 1929 for the OKeh label, which spawned his signature tune "44 Blues." He spent the rest of the 1930s recording for the Victor and Decca labels, sometimes under the pseudonyms of Easy Papa Johnson, Dobby Bragg, or Willie Kelly.

Sykes moved to Chicago in 1941. He fit in perfectly with the local scene, working with Memphis Minnie and recording with Jump Jackson's band. During the 1940s, Roosevelt was making solo records and working as a sideman for the Bluebird and Bullet labels. He formed his first band, the Honeydrippers, around then and toured the South regularly during and after World War II.

Sweet home New Orleans

Roosevelt left Chicago and moved to New Orleans in 1954. There he found plenty of work for a piano player and entertainer of his caliber and made the city his home for the rest of his days. He began touring Europe during the 1960s and kept up a full schedule of playing and recording for a variety of labels into the 1980s. Playing his brand of blues and boogie-woogie right to the end, Roosevelt Sykes died on July 17, 1983.

The Honeydripper (Original Blues Classics). This 1961 release finds Sykes in fine form, backed by a solid little combo including King Curtis on tenor saxophone playing a batch of great tunes.

Big Mama Thornton

By the time of the first blues heyday beginning in the mid-1940s, female blues singers were scarce and female singer-instrumentalists were even scarcer. Filling this musical void was Willie Mae "Big Mama" Thornton (1926–1984), a woman with a physical presence that proved her nickname was no boast. With a rough-edged voice that could peel paint, she blew a mean harmonica, and could pound out a drum beat to boot.

She was born Willie Mae Thornton on December 11, 1926, in Montgomery, Alabama, into a religious family. Her father was a minister and her mother was a featured vocalist in the church congregation. But after Willie Mae got a taste of the blues, she left home at 14 to become a performer. She made her show business debut with Sammy Green's Hot Harlem Revue based out of Georgia. The seven years spent with the troupe honed both her vocal and instrumental skills, which she demonstrated by blowing neck-rack harmonica and pounding the drums simultaneously.

Notching a hit with "Hound Dog"

Figuring Houston would be a good base of operations for furthering her career as a singer, Thornton moved there in 1948. In 1951, she signed up with Don Robey's Peacock label. Her moment of blues immortality came two years later when she recorded the original version of "Hound Dog" with bandleader Johnny Otis. The song hit Number One on the R&B charts and inspired a record in response from Rufus Thomas, the single "Bear Cat" on the Sun label.

But Big Mama didn't write "Hound Dog" and saw little in the way of royalties from her hit. In 1956, Elvis Presley, utilizing an arrangement he picked up from Las Vegas lounge rockers Freddie Bell and the Bellboys, turned the song into a million-selling rock 'n' roll record.

Although she never had another chart record, she stayed in demand as a live attraction, working many package tours with Johnny Otis, Little Esther Phillips, and Little Junior Parker. Big Mama (see Figure 5-15) continued to record with Peacock until 1957 until her career fortunes began to fade. She relocated to San Francisco and became a regular fixture on the club scene there. Thornton label-hopped during the early 1960s, doing one-off singles for Irma, Bay Tone, Sotoplay, and Kent, none of which sold all that well.

"Ball and Chain" and a record deal

In 1965, her career got a sudden boost when she toured Europe as a member of the American Folk Blues Festival package. While in England, she recorded with members of the troupe, including Buddy Guy and Mississippi Fred McDowell. The results of that session were released on the Arhoolie label. She recorded again for Arhoolie the following year in San Francisco with the Muddy Waters Band backing her up. A 1968 session for the label yielded her minor masterpiece "Ball and Chain."

This number was quickly adopted by Janis Joplin, who made it her set closer that same year at the Monterey Pop Festival with her band Big Brother and the Holding Company. When it appeared on Big Brother's *Cheap Thrills* album, the ensuing publicity helped secure Big Mama a two-album deal with Mercury Records in 1969.

Big Mama Thornton continued to record and perform into the 1970s, releasing records on Vanguard and Buddah. She appeared on the *Dick Cavett Show* and was heard on the soundtrack for the movie *Vanishing Point*. By the 1980s, after years of hard living, her once-massive frame was nearly skeletal, and she had to remain seated through her performances. Big Mama Thornton died on July 25, 1984, the same year she was inducted into the Blues Foundation's Hall of Fame.

Hound Dog: The Peacock Recordings (MCA). All of Big Mama's seminal recordings for the Peacock label are here to savor, with solid backing and that gruff roar of a voice soaring over it all.

Figure 5-15:
Big Mama
Thornton
(photo
courtesy of
Burton
Wilson,
Austin, TX).

T-Bone Walker

T-Bone Walker (1910–1975) stands as the originator of the modern electric blues guitar style. B.B. King and Clarence "Gatemouth" Brown both learned to play solo electric by immersing themselves in T-Bone's music, and his influence extends directly to early rock 'n' rollers, including Chuck Berry.

When he amplified his instrument in 1940, Walker changed blues guitar forever — both its sound and the way it was played. In addition to his innovative guitar playing, he was also a great singer and consummate showman. T-Bone incorporated many eye-popping guitar tricks into his live act that were later used by Jimi Hendrix and Stevie Ray Vaughan.

Blues done to a Texas T-Bone

Born Aaron Thibeaux Walker in Linden, Texas, on May 28, 1910, T-Bone's family moved to Dallas, and it was there that the youngster got his first guitar lessons from no less than the legendary blues guitarist Blind Lemon Jefferson. By the age of 19, Walker was well-known enough in the Oak Cliff section of Dallas to record his first single under the name "Oak Cliff T-Bone."

He spent most of the 1930s out on the road playing with several jazz bands and small combos. Legend has it that he started playing a prototype electric guitar by 1936. Three years later, he joined Les Hite's Orchestra and resumed his recording career with the classic "T-Bone Blues." By 1941, T-Bone had formed his own band, first recording for Capitol and then for Black & White Records, which produced his most enduring hit, "Call It Stormy Monday (But Tuesday Is Just As Bad)." Walker moved on to Imperial Records in 1950 and stayed long enough to leave more than 50 recordings behind. By 1955, he had signed with Atlantic Records, producing the album *T-Bone Blues,* which many consider to be among his best work.

The end of the road

During the 1950s, Walker was working dates with pickup combos with wildly fluctuating talent in place of his customary big band. He continued to record sporadically for a number of labels (even winning a Grammy for *Good Feelin'* in 1970), but was much more of a force as a live attraction on the United States and European blues festival circuit.

By the early 1970s, years of hard drinking had led to stomach problems. T-Bone retired in 1974 after a stroke and died from bronchial pneumonia the following year. In 1987, the Rock and Roll Hall of Fame recognized Walker as an Early Influence on rock. Without T-Bone Walker's contributions to the blues, it's hard to say what the electric blues guitar would sound like today.

T-Bone Blues (Atlantic). Walker's last great album is the perfect way to begin digesting the genius of this highly influential artist.

Muddy Waters

In the Chicago blues kingdom of the 1950s and 1960s, no one ruled the palace like Muddy Waters (1915–1983). He was one of blues music's very best slide guitarists and singers, a mesmerizing stage performer, a patriarch in the blues community, and a visionary bandleader beyond compare.

Muddy virtually invented the modern day blues band lineup as we know it. The list of musicians who flowed through the ranks of The Muddy Waters Band reads like a Who's Who of Chicago blues — harp players Little Walter, James Cotton, Junior Wells, Carey Bell, and Big Walter Horton; guitarists Jimmy Rogers, Pat Hare, and Luther "Guitar Junior" Johnson; pianists Otis Spann and Pinetop Perkins; and bassist Willie Dixon, and most of them can be heard on several of Muddy's best-known recordings.

Muddy was also a great ambassador for the music as well. He was a gentlemanly, sharply dressed man with strikingly good looks who carried himself with a regal dignity. An unselfish patron of the blues, he was always willing to lend a hand to any up-and-coming or down-on-his-luck blues artist.

His first "label" — the Library of Congress

Muddy Waters (see Figure 5-16) was born McKinley Morganfield on April 15, 1915, to a sharecropping family in Rolling Fork, Mississippi. He picked up the nickname Muddy Waters as a small child. When his mother died, he moved in with his grandmother to Stovall's Plantation in Clarksdale. Muddy's first musical heroes were local musicians Son House and Robert Johnson. By the age of 17, Muddy was working in a loosely collected group called the Son Simms Four. It was with this group and as a solo artist that he recorded for folklorist Alan Lomax and the Library of Congress in 1941 and 1942.

Muddy came to Chicago in 1943 and quickly became a fixture on the local blues scene with help from Big Bill Broonzy, then an established star. Waters never forgot the kindness and later recorded a tribute album in Broonzy's honor. After a couple of stray sessions that largely went nowhere, Muddy's next recording opportunity was courtesy of pianist Sunnyland Slim.

Slim had a session lined up with the Chess brothers' new Aristocrat label and invited Waters to sit in on guitar along with bassist Big Crawford. Muddy cut a couple of vocals that day with Crawford seconding his electric guitar. Their next session together in 1948 is where the Muddy Waters story truly begins.

Shaping the modern day Chicago blues band

The single from that 1948 session, "I Can't Be Satisfied," was an old Delta blues song Muddy had already recorded for the Library of Congress as "I'se Be Troubled." But in its new electric arrangement, it took on an entirely new character and people immediately took notice. In just one day, the Chess brothers sold every single copy they had pressed.

Leonard Chess wanted Muddy to continue to record with just his electric slide guitar and Crawford's string bass, but Waters was anxious to record with the larger band he worked with in clubs. It took a while for Chess to cave in, but once the label did, what followed for the next decade were the most important and definitive recordings in Chicago blues history.

Figure 5-16:
Muddy
Waters
(photo
courtesy of
Burton
Wilson,
Austin, TX).

Whether he was contributing his own material (such as "Long Distance Call," "Rolling Stone," "She Moves Me," and "She's 19 Years Old"), singing songs custom written for him by Willie Dixon (such as "I'm Your Hoochie Coochie Man," which is on the *Blues For Dummies* CD) "I Just Want To Make Love To You," and "I'm Ready"), or putting his personal stamp on other's artists material (such as Ann Cole's "I Got My Mojo Working"), Muddy's records shaped and defined the sound of Chicago blues and the structure of the modern day blues band.

The 1960s psychedelic flop and the 1970s masterpieces

By the early 1960s, Waters gained acceptance both here and in Europe with solid performances on the jazz and folk music festival circuits. His music broke through to a whole new audience of white music fans just discovering the blues. By the end of the 1960s, Muddy was adding rock festivals and ballrooms to his crowded schedule of play dates.

Chess Records released some ill-conceived albums during the late 1960s with Muddy attempting to sing rock music and psychedelic blues, but they weren't successful, either artistically or financially. As it turned out, he won a Grammy in 1971 for *They Call Me Muddy Waters,* a collection of older material.

Muddy moved over to CBS/Blue Sky in 1977 and recorded *Hard Again* with Johnny Winter producing. It was an inspired session that won him his second Grammy, and Waters and Winter continued to work together, both in the studio and live, into the 1980s. Muddy capped the 1970s with a command performance at the White House for President Carter and a one-song cameo in the Band's documentary, *The Last Waltz*.

In 1983, Muddy Waters died of a heart attack in his sleep. His death was mourned by music fans around the world. He was inducted into the Blues Foundation Hall of Fame in 1980 and the Rock and Roll Hall of Fame in 1987. His face was even on a U.S. postage stamp as part of a series honoring famous American blues artists.

"I used to just wait for Muddy to come out with another record! I wanted to hear what he was going to do next. As soon as I heard somebody say, 'Muddy's got a new record out,' I was the first one in the store looking for it. I'd even go to the radio station to see if they would make me a tape of it just so I could be the first one to play his new numbers on a bandstand."

His Best, 1947 to 1955 (MCA-Chess). This is one of the essential first buys for your blues collection simply because this is the spot where electric Chicago blues begins. Beyond essential.

Junior Wells

Junior Wells (1934–1998) was the dean of Chicago blues harmonica players. His flamboyant singing was wedded to a hard-as-nails harmonica attack and a tough and street-wise stage persona. Rather than soften his bad-boy stage image as he grew older, he continued to play it up for all it was worth.

Junior's harmonica style was firmly built on the twists and turns of the great Sonny Boy Williamson II. It was a style marked by short, rhythmic blasts that accented the beat. Junior Wells could accomplish more by blowing a couple of notes than most other harp players could achieve over several choruses.

Junior was also the first Chicago artist to infuse the blues with the contemporary sounds of mid-1960s soul music. He would recast old songs with a modern, funky beat and punctuate his vocals with soulful cries in the manner of R&B singers such as James Brown and Otis Redding.

Stepping into Little Walter's shoes

Junior Wells was born Amos Blakemore in Memphis on December 9, 1934. He was taught the rudiments of harmonica playing by Little Junior Parker. When the Blakemore family moved to Chicago at age 12, young Amos started playing on the streets for tips. He quickly graduated to house rent parties, playing with a band called the Aces. The Aces later became Little Walter's backing band (renaming themselves the Jukes). When Little Walter left Muddy Water's band, Junior Wells (then all of 18) jumped in to take Walter's place.

Wells recorded on his own throughout the 1950s and early 1960s for a batch of small Chicago-based labels including States, Chief, and Profile, often working with guitarist Earl Hooker. The recording partnership of Wells and Hooker produced a lot of great music and one small hit in 1962 — the enduring blues classic "Messin' With The Kid."

Partnering with Buddy Guy

Junior Wells finally came to national attention by teaming up with guitarist Buddy Guy in the mid-1960s and releasing a batch of brilliant landmark recordings for collector-oriented labels, including Delmark and Vanguard. Junior's 1966 *Hoodoo Man Blues* album stands as one of the first modern-day blues albums that helped launch renewed interest in electric blues.

Junior continued working with Buddy into the 1970s, and touring around the United States and Europe, when the two weren't holding down the fort at Theresa's Lounge back in Chicago. Performance footage of the duo in their prime exists in abundance, but the tape to see is the concert video *Messin' With The Blues* (Rhino Home Video), which features Wells and Guy working behind Muddy Waters.

During the 1980s and 1990s, Junior did more live performances than recorded work, but did rekindle his recording career toward the end with four new albums for the Telarc label, one of which, *Come On In This House,* won both the W.C. Handy award for Best Traditional Blues Album of the Year and the Living Blues award for Best Blues Album.

In 1997, Wells made an appearance in the movie *Blues Brothers 2000.* But then, the seemingly indestructible Wells began to get very sick. He was diagnosed with lymphatic cancer and later suffered a heart attack that put him in a coma for several weeks. Junior Wells, the harp-blowing toughie and the last of his kind, died on January 15, 1998, at the age of 63.

Hoodoo Man Blues (Delmark). Junior, Buddy Guy, and a crack rhythm section roam through a set of bandstand staples, and the result just happens to be one of the first great modern-day blues albums.

Junior is one of the greatest harp players of that brand of music we call "deep blues." He's also written some of the best blues classics, especially "Little By Little" and "Messin' With The Kid."

Bukka White

Bukka White (1905–1977) played down-home styled acoustic Delta blues with an emotional ferocity matched by few. He used his guitar almost as a percussion instrument to hammer home his message. White's compositional skills showed remarkable lyrical depth and true originality. His music was unadorned yet rhythmically complex, and his intense slide guitar work was a huge influence on his cousin, B.B. King.

Bukka was born Booker Washington White on November 12, 1909, in Houston, Mississippi. Bukka learned guitar basics from his father, a railroad worker who played music on the weekends. After moving to the Delta region of Mississippi in his teens, White fell under the musical spell of Charlie Patton, his biggest musical influence.

Supplementing his income with boxing and baseball

Bukka made his first records in 1930 for the Victor label, recording both blues and gospel numbers under the name of Washington White. Supplementing his income playing juke joints and parties, White also worked as a professional boxer and played baseball for the Negro leagues.

In 1937, he was arrested and sentenced to prison after a shooting incident. He jumped bail, fled to Chicago, and once there, managed to record a session for Vocalion before being captured and sent to Parchman Farm prison to serve out his term. After his release in 1940, he recorded for the OKeh and Vocalion labels, pairing up with Washboard Sam.

Rediscovered by John Fahey and recording for Arhoolie

Bukka quit playing by the late 1940s when country blues fell out of favor. He settled down in Memphis and worked as a laborer until his rediscovery in 1963 by folk guitarist John Fahey and blues fan Ed Denson. This led to recordings for the Arhoolie label and several successful appearances at folk clubs and college campuses around the country.

In 1966, Bukka appeared at the prestigious Newport Folk Festival, along with Son House and Skip James, to great acclaim. The following year saw White touring Europe for the first time as part of the American Folk Blues Festival troupe. Recording new albums into the 1970s, White stayed true to his original vision, keeping his unique approach to the music firmly intact. Bukka White passed away on January 26, 1977, and was inducted into the Blues Foundation's Hall of Fame in 1990.

The Complete Bukka White (Columbia/Legacy). This CD features all of Bukka White's 1940 sessions for OKeh and Vocalion Records and captures Bukka at his very best.

Sonny Boy Williamson II

Sonny Boy Williamson II (1899–1965) ranks among the greatest of the blues harmonica players. He represented the complete blues package — he was a terrific singer, a brilliant and innovative instrumentalist, and a songwriter of incomparable creativity.

Sonny Boy Williamson's life was truely well spent in the blues. He may be the only person featured in this book to have actually played with artists from all three major time periods of blues history, starting with Robert Johnson in the 1930s and ending with Eric Clapton in the mid-1960s.

A late bloomer

Sonny Boy's style made him readily identifiable the second you heard him. He didn't start recording until he was 50 years old, but even then, he sounded like someone decades older. That "old man playing on the front porch" sound to his voice made his lyrics seem even more eloquent and he delivered his songs almost as if they were poetry. If you ignore the occasional malaprop, each of his songs reads like a three-minute morality play as recited by Grandpa Sonny Boy.

His harmonica playing was unique in a number of ways. He rarely played an amplified harp as Little Walter and others did. He used the harmonica to insert musical punctuation between vocal phrases, using tidy little blasts that kept audiences on edge waiting for Sonny Boy (see Figure 5-17) to turn up the heat and blast out a chorus at full throttle.

A sketchy early history

Trying to construct any kind of early biographical information on Sonny Boy is where the going gets beyond tough. Sonny Boy considered being interviewed by blues fans and scholars an invasion of privacy equaled only by a tax audit. He believed every answer he gave would be information eventually used against him.

Figure 5-17:
Sonny Boy
Williamson II
(photo
courtesy of
MCA-Chess).

The best guess on his real name is that it was either Aleck or Alex Miller (the most likely choice) or Willie Ford. He was born in Glendora, Mississippi, in either 1897, 1899 (the most likely year), or 1909. At one time or another, Sonny Boy has supplied all of this contradictory information.

The next historical glimpse of Sonny Boy is during the 1930s, after he had become a professional musician. Hoboing around the Mississippi Delta region, Sonny Boy worked dances, country suppers, and juke joints under the name Little Boy Blue. Playing harmonica and kazoo, he would hook up a crude p.a. system that piped his playing through the club's jukebox.

He was also broadcasting over radio station WEBQ with a 15-minute program four times a week. Although his favorite musical partner turned out to be guitarist Robert Jr. Lockwood, Sonny Boy also logged playing time with Elmore James, Robert Johnson, and Robert Nighthawk.

Will the real Sonny Boy please sign on?

In the 1940s, Sonny Boy and Lockwood were made a broadcasting offer, with a catch to it. The Interstate Grocery Company (IGC) wanted to promote its King Biscuit flour with a local radio show and wanted to build the program around blues music. IGC figured that this new show would have more appeal to its African-American target audience if the artist hosting it was a bona fide blues recording star. A likely candidate was Chicago harmonica ace John Lee "Sonny Boy" Williamson (for the full story on *that* Sonny Boy, see Chapter 4).

But Sonny Boy the First wasn't interested in traveling south to do the show, so IGC enlisted Sonny Boy II (who was going by the name Rice Miller at the time) to pose as the Chicago bluesman in order to host KFFA's *King Biscuit Time* program. Even though Miller didn't sound a bit like Sonny Boy the First, he assumed his identity and the show was a huge hit.

John Lee Williamson's death in 1948 gave Miller clearance to use the name of the elder bluesman (and first Sonny Boy Williamson), and by the 1950s, the *King Biscuit Time* show was such a success that IGC came out with a new product, Sonny Boy Corn Meal, which featured a cartoon drawing of Sonny Boy II on the front of the bag.

With all his regional success, it would seem the logical time for Sonny Boy II to start making records. But he didn't seem to care one way or the other about recording, preferring to live off what he made from live performances and his gambling winnings.

A reluctant recording star

Sonny Boy did eventually record — for the Trumpet label out of Jackson, Mississippi. His first single for the label, which was released in 1951, also became his first hit, "Eyesight To The Blind," a number later included in The Who's rock opera *Tommy*. That same year, Sonny Boy blew harp on Elmore James's hit recording of "Dust My Broom." He would record for Trumpet until 1954 when his contract was eventually sold to Leonard Chess in Chicago. Assigning Sonny Boy to the label's subsidiary, Checker, Leonard brought his new acquisition north to record in the Chess studios in August 1955.

Sonny Boy's backing group on this first session was none other than Muddy Waters and his band. They complemented each other's style perfectly — Chicago blues by way of Mississippi at its very best. Sonny Boy's first Checker single from that session, "Don't Start Me To Talkin'," made the national R&B charts.

But rather than cashing in on all his newfound success, Sonny Boy continued his rambling and gambling ways, doing as he darn well pleased. He preferred playing small juke joints to submitting to the rigors of the road.

A restless spirit

Sonny Boy's restless spirit and taste for experiencing new places and new things reached its zenith when he toured Europe in 1963 as a member of the American Folk Blues Festival. European audiences went absolutely crazy over Sonny Boy's harp mastery and showboating tricks, and he fell in love with his new surroundings.

Sonny Boy began entertaining notions about moving to Europe, and over the next couple of years he toured with blues-rock groups, including the Animals and the Yardbirds. To put the icing on the cake, his most recent Checker recording of "Help Me" started making the charts all across Europe. What changed his mind at this point is anyone's guess. Instead of moving to London or Paris, Sonny Boy returned to the United States, back to Mississippi, and once again was hosting the *King Biscuit Time* program.

Surviving radio broadcasts from this time period show him in high spirits and in full command of his playing and singing abilities. But on May 25, 1965, Sonny Boy II died suddenly of a heart attack. He was elected to the Blues Foundation Hall Of Fame in 1980, and later a monument was also erected to Sonny Boy at his gravesite in the Whitfield Cemetery in Tutwiler, Mississippi.

His Best (MCA-Chess). The 20 tracks of blues dynamite from this harp wizard, coupled with stellar backing and some great song writing, makes this yet another essential purchase.

Other Notable Artists

Although the artists in this section of the chapter may not have been huge stars, or had as wide-ranging an influence as some other better-known blues artists, we'd be remiss in our duties if we didn't mention these folks. When you're talking about some of the great ones who carved out a piece of blues history for themselves, be sure to add the following names to your list.

James Cotton

James Cotton (born 1935) started his career blowing harmonica in Howlin' Wolf's band during performances broadcast over radio station KWEM in West Memphis, Arkansas. When Memphis producer-engineer Sam Phillips tracked down Wolf in order to make records with him, Cotton (see Figure 5-18) got his chance to cut his first sides as well. One of these was "Cotton Crop Blues," released on Phillips's Sun label, and long considered one of the classics of post-War blues.

Cotton moved to Chicago in 1955 and made his considerable reputation as a member of Muddy Waters band, appearing on several legendary recording sessions and famous live performances, including Waters's appearance at the Newport Jazz Festival in 1960. Cotton left Muddy's band to form his own group in 1966 and continues to perform and record to the present day.

Chicago/The Blues/Today! Volume 2 (Vanguard). Cotton shares this album with Otis Rush and Homesick James. The five tracks of his included here, with Muddy Waters band mates Otis Spann, "Pee Wee" Madison on guitar, and drummer S.P. Leary, are some of his best. All of them feature a harp sound as big as a Mack truck and Cotton's signature sledgehammer attack.

Figure 5-18:
James
Cotton
(photo
courtesy of
Burton
Wilson,
Austin, TX).

Guitar Slim

Even if he never did anything other than record the blues masterpiece "The Things I Used To Do" (a million-selling record in 1954 and the best-selling R&B single of that year), Guitar Slim (1926–1959) would still be a blues legend. With his gospel-styled vocals and brutally loud guitar, he was one wild showman. Performing in his cherry red suits, he strolled through clubs as he played, dragging around a 200-foot-long cord that was plugged into his guitar.

Buddy Guy, Jimi Hendrix, Stevie Ray Vaughan, and a host of others all learned from his onstage antics, either first-hand like Guy or through oft-told tales that helped set the stage for all the blues and rock guitar slingers that followed. A heavy drinker and carouser, Slim's wild ways got the best of him and he died of pneumonia at the age of 32.

Sufferin' Mind (Specialty). This single disc serves up 26 tracks recorded in 1953 to 1955 for Specialty Records — Slim's finest work. It includes his million-seller, "The Things I Used To Do," featuring a young Ray Charles on piano. Hear why he influenced everyone from Buddy Guy to Hendrix.

Wynonie Harris

An R&B shouter of the jump blues school, Wynonie Harris (1915–1969) combined lady-killer good looks, a commanding voice, and suggestive stage moves into one dynamite package. He enjoyed a run of hits from the late 1940s to the early 1950s, including "Good Rockin' Tonight," "Lovin' Machine" and "Bloodshot Eyes." Onstage and off, Wynonie's confidence at times bordered on arrogance, and he often showed little respect for older blues players, including his principal inspiration, Big Joe Turner. Subtlety wasn't his thing, but *nobody* rocked the blues as hard as Wynonie Harris.

His lyrics were as sexually charged as his stage movements. (The pelvic thrusts that prevented Elvis Presley from being filmed below the waist on the *Ed Sullivan Show* were borrowed from Wynonie Harris.) Unable to parlay his success into a lasting career or transition into the rock 'n' roll scene, Harris simply partied and drank the years away, eventually dying of cancer at age 53.

Bloodshot Eyes: The Best Of Wynonie Harris (Rhino). This 18-track best-of collection shows off this dynamic singer to great effect. Most of his big hits are here, including "Good Rockin' Tonight," "Lovin' Machine," and "Grandma Plays The Numbers."

Homesick James

A cousin of Elmore James, Homesick James Williamson (born 1910) brings his own brand of slide guitar stylings to the blues, full of unorthodox tunings and twists of timing. He learned to play guitar at age 10 and ran away from home to take up the life of a blues road musician. He settled in Chicago in the 1930s and made his first records in 1937 for the Bluebird label.

He didn't record again until the early 1950s, when he joined up with Elmore James as a member of his band, the Broomdusters, and released sides under his own name before and after Elmore's death in 1965. At the age of 87, James still continues to tour and record.

Chicago/The Blues/Today! Volume 2 (Vanguard). Homesick has four tracks on this 1966 album, playing his idiosyncratic brand of blues with support from Willie Dixon and former Bo Diddley drummer Frank Kirkland. James plays in a nice, relaxed manner and Dixon and Kirkland follow his every odd twist and move. Nice versions of "Dust My Broom" and "Set A Date" and some of his most cohesive recordings overall.

J.B. Hutto

Another disciple of Elmore James, J.B. Hutto (1926–1983) had a raw and slashing slide guitar style and irrepressible personality that made him a popular club performer for nearly 30 years. He cut his first records with his original band, the Hawks, in 1954. Those recordings are now regarded as Chicago blues classics and are highly prized collector's items.

After almost a decade away from the blues scene, Hutto returned to playing and recording in the mid-1960s with various versions of the Hawks, his huge voice and raucous style untouched by the passage of time. In 1977, Hutto moved to the Boston area and spent his final eight years touring around the world and recording for various labels, still capable of putting across music with a fierce, raw edge.

Chicago/The Blues/Today! Volume 1 (Vanguard). Hutto shares this album with Otis Spann, Junior Wells, and Buddy Guy. J.B.'s five tracks are some of his very best, featuring economical but driving rhythm playing from bassist Herman Hassell and drummer Frank Kirkland. Half the fun here is trying to figure out Hutto's mostly incomprehensible vocals. This is the place to start digging this raucous slide genius.

J.B. Lenoir

J.B. Lenoir (1929–1967) was equal parts deep blues artist and wild show-man. Lenoir (pronounced *Lenore*) could play both driving guitar boogies and slow, low-down stuff, and he wrote lyrics as powerful as any in the blues. J.B. (his given name, incidentally) was also one of the last contemporary blues artists from the 1950s and 1960s to address topical subjects in his compositions. Lenoir sang in a voice so high that many who listened to his recordings without knowing what he looked like frequently guessed wrong on his gender.

In a live setting, J.B. (see Figure 5-19) was the ultimate showman. He would wedge his vocal mike into a neck rack designed for a harmonica. Then, by dragging a long electrical cord behind him, it left his hands free to work a room "wireless." Luther Allison recalled seeing Lenoir "duck walking" long

Figure 5-19:
J.B. Lenoir
(CD booklet
photo
courtesy of
Jewel
Paula Ronn
Records, A
Division of
Sue
Records,
Inc.).

before Chuck Berry made the move famous. Ever outrageous, J.B. often performed onstage in a zebra skin dress coat with tails. His best known hit was the oft-revived "Mama, Talk To Your Daughter." He continued recording and experimenting with his music up until his death in 1967 at the age of 37.

The Parrot Sessions (Relic). J.B. Lenoir was at a creative peak when he waxed these sessions for Parrot Records in 1954 and 1955. Highlights include the topical "Eisenhower Blues," "Give Me One More Shot" (later recorded by *Blues For Dummies* author Lonnie Brooks) and "Mama, Talk To Your Daughter" (later recorded by *Blues For Dummies* author Cub Koda).

Snooky Pryor

Although he has never achieved the notoriety of fellow harmonica wizards Little Walter, Big Walter Horton, or Junior Wells, Snooky Pryor (born 1921) is synonymous with Chicago blues harmonica. Pryor (see Figure 5-20) was there at the beginning of the post-War era, recording some of the earliest classics in the new amplified style and helping to shape the sound of the electric blues harp.

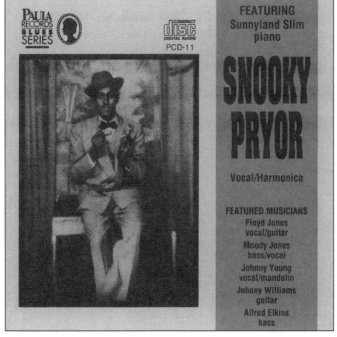

FEATURING
Sunnyland Slim
piano

SNOOKY PRYOR

Vocal/Harmonica

FEATURED MUSICIANS
Floyd Jones
vocal/guitar
Moody Jones
bass/vocal
Johnny Young
vocal/mandolin
Johnny Williams
guitar
Alfred Elkins
bass

Figure 5-20:
Snooky
Pryor
(photo
courtesy of
Jewel
Paula Ronn
Records, A
Division of
Sue
Records,
Inc.).

Pryor also claims to be the first harmonica player to play through a crude p.a. system or order to get a more massive sound — a technique quickly adopted by every harp player in the city, including Little Walter. Snooky gave up the blues life for 20 years, returning to it full time in 1987, and continues to record and perform to this day.

Snooky Pryor (Paula). This solid 20-track cross section of Pryor's earliest, and best, recordings includes "Keep What You Got," "Stockyard Blues," "Boogie Twist," and a spate of equally fine unreleased material.

Jimmy Rogers

Jimmy Rogers (1924–1997) was one of the original members of the Muddy Waters band, the group that plugged in the Chicago blues and changed the sound of the music forever. As a second guitarist to Waters's slide playing, Rogers worked out many of the complementary patterns and fills that are now standard in Chicago blues. Working and recording with Muddy for the first half of the 1950s, Jimmy (see Figure 5-21) played on several of Muddy's most famous sides, including "Hoochie Coochie Man," "I Just Want To Make Love To You," and "Honey Bee."

Figure 5-21:
Jimmy
Rogers
(photo
courtesy of
MCA-Chess).

As a solo artist in his own right, Rogers wrote and recorded the blues classics "That's All Right," "Sloppy Drunk," and "Walkin' By Myself," the latter tune becoming his only R&B chart hit in 1957. After a decade-long sabbatical from the music business, Jimmy eased back into it in 1973 and kept recording and touring until his death from colon cancer in December 1997.

The Complete Chess Recordings (MCA-Chess). This two-CD, 51-track collection contains everything Rogers recorded as a solo artist for Chess Records between 1950 and 1959. Besides the classics, you'll find a pile of rarities and alternate versions. This disc also serves as a mini-history of the best of Chicago blues with Muddy Waters, Little Walter, Willie Dixon, Otis Spann, Big Walter Horton, and Fred Below in strong supporting roles throughout.

On The Side: Sidemen (And Women) of Note

All the artists listed in this section recorded vocals under their own names, but their main contribution to the blues was through their prowess as instrumental accompanists. Time and again, they added a spark to many recording sessions and much of blues musical development is owed to their honest and soulful playing.

Fred Below

Fred Below (1926–1988) was Chicago's finest drummer when the music was in its heyday. The mainstay of Little Walter's band, the Jukes, Below's jazzy approach launched the small-combo blues format into a whole new direction. His versatility also made him one of the mainstays of the Chess Records house band. Below's impeccable drumming shows up on classic recordings by Little Walter, Muddy Waters, Chuck Berry, Howlin' Wolf, Sonny Boy Williamson, Elmore James, Otis Rush, and literally dozens of others.

Little Walter — *Blues With A Feeling* (MCA-Chess). To hear Fred Below driving the beat behind a small Chicago blues band, this double-disc set of rare and unissued Little Walter recordings is the perfect place to start. His fast-paced jazz excursions on material such as "My Kind Of Baby" and "Last Boogie" sit alongside rock-solid, mid-tempo romps like "That's It" and slow burners like "Blue Midnight" that feature his working with wire brushes in place of the customary sticks. Nobody could push a band like Fred Below and this CD also makes a worthwhile addition to anyone's Little Walter collection.

Lazy Lester

Lazy Lester (born 1933) was the king of swamp blues harmonica in Louisiana in the 1950s and early 1960s. Working with producer J.D. Miller, Lester (his real name was Leslie Johnson) played on numerous blues and swamp-pop sessions, doing everything from blowing harmonica solos to contributing percussion effects by beating on a cardboard box with a rolled-up newspaper. His best known work is behind guitarist Lightnin' Slim, answering Slim's signature call to "blow your harmonica, son" with countrified harp blasts that worked hand-in-glove with Lightnin's bare-bones style.

Lester also made several fine solo records under his own name, including the blues classics "I'm A Lover, Not A Fighter," "Sugar Coated Love," and "I Hear You Knockin'" (the latter two were later recorded by the Fabulous Thunderbirds). Away from the blues scene for almost two decades, Lester later resumed playing, made a pair of successful comeback albums in the late 1980s, and continues to perform today.

I Hear You Knockin'!!! (Excello-AVI). A rock-solid, 30-track collection of Lester's singles for the Excello label — with J.D. Miller's eerie swamp blues production touches in place and a mass of great songs and performances throughout, this is just about as good as Louisiana blues gets.

Robert Jr. Lockwood

Robert Jr. Lockwood's (born 1915) amazing career in the blues spans some six decades and is still going strong. His link to the Delta blues couldn't possibly be any stronger — he was taught guitar by his stepfather, Robert Johnson. Lockwood took Johnson's style and added amplification, jazzy fills, and an exploratory musical vocabulary.

Some of Lockwood's best guitar work graces the recordings of Little Walter, Sonny Boy Williamson II, and others. Since the 1940s, he's maintained a solo recording and touring career. Now in his 80s, he continues to follow his artistic muse and push the blues into new musical territory.

Steady Rollin' Man (Delmark). This relaxed 1970 session captures Lockwood playing, singing, and backed by Little Walter's former band mates, the Aces. With Fred Below laying down one comfortable groove after another, Lockwood trades solos with guitarist Louis Myers and performs a set that has touches of both Robert Johnson and Lockwood's jazzier leanings.

Pinetop Perkins

A Chicago blues band pianist with strong Delta roots, Pinetop Perkins (born 1913) is one of the last of the great old-time boogie-woogie piano players. Over the years, he's lent his considerable piano-pounding skills to the music of Robert Nighthawk, Sonny Boy Williamson II, Muddy Waters, and others.

Pinetop originally played guitar, but by age 20 switched to piano and was soon playing in Robert Nighthawk's band. His initial influence was boogie-woogie pianist Pinetop Smith, from whom he took his nickname. After splitting from Nighthawk in 1945, Perkins worked with Sonny Boy Williamson II, appearing on Sonny Boy's *King Biscuit Time* radio show. In 1951, Perkins moved to Chicago, and worked throughout the 1950s with Nighthawk, Earl Hooker, Albert King, and Little Milton.

In 1969, Muddy Waters invited Pinetop to replace Otis Spann in his band, and Perkins stayed for the next 11 years, recording and touring with the group. In 1980, the core of the Muddy Waters band, including Pinetop, left Muddy and became the Legendary Blues Band, recording two albums for the Rounder label. Perkins started recording as a solo artist in 1988 and continues to issue new albums, although he considers himself semi-retired.

Live Top (Deluge). A great live recording of Pinetop backed up by a hot little combo — Perkins pounds out the blues and boogie-woogie like a man half his age.

Otis Spann

Otis Spann (1930–1970) was the gentle piano-playing giant of post-War Chicago blues. As a charter member of the original Muddy Waters band, his solid boogie-woogie left-hand work, coupled with his rippling fills, made him the perfect ensemble player. Capable of holding a rhythm section together one minute and firing off a splendid solo the next, any blues recording he participated in benefited from his presence. He was a role model for what unselfish, supportive playing is all about. As a vocalist, his husky voice was imbued with a true blues flavor.

Otis (see Figure 5-22) joined the Muddy Waters band in 1953, playing on several classic recordings, including "Hoochie Coochie Man" and "Got My Mojo Working." Spann also appeared on Waters's landmark album, *Live At Newport—1960*. Although Spann had made a few solo records since 1954, he finally went out on his own in the late 1960s. But little time was left for the soft-spoken pianist. He died of cancer in 1970 at the age of 40.

Chicago/The Blues/Today! Volume 1 (Vanguard). Spann appears on this 1966 album with J.B. Hutto and the Hawks, Junior Wells, and Buddy Guy. Spann's five tracks are pretty potent stuff. He's backed by nothing more than the solid beat of drummer S.P. Leary, keeping the focus directly on his vocals and his amazing piano work. This is Chicago blues piano at its finest.

Figure 5-22:
Otis Spann (photo courtesy of Burton Wilson, Austin, TX).

Sunnyland Slim

With his booming voice and thundering keyboard figures, Sunnyland Slim (1907–1995) was one of the last great Delta blues piano players. Between his solo outings and his work as a sideman, Sunnyland played on more than 200 recordings in his long career, and some put the figure at more than 250.

Born Albert Luandrew in Mississippi, Sunnyland moved to Chicago in 1939 and quickly became an in-demand piano player, recording on his own as early as 1947. It was Sunnyland who steered Muddy Waters to Chess Records, using the young blues singer as a backup guitarist on one of his early sessions.

In the 1950s and 1960s, Slim recorded for more than 15 labels under his own name and various pseudonyms. He became a regular on the European blues circuit in the 1960s and recorded with Johnny Shines, Big Walter Horton, J.B. Hutto, and others. The following decades found him doing what he always did best, pounding the piano like nobody else and adding more recordings to his already lengthy resume. Musically active until the very end of his life, Sunnyland Slim died of kidney failure in 1995 at the age of 87.

Chicago Piano (Paula). Here, you'll find Sunnyland Slim on a half-dozen of his best 1950s recordings along with two fine examples of his excellent backing work for other artists. Slim's high falsetto whoops on "It's You, Baby" (along with some great harp work from Big Walter Horton) are alone worth the price. This 20-track collection also includes stellar tracks from other Chicago piano giants including Little Brother Montgomery, Eddie Boyd, Lafayette Leake, Memphis Slim, and Otis Spann.

Eddie Taylor

Every guitarist who uses the standard bass-string boogie figure that goes "bompa-bompa-bompa-bompa" may not realize it, but that's nothing but pure Eddie Taylor (1923–1985). The boogie rhythm and bottom string turnarounds came from Taylor's Delta roots, but he developed it into high art and the musical glue that held together all of Jimmy Reed's best-known recordings. What's known as the "Jimmy Reed beat" is actually the "Eddie Taylor rhythm." It was Eddie who acted as musical director on those sessions, keeping Reed focused and on the beat.

Taylor grew up in Mississippi and watched Charlie Patton and Robert Johnson play in juke joints when he was a small boy. Eddie came to Chicago in 1949 and hooked up with childhood friend Jimmy Reed in 1953. Two years later, he started making records under his own name, including the classics "Bad Boy," "Ride 'Em On Down," and "Big Town Playboy." He went on to record with John Lee Hooker, Elmore James, John Brim, and Snooky Pryor.

By the late 1950s, Taylor was in demand as a session player and remained so for the rest of his career. Taylor started recording on his own again in 1972 and kept touring and recording up until his death in 1985. He was elected to the Blues Foundation's Hall of Fame in 1987.

Bad Boy (Charly). This disc represents all of Eddie's output for Vee-Jay Records from 1955 to 1964 — 15 tracks in all. All the hits are here — "Bad Boy," "Ride 'Em On Down," and "Big Town Playboy" — along with other equally fine material such as "Lookin' For Trouble" and "Find Me A Baby." With wry, inventive writing, rock-solid rhythm playing, wild clusters of solo notes, and low-down vocals, this is patented Chicago blues.

Katie Webster

A two-fisted piano-pounder of the first order, Katie Webster (born 1939) is the swamp-boogie queen of Louisiana. An in-demand session player, her keyboard work graced many of the best bayou blues and swamp-pop recordings of the 1950s and 1960s. Katie (see Figure 5-23) also recorded some terrific sides under her own name between 1959 and 1961 for a variety of small labels and even introduced her own dance craze, "The Katie Lee."

Figure 5-23: Katie Webster (CD booklet photo courtesy of Jewel Paula Ronn Records, A Division of Sue Records, Inc.).

Webster also played on numerous recordings behind Lazy Lester, Clarence Garlow, and Lonnie Brooks in his early Guitar Junior days, and supplied the rolling piano behind Phil Phillips's million-seller, "Sea Of Love." From 1964 to 1967, she was the opening act for Otis Redding's stage revue. She left show business in the 1970s to care for her ailing parents, and returned to playing and touring in the early 1980s. She released three successful albums on Alligator and worked for another decade until she was sidelined by a stroke in 1993.

Katie Webster (Paula). For great Louisiana blues and R&B, check out this 20-track collection of Webster's solo recordings from the late 1950s through the early 1960s, done with swamp-blues producer J.D. Miller. Her own dance tune, "The Katie Lee" is here, along with the bluesy "No Bread, No Meat" and her own captivating take on "Sea Of Love."

Chapter 6

Artists on the Contemporary Blues Scene (1970 to Present)

In This Chapter

▶ Discovering who's at the forefront of today's blues scene

▶ Taking a peek at their career highlights

▶ Finding out about their finest recordings

*B*ig changes happened in the blues after 1970, marking a significant turning point in the music's history. Perhaps the biggest change during this period was the "discovery" of blues by a mainstream audience raised on rock 'n' roll. By the late 1970s, it wasn't uncommon to find integrated blues bands with large followings that cut across all demographic groups.

In the past couple of decades, we also lost a number blues legends who helped define the music — Luther Allison, Albert Collins, Slim Harpo, Earl Hooker, Howlin' Wolf, Lightnin' Slim, Jimmy Reed, Otis Spann, Hound Dog Taylor, Muddy Waters, and Junior Wells — every last one irreplaceable. But a new crop of talent has sprung up in recent decades — talented younger musicians schooled not only in blues but also hard rock, country, and even jazz. Influenced by the late greats, they work within the rich blues tradition, while putting their own spin on the music.

Today, blues is a big business with its own radio charts, music clubs, movies, festival circuits, and million-selling records. In this chapter, we tell you about many of the artists who've been instrumental in making blues music more popular than ever before.

Luther Allison

Few artists in the modern era brought as much fire and panache to their blues playing as did Luther Allison (1939–1997). His high-energy guitar work combined the best of Chicago West Side guitar legends Magic Sam, Freddie King, and Buddy Guy, while his soulful vocals and dynamic stage presence proclaimed him as a member of the "new breed" who filtered rock and funk styles into their music.

Luther Allison (see Figure 6-1) had one of the more mercurial careers in the blues. After his rise to fame in blues circles in the late 1960s, he went into a slump for nearly two decades, which finally prompted his move to France in 1984. It was there Allison found a mature style that showcased his enormous onstage energy and considerable songwriting skills. In fact, some of the very best records Allison ever made were done in the final years of his life.

From Widener, Arkansas, to the Windy City

Allison was born in Widener, Arkansas, on August 17, 1939, the fourteenth of fifteen children born to cotton-farming parents. Keeping his ears wide open to all sorts of music, he soaked up B.B. King's music on radio station WDIA, *King Biscuit Time* on KFFA, and the *Grand Ole Opry* on Saturday nights.

After his family moved to Chicago in 1952, Luther sang with a local gospel group, the Southern Travelers. The blues bug bit him around 1954 when his older brother Ollie Lee taught him the rudiments of blues guitar. Allison received more instruction from neighbor Willie James Lyons and also played bass with Jimmy Dawkins. Allison later honed his craft sitting in with Muddy Waters and others, and in 1963 took over the guitarist's spot in Freddie King's band.

In 1967, Luther recorded tracks with bassist Big Mojo Elem (produced in part by Magic Sam's uncle, Shakey Jake Harris). This session found its way onto a compilation released by Delmark Records called *Sweet Home Chicago.* Allison's first solo album for Delmark, *Love Me Mama,* was released in 1969 and was followed up with explosive performances at the Ann Arbor Blues Festival and other shows. Luther Allison seemed poised to become a star.

Allison was beginning to cross over musically, making a big hit with rock audiences who loved his unabashed energy and ability to flavor his music with rock pyrotechnics. In 1972, he had big break when he became one of the few blues artists to be signed by Motown Records.

Figure 6-1:
Luther
Allison
(photo by
David
Lucinger;
courtesy of
Alligator
Records).

From Motown to Paris

Luther remained with Motown's Gordy label for four years, where he released three albums. Despite almost constant touring (including numerous dates in Europe and Japan) and the efforts of the Motown promotional machine, his albums failed to achieve commercial success.

By the late 1970s, Allison was spending more and more time touring in Europe. He released album after album on a variety of labels including Black and Blue, Encore, and Rumble. By the mid-1980s, Luther had built up such a solid following overseas that he moved to France where he took up permanent residence.

The move seemed to suit him well. By the 1987 release of the album *Serious* on Blind Pig, it was obvious that Allison had found a way to tap musical sources as diverse as funk, rock, and reggae while still sounding like nobody else except Luther Allison.

In the 1990s, Luther hit his stride with a trio of albums released on Alligator Records. He came home to his American blues audiences with a vengeance. On the strength of those recordings and his live shows, he won the Living Blues Artist of the Year award and the W.C. Handy award for Entertainer of the Year in both 1996 and 1997, nine other Living Blues awards, and six other Handys.

On July 10, 1997, Allison was diagnosed with lung cancer and inoperable brain tumors. He was undergoing treatment in Madison, Wisconsin, when he died on August 12, 1997.

Reckless (Alligator). This record, Allison's final album, shows him at the peak of his powers.

"Luther Allison was a guy who *always* took care of business. But it seemed to me that when he moved to Europe, he became very serious about his music and about life in general. He wasn't around too many people who spoke English, so he had nowhere to go *except* to his music to get his feelings out. He seemed to find that person he had been looking for inside of himself when he moved there. And when he came back here to America, that's what the people saw and heard."

Lonnie Brooks

The long and varied career of Lonnie Brooks (born 1933) has spanned four decades of playing not just the blues, but also zydeco, rock, and soul music. With a style that combines his Louisiana swamp music heritage with Texas swing, Memphis soul, and Chicago blues, Lonnie has carved out a piece of blues music territory that's uniquely his own.

Lonnie was born Lee Baker, Jr. on December 18, 1933, in Dubuisson, Louisiana. Although the music of Lightnin' Hopkins, B.B. King, and John Lee Hooker stirred an early interest in the blues, he didn't start playing guitar until in his early twenties after he had moved to Port Arthur, Texas.

His entry into show business occurred when zydeco legend Clifton Chenier heard young Lee Baker playing on the porch of his house and offered him a job in Chenier's Red Hot Louisiana Band. At that time, he also worked with guitarist Lonesome Sundown, who later recorded for Excello.

Back when he was "Guitar Junior"

In 1957, Lonnie cut his first records for the Goldband label in Lake Charles, Louisiana. He scored a regional hit on his first try with the swamp-rock ballad "Family Rules." That record and other early singles were issued under the name of "Guitar Junior." Another big regional hit for Guitar Junior was "The Crawl," later recorded by both Johnny Winter and the Fabulous Thunderbirds.

The Guitar Junior singles were kicking up enough noise to get Lee Baker plenty of work on various R&B package shows and tours. By the late 1950s, he was working as a member of Sam Cooke's touring show. When the tour reached Chicago, Guitar Junior decided to put down new roots. He faced two immediate challenges in the Windy City — the town already had an established guitarist named Guitar Junior and the swamp-rock hits he scored in Louisiana didn't seem to go over with Chicago audiences accustomed to a rougher style of blues. Nevertheless, within a year, he was working as a sideman to Jimmy Reed and had acquired a new name — Lonnie Brooks.

But the Guitar Junior name wasn't put to rest quite yet. Lonnie recorded a pair of singles for Mercury and Midas Records under his old alias, while releasing new 45s as Lonnie Brooks for local Chicago labels including USA, Chirrup, and Palos. He ended up on Chess Records in 1967 and scored a small hit with "Let It All Hang Out" and dusted off the Guitar Junior handle once last time for a 1969 album for Capitol, *Broke and Hungry*.

The Voodoo Daddy

Lonnie spent most of the 1970s working around Chicago and honing his songwriting craft. In 1975, he played Europe for the first time as a member of the Chicago Blues Festival, and recorded an album for the Black and Blue label while on the tour with Willie Mabon, Little Mack Simmons, and others.

By 1978, Brooks had stockpiled an impressive collection of original tunes and was ready to record. Four of his tunes turned up on an Alligator Records *Living Chicago Blues* anthology and that paved the way for Lonnie's first full-length album for the label, *Bayou Lightning*. During the 1980s and 1990s Lonnie toured extensively and released six new albums on Alligator, culminating with the 1997 release of the *Lonnie Brooks Deluxe Edition* collection.

Lonnie's performing credits remain as diverse as ever, ranging from the Montreux Jazz Festival, to a guest shot on TV's *Hee-Haw,* to headlining the 1996 Chicago Blues Festival, to appearing in the *Blues Brothers 2000* movie. With his son Ronnie Baker Brooks, a regular guitarist in his touring band, and son Wayne joining in for a three-guitar attack, The Lonnie Brooks Band tours as a tightly knit family group and one of the most successful and popular acts now working in the blues.

The Deluxe Edition (Alligator). Start here for a sample of Lonnie's work — a great overview of Lonnie's best sides for the Alligator label.

R.L. Burnside

R.L. Burnside (born 1926) is the preeminent modern-day practitioner of Mississippi juke joint blues. His droning, modal playing style hearkens back to the music of the earliest country blues singers, while his guitar sound is as amped up and nasty as any heard in the juke joints where he's honed his craft for the past 30 years.

Burnside was born November 23, 1926, in Oxford, Mississippi. As a youngster he moved to Mississippi's hill country, settling in the town of Holly Springs, where he has lived ever since. R.L.'s main mentor and early influence was neighbor and blues legend Fred McDowell. R.L.'s country style of playing was also influenced by Lightnin' Hopkins, John Lee Hooker, and Muddy Waters.

Early exposure through field recordings

R.L. spent most of his adult life working as a fisherman or farmer, playing his music on weekends at neighboring roadhouses, house parties, and juke joints. Burnside had done some "field" (non-studio) recordings in the 1960s and a few of his songs turned up on an Arhoolie label compilation album. He toured Europe for the first time in 1971, eventually recording albums for the European-based Swingmaster, Arion, and Vogue labels. He toured only sporadically until the late 1980s, when his raw sound suddenly seem to catch on with a new audience.

Burnside's career got a boost in 1992 when he appeared in the documentary *Deep Blues* with his neighbor and friend, guitarist Junior Kimbrough. The soundtrack from the movie featured two solo tunes by Burnside. The following year he released *Bad Luck City,* backed by a small electric combo featuring his son Dwayne on bass and son-in-law Calvin Jackson on drums.

Make way for the entire Burnside clan

Burnside's current band, dubbed the Sound Machine, features various members of the Burnside clan — R.L. has eight sons and they all play guitar or bass with the band! The group has been a family affair for several years now, helping to keep the blues alive for successive generations.

Recently, Burnside has recorded new albums for the Mississippi-based Fat Possum label, including *Too Bad Jim* and *The Wizard,* and is touring more extensively than ever before. In a world full of demographic studies and target-group marketing, it's comforting to know that true, old-time Mississippi blues is alive and well in the hands, heart, and soul of R.L. Burnside.

Too Bad Jim (Fat Possum). Modern-day Mississippi juke joint blues comes to life in this inspired recording session.

Eric Clapton

Few guitarists in any field of music have earned as much acclaim as Eric Clapton (born 1945). He's long been regarded as rock's best-known and finest guitarist — with only the late Jimi Hendrix getting an equal nod in his time — yet all the while his music has remained strongly rooted in the blues.

During the 1960s when he was barely out of his teens, Clapton was already the most famous and respected blues guitarist in Great Britain. He was also Britain's first bona fide guitar hero. After consecutive tenures with the Yardbirds, John Mayall's Bluesbreakers, and rock's first "supergroup," Cream, Eric almost single-handedly built the foundation of blues-rock music.

The birth of "Slowhand"

Eric Patrick Clapp was born in Ripley, Surrey, England, on March 30, 1945. He didn't start playing guitar until he was 17. A year later, he formed his first band, the Roosters. After a brief stint with Casey Jones and the Engineers, Clapton joined the Yardbirds, who had replaced the Rolling Stones as Britain's number-one R&B club band.

By this time Eric had totally immersed himself in the blues, isolating himself for long periods of time to study the guitar techniques of Muddy Waters, Robert Johnson, and the Kings B.B., Freddie, and Albert. He remained with the Yardbirds until 1965, playing on their first hit "For Your Love."

When the Yardbirds's music became more pop oriented, Clapton left to join Britain's esteemed blues band, the John Mayall's Bluesbreakers. Armed with a Les Paul guitar and a blisteringly loud Marshall combo amp, Clapton stole the show on the Bluebreakers album released in 1966.

The graffiti said so: Clapton Is God

The album *Bluesbreakers — John Mayall with Eric Clapton* shook up both the blues and rock scenes when it was released. Eric's versions of "Hide Away," "All Your Love," and other classics announced the presence of a guitarist who could artfully combine a powerhouse hard-rock sound with the plaintive beauty of the blues.

Clapton quickly became Britain's number-one guitarist. Graffiti sprayed across London's subways walls proclaimed that "Clapton Is God." But, Eric became restless within the confines of Mayall's group and within a year formed a trio called Cream with bassist Jack Bruce and drummer Ginger Baker. Cream scored as the first major psychedelic blues band. Their early song list included souped-up renditions of the blues standards "Rollin' and Tumblin'," "Born Under A Bad Sign," "Spoonful," "Cat Squirrel," and Robert Johnson's "Crossroads," a tune that would eventually serve as a signature piece for the young Clapton.

The supergroup years

Cream broke up in 1968 and Eric formed the ill-fated supergroup Blind Faith with keyboard player and singer Stevie Winwood, Ginger Baker, and bassist Rick Grech, which lasted for only one album and a brief tour. Clapton then ducked out of the spotlight by playing behind Delaney and Bonnie Bramlett, an R&B-based group that had opened shows for Blind Faith.

After recording his debut solo album in 1970, Eric enlisted the core rhythm section of the Bramlett band to form Derek and the Dominos. That year, Clapton released the rock masterpiece, *Layla And Other Assorted Love Songs*, which featured the title track and his renditions of the blues classics "Have You Ever Loved A Woman" and "Key To The Highway."

Clapton disbanded the group after that landmark album, returning to England to deal with his well-publicized drug and alcohol problems. Having recovered, he returned to performing and recording in 1973. The records Eric produced for the next 15 years included largely rock and pop tunes with only a stray blues track here and there.

Back to the blues

In the late 1980s, Clapton's interest in the blues was rekindled by the mainstream success enjoyed by Stevie Ray Vaughan and Robert Cray. Clapton's annual music shows at London's Royal Albert Hall featured both of those artists plus Buddy Guy, Stevie Ray's brother Jimmie Vaughan, and others.

In 1992, Clapton released an album of songs culled from his concert for MTV's *Unplugged* series. It became his biggest-selling album ever and dominated the 1993 Grammys by winning six awards. That year, Clapton was inducted into the Rock and Roll Hall of Fame as a member of the group Cream. In 1994, Clapton released his first all-blues album, *From The Cradle*. It reached the top of *Billboard* magazine's new blues chart and showed the guitarist to be as a great blues artist as he'd ever been.

Bluesbreakers — John Mayall with Eric Clapton (Mobile Fidelity). Clapton really came into his own as a blues artist on this seminal blues-rock album loaded with great guitar playing.

William Clarke

William Clarke (1951–1996) was the brightest new stylist in the modern blues harmonica era. He built his lyrical ideas on the foundation laid by harmonica masters Little Walter and Big Walter Horton. With compositions full of ceaseless invention, Clarke blasted harp playing into new territory while never losing sight of its traditional blues roots.

Clarke (see Figure 6-2) was born in Inglewood, California, on March 29, 1951. His interest in blues music was first ignited by hearing cover versions of Chicago blues classics done by the Rolling Stones. He started out playing guitar and drums, but by 1967 had devoted himself entirely to playing harmonica.

Forging a new style

During the 1960s, Clarke immersed himself in the music of Sonny Boy Williamson II, James Cotton, Big Walter Horton, and Little Walter and soaked up the jazz organ combo stylings of Jimmy McGriff, Richard "Groove" Holmes, and Jack McDuff. By combining the hard, aggressive Chicago blues harp style with organ-trio swing, William formed the basis of a unique harmonica style.

Figure 6-2:
William
Clarke
(photo
courtesy of
Alligator
Records).

Undoubtedly the biggest influence on Clarke's playing was his apprentice-ship with harmonica ace George "Harmonica" Smith. Smith's mastery of the chromatic harp was unmatched and William felt reverential respect for the elder harp wizard. The two formed a strong friendship (cemented with plenty of harmonica lessons) that lasted until Smith's death in 1983.

The hardest-working harp player in the blues

Although he worked for 20 years as a machinist to support his family, Clarke was no mere weekend musician. He regularly traveled from one club to another, playing until closing time. Then, on those same nights, he'd sit in with bands at after-hours clubs playing until morning. Even with all this performing, he still held down his regular day job!

Clarke cut his first records on small California-based labels beginning in 1978. His debut was *Hittin' Heavy,* followed by *Blues From Los Angeles* in 1980, *Can't You Hear Me Calling* in 1983, and *Rockin' The Boat* in 1988.

Clarke garnered his first Handy award nomination with 1987's *Tip Of The Top,* a tribute to his mentor and friend George "Harmonica" Smith. After signing with Alligator Records in 1990, the label issued Clarke's first CD, *Blowin' Like Hell.* The tune "Must Be Jelly" from that album won the 1991 Handy award for best blues song of the year.

Clarke continued his winning streak with 1992's *Serious Intentions* and 1994's *Groove Time,* racking up six Handy nominations. His fourth album for Alligator, 1996's *The Hard Way,* found him exploring jazzier grooves and new themes while expanding the vocabulary of the blues harmonica. But sadly, Clarke wouldn't have much time left to enjoy his artistic success. After recovering from congestive heart failure, he resumed playing for a brief while before dying from a bleeding ulcer on November 3, 1996.

The Hard Way (Alligator). This CD, his final album, found Clarke exploring yet more new musical territory.

Albert Collins

Dubbed "The Master of the Telecaster," The Razor Blade," and "The Iceman," no blues guitarist could evoke a chillier and crisper tone from his instrument than Albert Collins (1932–1993). With his sparse, lean solos he made every note count. His influence extended to a number of modern players including Jimi Hendrix, Robert Cray, and Debbie Davies.

Collins (see Figure 6-3) was a leading exponent of traditional Texas blues guitar. Even though he'd been recording and touring since the late 1950s, it wasn't until the 1980s Texas blues revival, which made Robert Cray and Stevie Ray Vaughan into stars, that Albert achieved his greatest success.

Collins was born in Leona, Texas, on October 1, 1932, and moved to Houston when he was 7. A gifted musician from childhood, Albert's heavy influences included his cousin Lightnin' Hopkins, Clarence "Gatemouth" Brown, and T-Bone Walker. By the time he was 18, Collins was working the same clubs where he used to watch those guitar legends (as well as John Lee Hooker and Johnny "Guitar" Watson) perform.

"The Freeze" and other chilly titles

Collins formed a ten-piece band, the Rhythm Rockers, and cut his first record in 1958. That single, "The Freeze," became a regional hit, and lead to the instrumental follow-ups "Sno-Cone," "Defrost," "Don't Lose Your Cool," and "Icy Blue."

Figure 6-3:
Albert
Collins
(photo by
Paul Natkin/
Photo
Reserve;
courtesy of
Alligator
Records).

In 1962, Albert had his biggest hit with the instrumental "Frosty" (which is on the *Blues For Dummies* CD), a million-selling single for the small Hall-Way label out of Beaumont, Texas. Even after his recording success, Collins continued to work various day jobs while going out for short regional tours and recording for small regional labels.

Collins's unique style and sound was achieved through unorthodox minor key tunings and by clamping a capo high on the guitar neck. (A *capo* is a device attached to the neck of a guitar that allows a guitarist to uniformly change the pitch of a chord without changing any fingering positions.) Collins also used his bare fingers for a percussive picking attack that really cranked things up.

Hooking up with Canned Heat

In 1968, Collins befriended Bob Hite from the blues-rock group Canned Heat. Impressed with Albert's style, Hite brought him over to Imperial Records, which released three albums with the guitarist. Collins moved to Los Angeles, left Imperial for the short-lived Tumbleweed label in 1972, and recorded several sessions produced by rock guitarist Joe Walsh.

Albert didn't record again until 1977 when he was signed to Alligator Records. The move was a good one, with Collins's *Ice Pickin'* album setting the stage for five more acclaimed albums for the label, including *Frostbite, Frozen Alive, Don't Lose Your Cool, Live In Japan,* and *Cold Snap,* the last being nominated for a Grammy award.

In 1985, Collins also participated on the Alligator album *Showdown!* — a combination summit meeting/jam session including Collins, Johnny Copeland, and Robert Cray that won Grammy awards for all three participants.

Suddenly, a media star

After years of scuffling and driving his own bus to make the next show, in the mid-1980s Albert Collins rode the crest of renewed interest in the blues for all it was worth. He played Carnegie Hall, appeared on *Late Night with David Letterman,* made a cameo appearance in the teen movie *Adventures In Babysitting* and even made a wine cooler commercial with Bruce Willis — suddenly, Albert Collins was everywhere.

In 1989, Collins moved from Alligator to ink a deal with the Pointblank label (a subsidiary of the major label Virgin Records). Albert's first album for the label was 1991's *Iceman.* In the wake of that release, he toured relentlessly to appreciative audiences around the world.

LONNIE SAYS

No mean guitar feat

"The first time I ever saw Albert Collins play was around 1953 or 1954 down in Beaumont, Texas, in a guitar battle with Clarence 'Gatemouth' Brown's nephew Curly Mays. I don't think either one of them had a record out at that time.

"Curly could do a lot of tricks with the guitar and back in Texas, that was the thing. You had to do more than just play. That night, Albert finished his show by playing his guitar with one hand and dribbling a basketball between his legs with the other. The house went crazy for that! Curly waited until Albert was through, then he brought a chair out onstage. He took off his shoes and socks, put some picks between his toes, and started playing the guitar with his feet! Oh man, I'll never forget that. That may have been the best guitar move of them all."

But in the midst of this long-awaited success, Albert was diagnosed with liver cancer and time was running out for this much-loved blues artist. He finished up another album for Pointblank — 1993's *Collins Mix* — and kept up a heavy touring schedule until he died of cancer on November 24, 1993, a month after the record's release. Albert Collins was 61 years old.

Ice Pickin' (Alligator). This was Collins's first album for Alligator and makes a perfect introduction to his explosive style.

Johnny Copeland

Texas guitarist and singer Johnny Copeland (1937–1997), who enjoyed a career that spanned five decades, was a product of the same fertile Houston blues scene that gave rise to the careers of Albert Collins and Johnny "Guitar" Watson. Although Copeland began recording in the late 1950s, his career really didn't take off until the 1980s, when he signed on for a series of albums for the Rounder label.

Copeland was born on March 27, 1937, in Haynesville, Louisiana, a town near the Arkansas border, the son of sharecropping parents. When Johnny's father died, he left behind an old guitar that the youngster taught himself to play.

After Johnny and his mother moved to Houston, Copeland began taking his more music seriously and started working the local club circuit. His first professional job was playing behind his friend Joe "Guitar" Hughes. When Hughes got sick one night, Johnny stepped up to the microphone and discovered he could front a band as well as anyone on the local scene.

Backing up the legends

Copeland cut his first records in 1958, starting with the regional hit "Rock 'n' Roll Lilly." In the 1960s, he recorded some 30 singles with marginal success for a variety of small labels. Copeland's group, the Dukes of Rhythm, toured throughout the Southwest, working with, and sometimes providing backup for, Big Mama Thornton, Freddie King, and Sonny Boy Williamson II.

But the Houston blues scene went fallow by the early 1970s. Rather than make the usual Texas blues artist move and head to the West Coast, Johnny decided to move to New York City instead. Keeping a day job at the Brew 'n' Burger restaurant and playing his blues at night, Copeland found a whole new audience for his brand of Texas blues in the Greenwich Village and Harlem nightspots.

Touring and recording in Africa

Johnny then inked a deal with Rounder Records in 1980, and in 1981 released his debut album, *Copeland Special,* followed by *Make My Home Where I Hang My Hat* in 1982. Following the critical acclaim showered on those two albums, Copeland toured the United States and Europe, and did a ten-nation tour of Africa. Inspired by his African trip, Copeland recorded his third album for Rounder, *Bringing It All Back Home,* in Nigeria using native African musicians.

Copeland hit his stride in 1985 with the album *Showdown!,* recorded with fellow Texan Albert Collins and newcomer Robert Cray. The album, released on Alligator, finally made him a national name on the blues scene and won both W.C. Handy and Grammy awards.

Johnny kept up a frantic pace of touring and recording for Rounder, releasing the Grammy-nominated live album *Ain't Nothing But A Party* in 1988 and *Boom Boom* in 1990. He moved over to the Verve label in 1992 for *Flyin' High,* followed by *Catch Up With The Blues* in 1994, and *Jungle Swing* in 1996.

In the middle of a tour in 1994, Copeland was diagnosed with a heart condition that required costly transplant surgery. He returned to touring and recording, all the while waiting for a heart donor, which he finally found on New Year's Day, 1997. But Johnny Copeland's new heart gave out and he died on July 3, 1997, after an unsuccessful operation to repair a leaky valve.

Copeland Special (Rounder). This debut album for Rounder Records puts Johnny Copeland's name on the blues map.

"Johnny Copeland was *serious* when he was on the bandstand. You'll see some artists joke around with their bands onstage, but when Johnny got up there, he just *played,* one tune after another in a real intense way. Johnny was all business; you didn't see him mingling with the crowd or stuff like that. When he got off the bandstand, he went right to his dressing room. He fascinated me. He was like a preacher when he sang and I watched every move he made up there."

Robert Cray

Along with Stevie Ray Vaughan, the Fabulous Thunderbirds, and Albert Collins, Robert Cray (born 1953) is one of the pivotal figures in blues music's ascent into mainstream popularity during the 1980s. Cray's stinging guitar lines, smooth vocals, and strong song selection helped the blues to reach its largest crossover audience ever.

Born August 1, 1953, in Columbus, Georgia, Cray was a quintessential Army brat who spent his childhood in Virginia, California, and Germany before his family settled in Tacoma, Washington, in 1968. Robert had studied piano while living in Germany but switched to guitar when the British Invasion swept America in the mid-1960s. Cray was well-versed in both soul and rock music (his major influences include O.V. Wright, Howlin' Wolf, Jimi Hendrix, the Beatles, Sam Cooke, and Ray Charles) and like most successful musicians, he paid his dues playing in various local bands.

The influence of Albert Collins

Robert's interest in the blues was sparked when Albert Collins played at his high school graduation party. Cray immediately fell in love with the elder blues artist's economical and forceful guitar style and after that immersed himself in the blues. With bass player Richard Cousins, he assembled the first edition of the Robert Cray Band in 1974.

During the time Cray was backing up Collins and other blues artists, Cray met actor John Belushi and scored a bit part in *National Lampoon's Animal House* as the bass player in the group Otis Day and the Knights. In 1978, Cray signed with Tomato Records and the following year recorded his first album, *Who's Been Talkin.* Shortly after the album's release, Tomato Records went out of business and so the album never got the marketing push it deserved.

Cray moved to Hightone Records in 1983 for his next release, *Bad Influence,* an album that showed off his hybrid soul-blues sound to good effect. He followed this with the equally strong *False Accusations* in 1985. His one-off album for Alligator Records — *Showdown!* with Johnny Copeland and Albert Collins — earned Cray his first of several Grammy awards.

Make way for the Strong Persuader

Cray crossed over to the pop charts in a big way with the 1986 album *Strong Persuader,* which featured the hit song, "Smoking Gun." Cray won a Grammy award the second straight year in a row and suddenly found himself on top of the pop charts and a regular on MTV video playlists.

Cray's success had him touring all over America, Europe, Canada, and the Far East, and he appeared with Eric Clapton, Keith Richards, and Chuck Berry in the movie *Hail! Hail! Rock'n'Roll.* Now a force to be reckoned with in contemporary blues, Cray's next album, *Don't Be Afraid Of The Dark,* sold more than a million copies and won Robert his third Grammy award in 1989.

Cray's more-recent releases — *Midnight Stroll* in 1990, *I Was Warned* in 1992, *Shame + A Sin* in 1993, *Some Rainy Morning* in 1995, and *Sweet Potato Pie* in 1997 — have found Cray alternating quite successfully between his two major playing styles, soul music and the blues. Even as a well-established major player on the modern blues scene, Robert Cray continues to redefine his art.

Strong Persuader (Mercury). This is Cray's breakthrough album and a great introduction to his engaging blues style.

"Robert Cray has a voice that, when I first heard it I thought, *here* was the voice I had been dreaming about. I would put him right up there with Sam Cooke. Robert can do exactly what he wants to do with his voice. He's always been a great rhythm guitar player and now his soloing is starting to become as exciting as his singing and songwriting."

The Fabulous Thunderbirds

Other white blues bands made their mark before the Fabulous Thunderbirds came along, but the T-Birds were especially important to the blues not only because of their engaging sound and excellent taste in material, but because they changed the way a blues band is supposed to *look*. After the T-Birds burst onto the scene, bell bottoms were out and pleated pants were in. Long hair was out, and pompadours were in. Tams, berets, and turbans were in, and so were baggy suits from the 1940s and 1950s. And everybody wore shades, even at night.

But the Fabulous Thunderbirds were more than just fashion plates — they always had great music to back up the look. They're schooled in the music of Lightnin' Slim and Jimmy Reed, are adept at Texas shuffles and rocking Cajun music, and exhibit a deep knowledge of 1950s Chicago blues. Nobody covers as many blues and roots-music bases and does it as well as the Fabulous Thunderbirds.

The Fabulous Thunderbirds were formed in 1974 in Austin by guitarist Jimmie Vaughan and vocalist-harmonica player Kim Wilson. The other two original members were bassist Keith Ferguson and drummer Mike Buck. For a brief time early on, singer Lou Ann Barton was also a member of the band.

Austin's premiere club band

Austin was a fertile environment for music and musicians in the 1970s, and within a few years, the Thunderbirds were established as the house band at Antone's, the city's number-one blues club. Between playing sets of their own and backing up nearly every blues artists that worked the club, the band quickly established themselves as the premiere band in the area.

In 1979, the group recorded its first album and embarked on their first cross-country tour in support of it. The Fabulous Thunderbirds were a powerful live act, and the combination of Wilson's front-man abilities, Vaughan's self-assured playing, and the solid rhythm section work of Buck and Ferguson made a strong impression on both musicians and audiences alike.

By 1980, the band had worked up enough attention to get signed by Chrysalis Records and started in on their next record, *What's The Word?* During the making of that album, Mike Buck left the band and was replaced by Fran Christina, formerly of Roomful Of Blues. For their next album, *Butt Rockin',* the T-Birds brought in members of the Roomful Of Blues horn section to broaden their sound.

But that album and its 1982 follow up, *T-Bird Rhythm,* didn't sell well and Chrysalis dropped the band, leaving them without a record label for the next four years while they continued to tour relentlessly. During this period, Keith Ferguson left the band and was replaced by another Roomful Of Blues alumni, bassist Preston Hubbard.

"Tuff Enuff" to break through

The group signed with Epic Records in late 1985 and released their break-through album, *Tuff Enuff,* the following year. Produced by Dave Edmunds, the album spawned two hit singles, sold more than a million copies, and won the group the 1986 Handy award as best blues band.

The T-Birds' follow-up albums, 1987's *Hot Number* and 1989's *Powerful Stuff,* sold well, but their more rock-oriented sound turned off long-time fans of the band's earlier and bluesier style. After these two albums failed to match the success of *Tuff Enuff,* Jimmie Vaughan left the band in 1989 to do a project with his brother, Stevie Ray. After Stevie Ray's death in 1990, Jimmie officially began his solo career with his 1994 debut *Strange Pleasures.*

By 1990, Kim Wilson was the only remaining original member. Replacing Jimmie Vaughan with two guitarists — Duke Robillard and Kid Bangham — the band soldiered on with 1991's *Walk That Walk, Talk That Walk.* It would be the last record for Epic and the last album from the band for a while. Kim Wilson released two solo albums, 1993's *Tigerman* and 1994's *That's Life.*

The band reformed in late 1994 and recorded a new album for the Private Music label, *Roll Of The Dice.* With Kim Wilson still at the helm and numerous personnel changes in their wake, the Fabulous Thunderbirds continue to tour, ready to record again.

The Essential Fabulous Thunderbirds (Chrysalis). A fine collection of the band's early recordings. Many of the tracks feature the original lineup.

"The first time I ever heard the Fabulous Thunderbirds was down in Austin. They were playing at a club that I was going to play at the next night and I went to check the place out. They sounded great, but what really caught my ear was when they went into "The Crawl," one of my old Guitar Junior numbers. I went over and talked to them and that's when I found out they played a whole mess of my songs."

James Harman

If a sincere appreciation of blues-roots music combined with an offbeat sense of humor sounds like an intriguing combination, then harmonica player-singer-songwriter-bandleader James Harman (born 1946) is your man. But, Harman is far from being a novelty act. His bands consistently have been solid combos featuring a host of great players.

Harman was born June 6, 1946, in Anniston, Alabama, and moved around the country before putting down roots on the West Coast in the early 1970s. Perfecting a harmonica style that combined equal parts Sonny Boy Williamson II and George "Harmonica" Smith, Harman hit the club scene with his first combo, the Icehouse Blues Band, which eventually coalesced into the James Harman Band. Harman's new group quickly became a cult favorite with West Coast bar patrons. Harman tightened the band's chops by securing gigs backing up blues legends such as Freddie King, Big Joe Turner, and T-Bone Walker.

The band that won't behave

Harman's first recording was released on his own Icepick label in 1981. It was a four-song, extended-play 45 record entitled *This Band Won't Behave.* In 1983, James cut his first full-length album for the Enigma label, *Thank You Baby,* followed by 1987's *Those Dangerous Gentlemens,* released on Rhino Records.

In 1988, Harman and his combo hooked up with the fledgling Rivera label to release their first "concept" album, *Extra Napkins,* which provided a glimpse into Harman's far-reaching blues vision.

Finding a following overseas

Harman's career got a boost when his tune "Kiss Of Fire" was included on the soundtrack of the Jodie Foster movie, *The Accused.* This kicked up enough interest in him to land James his first tour of Europe in 1989. Always a crowd pleaser overseas, he's regularly toured Europe ever since.

The long awaited *Strictly Live . . . In '85,* a stunning document of Harman's powers as a live performer, was released in 1990. James switched labels to Black Top Records, where he's released a top-notch batch of albums including 1991's *Do Not Disturb,* 1993's *Two Sides To Every Story,* 1994's *Cards On The Table,* and 1995's *Black And White.*

Extra Napkins was reissued on CD in 1997 on the Cannonball label, this time with bonus tracks included from the original sessions. In the meantime, James Harman keeps on playing and making new records, bringing his quirky but hip slant to the deepest of blues.

Strictly Live . . . In '85 (Rivera). This live set illustrates Harman's offbeat yet effective approach to traditional blues.

Etta James

Etta James (born 1938) has been belting out her brand of the blues, R&B, and jazz ballad stylings for more than 40 years and shows no signs of slowing down. Her signature gritty vocals can convey the sultriest of moods one minute, and absolute pain and heartbreak the next. "Miss Peaches" — her original show-business moniker — is equally adept at Billie Holiday ballads, Little Richard–styled rock 'n' roll hollering, and everything in between. Few singers can put an individual stamp on a song the way Etta James does — she's a song stylist of the first order.

Born Jamesetta Hawkins in Los Angeles on January 25, 1938, Etta was something of a child prodigy, singing gospel music in a church choir when she was only 5. In 1950, she moved with her mother to San Francisco and turned to secular music, forming a musical group with two other girls while still in her early teens.

"The Wallflower" rocks

Etta (see Figure 6-4) and her two friends auditioned for West Coast bandleader Johnny Otis in 1954. They worked together on a tune Etta had composed as an answer to Hank Ballard's "Work With Me, Annie." It was titled "Roll With Me, Henry." Otis took the girls, his band, and vocalist Richard Berry (the R&B singer who wrote "Louie Louie") into a Los Angeles studio to cut the new song for Modern Records.

Otis changed Jamesetta's name to Etta James and dubbed her group The Peaches. "Roll With Me, Henry" was changed to "The Wallflower" after radio programmers deemed the original title too suggestive, but the song hit the number-one spot on the R&B charts anyway. (The pop singer Georgia Gibbs changed the title and much of the meaning of the song when she recorded "Dance With Me, Henry" and scored a number-one *pop* hit with it in 1955.) Soon after that, Etta began her solo career and continued to record for Modern for the rest of the 1950s, scoring one more R&B hit in 1955 with "Good Rockin' Daddy."

Figure 6-4:
Etta James
(photo
courtesy of
MCA-Chess
Records).

The Chess years

In 1960, Etta moved from Modern Records to Chess, signing with their Argo subsidiary. After a five-year drought, Etta began scoring hits once more on both the R&B and pop charts including 1960's "All I Could Do Was Cry," 1961's "At Last," 1962's "Something's Got A Hold On Me" and "Stop The Wedding," and 1963's "Pushover."

She continued to record for Chess, moving over to their new Cadet subsidiary. In 1967, she released the classic "Tell Mama." Backed by the equally fine "I'd Rather Go Blind," it became her biggest pop hit, reaching Number 23 on the charts. She stayed with the Chess label until 1975, moving in the direction of pop and rock toward the end of her stay with the label.

A rage to survive

The next decade was a tough one for Etta James. For many years, she had no recording contract and was fighting two long-time personal demons, drug use and weight problems. But with the courage of a true survivor, she emerged drug-free and began working again on the R&B circuit, her voice still a powerful instrument.

In 1978, Etta opened for the Rolling Stones and started to put her career on track again. In 1984, Etta sang at the opening of the Los Angeles Olympic Games. She went back to recording in 1988 for the Island label, starting with the classic *Seven Year Itch* and has since released new material that's taken her in a variety of directions.

Etta James was inducted into the Rock and Roll Hall of Fame in 1993. In the early 1990s, she also wrote an amazing autobiography, *Rage To Survive*. Etta continues to deliver her brand of blues, R&B, soul, jazz, and pop music, and remains a true legend and consummate original stylist.

The Essential Etta James (MCA-Chess). A sumptuous dual-disc set containing 44 of Etta's best recordings for the Chess label.

A Rage To Survive by Etta James with David Ritz (Knopf). Etta's life has been a rough one and she pulls no punches in telling about it. This is a non-stop page turner that keeps you rooting for her every step of the way and one of the best show business autobiographies you're likely to run across.

Taj Mahal

Over the past four decades, singer-songwriter-guitarist Taj Mahal (born 1942) has been an active force in preserving traditional blues and African-American roots music and bringing it to a large and very appreciative audience. Taj Mahal has the ability to play various styles of traditional music on any number of instruments, provide scholarly insight on every aspect of those styles, and thoroughly entertain you, all at the same time.

He was born Henry Saint Clair Fredericks in New York City on May 17, 1942. His parents raised him in Springfield, Massachusetts, and young Henry grew up in a musical family — his mother was a gospel singing schoolteacher and his father a West Indian jazz musician.

Musical historian and versatile multi-instrumentalist

Taj Mahal's interest in the blues was sparked while he was a student at the University of Massachusetts in the early 1960s during the middle of the folk music revival. His personal research led him to more archaic forms of music. He decided that by working to preserve the music he would be keeping his African heritage alive for future generations. He jumped headlong into the study of blues history and taught himself to play the guitar, piano, banjo, mandolin, dulcimer, and various woodwind instruments.

He has said that the name Taj Mahal came to him in a dream and early on he worked the local Boston folk music circuit under that name. After he graduated with a B.A. in agriculture in 1964, Taj moved to Los Angeles and put together his first band, the Rising Sons, with guitarist Ry Cooder. The group broke up before their first album was released. But Taj Mahal's self-titled debut album followed in 1968, featuring both Cooder and guitarist Jesse Ed Davis.

A world of music in his brand of the blues

Taj Mahal's music underwent some interesting changes. In addition to his mastery of old-time country blues styles, he was also incorporating strains of West African, Caribbean, reggae, R&B, and rock 'n' roll into his sound as well. Over the next two decades, he used all of these styles on his records to create a musical hybrid all his own.

In the early 1970s, Taj Mahal contributed music to (and also appeared in) the movie *Sounder* and was on the soundtracks of *Brothers* and *Sounder II*. He also created television music scores for *The Man Who Broke A Thousand Chains* and *Brer Rabbit* and original music for the 1991 production of *Mulebone,* a long-lost Langston Hughes and Zora Neale Hurston play from the 1930s.

The 1990s have found Taj Mahal staying true to his eclectic musical vision. He's recorded everything from children's albums to progressive experiments such as 1996's *Phantom Blues,* which featured guest appearances from Eric Clapton and Bonnie Raitt. With more than 35 albums to his credit and a full touring schedule, Taj Mahal remains a leading exponent of highly experimental blues.

The Best Of Taj Mahal, Volume 1 (Columbia). On this CD, you'll find a collection of blues and roots music tracks as eclectic as the artist who made them.

Gary Primich

Gary Primich (born 1958) is one of the top harmonica players working in the blues today. His big, rich harmonica sound is reminiscent of his number-one idol, Big Walter Horton, while his clutch of solo albums demonstrate an artist willing to extend the boundaries of the blues without ever losing touch with its down-home roots.

Hanging out on Maxwell Street

Primich (see Figure 6-5) was born in Chicago on April 20, 1958, but grew up in neighboring Gary, Indiana. By the time he was a teenager, Gary was learning harmonica first-hand from the blues players working Chicago's Maxwell Street outdoor market. But the Chicago blues club scene at the time didn't offer much of a chance for Primich to break into its ranks, so after getting a degree in radio and television from Indiana University in 1984, Primich moved to Austin to try his luck in that city's burgeoning blues scene.

Pairing up with former Mothers drummer

After working around Austin as a sideman, Gary met up with former Mothers Of Invention drummer Jimmy Carl Black. The two formed a group, the Mannish Boys, and recorded an album for the Texas-based Amazing label, *A Li'l Dab'll Do Ya.* Black left the Mannish Boys, but Primich did one more album with the group for Amazing, *Satellite Rock.*

Figure 6-5:
Gary
Primich
(photo
courtesy of
Black Top
Records).

Gary decided to form his own group and released his debut album for Amazing in 1991. His follow up album, 1992's *My Pleasure,* was produced by fellow harmonica wizard James Harman. When Amazing Records went of business, Primich moved over to the Chicago-based Flying Fish label and released two fine albums for them, 1994's *Travelin' Mood* and *Mr. Freeze* in 1995. A move over to Black Top Records produced the following year's album, *Company Man.*

Gary Primich's music continues to evolve while he tirelessly promotes it with a non-stop touring schedule that takes his music around the world. Primich's abilities on harmonica, coupled with his smooth vocals and songwriting talents, makes him a blues artist to watch in the coming years.

Company Man (Black Top). Primich blows great harp, writes great songs, and sings his heart out on this fine release.

Bonnie Raitt

Whether it's a rock number, a pop tune, or the tenderest of ballads, Bonnie Raitt (born 1949) puts her blues-roots stamp on everything she plays. Her singing is soulful and deep and she always gets a song across without having to resort to vocal histrionics. Her guitar playing (especially her work on slide) with its economy, strong sense of rhythm, and unerring note placement is top notch.

Raitt (see Figure 6-6) was born on November 8, 1949, into a show business family (her father is Broadway musical star John Raitt). She started playing guitar in her teens and became immersed the blues in the mid-1960s while at college in Cambridge, Massachusetts. There she made a name for herself working the local coffeehouses and folk clubs around campus.

Catching the attention of several blues legends

It was her solo act in which she accompanied herself on acoustic slide guitar that caught the attention of legendary blues artists Son House and Mississippi Fred McDowell. (Both men would eventually pass on some of their slide secrets to the young singer.) Older blues artists such as House, McDowell, Rev. Gary Davis, and singer Sippie Wallace appreciated Raitt's strong commitment to the music, as well as her ability to sing and play the blues so well.

Figure 6-6: Bonnie Raitt, shown here in the studio with B.B. King (photo courtesy of MCA Records).

Her career got a boost when Dick Waterman, who also managed Son House and Mississippi Fred McDowell, took her on as a client. Bonnie was soon out of the coffeehouses and on the blues and folk festival circuit, establishing her reputation as an up-and-coming artist. She was signed to Warner Brothers Records and released her self-titled debut album in 1971, which featured guest appearances from A.C. Reed and Junior Wells. Bonnie continued to work the folk and blues festivals and blues clubs around the country throughout the 1970s.

Raitt's follow-up albums, 1972's *Give It Up,* 1973's *Takin' My Time,* and 1974's *Streetlights,* demonstrated interpretive skills that went well beyond country blues as she tackled the work of modern songwriters, including Jackson Browne and Randy Newman. Bonnie eventually scored a hit with her rendition of Del Shannon's "Runaway" from the 1977 album *Sweet Forgiveness.* But as Bonnie steered her music down an increasingly eclectic path in the 1980s, and had diminishing sales to show for it, her record company began exerting more control.

In the nick of time, the breakthrough recording

For her ninth and final album for Warner Brothers, 1986's *Nine Lives,* the higher-ups at the label pasted together an album out of two sessions recorded three years apart. After 15 years of recording for Warner Brothers Records, the label unceremoniously dropped Bonnie Raitt from its roster of artists.

With no record company for support and no new records to promote, times got rough for Bonnie. She couldn't afford a band anymore and went back to working small clubs as a solo act. For a while in the 1980s, Raitt battled problems with alcohol and substance abuse. But the turnaround in her life, both personally and professionally, came with dramatic swiftness.

Bonnie signed with Capitol Records in 1989 and released *Nick Of Time,* an album that went on to win six Grammy awards. With her worldwide breakthrough finally achieved, Raitt piled one hit album on top of another, including *Luck Of The Draw* and *Longing In Their Hearts.* A fine example of her modern-day live sound appeared on 1995's *Road Tested.*

With guest slots on albums by John Lee Hooker, Ruth Brown, and B.B. King, Bonnie Raitt continues to sing and play the blues with authority. Her 1998 release, the album *Fundamental,* has garnered some of the best reviews of her career. A true ambassador for blues music, Bonnie also donates her time to promoting the blues community as an active member of the Rhythm and Blues Foundation.

Give It Up (Warner Brothers). Bonnie Raitt's second album, released in 1972, showcases her considerable interpretive skills.

"Bonnie Raitt is a spell-binding slide guitarist and singer. But, more important than that, her work is really honest. When she says she's dedicated to the blues, she means it, and it comes through in her playing."

Kenny Wayne Shepherd

A child prodigy with instrumental chops galore, Kenny Wayne Shepherd (born 1977) recorded his debut album in 1995 when he was only 18 years old. Almost overnight, Shepherd became the hot young guitar slinger in modern blues-rock, filling the void left by the death of Stevie Ray Vaughan. But Shepherd's youthful demeanor is deceiving — he doesn't play like a kid, but more like an "old soul."

A self-taught prodigy

Kenny Wayne was born in Shreveport, Louisiana, on June 12, 1977. He taught himself the guitar when he was 7 by playing along with records from his father's blues collection. Although his playing is reminiscent of Stevie Ray Vaughan, Shepherd is quick to point out that Robert Cray, Albert King, B.B. King, Hubert Sumlin, and Muddy Waters are his main influences.

By the time he turned 13, Shepherd had kicked up enough noise as a novelty act on the jam session circuit that he made up his mind to become a full-time musician. He put together his first band, and Kenny Wayne's father became his manager. An early recording session in Shreveport had the teenage Shepherd overdubbing his guitar on an unreleased Willie Dixon song for Jewel Records. It was released as a 45 single titled "Sex Appeal" with the credits "by Willie Dixon — vocal — with Kenny Wayne on guitar."

Scoring a cross-over hit

Kenny Wayne's reputation as young guitar hotshot was expanding beyond the confines of Shreveport when he landed a record deal with major label Giant Records. Shepherd's debut album, *Ledbetter Heights,* was released in 1995. The album showcased Kenny Wayne's blazing guitar chops in a number of stylistic settings, with even some acoustic work. By 1996, the album had crossed over to the pop charts, selling more than a half-million copies. Shepherd has toured extensively since then, taking time off to record his second album, *Trouble Is...,* released in 1997.

Ledbetter Heights (Giant). The debut album from this young artist shows much promise and features loads of hot guitar work.

Hound Dog Taylor

No one enjoyed playing slide-guitar blues for an audience more than Hound Dog Taylor (1915–1975). While perched on a rickety folding chair armed with a cheap pawnshop guitar, Hound Dog would churn out nonstop boogies, shuffles, slow blues, and rocking rhythms in the course of a single night.

Equally important to Hound Dog's sound was his backup band, the HouseRockers. Brewer Phillips (who played bass lines on his six-string guitar) and drummer Ted Harvey knew every twist and turn in Hound Dog's music, and came up with a sound that was equal parts deep blues and 1950s-style rock 'n' roll.

Hound Dog was born Theodore Roosevelt Taylor on April 12, 1915, in Natchez, Mississippi. Originally a piano player (he was born with six fingers on each hand), Taylor started playing slide guitar at 20, working various juke joints and country suppers in the area. He also made a few guest appearances on the King Biscuit Time radio show on KFFA in Helena, Arkansas, before moving to Chicago in 1942.

"Let's have some fun!"

Taylor didn't pursue a full-time blues career until 1957, when he put together his first version of the HouseRockers and started working the club circuit on Chicago's West and South sides. With his raucous music and onstage cry of "Let's have some fun!" Hound Dog quickly became an inner-city club favorite. He also influenced other blues artists as well (an untitled instrumental he frequently played live became the basis for Freddie King's hit, "Hide Away").

Hound Dog made his first record in 1960, releasing one of his signature tunes, "Take Five," on the Bea & Baby imprint. Two years later, he released another single, "Christine," for the Firma label. His only other 1960s recording was another single for Chess's Checker subsidiary, 1967's "Watch Yourself." Although the three 45s captured only a glimmer of his good-time style, all are sought-after collector's items today.

The first Alligator recording artist

Someone who did see the potential in Hound Dog's music was Bruce Iglauer, then working as an employee at Delmark Records. Iglauer tried to convince Delmark owner Bob Koester to record Taylor. When his request was denied, Bruce started up the Alligator label, releasing Hound Dog Taylor and the HouseRockers in 1971.

Taylor's debut album received critical acclaim and the group started making waves touring across the country, working every blues club and festival out there. European tours brought Hound Dog's intense slide work and the HouseRockers' gritty blues to a global audience. Even more successful was their follow up album, *Natural Boogie,* released in 1973.

A live album, *Beware Of The Dog!* perfectly captures the band's raw, distortion-filled style, but Hound Dog didn't live to see the record's release. He died of cancer on December 17, 1975.

Taylor was inducted into the Blues Foundation's Hall of Fame in 1984. In 1998, Alligator Records released *Hound Dog Taylor — A Tribute* featuring Luther Allison, Son Seals, Magic Slim, *Blues For Dummies* author Cub Koda, and others paying homage to the slide guitar master.

Hound Dog Taylor and the HouseRockers (Alligator). Hound Dog's debut album is still the one to beat, loaded with the kind of crazy, juke joint music that seldom finds its way onto record.

"With Hound Dog, you really enjoyed just *watching* him. I never saw anybody on a bandstand who enjoyed himself as much as Hound Dog Taylor. He was always smiling, just stamping his feet and playing that guitar. He was having more fun than the audience! He loved playing for other musicians and all the other blues musicians just loved him. His music gave you the feeling that you sometimes get in church, when you feel the spirit and get happy because of it."

Koko Taylor

Koko Taylor (born 1935) reigns as the undisputed "Queen of the Chicago Blues," a title she's held since the mid-1970s. With her powerhouse voice and no-nonsense style, Koko (see Figure 6-7) has a lock on the top spot among Chicago blues vocalists.

Taylor was born Cora Walton on September 28, 1935, in Memphis. (When she was a kid, a relative of hers called her Koko by mistake and the nickname stuck.) She grew up on a farm her family sharecropped, started singing gospel music in church, and was singing professionally by the time she was 15.

Figure 6-7:
Koko Taylor
(photo by
Peter Amft;
courtesy of
Alligator
Records).

The blues she heard on the radio (especially the tunes that disc jockey B.B. King played on Memphis station WDIA) convinced her to switch musical directions. She then met Robert "Pops" Taylor, a fixture on the local Memphis blues scene, and the two were married and moved to Chicago in 1953.

Finding a mentor in Willie Dixon

Taylor worked as a domestic for 15 years while pursuing her musical career on the side. Koko and Pops started making the local club scene, meeting all the famous artists and the lesser lights, and sitting in at every opportunity. After producer-songwriter-bassist Willie Dixon heard her sing, he became her mentor while Pops worked as her manager.

Taylor cut her first record, "Honky Tonky," under Dixon's direction for the USA label in 1963. Willie then moved her over to Chess Records where she scored her first big hit in 1966 with Dixon's "Wang Dang Doodle." The song made it to Number Four on the R&B charts and remains a staple of her stage show to this day.

Koko continued to record for Chess, producing several singles, her self-titled debut album in 1969, and 1972's *Basic Soul.* Even though Dixon's involvement ensured top-flight songs, arrangements, and brand-name players, none of these recordings hit the top of the charts.

Earning more Handy awards than anyone else

Koko worked the local club and festival circuit, turning in devastating sets at the Montreux Jazz Festival and the Ann Arbor Blues and Jazz Festival, and appearing in the film documentary *The Blues Is Alive And Well In Chicago.* Bruce Iglauer signed her to his Alligator label, and her 1975 album *I Got What It Takes* was nominated for a Grammy award. Koko Taylor was back.

Since then, Taylor has released one solid album for Alligator after another, including 1987's *Queen Of The Blues, The Earthshaker, Live From Chicago,* and 1993's *Force Of Nature.* In 1989, she fought to recover from injuries sustained in a near-fatal automobile accident. In 1990, she appeared in the David Lynch film *Wild At Heart* and buried her husband of 37 years, the beloved Pops Taylor.

With more W.C. Handy awards to her credit than anyone else, the tightest of backing groups in her Blues Machine, and a schedule as full as she wants it to be, Koko Taylor continues her reign and shows no signs of abdicating the throne any time soon.

The Earthshaker (Alligator). Koko shines in her second album for Alligator, delivering songs you can still hear in her nightly stage shows.

"Koko Taylor is the bluesiest, hardest-working, and most soulful female singer out there today. She has the biggest voice and the biggest heart to go with it."

George Thorogood

Largely through the strength of his raucous brand of high-voltage blues-rock, George Thorogood (born 1952) has enjoyed one of the largest mainstream followings in the blues. In the 20 years since the release of his debut album for Rounder Records, Thorogood has toured incessantly in venues large and small, always delivering a show that's loaded with energy.

Thorogood was born in Wilmington, Delaware, on December 31, 1952. He spent most of his childhood dreaming of becoming a professional baseball player, and even played for a while in the minor leagues. But after seeing a John Hammond, Jr. concert in 1970, he decided on a career in music instead. Armed with an acoustic guitar, he moved to California, but at first had little luck breaking into the blues scene.

The Delaware Destroyer

In 1973, Thorogood moved back to Delaware and went electric, forming his first band, the Delaware Destroyers. He moved the band to Boston, and after opening shows for Hound Dog Taylor and the HouseRockers, fashioned a repertoire that was part Taylor, part Chuck Berry, and a whole lot of Bo Diddley.

The group developed a strong local following and recorded several demos before inking a deal with Rounder Records. The band's debut album, *The Destroyers,* set the pattern for every Thorogood album that followed — loud, brash, in-your-face blues that unashamedly plays to a rock audience.

Thorogood's second album, *Move It On Over,* became his nationwide calling card. His version of the Hank Williams title song became a surprise hit single and the album went gold. MCA Records released a batch of the pre-Rounder demos as *Better Than The Rest* and Rounder released *More George Thorogood* in 1980.

He opened shows for the Rolling Stones in 1981 and in 1982, Thorogood signed with EMI Records and released his major label debut, *Bad To The Bone.* The title song was built on the chassis of Bo Diddley's "I'm A Man," and Thorogood rode it for all it was worth. It became a major hit and his best-known song.

Born to be bad to the bone

Thorogood's next three albums — 1985's *Maverick,* 1986's *Live,* and 1988's *Born To Be Bad* — all went gold and continued his run of success. He had videos on MTV and even made a cameo appearance in a video for country artist Hank Williams, Jr.

Thorogood's 1990 album *Boogie People,* a 1992 greatest hits package, and 1993's *Haircut* didn't quite notch the sales that his previous releases had. While his recording career may be in a state of flux, Thorogood continues to draw big crowds to his shows and boasts a large number of European fans.

Move It On Over (Rounder). Thorogood's second album contains many of the songs that made him one of the biggest draws in the blues-rock scene.

Stevie Ray Vaughan

If modern-day blues has a true guitar hero to call its own, it's the late Stevie Ray Vaughan (1954–1990). With a dazzling technique reminiscent of Albert King, Lonnie Mack, and Jimi Hendrix, Stevie Ray's guitar style became, and continues to be, the most widely copied of the modern era.

Stevie Ray's high-volume playing and musical nods to Hendrix made him immediately accepted by rock audiences. In fact, no artist did more to bring blues to its current level of popularity than Vaughan. But Stevie Ray was no blues dilettante — his music was always firmly rooted in the blues tradition.

Like Hendrix, Vaughan favored a Fender Stratocaster guitar, used impossibly heavy guitar strings to acquire a larger tone, and played the guitar with both wild abandon and quiet beauty. As a showman, he was heavily indebted to Hendrix, Guitar Slim, and Buddy Guy, while his ability to produce a multitude of notes by stretching a single string could be bettered only by his hero, Albert King.

Forming Double Trouble in Austin

Stevie Ray was born in the Oak Cliff section of Dallas on October 3, 1954. His first influence was his older brother Jimmie, who turned the younger sibling on to what would become his two great loves, the guitar and the blues. As a youngster, Stevie Ray played in local Dallas bands The Blackbirds and The Chantones. When Jimmie Vaughan moved to Austin to form the Fabulous Thunderbirds, young Stevie quit high school in his junior year and followed his brother's trail, joining local band The Cobras in 1975.

In 1977, Stevie Ray hooked up with singer Lou Ann Barton, forming the Triple Threat Revue. A year later when Barton left the group, Vaughan assumed the lead-singing duties. The band was stripped down to a trio named "Stevie Ray Vaughan and Double Trouble," after an Otis Rush song.

The Texas flood of attention

Everything started falling into place for the young guitarist in 1982. A videotape of one of the band's performances got into the hands of Mick Jagger, who hired Double Trouble to play a private party. Producer Jerry Wexler caught the band live and hired them to play at the Montreux Jazz Festival, the first time an unsigned band had ever been tapped to play the prestigious event.

In the audience were rock stars David Bowie and Jackson Browne. Bowie hired Stevie to play on his *Let's Dance* album while Browne offered the band free recording time at his California studio. Shortly after Montreux, producer John Hammond, Sr. signed Stevie Ray to Epic Records and helped supervise the recording of Double Trouble's debut album, *Texas Flood.*

Texas Flood became a surprise success, earning two Grammy award nominations and hitting Number 38 on the pop charts, an unprecedented achievement for a straight blues album. The follow-up album, 1984's *Couldn't Stand The Weather,* was even more successful, hitting Number 33 on the charts and going gold the following year.

The critical praise and accolades kept coming as Stevie Ray released *Soul To Soul* in 1985 and *Live Alive* the following year. Vaughan won *Guitar Player* magazine's poll for best electric blues guitarist every year from 1983 to 1989. His name was big enough that he started guesting on other artists' albums. He played and coproduced *Strike Like Lightning,* recorded by his early inspiration, guitarist Lonnie Mack.

Getting back in step

In 1986, Stevie Ray's long-time battle with alcohol and substance abuse began to take its toll and the artist collapsed onstage at a concert in London. He went ahead with an extensive tour of the United States in the early part of 1987 but after the last date was played, Vaughan checked into a rehab clinic.

He spent most of the year cleaning up and reprioritizing his life. His new outlook resulted in his best music yet — 1989's *In Step.* Full of inspired vocals, incredible guitar playing, and his best songwriting to date, it also became his best-selling album, winning a Grammy award and selling a million copies just six months after its release.

Stevie Ray went back on the road with a vengeance, while taking some time out in early 1990 to record an album with his brother Jimmie. The album was to be called *Family Style* and featured both brothers working with musical formats that differed from the usual Fabulous Thunderbirds or Double Trouble sound.

A foggy night and a helicopter crash

On August 26, 1990, Stevie Ray and Double Trouble were part of a blues superstar show in East Troy, Wisconsin, that concluded with an onstage jam featuring Stevie Ray, Buddy Guy, Eric Clapton, Robert Cray, and Jimmie Vaughan. Stevie's playing was inspired. After the show, Stevie Ray boarded a helicopter headed for Chicago. Minutes after takeoff, the helicopter crashed in a dense fog, killing all five people aboard.

Family Style was issued posthumously in January 1990 and paved the way for a series of releases that have consistently sold well and have added to the Stevie Ray legacy. Fender issued their popular SRV signature model Stratocaster shortly after Vaughan's death, and the guitar is still in production. Nearly a decade after his death, Stevie Ray is still the guy to emulate. Nearly every kid who straps on a Strat to play the blues hopes some day to sound like Stevie Ray Vaughan.

Texas Flood (Epic). You can't overestimate the importance of this album to modern blues history. Great songs, a swinging rhythm section, and, oh, that guitar!

Johnny Winter

When Johnny Winter (born 1944) burst out of Texas and onto the national scene, he was hailed by the rock press as America's answer to the British-invasion guitar heroes. The playing and singing that made Winter a star was raucous, hyperkinetic, and unrelenting. Although his style shifted from blues, to blues-rock, to hard rock, and back to the blues again in a period of a decade, his true blues roots were never in doubt.

Johnny (see Figure 6-8) was born John Dawson Winter III on February 23, 1944. He taught himself the guitar at age 11 and at the same time was tuning in regularly to hear the blues on disc jockey Clarence Garlow's radio show. Johnny and his younger brother Edgar (both of whom were albinos) got involved in the local music scene, and by the time Johnny was 14 and Edgar was 12, the Winter brothers had formed their first band, Johnny and the Jammers. The band recorded a few singles that got some local airplay and Johnny's career was launched.

Figure 6-8:
Johnny
Winter
(photo by
Burton
Wilson,
Austin, TX).

Johnny and Edgar worked the local circuit together until 1963, when Johnny took off for Chicago to try to make it in the local blues club scene. He was unsuccessful at the time and soon returned home, putting together a new band that played a combination of blues and Top 40 rock. Johnny eventually jettisoned the pop music and started concentrating on nothing but the blues.

The blues guitarist as rock star

In 1968, *Rolling Stone* magazine published an article about the music scene in Texas, describing Johnny Winter in glowing terms. The article caught the attention of rock manager Steve Paul, who signed Winter and moved him to New York City, where Johnny instantly became *the* new hot act.

He signed a multi-album deal with Columbia Records and released a self-titled debut album in 1968. The record was a huge success and turned many rock listeners on to the blues as it's played, minus any of the psychedelic trappings. Winter hit the festival circuit and quickly gained a large rock following. His second album, *Second Winter,* found him playing in more of a blues-rock format.

After letting his original rhythm section go, Winter formed a new band called Johnny Winter And made up of former members of the rock group the McCoys. The group recorded two albums in 1971, *Johnny Winter And* and *Johnny Winter And Live,* and the Texas guitarist's star was on the rise. But near-constant touring and the pressures of success contributed to Winter's drug problem, and he spent 1972 kicking his habit. He returned in 1973 with *Still Alive And Well,* then moved over to Steve Paul's Blue Sky label to release the more rock-oriented *Saints and Sinners* and *John Dawson Winter III.*

Award-winning producer for Muddy Waters

In 1977, Johnny moved back to his first musical love with the release of *Nothing But The Blues,* followed by *White Hot and Blue* the following year and *Raisin' Cain* in 1980. His stock in the blues community shot up considerably when he produced four albums for Muddy Waters for the Blue Sky label. Two of the albums won Grammy awards and it's generally conceded that the albums Johnny produced (which included the classic *Hard Again*) were the finest Muddy had recorded in years.

Johnny went four years without a recording contract before signing up with Alligator Records in 1983. He made four albums for the label, including *Whoopin'* with Sonny Terry and Willie Dixon, *Serious Business, Third Degree,* and *Guitarslinger,* the last three loaded with Winter's patented blend of blues and rock.

In 1986, Winter became the first white artist ever inducted into the Blues Foundation's Hall of Fame. Two years later, he moved over to MCA/Voyager Records for one album, then joined Pointblank Records in 1991. He's released two fine albums for the label and continues to tour extensively, still capable of bringing that Texas heat to anything he touches.

White Hot Blues (Columbia). Head here to find a solid collection of Winter's blues-rock excursions featuring his high-energy style.

Other Notable Artists

In this section, we include other blues artists who, while not major stars (at least not yet), are nevertheless talented blues performers who play with brilliance and true feeling for the music. Many of these folks are still defining their art, making important contributions to the blues with each new record release.

Marcia Ball

Marcia Ball (born 1949) is a triple-threat blues talent — she combines powerful piano playing, soulful vocals, and great songwriting and mixes it into a musical gumbo loaded with strong bayou rhythms that pay homage to her Texas-Louisiana roots. Ball (see Figure 6-9) credits pianist Professor Longhair and singers Irma Thomas and Etta James as major inspirations.

After a brief stint in a psychedelic rock band while at Louisiana State University, Ball moved to Austin, found the city's musical scene to her liking, and has been based there ever since. Marcia's recording career began in 1984 with her debut album *Soulful Dress* on Rounder Records. She's followed it with top-notch albums, including 1986's *Hot Tamale Baby,* 1989's *Gator Rhythms*, and 1997's *Let Me Play With Your Poodle*. Also noteworthy is her 1990 collaboration with Angela Strehli and Lou Ann Barton, *Dreams Come True*. She continues to write, record, and perform, bringing her blend of boogie-woogie and Louisiana swamp rock to clubs and festival audiences in Europe, Canada, and the United States.

Let Me Play With Your Poodle (Rounder). Marcia pounds out boogie-woogie piano like nobody's business on this fine release.

Figure 6-9: Marcia Ball with her band (photo by Burton Wilson, Austin, TX).

Lou Ann Barton

Big-voiced Lou Ann Barton (born 1954) is one of the best-known figures on the Texas blues scene. Early in her career, she was a member of the Fabulous Thunderbirds, an early incarnation of Stevie Ray Vaughan's band, and Roomful Of Blues. She hasn't recorded nearly as much as she should, but her live shows remain the stuff of Austin legend.

Born in Fort Worth, Lou Ann's early influences include Irma Thomas and rockabilly singer Wanda Jackson (you can hear a touch of Jackson in Barton's Texas twang). After perfecting her craft playing in dozens of Texas dance halls, Lou Ann moved to Austin in the 1970s.

A fixture at Antone's and other music clubs in Austin, Barton's first recording was 1982's *Old Enough* on the Asylum label, followed in 1986 with *Forbidden Tones* on the Spindletop label, and *Read My Lips,* released in 1989 on Antone's label. The following year she joined Angela Strehli and Marcia Ball for their *Dreams Come True* album. She continues to perform while her fans eagerly wait for her next album.

Read My Lips (Antone's). Barton's R&B belting and Texas twang invigorate this aces-up collection of bluesy and soulful material.

Carey Bell

Combining the inventiveness of Little Walter with the lyricism of Big Walter Horton, Carey Bell (born 1936) is one of the last great originators of the Chicago electric harmonica sound. Long a fixture around Chicago as a backup musician extraordinaire (he also plays guitar and bass), Carey has recently come into his own as a front man with his brace of excellent albums.

Born in Mississippi, Carey was blowing harp by the age of 8 and was playing clubs by the time he was 13. At 20, Bell was spirited off to Chicago and started working around the local scene, getting lessons from Little Walter, Big Walter Horton, and Sonny Boy Williamson II.

In 1969, Bell recorded his first album for Delmark and in the 1970s he was a member of Muddy Waters' band. He cut an album for Alligator Records in 1972 with mentor Walter Horton, then recorded four sides on his own for the label's *Living Chicago Blues* anthology series in 1978.

Also noteworthy is 1990's *Harp Attack,* which teamed Bell with James Cotton, Junior Wells, and Billy Branch. Carey has since released several fine solo albums including 1991's *Mellow Down Easy* for Blind Pig and 1995's *Deep Down* for Alligator. He continues to record and tour and blow that harmonica like nobody else.

Deep Down (Alligator). Carey Bell's mastery of the harmonica shines brightly on this great session.

Rory Block

Acoustic blues is Rory Block's specialty. Adept at replicating the styles of early Mississippi Delta artists such as Son House and Robert Johnson, Block is no mere imitator — she always puts her individual stamp on the music.

Born in 1949 and raised in Greenwich Village, Rory began playing guitar at the age of 10 and later took occasional guitar lessons from blues legends Son House, Rev. Gary Davis, and Mississippi John Hurt. After a move to California in the mid-60s, Block dropped out of music for several years to raise a family.

She returned to active performing in 1975, signing with Blue Goose Records and releasing her debut album. After cutting two pop-oriented albums for Chrysalis in the late 1970s, she signed with Rounder in 1981 and returned to the sound she originally fell in love with, solo acoustic country blues.

The dozen or so albums Block has released since then (including a couple "best of" collections) have firmly established her as one of the brightest stars working in the modern-day country blues idiom. Rory Block continues to record and tour, always looking to expand into new musical areas.

Gone Woman Blues (Rounder). This CD is a fine collection of Block's interpretations of traditional country blues.

Women in the blues — the new breed

Back in the 1920s *all* the blues singers making records were women. The pioneering work of Ma Rainey, Bessie Smith, and others brought mainstream popularity to the blues. But that changed in the 1930s when male artists playing guitars, harmonicas, and pianos began dominating the blues music scene. The classic female blues singers of the 1920s either moved into cabaret work or retired, and blues essentially became an exclusive "boys club," with a few rare exceptions, such as guitar-wielding female singer Memphis Minnie.

The following decades produced notable female blues artists, including Koko Taylor and Etta James. But the fact was, during the 1950s and 1960s, most female singers worked in jazz, R&B, or pop, and women instrumentalists were relatively rare.

But in the last two decades, things have really begun to turn around. Many female blues artists have marched through the door opened during the late 1960s by Bonnie Raitt, Janis Joplin, and others. Several of the women featured in these pages are blues veterans who have been playing professionally and recording for two decades or more. But also keep an eye out for some new and exciting talent to emerge out of the current crop of quality female guitar players — a signal of one of the most interesting trends in the blues.

Sarah Brown

Sarah Brown (born 1951) is an American music dynamo. A consummate bass player and spark plug for any rhythm section she's in, Sarah has recorded or played behind Albert Collins, Buddy Guy, Otis Rush, Memphis Slim, Dr. John, and others. Brown is also one of the most in-demand songwriters in blues and R&B music circles and does an equally fine job as a solo artist interpreting her own material.

Sarah (see Figure 6-10) was born and raised in Ann Arbor, Michigan, and caught the blues bug after seeing Buddy Guy in concert in 1965. Brown purchased her first bass at a local pawnshop and taught herself how to play. After a stint at Boston's Berklee College of Music, Sarah moved back to Ann Arbor and dived headlong into that city's burgeoning blues scene.

Her recording debut found her backing up Detroit blues singer-guitarist Bobo Jenkins on his version of the old classic, "Shake 'Em On Down" in 1971. After a stint with Chicago harmonica legend Big Walter Horton, Brown pulled up stakes and moved back to Boston, playing up and down the New England Coast in the Rhythm Rockers with John Nicholas and Ronnie Earl, and recording for the Baron label in the late 1970s. After a 1982 tour of Europe, playing behind slide guitar legend J.B. Hutto, Sarah moved to Austin and once again plugged into a thriving local music scene.

After logging a couple of decades' worth of solid work as a sideperson in a variety of musical settings, Brown decided to go out on her own as a singer and songwriter. Her tunes have been recorded by Lou Ann Barton, Ruth Brown, Angela Strehli, and the trio of Tracy Nelson, Marcia Ball, and Irma Thomas, but most impressive of all was Sarah's interpretations of her own material on her 1996 debut album, *Sayin' What I'm Thinkin'*. As busy as ever, Sarah Brown continues to write great songs, make new records, and plug in her bass wherever a band needs a solid, swingin' groove.

Sayin' What I'm Thinkin' (Blind Pig). Sarah's fine songwriting and assured vocals are framed by a top-notch band on this fine outing.

Eddy Clearwater

With his Magic Sam-influenced West Side sound, his penchant for cranking out Chuck Berry-styled rock 'n' roll, the native-American headdress he regularly wears onstage, and his upside-down and left-handed guitar playing, Eddy Clearwater (born 1935) definitely stands out from the rest of the blues crowd.

Born Eddy Harrington, Jr. in Macon, Mississippi, he grew up in Birmingham, Alabama, before moving to Chicago in 1950. There, he initially billed himself as Guitar Eddy until he started recording in the late 1950s as Clear Waters (spoofing the name Muddy Waters) for his uncle's Atomic H label. Eddy also cut singles for LaSalle and Federal in the early 1960s.

After changing his name to Eddy Clearwater, he worked both the rock 'n' roll and blues sides of the fence until the late 1970s. He recorded his first U.S. album in 1980, *The Chief,* for the Rooster Blues label. Follow-up albums included 1986's *Flimdoozie,* 1990's *Real Good Time: Live!,* 1992's *Help Yourself,* and 1997's *Mean Case Of The Blues.* A consistently entertaining live performer, Eddy continues to record and tour.

The Chief (Rooster Blues). Eddy Clearwater's debut album is a wonderful introduction to his rocking, good-time blues style.

Deborah Coleman

Deborah Coleman (born 1956) is one of the most exciting musicians currently on the blues scene. As a singer, songwriter, and lead guitarist, she mixes contemporary blues stylings with elements of funk and rock.

Born in Portsmouth, Virginia, into a music-loving military family, Deborah (see Figure 6-10) began dabbling with the guitar when she was 8. (She was inspired to become a musician from watching *The Monkees* TV show.) Coleman began playing professionally at 15, first on bass, then guitar, in a variety of rock and soul bands. She took some time off to raise a family and pursue careers as a nurse and an electrician before turning to music full time in the mid-1980s. After working in a female rock band called Moxxie, Coleman played blues with a trio called Misbehavin'.

Her big break came when she entered and won the Charleston, South Carolina, Blues Festival's National Amateur Talent Search. She landed a deal with the local New Moon label and released her debut album, *Takin' A Stand,* in 1994. Her second album, *I Can't Lose,* came out in 1997 on the Blind Pig label.

I Can't Lose (Blind Pig). Check this CD for a fine introduction to the deft musicianship of this bold new artist.

Figure 6-10:
Some of the best of the current crop of female blues artists. Clockwise from upper left: Sarah Brown; Deborah Coleman; Debbie Davis; and Joanna Connor. All photos courtesy of Blind Pig Records.

photo by Reagan Bradshaw

photo by Jim Purdin

photo by Pat Johnson

photo by Chris Jacobs

Joanna Connor

Joanna Connor (born 1962) plays a ferocious blues-rock slide guitar with a tone as nasty as the law will allow. Her approach to the blues has been likened to Johnny Winter's high-voltage style, but the sound is still uniquely Joanna's.

Connor (see Figure 6-10) was born in Brooklyn but grew up in Worcester, Massachusetts. She got her first guitar at the age of 7 after hearing her mother's Taj Mahal and Jimi Hendrix albums, and sang in various bands during high school before turning pro in 1981.

Joanna headed to Chicago in 1984, ready to jump into the local blues circuit. She joined up with slide guitarist Johnny Littlejohn, then became a featured member of Dion Payton's 43rd Street Blues Band. By 1987, Connor put the first edition of her own band together, and two years later released her debut album for Blind Pig Records, *Believe It!*

Connor has issued four albums since then, including her debut follow-up *Fight* and 1996's *Big Boy Blues*, both on Blind Pig. As her fame on the festival and club circuit continues to grow, so does Joanna Connor's reputation as a first-rate guitarist and songwriter.

Big Boy Blues (Blind Pig). Connor's slide guitar on this torrid session cuts through these tracks like a knife.

Debbie Davies

Debbie Davies (born 1952) plays no-nonsense blues for the '90s and has been grabbing a lot of attention since her days of playing with her mentor, the late Albert Collins. Debbie's skills in both single-string guitar soloing and slide playing are astounding.

Born in Los Angeles into a musical family, Davies (see Figure 6-10) grew up in a show-business environment. As a child, she sang in commercials and in Walt Disney productions and by her 20s was performing in a number of San Francisco rock and blues bands.

She moved back to Los Angeles in 1984 and landed the lead guitar spot in Maggie Mayall and the Cadillacs, an all-female R&B band. After the breakup of the Cadillacs several years later, Davies started performing under her own name. Six months after being introduced to guitar master Albert Collins, she was invited to join his band, the Icebreakers. She opened Albert's shows for the next four years.

In 1991, Davies struck out on her own with a new band, recording her first album for Blind Pig Records, *Picture This*. It earned rave reviews and cuts from the album were hits on blues radio stations for months. Debbie followed it with *Loose Tonight* and 1997's *I Got That Feeling*. With four Handy award nominations under her belt, Davies is a potent blues force.

Picture This (Blind Pig). Debbie Davies's debut album was the calling card announcing that a fine new guitarist was on the scene.

Long John Hunter

For years, Long John Hunter (born 1931) was a Texas underground legend. He is an amazing showman in a state loaded with amazing performers. Patrons of blues clubs from El Paso to Juarez, Mexico, can tell stories of Hunter's hanging from the ceiling rafters with one hand while playing the guitar with the other. A major influence on Lonnie Brooks, Hunter is just now beginning to find a wider audience for his brand of Texas blues.

While working in a box factory in Beaumont, Texas, Hunter became interested in the blues after watching B.B. King on TV. He went out and bought a guitar the very next day and a year after that was playing the same club that B.B. had once played. He recorded a few singles for the Duke and Yucca labels in the 1950s and early 1960s while holding down a 13-year gig at the Lobby Bar in Juarez from 1957 to 1970.

Long John finally moved beyond his local legend status with his first album in 1992, *Ride With Me,* for the now defunct Spindletop label. In 1996, Hunter grabbed national attention with his first album for Alligator Records, *Border Town Legend,* followed by *Swingin' From The Rafters.* After decades of local celebrity, Long John Hunter is finally getting the audience he's long deserved.

Swingin' From The Rafters (Alligator). Hunter's brand of Texas blues packs a wallop on this album.

Jimmy Johnson

Over the past two decades, Jimmy Johnson (born 1928) has moved to the front ranks of Chicago's contemporary blues field. He got a late start in the blues. He was primarily a soul performer until the mid-1970s when he changed career goals and scored a gig as Jimmy Dawkins's rhythm guitarist.

Johnson was born in Holly Springs, Mississippi, and is the older brother of blues musician Syl Johnson. (Another brother, the late Mack Thompson, played bass with Magic Sam's band for many years.) In 1950, Jimmy moved to Chicago to work in a sheet metal factory on the city's south side. In 1958, after years of playing and singing, Johnson landed his first professional gig. He was eventually hired by Harmonica Slim, who helped launch Jimmy's career.

It was Jimmy's albums for Delmark and Alligator that made his name. *Bar Room Preacher* was issued in 1985 on Alligator, although it was released earlier overseas. Jimmy also recorded *I'm A Jockey* for Verve in 1995, which featured a more orchestrated style and horn arrangements.

Bar Room Preacher (Alligator). This record from the early 1980s is an excellent example of Johnson's gutsy blues style.

Syl Johnson

Syl Johnson (born 1939) is probably best known as a soul music artist, but his early work in the blues later resurfaced in the fine soul-blues records he released late in his career. Syl was born in Holly Springs, Mississippi, and is the younger brother of blues musician Jimmy Johnson. After moving to Chicago in 1950, young Syl played in bands led by Junior Wells, Billy Boy Arnold, and Eddie Boyd.

Johnson's first national hit, "Come On Sock It To Me," released in 1967 on the Twinight label, was a hard-soul sensation and made Syl a star. His biggest hit, 1975's "Take Me To The River," was given to him by Al Green and produced by Memphis legend Willie Mitchell for the Hi label. In 1980, Syl recorded *Brings Out The Blues In Me* on his own Shama label. Today, Johnson is busy recording with young artists, including Jonny Lang and his daughter, Syleena Johnson, a 19-year-old vocalist.

Back In The Game (Delmark). This wonderful 1994 comeback album beautifully spotlights Syl Johnson's soul-blues synthesis.

Eddie Kirkland

Eddie Kirkland (born 1928) is a long-time popular fixture on the blues scene with a recording career dating back to the 1950s. This 70-year-old blues artist shows no signs of slowing down — his music is always fresh and continually evolving.

Born in Jamaica, Kirkland moved to Dothan, Alabama, where he soaked up blues music firsthand. A move to Detroit in 1943 resulted in his working and recording with John Lee Hooker. Kirkland's own recording career began around that time when he issued some singles for RPM, King, and Fortune.

He recorded his first album, *It's The Blues, Man!*, in 1961 for the Prestige label. He moved to Macon, Georgia, in 1962 and played in Otis Redding's band for a short time and also recorded for Stax Records. Albums for the Trix label followed in the 1970s as Eddie's music moved toward a more soul-oriented style.

Eddie's kept recording ever since, turning out a spate of albums for the Deluge label. His recent effort for Telarc, 1997's *Lonely Street,* was released in an enhanced CD-ROM format.

Lonely Street (Telarc). Eddie Kirkland's eclectic mix of blues, soul, and rock gets a workout in this 1997 outing.

Lil' Ed and the Blues Imperials

Lil' Ed (born 1955) and the Blues Imperials continue the proud and long-standing tradition of no-nonsense, hard-rocking blues bands started by Hound Dog Taylor and the HouseRockers and Magic Slim and the Teardrops.

Lil' Ed Williams formed the Blues Imperials with his half brother, bassist James Young. (Williams learned his slide guitar technique from his uncle, Chicago blues artist J.B. Hutto.) After years of working in a car wash and playing their music on the side, the Blues Imperials successfully auditioned for Alligator Records and released their debut album, *Roughousin',* in 1986. Two more albums for Alligator followed, 1989's *Chicken, Gravy and Biscuits* and 1992's *What You See Is What You Get.* Surviving numerous personnel changes in his backing unit, Lil' Ed continues to record and perform on the blues club circuit.

Chicken, Gravy and Biscuits (Alligator). On this CD, Lil' Ed and his band put together a roaring set of slide guitar boogie and good-time party music.

Magic Slim

Nobody on the modern scene exemplifies the classic raw Chicago blues sound like Magic Slim (born 1937) and his band the Teardrops. Slim and his band deliver spontaneous juke joint blues through an ever-expanding repertoire of music.

Magic Slim was born Morris Holt in Grenada, Mississippi. He moved to Chicago in the early 1950s to become a part of the local blues scene, but found the competition tough. He moved back to Mississippi and kept working at his music. In 1965, he tried the Windy City again with a new band featuring his brothers.

Magic Slim and the Teardrops quickly established themselves as blues club fixtures on Chicago's South Side, taking over Hound Dog Taylor's gig at Florence's for a number of years. Their first opportunity to record came with a batch of tunes for Alligator's *Living Chicago Blues* series in 1978. The records have come fast and furious since then, with Slim recording for Alligator, Wolf, Rooster Blues, and Blind Pig. He continues to record and tour, bringing his unvarnished brand of blues to audiences the world over.

Raw Magic (Alligator). On this record, Magic Slim and the Teardrops deliver great Chicago blues that's as low down and nasty as any around.

Charlie Musselwhite

Charlie Musselwhite (born 1944) burst onto the national scene in the mid-1960s with his debut album, *Stand Back! Here Comes Charlie Musselwhite's Southside Band*, one of the first successful albums released by a non-African-American artist during the '60s blues revival. Since then, he's earned the respect of blues artists the world over and continues to surprise blues fans with each new release.

Born in Kosciusko, Mississippi, of Native-American parents, Musselwhite moved to Memphis and honed his harmonica skills playing with traditional country blues artists, including Furry Lewis and Big Joe Williams. Moving up to Chicago in the early '60s, Charlie soon became a presence on the local club scene, sitting in with and getting pointers from Little Walter, Big Walter Horton, and Sonny Boy Williamson II.

Before forming his first band, Charlie recorded with Tracy Nelson and John Hammond, Jr., and paired with Walter Horton on a session for Vanguard. After the *Stand Back!* album began receiving FM airplay, Musselwhite moved to San Francisco. Over the years, he's assembled one top-notch band after another, recording for a variety of labels and playing around the Bay area.

After conquering a long-time drinking problem, Charlie Musselwhite started touring the world in the 1980s to sparkling reviews. His recording career also started back up with a vengeance, having cut fine albums for Alligator, Blue Rock-It, and Pointblank in the 1980s and 1990s. In total command of his music and his life, Charlie Musselwhite is better than ever.

Ace of Harps (Alligator). This CD presents a fine selection of Charlie Musselwhite's mature playing style.

Saffire—The Uppity Blues Women

Saffire—The Uppity Blues Women are both delightful throwbacks to the heyday of the classic female blues singers of the 1920s and strong 1990s-styled feminist artists. They combine their all-acoustic sound with great songs filled with bawdy lyrics that address topical subjects not usually found in the blues.

Based out of Fredericksburg, Virginia, pianist-vocalist Ann Rabson (born 1945) and guitarist-vocalist Gaye Adegbalola (born 1944) met while both were working the local club circuit as solo acts. Teaming with bass player-vocalist Earlene Lewis, the three musicians pooled their resources, and Saffire was formed in 1984 as a weekend project, eventually going full time in 1988.

In 1989, the group recorded a demo tape that caught the attention of Bruce Iglauer, who signed them to his Alligator Records label. Their self-titled debut album came out the next year to great reviews and healthy sales. Saffire was nominated for five Handy awards and won the award for blues song of the year for their "Middle-Aged Boogie."

Their follow-up album, *Hot Flash,* was released in 1991, and their third album, *Broadcasting,* witnessed the first personnel change in the band when Lewis left and was replaced by Andra Faye McIntosh. This version of the group recorded in 1994, producing the album *Old, New, Borrowed & Blue.* Since that time, Ann Rabson has also recorded her first solo album for Alligator, *Music Makin' Mama,* while the group continues to tour and record.

Saffire—The Uppity Blues Women (Alligator). The group's debut album is loaded with great original tunes full of sass, wit, and verve.

Son Seals

As one of the leading lights of the modern Chicago scene, guitarist Son Seals (born 1942) brings razor-sharp lead work and strong songwriting to his brand of the blues. Long a favorite with critics, Seals's albums for Alligator in the 1970s featured some of the fiercest blues guitar playing to be heard on record during that decade.

Son was born Frank Seals in Osceola, Arkansas. Originally a drummer, young Frank honed his skills sitting in with traveling blues artists at his father's juke joint. It was Albert King who taught Seals the basic rudiments of guitar playing. By his teens, Seals had formed his first band.

A trip to Chicago netted him a slot in Earl Hooker's Roadmasters band in 1963 and Son went behind the drums once again to record and tour with Albert King in 1966. He moved to Chicago in 1971, working briefly with Hound Dog Taylor before forming his own band.

When blues fan Wesley Race spotted Seals playing at the Expressway Lounge in Chicago, he immediately called Bruce Iglauer at Alligator Records who jumped at the chance to record this new blues artist. Son Seal's debut album was released in 1973, followed by six more for Alligator, including 1977's *Midnight Son,* 1978's *Live & Burning,* and 1994's *Nothing But The Truth.* While he keeps his touring to a bare minimum, Seals continues to play regularly around the Chicago area.

The Son Seals Blues Band (Alligator). Son's debut album features great originals and savage guitar playing.

Angela Strehli

Angela Strehli (born 1945) was one of the founding members of the Austin, Texas, blues scene of the 1970s along with the Fabulous Thunderbirds, Lou Ann Barton, Stevie Ray Vaughan, and others. Equal parts blues fan, blues historian, singer, and songwriter, Strehli is much more than just another vocalist fronting a blues band.

Born in Lubbock, Angela started out playing harmonica and bass before deciding to devote herself to singing. After spending some time in California, Angela relocated to Austin and quickly became a popular member of local music scene as a singer with the group Southern Feeling. In 1975, she hooked up with the city's top blues club, Antone's, working behind the scenes and sitting in with bands on occasion.

In 1982, Strehli organized her first band and four years later released an EP, *Stranger Blues,* which also doubled as the debut release for Antone's Records. In 1987, she released her first full-length album for the label *Soul Shake.* Three years later, she relocated to San Francisco and participated in the *Dreams Come True* project with Marcia Ball and Lou Ann Barton. In 1993, she signed with Rounder and released her second album, *Blonde and Blue.* Strehli continues to perform while her fans await her next release.

Soul Shake (Antone's). Angela Strehli's debut release serves as a great introduction to her soulful style.

Hubert Sumlin

A great deal of Hubert Sumlin's (born 1931) reputation in blues circles comes from his long tenure as Howlin' Wolf's guitarist. His wild, skittering solos graced many of the elder blues artist's finest recordings and Sumlin's influence on a whole generation of younger blues and rock artists cannot be overestimated.

Sumlin was born in Greenwood, Mississippi, and grew up near West Memphis, Arkansas. He became fascinated with the blues, teaming early on with harmonica player James Cotton. But his greatest obsession was with blues legend Howlin' Wolf. Sumlin would sneak into clubs to watch him, and the two eventually formed an almost father-son relationship. (When Wolf moved to Chicago in 1954, he arranged for Sumlin to move up as well.)

Hubert started out on rhythm guitar in Wolf's band, eventually moving over to the lead guitar spot by the early 1960s. Sumlin provided the guitar spark on classic tracks including "Wang Dang Doodle," "Shake For Me," Goin' Down Slow," and "Killing Floor." He stayed on with Wolf until the elder bluesman's death in 1976.

Sumlin made a few solo recordings, mostly for European labels, before Wolf's death, but his solo career didn't really blossom until the late 1980s. Recording albums for Black Top and Blind Pig into the 1990s, Hubert Sumlin's whispery voice and stinging guitar continue to delight fans around the world.

Heart and Soul (Blind Pig). Hubert catches fire on this solo outing, featuring fine support from James Cotton.

Part III
Listening to the Blues

The 5th Wave   By Rich Tennant

BLUES CLUBS TO AVOID

HAMPTONS BLUES BISTRO

Special guest appearance...
Steven Spielberg
on harmonica

TONIGHT
MARTHA STEWART & the ARUGULAS
Featuring
"I've got the blues— and that's not a good thing"

In this part . . .

We applaud your tremendous taste and wisdom in reading a book about the blues, but now it's time to get out there and listen to it. Blues recordings are available in abundance and we figure you want get the biggest bang for your musical buck. So, in this part of this book, we steer you to some of the best blues CDs currently available. We also fill you in on some of the best places to hear the blues — both live and on the radio.

Chapter 7

The Best Blues Recordings and Record Labels

· ·

In This Chapter

▶ The top places to shop for blues records

▶ The best contemporary blues labels

▶ The 25 all-time classic blues tunes

▶ The 55 best blues albums and collections

· ·

You have a real bad case of blues fever and you crave a cure. One remedy is to build your own blues collection. Blues music has never been more plentiful, better documented, or more available than it is right now, but you may have to do a little digging to get *exactly* what you want.

The record retailing business still considers the blues a fringe commodity, despite the recent success the genre enjoys with its growing audience. Even the best-selling blues artist doesn't move anywhere near the number of discs that a chart-topping pop, rock, or country artist does. Big chain stores that have a blues section generally keep the selection to newer releases and a stray box set or two — a scant fraction of the blues titles that are actually released.

So, you aren't likely to find a Muddy Waters or John Lee Hooker box set sitting next to Garth Brooks or Mariah Carey at your local Kmart or Wal-Mart. If you want some blues — the real thing — in your record collection, you have to get out and look for it.

For the Record: Who's Got the Blues

Check out your local record stores and bookstore diskeries. Try to find an establishment that caters to a *roots music* clientele (customers who appreciate artists who are at the roots of current musical forms), and that has a good-size blues section with a wide variety of records to browse through. The record collectors' network relies on stores like these, partly because they usually can special-order obscure items on small labels that many of the bigger chain stores swear they can't find.

Don't be surprised at *where* you can run into the blues. You may find a very cool cassette sitting in a gas station display rack or discover that the chain bookstore at the local mall actually has an exemplary blues selection (sort of like finding money in a pocket of a seldom-worn jacket).

You can also sometimes find vintage blues singles and albums, should your collecting desires and cash flow lean in that direction. However, your best bet is sticking with newer issues on compact discs if you want to assemble a really nice collection of titles that costs something less than the national debt.

If you can't find a disc emporium in your area that carries blues records, don't be discouraged. Many record stores offer superior mail-order services. You also can find mail-order companies plying their wares in blues and collectors magazines such as *Living Blues, Blues Access,* and *Discoveries.*

If you live in a remote location, you can surf the World Wide Web for blues recordings. For example, Tower Records has a Web site (`www.towerrecords.com`), and so do several other companies and record dealers.

If you live in a remote location, you can surf the World Wide Web for blues recordings. For example, Tower Records has a Web site (`www.towerrecords.com`), and so do several other companies and record dealers.

Another Internet record retailer is CDnow (`www.cdnow.com`). Its Web site is driven by a search engine that enables you to enter any musical artist, song title, or record label in keyword format. The system immediately displays very complete search results.

The fake "live" album and the bottom line

As you may know, a *live album* is a non-studio-recorded document of a live performance. You can find several great live blues albums on the market (we list some of them in this chapter). But, watch out: Bootleggers very easily can take a second- or third-generation cassette of dubious quality, slap a color photo of the artist on the package, and pass it off as a legitimate and fully sanctioned live album.

Many bootleg "live" cassettes are created on a *mixing board,* the piece of equipment that's used to balance the sound sent out through an audience p.a. system. The board usually includes a cassette player-recorder that can play music between sets as well as record the music as it's being played onstage. Recordings from a mixing board can range from muddy sounding to just plain awful; they're usually very heavy in the bass tones and the vocals are mixed way up with very little real music that you can hear clearly. Nothing can break an artist's heart faster than being handed one of these things to autograph, knowing full well he or she isn't making a dime off of it.

The bottom line with bootlegged music is that the artists don't get paid, the session musicians (if any) don't get paid, the publishers and the songwriters don't get paid, and the producer or record company that financed the session doesn't get paid. The only person making money is the person bootlegging the material. You, the consumer, end up with a very low-quality recording that only provides a glimmer of what the actual performance really sounded like. End result: Both the artist and the consumer get burned.

You're outta here: Bootlegs and pirated recordings

You have more blues records to choose from than ever before, and sadly, that also includes *bootleg* and *pirated* recordings, which have never been more numerous.

Bootlegs are recorded without the artist's permission on inferior equipment, so not only is the sound quality poor, but the artist fails to receive royalties on bootleg record sales. Pirated recordings are literally just that — recordings taken or copied from the holdings of other record companies, which are then released or reissued without those companies' consent or knowledge.

Over the years, small record companies have been bought up by other larger record companies that can legally reissue the *master holdings* (that is, the original recordings, also known as *masters*) of the acquired label. But with the advent of digital tape and compact discs, almost anyone can copy an artist's material and end up with reasonably decent fidelity, and then turn around and put out a CD or cassette that seems to be a legitimate issue.

Anybody with even a beat-up vinyl copy of a rare album in his or her collection can make a digital tape of the album and get a compact disc pressed. The original art work is duplicated with a copier or computer and the sloppy, shoddy packaging and sound are passed straight on to you. At a convenience store tape rack, for instance, you can find street-legal budget cassettes of B.B. King sitting right next to low-fidelity rip-offs of Jimmy Reed (one of the great blues artists of all time).

And, don't buy the old saw that foreign pressings are always of superior quality. Some foreign countries' copyright laws have loopholes that exclude compact discs from the royalty payment equation. Therefore, pirated discs of material from U.S. record companies are rampant in those far-away places because they can usually be taped right out of a bootlegger's record collection. (Not all European issues are illegal, but a surprising number are.)

The bootlegging "industry" doesn't stop with just pirating recordings of previously released material. This rip-off game takes on many variations and one of the worst of all is the fake "live" album, the subject of another sidebar earlier in this chapter.

Didn't the guy notice the hat?

I remember one time this street vendor in Chicago was selling cassette tapes from his station wagon. I was going through his tapes when I ran across one with my name on it. It was a bootleg of an album I had made for Alligator Records. So he points to the tape and says, "Oh, that's Lonnie Brooks! He's great, you *oughta check him out." So I asked him how much he wanted for it and he said $5. I told him I didn't have that much on me, so he knocked the price down to $2.50. My own tape! I ended up buying it and took it right over to Alligator. I said, "Look what they're doin' to us, man." Oh yeah, and the tape sounded horrible!*

The Format Wars: Vinyl versus CDs versus Tapes

Most long-time blues aficionados and record collectors, if you give them the chance, can wax effusive (no pun intended) on the superiority of vinyl. In the early days of blues recordings, the music came out on 78 rpm discs pressed on shellac. After World War II, the *microgroove* format was adopted by the industry, which produced the long-playing album (usually called an *LP* or just plain *album*) and the 45 rpm *single* on vinyl plastic.

Today, music buyers can choose from among several recording formats, each of which has its pros and cons.

It must be vinyl!

Some audiophiles claim that vinyl recordings have a richer sound (with truer bass tones and a more realistic aural ambiance) than compact disc recordings. Collectors also say that the original vinyl is worth more than a compact disc reissue, and they're correct. The early 78 rpm records were made of very brittle material (so many of the 78 rpm records didn't survive) and blues music in any format (45s and LPs, as well as 78s) was never manufactured in great quantity in past decades because the blues audience was considered a small and highly specialized market. Their scarcity makes those original recordings highly collectable, commanding high-dollar figures that put them out of the price range of most fans who care more about listening to the music than owning a collector's item.

Some companies still have vinyl titles available, and if you haven't sold your old turntable at your last yard sale, you may want to ask your local record store if a certain title that you're looking for is still available in the vinyl format. If you care to, buy them in different formats and make the vinyl-versus-CD-versus-tape audio comparison yourself.

Everybody listens to CDs now!

If you're building a blues collection from the ground up, compact discs are definitely the way to go, partly for obvious ease of handling and greater portability. Recently developed audio improvements make many older recordings sound much better than their original vinyl (or shellac) counterparts. Plus, you can buy a CD of Muddy Waters's best recordings for a scant fraction of what the originals cost, if you're lucky enough to track down those originals.

While not every blues recording is currently available on CD, a great many recordings are, and every year, more and more titles are reissued on compact disc.

Tapes are cheap and handy!

As far as tape cassettes go, they're generally considered to be at the low end of the high-fidelity spectrum. Tapes are cheaper than CDs, but a defective prerecorded cassette is generally more difficult to return to a store than a CD (the reason being that sales clerks usually blame the problem on your tape player, not on the defective tape itself). But, if you really want a tape for your car, boombox, or Walkman, we suggest buying a bunch of high-quality, blank audiocassettes and taping your favorites from CDs or vinyl.

Another thing: With cassette tapes, you get what you pay for. That $2 convenience store tape may get you through a road trip in a pinch, but don't expect that tape to sound like much after a few dozen plays, if it lasts that long.

The Best Blues Labels

In the beginning, there existed nothing but major label involvement in documenting, recording, and selling the blues. Labels such as Columbia, (RCA) Victor, and Decca all recorded copious amounts of blues from the 1920s through the 1940s. Those records were usually released on the companies' budget labels such as Vocalion, Okeh, and Bluebird, which catered to a specialized market and priced below the pop and classical fare on their main imprints.

After World War II, the rise of the independent recording label brought a flood of blues releases from small outfits and even tiny one-person operations. Suddenly, blues records were available in abundance.

Independent labels

Every so often, a major label actually records, releases, and even has some success with a contemporary blues performer (Robert Cray and Stevie Ray Vaughan come to mind). However, a large chunk of new blues music that gets on disc comes from small or burgeoning record labels that major label recording outfits don't own or distribute.

These independent (or *indie*) labels play a mighty big role in keeping the blues alive. The indies record new artists and preserve older traditions by keeping the music available in reissued form. The following list includes information on the best of the indie blues labels.

Ace Records

Ace Records in London, England, specializes in brand-name reissues of classic '50s and '60s American rock 'n' roll, rhythm and blues, and rockabilly records. Ace's catalog also includes several fine collections of vintage blues material by both famous and obscure artists that's unavailable elsewhere.

Alligator Records

Alligator Records is the dominant label in the modern blues recording scene and the essence of the contemporary blues label. Bruce Iglauer — a former sales clerk at Chicago's famed Jazz Record Mart, formed the company in 1971, shortly after he arrived in the city from his hometown of Ann Arbor, Michigan. At the time, Bruce went to bat for his favorite band — Hound Dog Taylor and the HouseRockers — trying unsuccessfully to get Delmark Records founder Bob Koester to record the band. Iglauer decided to record Hound Dog Taylor himself, thus starting Alligator as a one-man, one-artist operation, working out of his apartment and the trunk of his beat-up Chevrolet. Soon, more releases from Hound Dog, and releases from Fenton Robinson, Son Seals, and Koko Taylor, quickly established the label as the true, modern-day home of the blues.

Alligator hit its stride in the 1980s with great modern-day albums from Albert Collins and *Blues For Dummies* author Lonnie Brooks, and the label was soon collecting Grammy nominations and other awards for its efforts. Over the years, Alligator became more musically diverse, issuing albums by white blues-rock artists such as Roy Buchanan, Lonnie Mack, and Johnny Winter, along with new acoustic artists such as Corey Harris and Saffire — The Uppity Blues Women. Still based in Chicago, the label's motto — "Genuine Houserockin' Music" — states its intentions loud and clear, as Alligator stands poised as the label that will take electric Chicago blues straight into the 21st century.

Chess Records

Two visionary brothers, Leonard and Phil Chess, started the label in 1947 under the name Aristocrat. The label's name changed to Chess Records in 1950 and by then, the label had a firm reputation as Chicago's finest for blues recordings. Chess (and its various subsidiaries) is the one label that all blues collectors go after, paying exorbitant sums for the original 78 and 45 rpm singles and albums. Chess was the biggest label on the Chicago blues scene with the most promotional clout, which also happened to be issuing the best blues records by the best blues artists.

At one time or another, just about every blues musician in Chicago passed through Chess Records's door. Many people know Chess as the label that brought the music of Muddy Waters, Little Walter, Howlin' Wolf, Sonny Boy Williamson, John Lee Hooker, Jimmy Rogers, Buddy Guy, and Willie Dixon to the world. The label also made its mark in the early days of rock 'n' roll history with classic recordings by Chuck Berry and Bo Diddley.

Delmark Records

Delmark Records grew out of Bob Koester's Jazz Record Mart in Chicago, a haven for blues and folk musicians and second home for part-time employees (and famous bluesmen) Michael Bloomfield and Charlie Musselwhite. Delmark was one of the first labels to successfully translate the onstage energy of modern blues onto albums for the burgeoning folk market in the '60s.

With the issuance of Junior Wells's *Hoodoo Man Blues* and Magic Sam's *West Side Soul* albums, the story of the modern-day blues album begins with this label. Today, Delmark continues to thrive by reissuing its extensive back catalog and releasing new LPs by older, more traditional artists such as Brewer Phillips and Jimmie Lee Robinson.

Fat Possum Records

Fat Possum specializes in Mississippi blues (the label hails from the town of Oxford). This label offers the *real* stuff, the music that you hear in the juke joints on Saturday nights. With Fat Possum, you don't get dusty, archival recordings but rather that deliciously nasty electric blues played by artists laying it down for their neighbors and friends. The albums, as a result, are some of the crudest, most raw, and unvarnished music you're likely to hear in a contemporary blues recording context.

Classic juke joint performers, such as R.L. Burnside, Paul "Wine" Jones, and Junior Kimbrough, and off-the-wall delights like Cedell Davis, are the driving forces of the label.

Dig it, man! The happening '60s indie label scene

With the overwhelming popularity of rock 'n' roll, blues recording ground to a virtual halt by the mid-'50s. The indie record label business — at least the blues music end of it — came to life again in the early '60s, when folk and jazz labels such as Vanguard, Prestige Bluesville, and Elektra released albums from country-blues artists in the style of folk-music archives.

The labels created these albums as if they were preserving a long-lost tradition — which the blues, as a commercial entity, almost was at that time. This scholarly approach was evident in the liner notes (often dryly written by academics) and in the spartan production, often done intentionally to achieve a quaint, folky ambiance.

A blues revival hit by the mid-'60s when college students and other intellectual types started listening to the blues. The acoustic-based labels began issuing hard electric blues, as well, by a variety of artists as diverse as Buddy Guy and the original Paul Butterfield Blues Band. (Take a look at Chapter 3 for all the details on acoustic and electric blues.) At the same time, labels such as Testament and Arhoolie were issuing LPs that almost sounded like field recordings, documenting both acoustic and electric artists. The small indie reissue label also started up during this period — spearheaded by Yazoo — bringing rare recordings from the 1920s and 1930s to a new audience.

Malaco Records

Malaco Records, located in Jackson, Mississippi, takes the least traditional approach to the blues of all the contemporary labels. The company's main audience is one that likes their blues served with a large dollop of soul and R&B music. Malaco's *Down Home Blues* album by the late Z.Z. Hill proved that a whole new market existed for the blues, and the label has since become home to R&B stalwarts Bobby "Blue" Bland and Johnnie Taylor.

Rooster Blues Records

Living Blues magazine founder Jim O'Neal runs this label, which has its base in Clarksdale, in the heart of Mississippi. Intensely involved with the local blues scene, O'Neal sees the label as filling a void in the blues field. Rooster Blues issues recordings by artists who normally don't get a chance to get on disc, either because their respective styles are considered not commercial enough even by blues standards, or they're simply great artists who haven't recorded as much as they should. Excellent recordings by Robert "Bilbo" Walker, Eddie Shaw, Eddie C. Campbell, and Eddy Clearwater pepper the unique Rooster Blues catalog.

Rounder Records

Rounder, out of Cambridge, Massachusetts, isn't a blues label in the strictest sense, but nevertheless it's done much to further the cause. Basically a folk/world music imprint, Rounder's catalog took on a bluesier bent with the success of guitarist and singer George Thorogood. Rounder's release schedule includes issues by several fine blues artists, such as current favorites Johnny Adams, Marcia Ball, and Rory Block.

Sun Records

Sun Records was the artistic vision of one man, Sam Phillips, who was best known for discovering Elvis Presley, Johnny Cash, Roy Orbison, Carl Perkins, Charlie Rich, and Jerry Lee Lewis. Launching the rockabilly revolution in the '50s, Sam Phillips was a recording engineer who started a one-person operation called the Memphis Recording Service, better known as the Sun Studio, which is still a tourist attraction in Memphis today.

Phillips recorded all the local blues talent (Howlin' Wolf, B.B. King, Bobby "Blue" Bland, Ike Turner, and Doctor Ross among them). Then, he leased the results to the Chess brothers (and their Chess Records label in Chicago) and to the Bihari brothers (Jules, Joe, and Saul) who ran Modern/RPM Records in Los Angeles and recorded Elmore James, B.B. King, John Lee Hooker, and Etta James during the '50s and early '60s.

After starting the Sun label in 1952, Phillips produced, engineered, and released classic *sides* (the recording industry slang for the actual recording of a single performance — one *side* of the record) by Little Junior Parker, Doctor Ross, Joe Hill Louis, Little Milton, Billy "The Kid" Emerson, Big Walter

Horton, and James Cotton. In 1956, the twin successes of the Elvis Presley and Carl Perkins recording of "Blue Suede Shoes" made the label change its entire focus from blues to rockabilly and rock 'n' roll, writing a whole new chapter in American music history.

Vee-Jay Records

Vee-Jay wasn't the first African-American-owned record company, but it was the one of the most successful record companies of the modern era. Run by the husband and wife team of Vivian and James Bracken and located near Chess Records in Chicago, the initials of their first names became the company's logo.

The Vee-Jay catalog featured R&B (rhythm and blues) artists including the Dells, Dee Clark, Jerry Butler, and the Impressions. The peak of the label's blues output came with the recordings of John Lee Hooker and Jimmy Reed.

Major labels

With the advent of the compact disc, most of the major labels have reissued much of their back catalogs of previously recorded albums. All five of the blues majors own quite a bit of the old masters and have done a fair amount of buying up of smaller labels over the years. The major labels now have extensive blues catalogs to produce in the new CD format. The majority of these reissues come with detailed notes, vintage photos, and superior sound. The following is a look at what the majors have to offer the blues fan.

BMG

BMG owns RCA Victor, a label that recorded almost no blues music in the '50s and '60s. However, in the late '30s and through the '40s, the Victor (as it was know then) Bluebird subsidiary was the most popular of all blues labels underwritten by a major company. BMG's reissue series is just now starting to bring back great classic collections by Tampa Red, John Lee "Sonny Boy" Williamson, and Big Maceo Merriweather.

EMI

EMI is an English-based company that owns blues labels large and small — with most of them located on the West Coast. EMI's range includes the master holdings from Capitol (T-Bone Walker); Aladdin (Amos Milburn, Charles Brown, Papa Lightfoot); Imperial (Pee Wee Crayton, Lightnin' Hopkins, Lil Son Jackson); and later recordings on World Pacific (George "Harmonica" Smith).

MCA

MCA probably owns more labels holding blues material in their vaults than just about any other music company. MCA also boasts the most extensive blues reissue work of any major label. The reason for such productivity? MCA owns the Chess catalog, a treasure trove of blues history. You can't go wrong with just about anything in MCA's large Chess catalog. The MCA conglomerate offers blues on both budget and full-priced cassettes and disks.

But what's really impressive is MCA's other master holdings besides the Chess catalog. The company has masters from Duke/Peacock (Bobby "Blue" Bland, Gatemouth Brown, Junior Parker); ABC Paramount and Bluesway (B.B. King, John Lee Hooker, and Jimmy Reed); Excello (Slim Harpo, Lightnin' Slim), and earlier country-blues catalogs from labels such as Decca reposing in its vaults.

Sony

Sony owns Columbia Records, and that covers nearly everything from Robert Johnson's classic recordings to Johnny Winter's blues-rock sides of the early 1970s and lots more in between. Sony's Roots 'n' Blues series features extensive collections of Robert Johnson, Bessie Smith (several box sets), Mississippi John Hurt, and Blind Willie Johnson, as well as several artists' compilations.

Virgin

Virgin is a global concern with a large presence in straight-ahead pop music. Nevertheless, the company found it in its best interest to purchase the master holdings of several West Coast-based labels originally owned by the Bihari brothers. The holdings include RPM (Howlin' Wolf), Kent (B.B. King), Flair, Meteor (Elmore James), and Modern (John Lee Hooker). Now reissuing older material on its reactivated Flair label, this international label is making extremely tough-to-find sides available once again.

Other labels worth checking out

The following is a list of independent labels (and some noteworthy artists on those labels) that you can trust to deliver top-notch albums by contemporary electric blues bands and solo artists, and worthwhile reissues of rare material.

- Antone's (Kim Wilson, Lou Ann Barton, Snooky Pryor)
- Black Top (Gary Primich, Robert Ward, Snooks Eaglin)
- Blind Pig (Debbie Davies, Tommy Castro, Deborah Coleman)

- Blue Wave (Kim Lembo, Kim Simmonds, King Biscuit Boy)
- Bullseye Blues (Ronnie Earl, Pat Boyack, Smokey Wilson)
- Hightone (new releases and reissues of the Testament catalog)
- Ichiban (Jerry McCain, Luther "Houserocker" Johnson, Sandra Hall)
- Tone-Cool (Rod Piazza, Monster Mike Welch, David Maxwell)
- Yazoo (reissues of country blues: Charlie Patton, Son House, Blind Blake)

The 25 All-Time Classic Blues Numbers

Almost every song in this section is better known through numerous cover versions by rock groups and blues-rock artists. (A *cover* is one artist's version of another artist's record or song.) What helps to makes these tunes classics is that most audiences love these numbers and request them . . . a lot, which is also one of the reasons these songs are recorded so often. Here, we try to steer you to the best and original blues versions of these classic tunes.

The tunes listed in Table 7-1 are all classics of the first rank and are the ones that most blues folks like to jam on when they get together. If you're armed with the title of that song you want, the name of the artist, and the label the song was recorded on, almost any record clerk should be able to locate its current catalog number and steer you right to it, or special order the record if it's not in stock. (Some of these numbers are on the Blues For Dummies CD — "I'm Your Hoochie Coochie Man," "Killing Floor," "Let the Good Times Roll," and "Sweet Little Angel.")

Table 7-1	The Best of the Classics
Song	*Best Versions and Their Labels*
"Baby What You Want Me To Do"	Jimmy Reed (Vee-Jay)
"Back Door Man"	Howlin' Wolf (MCA-Chess)
"Boogie Chillen"	John Lee Hooker (Rhino)
"Born Under A Bad Sign"	Albert King (Rhino)
"Dust My Broom"	Elmore James (Rhino), Robert Johnson (Columbia), Hound Dog Taylor (Alligator)
"Everyday I Have The Blues"	Joe Williams (Verve), B.B. King (MCA), Lowell Fulson (Night Train)
"Got My Mojo Workin'"	Muddy Waters (MCA-Chess), Ann Cole (Flyright)

(continued)

Table 7-1 *(continued)*

Song	Best Versions and Their Labels
"Help Me"	Sonny Boy Williamson (MCA-Chess), Junior Wells (Vanguard)
"Hide Away"	Freddie King (Rhino), Eric Clapton (with John Mayall) (Mobile Fidelity), Lonnie Brooks (Alligator)
"I Just Want To Make Love To You"	Muddy Waters (MCA-Chess), Etta James (MCA-Chess)
"I'm A Man"	Bo Diddley (MCA-Chess), Muddy Waters (as "Mannish Boy") (MCA-Chess)
"I'm Your Hoochie Coochie Man"	Muddy Waters (MCA-Chess)
"It Hurts Me Too"	Elmore James (Rhino), Tampa Red (RCA)
"Key To The Highway"	Big Bill Broonzy (various pre–WWII labels), Little Walter (MCA-Chess), John Lee Hooker (Modern-Flair/Virgin)
"Killing Floor"	Howlin' Wolf (MCA-Chess)
"Let The Good Times Roll"	Louis Jordan (MCA), B.B. King (MCA), Koko Taylor (Alligator)
"Little Red Rooster"	Howlin' Wolf (as "The Red Rooster") (MCA-Chess), Big Mama Thornton (Arhoolie)
"Mama Talk To Your Daughter"	J.B. Lenoir (MCA-Chess), Magic Sam (Delmark)
"Rock Me Baby"	B.B. King (Flair), Muddy Waters (MCA-Chess), Hound Dog Taylor (Alligator)
"Rollin' And Tumblin'"	Baby Face Leroy (Delmark), Muddy Waters (MCA-Chess), Elmore James (Capricorn), Hambone Willie Newbern (as "Roll and Tumble Blues") (Yazoo)
"Stormy Monday Blues"	T-Bone Walker (Capitol), Bobby "Blue" Bland (MCA)
"Sweet Home Chicago"	Robert Johnson (Columbia), Magic Sam (Delmark)
"Sweet Little Angel"	B.B. King (MCA-Chess), Robert Nighthawk (as "Sweet Black Angel") (MCA-Chess)
"The Thrill Is Gone"	B.B. King (MCA)
"Wang Dang Doodle"	Howlin' Wolf (MCA-Chess), Koko Taylor (MCA-Chess)

The 25 Best Blues Albums (And a Couple Dozen Others Worth Owning)

You blues collectors who've had these recordings on your shelves for as long as you can remember may feel obliged to skip this section altogether (but then you'd have less to brag about your collection). For the rest of you, this list is where you can begin to build an assortment of essential blues recordings.

We list 25 smart purchases to get you started in collecting a variety of blues musical styles. Following each selection, we list another album in the "also recommended" category. If you purchased the main selection and found that you enjoyed it, you may want to pick up the "also recommended" selection, even if it's by another artist. It's not a second-rate selection, by any means, and it's a pretty safe bet you'll enjoy that one, too.

This section of the book also lists some collections (compilations and box sets) worthy of your attention. Compilations that include selections by several artists are an economical way to get an overview of various blues styles. Because blues music was primarily a singles-driven marketplace before the 1970s, many blues artists either didn't get a chance to record full albums or they didn't leave behind enough material to fill an entire LP. This means a large number of great one-off blues performances are littered throughout blues recording history and collections of these singles provide the easiest way to locate great performances in quantity.

Some long-time aficionados claim that blues was never meant to be listened to on a long-play configuration of any format (10-inch vinyl, 12-inch vinyl, cassettes, eight-tracks, or CDs), but only on singles and preferably on old, scratchy, and easily breakable 78s. Although some collectors have a romantic fascination with original blues recordings (and we admire their taste), in this chapter, we pretty much stick to albums and collections available on CD. That way, you can enjoy the music without having to devote your life to finding it.

We listed the following albums alphabetically because we consider *all* of them essential to digging the musical message and getting the blues story straight. Obtaining any of these albums from a well-stocked record store is fairly easy to do.

1. **Lonnie Brooks, *Bayou Lightning* (Alligator):** Every artist has a defining moment in his or her career, and this is when it all came together for this *Blues For Dummies* author. An album full of great songs played and sung from the heart, including the classic "You Know What My Body Needs."

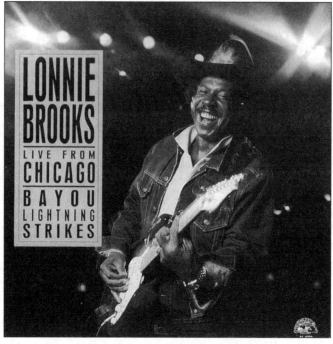

Also recommended: *Live From Chicago* (Alligator). Cut before an enthusiastic crowd at the B.L.U.E.S. Etcetera nightclub in the Windy City, this album captures great live renditions of many of Lonnie's best Alligator sides along with new material. His playing on "Hide Away" is textbook in its scope, pulling out every guitar virtuoso trick in the book.

2. **Ray Charles, *The Birth of Soul* (Rhino):** This is a very deluxe three-disc box set covering Ray Charles's unique style, which combines gospel, jazz, and heavy blues elements, to create just what this collection's title says. Plenty of blues among the early hits and a fine booklet with all the amenities make this an essential purchase.

Also recommended: Bobby "Blue" Bland, *I Pity The Fool/The Duke Recordings, Volume 1* (MCA). Another very important artist who mixed his brand of R&B with a large portion of the blues, Bland could shout or croon with equal authority. This two-CD set collects 44 tracks of intensely soulful music with blues sauce bubbling on top.

3. **Eric Clapton, *John Mayall's Bluesbreakers with Eric Clapton* (Mobile Fidelity):** You can hear Clapton very early in his career (1966 and fresh from defecting from the Yardbirds) and at the top of his game. This record includes great versions of "Hide Away" and "All Your Love" with a guitar tone that makes your stereo speakers positively sizzle.

Also recommended: *From the Cradle* (Reprise). In Eric's modern-day blues tribute album, he tips his hat to several of his early heroes (the influence of Buddy Guy's style is all over this album). This record captures the British guitar icon ripping up the fret board.

4. **Albert Collins, *Ice Pickin'* (Alligator):** Albert Collins had been recording for 20 years before this record came out and had the regional hits to show for it. But this 1978 session for Alligator was the one that introduced his sound to a large-scale audience. Although Albert Collins would go on to make several other successful albums in his career, *Ice Pickin'* was the one recording in which all the elements of his unique style came together like three cherries on a slot machine.

Also recommended: *Truckin' with Albert Collins* (MCA). These are Collins's earliest sides recorded in Texas. The album includes several of his signature instrumentals ("Frosty," "Frostbite") that made his reputation as the Master of the Telecaster.

5. **Buddy Guy, *The Very Best Of* (Rhino):** Buddy has survived to become the elder statesman of Chicago Blues, with his own nightclub and Grammy awards to show for it. This 18-track collection provides a nice introductory overview to his early recordings that established him as a Chicago legend back in the late '50s. Highlights include sides with Junior Wells in the late '60s and sessions with Eric Clapton and Dr. John in 1972. Nobody tears up a guitar quite like Buddy Guy. Just ask Eric.

Also recommended: Junior Wells, *Hoodoo Man Blues* (Delmark). The first electric Chicago blues band album geared for the modern-day market. Just a regular working band doing what they did in the clubs, laying it down hard, heavy, and real. Buddy Guy shining brightly on lead guitar makes this one very inspired session.

6. **John Lee Hooker, *The Ultimate Collection* (Rhino):** A two-CD set that begins with the early Detroit recordings ("Boogie Chillen," "Teaching the Blues," "Crawling Kingsnake") that knocked the blues world for a loop in the late '40s. The set finishes with a 1990 duet with Bonnie Raitt on "I'm In The Mood." The best introduction available to this ultra-important artist, covering all the high points of one of the most prolific recording careers in the history of the blues.

Also recommended: Charlie Patton, *Founder of the Delta Blues* (Yazoo). Robert Johnson's predecessor and the first great star of the Delta style back in the 1920s, Charlie Patton was a masterful guitarist and a singer with a powerful voice. A major influence on both John Lee Hooker and Howlin' Wolf, this album gives you a nice cross section of Charlie Patton's best-known tunes.

7. **Lightnin' Hopkins, *Mojo Hand: The Lightnin' Hopkins Anthology* (Rhino):** A two-CD set that follows 21 years of Lightnin' Hopkins's recording career for 21 different labels! You can't find deeper Texas blues than that of Lightnin' Hopkins, and this collection finds him working solo, with various band configurations and even a tap dancer on one tune! He's the man who made Lonnie Brooks want to play a guitar.

Also recommended: Frankie Lee Sims, *Lucy Mae Blues* (Specialty). Another Texas blues artist who mined similar turf with a distinctly electric bent to his playing, Frankie Lee Sims sounds like a more rock 'n' roll version of Lightnin' Hopkins, but every bit as country and lowdown. If you want great lyrics and a driving beat, this is it.

8. **Howlin' Wolf, *His Best* (MCA-Chess):** The blues has no sound heavier or scarier than in the recordings of Howlin' Wolf. This album collects 20 of the very best with superlative audio. Several tunes ("Killing Floor," "Smokestack Lightnin'," "Spoonful," "Back Door Man," "Goin' Down Slow," and "The Red Rooster") have since become blues classics.

Also recommended: *Howlin' Wolf Rides Again* (Flair). These 1951–1952 recordings that Howlin' Wolf made in Memphis for Sam Phillips at the Sun studios feature the wildly distorted guitar work of Willie Johnson, plus a small band pounding the beat home like there's no tomorrow, and a ferocious excitement that jumps out of your speakers. This is Wolf at his early best.

9. **Elmore James, *The Sky Is Crying: The Best Of* (Rhino):** The father of amplified slide guitar, Elmore James had a sound and style that influenced both first-generation electric Chicago blues artists and rock musicians a whole ocean away. All of his classics (with "Dust My Broom," "It Hurts Me Too," and "The Sky Is Crying," among them) are on this collection, which makes it a perfect introduction to his music and to electric slide guitar in general.

Also recommended: J.B. Hutto, *Hawk Squat* (Delmark). This record features J.B. Hutto, one of Elmore's most explosive disciples, ripping it up with a band that includes Sunnyland Slim and Bo Diddley's original drummer, Frank Kirkland. Its highlights include "Hip Shakin'" and the title track.

10. **Robert Johnson, *The Complete Recordings* (Columbia/Legacy):** The ultimate country-blues artist and the ultimate introduction to the fullest flowering of the Mississippi Delta blues style. (Check out Chapter 3 for more information on Delta Blues.) You get all the great songs that made Robert Johnson a legend ("Crossroads," "Sweet Home Chicago," "Love In Vain," and "Dust My Broom") and helped plant the seeds of electric Chicago blues.

Also recommended: Various Artists, *The Roots of Robert Johnson* (Yazoo). This collection offers 14 tunes that shaped a large part of Robert Johnson's repertoire. Son House is the major highlight with two of his original recordings from 1930, "My Black Mama" and "Preachin' the Blues," laying them down with a delivery that can only be described as ferocious. (Head over to Chapter 8 for more information on Robert Johnson and Son House.) The collection also includes original versions of Kokomo Arnold's "Milk Cow Blues" and Hambone Willie Newbern's "Roll And Tumble Blues," making this a one-stop Delta Blues primer.

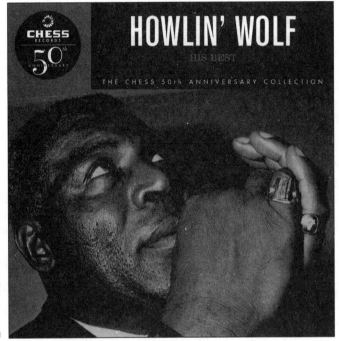

Figure 7-2:
The perfect
introduction
to one of
the true
blues
originals
(photo
courtesy of
MCA-Chess
Records).

11. **Albert King, *The Ultimate Collection* (Rhino):** Next to B.B. King, Albert King was the most influential single-string soloist in the blues field. Just *how* influential is easy to discern in this 2-CD, 39-track anthology. You can find all the hits and a nice cross section of material that starts with his early sessions in 1954 and goes up to 1984's "Phone Booth."

    Also recommended: *Born Under a Bad Sign* (Mobile Fidelity). After Albert cut this album with Booker T. and the MGs in the mid-'60s, the blues turned a corner. The music reached a whole new audience while simultaneously creating a new sound and style in the bargain. When you're talking influential modern-day blues albums, make sure that this one's near the top of the list.

12. **B.B. King, *Live at the Regal* (MCA):** One of the first great live blues albums, it's chockful of some of B.B. King's best playing. This album was as influential to a new generation of blues players as his early sides were to his contemporaries in the black community. A whole new generation of white players were convinced to try their hand at the blues. File under Essential.

Also recommended: *Singin' the Blues/The Blues* (Flair). Two of B.B. King's early LPs on one CD. These are his 1950s recordings for the Bihari brothers (see the section on "Sun Records" earlier in this chapter) that were so very influential in shaping modern electric blues. These recordings are full of nasty, distorted, stinging guitar work, fierce vocals, and classic songs galore.

13. **Freddie King, *Hide Away: The Best Of* (Rhino):** Freddie had a pile of hits in the early 1960s, mostly catchy instrumentals like "Hide Away." He was a fine vocalist, as well, and this 20-track album takes you through all the highlights, straight into his later blues-rock style of the early 1970s with classics like "Going Down."

    Also recommended: *Just Pickin'* (Modern Blues). Two of Freddie King's best instrumental albums recorded for King Records in the early- and mid-1960s on one disc. It features catchy, snappy little compositions with loads of high-voltage picking. Eric Clapton must have worn these records down to the labels studying King's style.

14. **Magic Sam, *West Side Soul* (Delmark):** Magic Sam was already a Chicago West Side legend when this album introduced him to the burgeoning blues revival crowd the world over. Considered a high-water mark of modern-day blues recordings simply because it is such an inspired session.

    Also recommended: *Magic Sam Live* (Delmark). You hear some amazing recordings of Sam working his magic at the Alex Club in Chicago in 1963–1964 and at the 1969 Ann Arbor Blues Festival. The recordings (both done by fans) are low-fidelity, but Sam's whiplash exuberance throughout makes it Class A all the way, negating any concerns audiophiles may have.

15. **Robert Nighthawk, *Live On Maxwell Street* (Rounder):** With Nighthawk playing raw, highly amplified slide guitar (accompanied by a second guitarist and a drummer) and recorded right on Chicago's Maxwell Street, this is one of the most amazing live blues albums of all time. Seldom do records come loaded with this much ambiance — you can hear cars driving by while the musicians play over the noise of the traffic.

    Also recommended: Earl Hooker, *Blue Guitar* (Paula). A true guitar virtuoso, Hooker learned how to play from Nighthawk, but could also play in a multiplicity of styles besides slide, usually backing other vocalists or playing instrumentals. This is one for the guitar connoisseurs.

16. **Jimmy Reed, *Speak The Lyrics To Me, Mama Reed* (Vee Jay):** No blues artist made the pop charts as many times as Jimmy Reed, and no one's songs were easier to play and sing. His simple, unfettered style yielded one blues classic after another ("Big Boss Man," "Baby What You Want Me To Do," "Honest I Do," "Going To New York," and "Bright Lights, Big City"), and the best of them are all right here.

Also recommended: Slim Harpo, *The Best Of Slim Harpo* (Excello/Hip-O). Slim Harpo was Jimmy Reed's Louisiana counterpart who contributed hits of his own with the classics "I'm A King Bee," "Raining In My Heart," "Shake Your Hips," "Got Love If You Want It," and "Baby, Scratch My Back," all of which are included in this 16-track collection.

17. **Otis Rush,** *1956–1958 Cobra Recordings* **(Paula):** Rush was always one of the most intense of the Chicago blues players and these are the recordings that made his reputation. Includes the original versions of "Double Trouble" and "I Can't Quit You, Baby" that would later inspire younger blues-rockers, among them Jimmy Page and Stevie Ray Vaughan.

   Also recommended: *So Many Roads–Live* (Delmark). Otis Rush comes to Japan, playing and singing his heart out. Loaded with great solos and impassioned singing, this is one of the best modern-day live blues albums.

18. **Bessie Smith,** *The Bessie Smith Collection* **(Columbia):** The Empress of the Blues has several box sets of her complete recordings available, but this 16-track, single-disc collection makes the perfect introduction to one of the all-time greatest voices in musical history.

   Also recommended: *Ma Rainey* (Milestone). As a staple act on the tent show circuit, Ma Rainey predated Bessie Smith. While she didn't have the amazing chops of Bessie, she could flat out sing the blues with a big, contralto voice that filled up a room without any amplification. This 24-track compilation features all her best tunes, making it another classic female blues purchase of the highest order. (For more on Ma Rainey and Bessie Smith, see Chapter 5.)

19. **Hound Dog Taylor,** *Beware Of The Dog!* **(Alligator):** Hound Dog and the HouseRockers were Chicago's ultimate party band, and this live album captures their no-holds-barred approach to great effect. Nobody made a slide guitar sound this nasty, ever.

   Also recommended: *Hound Dog Taylor & The HouseRockers* (Alligator). With a sound straight out of the juke joints, this raw, unvarnished debut album helped introduce Hound Dog and Alligator Records to the world.

20. **Koko Taylor,** *Queen of the Blues* **(Alligator):** The big-voiced Ms. Taylor has cut several fine albums, but guest appearances from James Cotton, Lonnie Brooks, Albert Collins, and Son Seals make this one a particular standout.

   Also recommended: *Etta James Rocks the House* (MCA-Chess). Etta James gets down and dirty with a pickup band in a Nashville club in 1964. It includes great versions of "Sweet Little Angel" and Jimmy Reed's "Baby What You Want Me to Do," in which she spot-on imitates the harmonica solo with nothing more than her singing voice.

21. **Stevie Ray Vaughan,** *Greatest Hits* **(Epic):** This single-disc collection is a perfect introduction to this Texas legend — Epic picked the very best from Stevie's various albums. This is the guitarist who changed the course of blues music in the 1980s and is still influencing it today.

Figure 7-3:
One of the
great blues
party
albums
(photo
courtesy of
Alligator
Records
and Artist
Manage-
ment, Inc.).

Also recommended: *Texas Flood* (Epic). Stevie's 1983 debut not only made the *pop* charts (hitting Number 38) and was nominated for two Grammy awards, but also truly signaled a whole new direction for blues to head. His guitar introduction on "Pride and Joy" alone is worth the price of admission.

22. **T-Bone Walker, *The Complete Imperial Recordings* (EMI):** Before B.B. King or Freddie King, Albert King or Albert Collins, Gatemouth Brown, or even Chuck Berry, for that matter, there was T-Bone Walker, plugging in and chopping his way through the forest so that all who followed could venture down the blues highway. This box set captures some good examples of much of that wood cutting that forged a new chapter in the blues. File this one under Textbook Playing.

Also recommended: Clarence "Gatemouth" Brown, *The Original Peacock Recordings* (Rounder). Gatemouth was one of T-Bone's most inspired (and eclectic) students. These are Gatemouth's earliest recordings and, as such, are classic examples of electric Texas blues. (For more on the Texas blues sound, see Chapter 3.)

23. **Little Walter, *His Best* (MCA-Chess):** This 20-track anthology pinpoints the place where modern amplified blues harmonica playing began. While working in the original Muddy Waters band, Little Walter inno-vated and brought to perfection the *now* standard Chicago harp-playing

technique of honkin' through a cheap mike that's plugged into a guitar amp. These are the sides that made him the Charlie Parker of blues harmonica and the place where all amplified blues harp players start going to school. Twenty classics of Chicago blues in its golden era, loaded to the brim with textbook classic playing. It really *doesn't* get any better than this.

Also recommended: Jimmy Rogers, *The Complete Chess Recordings* (MCA-Chess). The other great star of the Muddy Waters band was guitarist-vocalist Jimmy Rogers, whose solo career began in 1950 with the now classic "That's All Right." This two-CD set features a truckload of great songs from Jimmy Rogers and equally great harmonica playing from Little Walter Jacobs and Big Walter Horton, whose high-compression solo on "Walkin' By Myself" is alone worth the sticker price. This is classic Chicago blues.

24. **Muddy Waters,** *His Best, 1947 to 1955* **(MCA-Chess):** These recordings changed the blues world forever. You can hear Muddy Waters progress from a Delta blues guitar soloist to the architect of the first great electric Chicago blues band. This is the sound of electric blues history being made. (There's also a companion volume to this set that picks up Muddy's career from 1956 to 1964.)

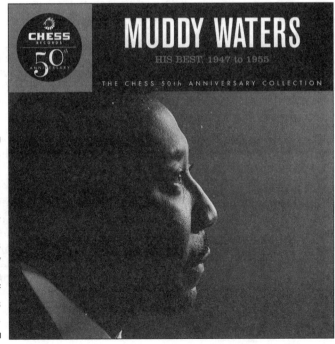

Figure 7-4:
A solid collection of the performances that made blues history (photo courtesy of MCA-Chess Records).

Also recommended: *Live At Newport–1960* (MCA-Chess). Muddy Waters with one of his greatest bands — including James Cotton, Pat Hare, and Otis Spann — show the jazz crowd how it's done in Chicago. This recording features the definitive version of Muddy's signature tune, "Got My Mojo Working."

25. **Sonny Boy Williamson,** *His Best* **(MCA-Chess):** One of the great stylists of the blues, Sonny Boy simply blew the best old-time harmonica, wrote the most interesting songs, and delivered them with a voice that was totally unique and instantly recognizable.

Also recommended: *King Biscuit Time* (Arhoolie). Sonny Boy's first recordings in 1951 for the Jackson, Mississippi-based Trumpet label. Includes the original version of "Eyesight to the Blind."

You may also want to check out these blues compilations, which are not only a good place to start a blues record collection, but give you lots of bang for your record-buying buck.

- ✔ *The Alligator 25th Anniversary Collection* **(Alligator):** A good cross section of modern-day blues and a great introduction to the Alligator label and its artists.

- ✔ *Blues Classics 1927–1969* **(MCA):** A really nice three-CD set of some of the most influential blues songs of all time in their original versions. Great sound restoration, informative notes, and attractive packaging make this a must-have.

- ✔ *Blues Masters, Volumes 1–15* **(Rhino):** A cross section of nearly all the styles and genres covered in this book and a perfect introduction to each of them. By the way, three of the volumes in the series (*Harmonica Classics, Slide Guitar Classics,* and *Blues Originals*) were compiled and annotated by author Cub Koda.

- ✔ *Chess Blues Box* **(MCA-Chess):** All the essential tracks and rarities from this legendary label are here for you to savor on this deluxe four-CD set; plus it comes with a booklet full of great photos and all the information that you need to get the big Chicago blues picture.

- ✔ *Chicago/The Blues/Today!, Volumes 1, 2 and 3* **(Vanguard):** These sessions include dynamic performances from Otis Rush, Junior Wells, Buddy Guy, Otis Spann, J.B. Hutto, Johnny Shines, Johnny Young, and the achingly beautiful harp work of Big Walter Horton. A highly influential set at the time of its release, it introduced many of these artists to a whole new audience. Rough, raw-sounding takes that represent authentic South Side Chicago music from the mid-'60s are captured in these volumes.

Chapter 8

Where to Head to Hear the Blues

● ●

In This Chapter

▶ Checking out blues clubs

▶ Catching up on festivals around the country

▶ Tuning in to the blues on the radio

● ●

*W*e're happy to report that blues is alive, thriving, and more popular than ever (but then we're partial to the blues). You don't have to search very far to hear quality blues music, but to save you some legwork, we've assembled information in this chapter that will help guide you to where the best blues music is playing.

Hear It Live: Blues Clubs

So, maybe you own some totally classic blues CDs that you play at maximum volume every Friday night. Or, you've been known to sing the blues in the shower or while driving to work. Maybe you've seen those blues legends specials on VH-1 at midnight. But isn't it time you ventured out to hear the blues the best way possible — performed live while you're surrounded by other blues lovers?

To encourage you in that endeavor, we provide a list of some of the best blues clubs in the country, including several of our favorite smaller clubs and venues that are off the beaten track for those of you who are more adventurous. We didn't have room to include all the great places that offer blues music entertainment, but this chapter should give you a good start on exploring the live blues music scene in the U.S. Your town probably has an excellent live blues venue or two, so get out there and check them out!

Nationwide chains

If you're ever in doubt about the continued popularity of the blues, just keep your eye on the growth of blues club chains across the land.

B.B. King's Blues Club

B.B.'s two large and friendly club and restaurant facilities host the best of the blues nightly. You just may see B.B. pop his head in, too.

> 1000 Universal Center Drive, Suite 222, Universal City, CA 91608; 818-622-5464

> 143 Beale St., Memphis; 901-524-KING

Chicago B.L.U.E.S.

These may be the best-known blues clubs in Chicago. The original B.L.U.E.S. is a small place with big sounds that packs them in almost every night. The sister club ETCETERA was built to handle larger crowds.

> B.L.U.E.S., 2519 N. Halsted St.; 773-528-1012

> B.L.U.E.S. ETCETERA, 1124 W. Belmont; 773-525-8989

The New York City branch features Chicago-style blues with local and national acts nightly.

> Chicago B.L.U.E.S., 73 Eighth Avenue, New York; 212-924-9755

House of Blues

Founded by Isaac Tigrett, who started the Hard Rock Cafe in London in 1971, the first House of Blues opened in Cambridge, Massachusetts in 1992. (Actor Dan Aykroyd is an investor in the chain.) Now with six locations, the House of Blues features rock, country, and R&B bands, as well as blues acts.

> 96 Winthrop St., Cambridge; 617-491-BLUE

> 329 N. Dearborn, Chicago; 312-527-2583

> 8430 Sunset Blvd., Hollywood; 213-848-5100

> 225 Decatur St., New Orleans; 504-529-2583

> 4640 Highway 17 South, North Myrtle Beach; 803-272-3000

> 1490 East Buena Vista Drive, Orlando; 407-934-BLUE

Clubs listed by city

With hundreds of gigs a year among us, we get to know what's out there on the blues scene. In this chapter, we list some of the clubs we know best, so your first live blues experience is as awe-inspiring as it should be.

Our apologies to all the blues venues out there that we didn't have room to list. But, we'll make it up to you by telling our readers to check out some other information resources on blues clubs, which we note at the end of this section of the chapter.

Atlanta

Blind Willie's: 828 N. Highland Avenue; 404-873-BLUE. Blind Willie's stages the best of the national and local blues acts. The club is named after one of Atlanta's most-famous blues players, Blind Willie McTell, and features blues, zydeco, and folk music nightly.

Austin

Antone's: 213 W. 5th Street; 512-474-5314. The famed Antone's has been a blues mecca for decades. Dozens of blues legends have performed here at one time or another in their careers. Antone's features three music rooms, a patio, a restaurant, and music nightly.

Bethesda

Twist and Shout: 4800 Auburn Ave.; 301-652-3383. This club in the Washington, D.C., suburb features live blues music, plus rock, Cajun, and zydeco on weekend nights.

Boston

Johnny D's Uptown Restaurant and Music Club: 17 Holland St., Somerville; 617-776-9667. This club was the 1992 winner of the W.C. Handy "Keeping the Blues Alive" Club of the Year Award. The club features national acts almost every night.

Buffalo

Lafayette Tap Room: 320 Pearl; 716-855-8800. Grab a meal in the restaurant downstairs, and then head upstairs to boogie. Live blues is played every night of the week.

My name is on the door

It seems to be a trend of late. Recently Buddy Guy did it. Then B.B. King followed suit. And now, John Lee Hooker's gotten into the act. Blues artists are opening their own clubs in greater numbers than ever before.

"It's important for a blues musician to own a club," says B.B. King, whose name is on the door of B.B. King's Blues Bar & Restaurant in Los Angeles and Memphis. "We know how important it is to increase the number of venues for blues musicians. Every club that opens gives blues musicians another opportunity to play."

John Lee Hooker says he's "real proud" of his place, John Lee Hooker's Boom Boom Room in San Francisco, which opened in October 1997. John Lee occasionally visits the club to meet and greet patrons whenever he's in town. "The club is something I dreamed about for a long time," he said.

Buddy Guy, who has made Buddy Guy's Legends into a Chicago institution, plays a series of concerts every January and is at the club most nights when he's not touring.

Charlotte

Double Door Inn: 281 E. Independent; 704-376-1446. National and local acts play here nightly. Stevie Ray Vaughan, Eric Clapton, and other blues guitar heroes have plugged in their axes here at one time or another.

Chicago

Blue Chicago: 736 N. Clark St.; 312-642-6261, and **Blue Chicago on Clark:** 536 N. Clark St.; 312-661-0100. Two popular sister clubs on the city's near north side. Between the two, they offer live blues music every night of the week. On most nights, a single cover gets you into both places.

Buddy Guy's Legends: 754 S. Wabash Ave.; 312-427-0333. This spacious South Loop club hosts top-notch performers. Buddy hangs out whenever he's in town and usually plays a series of concerts every January.

Checkerboard Lounge: 423 E. 43rd. St.; 773-624-3240. This Chicago blues music institution on the city's south side offers great live music Thursday through Monday.

Kingston Mines: 2548 N. Halsted Ave.; 773-477-4646. A well-known blues club that's open Sunday through Friday until 4 a.m.; on Saturday, Kingston Mines stays open until 5 a.m.

Cleveland

Wilbert's: 1360 W. 9th; 216-771-2583. This clubs holds 300 patrons, but you can still get right up front and close to the bands on stage. The menu is tops.

Dallas

Blue Cat Blues: 2617 Commerce; 214-744-2287. Situated on the east edge of downtown Dallas, this club features local and national blues acts nightly.

Denver

Brendan's: 1624 Market; 303-595-0609. Shoot some pool, order some grub from the inventive menu, and partake of the blues played nightly, featuring local and national acts.

Delray Beach

Backroom: 16 Atlantic Ave.; 561-243-9110. One of the top blues clubs in Florida, featuring local acts during the week and touring acts on the weekend.

Detroit

Soup Kitchen: 1585 Franklin; 313-259-1374. This club has the distinction of being the place where _Blues For Dummies_ authors Lonnie Brooks and Cub Koda first met when they jammed here in 1984. One of the oldest saloons in Detroit and one of the premier blues clubs in town.

Ft. Lauderdale

Musician's Exchange Café: 729 W. Sunrise Blvd.; 954-764-5079. This club features blues and jazz on Wednesday nights and again on Friday through Monday nights in a space resembling an old-style Greenwich Village bistro.

Houston

Billy Blues: 6025 Richmond Avenue; 713-266-9294. This club seats 150 in the main bar and restaurant; a separate blues room accommodates 250. Blues is featured every night except Sunday.

Indianapolis

Slippery Noodle Inn: 372 S. Meridian St.; 317-631-6974. This is not only the largest and best-known blues club in Indy, the Slippery Noodle is also the oldest bar in town — it's been in business since 1850.

Kansas City, Missouri

Grand Emporium: 3832 Main St.; 816-531-1504. Known for its prize-winning barbecue sauce and Creole menu, this club is host to everyone who's anyone in the blues world. You can hear mostly blues and some jazz music Monday through Saturday.

Lincoln

Zoo Bar: 136 N. 14th St.; 402-475-3094. This venerable blues venue plays host to local and national acts every night of the week except Sunday.

Los Angeles

Blue Café: 210 Promenade North, Long Beach; 562-983-7111. This beach-front club features blues music six nights a week.

Harvelle's: 1432 Fourth Street, Santa Monica; 310-395-1676. Operating since 1931, this club has a down-home atmosphere and features live music nightly.

Jack's Sugar Shack: 1707 N. Vine St., Hollywood; 213-466-7005. This club is large, well-lit, and located in what once was a tropical-theme restaurant. Many Alligator Records artists have played here.

Lighthouse: 30 Pier Avenue, Hermosa Beach; 310-376-9833. A nautical-theme club close to the beach, the Lighthouse features blues on a regular basis.

Memphis

Blues City Cafe/Band Box: 138 Beale St.; 901-526-3637. This club is located across the street from B.B. King's place. It has a down-to-earth, comfortable atmosphere, and features music nightly.

Rum Boogie Café: 182 Beale St.; 901-528-0150. Load up on red beans, rice, and cornbread while you take in acts on two separate stages — one devoted to R&B acts, and one for strictly the blues. Live music nightly.

Miami

Tobacco Road: 626 S. Miami Avenue; 305-374-1198. This downtown tavern dating from the early 1900s has welcomed the biggest names in the blues and R&B world.

Minneapolis

The Blues Saloon: 601 Western Ave. North; 612-228-9959. The best blues joint in the area is tucked away in what used to be the ballroom of a neighborhood bar and features a large dance floor.

The Cabooze: 917 Cedar Ave., S.; 612-338-6425. Two doors down from Whiskey Junction, this club is long on atmosphere and features blues acts regularly.

Whiskey Junction: 901 Cedar Ave., S.; 612-338-9550. This club offers a steady stream of local blues talent and a blues jam on Monday nights.

Nashville

Boardwalk Café: 4114 Nolanville Road; 615-832-5104

Bourbon Street Blues Bar: 220 Printer's Alley; 615-242-5837

Third and Lindsley: 818 Third Avenue South; 615-259-1597

These three clubs are our favorites in Nashville, and all feature blues music nightly.

New Orleans

Muddy Water's: 8301 Oak St.; 504-445-2582. This large neighborhood club near Tulane University features blues music two days a week.

Tipitina's: 501 Napolean Ave.; 504-895-8477. Countless major blues acts have passed through Tipitina's, the legendary New Orleans nightclub that features music nightly.

New York

Blue Note: 131 W. Third St.; 212-475-8592. New York's premier blues and jazz supper club has featured leading blues artists including B.B. King and Koko Taylor.

Manny's Car Wash: 1558 Third Avenue; 212-369-BLUES. Manny's is a small club that books well-regarded national and local blues acts and features Chicago blues sounds, New Orleans blues, jam sessions, and zydeco.

Tramps: 51 W. 21st Street; 212-727-7788. A large, loft-like space featuring music nightly, including blues, rock, and zydeco.

San Francisco

John Lee Hooker's Boom Boom Room: 1601 Fillmore St.; 415-673-8000. When he's not touring, John Lee occasionally visits his club, which opened in October 1997.

Larry Blake's R&B Café: 2367 Telegraph Ave., Berkeley; 510-848-0886. Well-known blues artists have been known to drop in on the club's Monday night blues jam.

Slim's: 333 11th Street; 415-522-0333. This fashionable bar and restaurant seats 300 and serves California cuisine. Slim's specializes in homegrown music including jazz, blues, and alternative rock. ("Slim," by the way, is musician Boz Scaggs.)

Memorable nights at Buddy Guy's Legends

Clapton's three-night stand: In November 1994, as part of a four-city, small-club tour, Eric Clapton played three sold-out shows. This was a once-in-a-lifetime chance to see Clapton play the music he loves in an intimate setting and jamming with Lonnie Brooks and Otis Rush.

Buddy jams with Jeff Beck and Stevie Ray Vaughan: During the Chicago portion of Beck and Vaughan's "The Fire and The Fury" tour, these two guitar greats stopped by the club in August 1989. The impromptu jam was one of the best in the club's history.

Albert Collins and Buddy Guy pair up: This 1990 jam featured two of blues music's most influential and entertaining guitarists. It was filmed and released on video as *Blues Alive*. Junior Wells also joined in.

The return of Luther Allison: Luther's appearance at Legends on February 20, 1993, was his first in Chicago after a long hiatus in Europe. Luther played one of the club's best shows ever to a sold-out crowd.

Buddy records *The Real Deal*: Recorded live during a three-night stretch in May 1994, Buddy, G. E. Smith, and the Saturday Night Live Band, along with special guest Johnnie Johnson, were at the top of their game. *The Real Deal* became one of the most popular Buddy Guy albums.

Stanhope, New Jersey

Stanhope House: 45 Main St.; 973-347-0458. Just about all the greats, including Muddy Waters, Willie Dixon, James Cotton, and Junior Wells, have played here over the past 25 years. The club is housed in a 200-year-old building.

Tampa

Skipper's Smoke House: 910 Skipper Road; 813-977-6474. This indoor/outdoor club can accommodate 800 people and features blues music eight times a month.

Off the beaten track

Artis's: 1249 E. 87th Street, Chicago; 773-734-0491. This bright and modern club features a large horseshoe-shaped bar and a stage situated in the middle of the room.

Big Cities: 905 E. State, Rockford, IL; 815-965-6026. This club features local and national blues acts Fridays and Saturdays.

The Blue Bouquet: 1010 Main Street, Boise; 208-345-6605. This Idaho club features blues nightly.

Continental Club: 1315 S. Congress Ave., Austin; 512-441-2444. An Austin institution since the 1950s, this club presents blues on weeknights from 5 p.m. to 8 p.m.

The Crossroads: Sunflower Avenue, 705 North State, Clarksdale, MS; 601-624-5108. This popular blues club is right in the heart of the Mississippi Delta region.

Fitzgerald's: 6615 Roosevelt, Berwyn, IL; 708-788-2118. This club features all types of American music and has long supported the blues community.

Rhythm Kitchen Café: 125 Ottawa, Suite 100, Grand Rapids, MI; 616-774-4199. Blues is featured here nightly.

Rosa's: 3420 W. Armitage Ave., Chicago; 773-342-0452. This venerable blues club has an intimate atmosphere and terrific blues music nightly. A must if you're doing the Chicago blues club circuit.

Subway Lounge: 619 W. Pearl Street (basement of the Summers Hotel), Jackson, MS; 601-353-2408. One of the oldest clubs in Jackson, it frequently features live blues on the weekend.

If you want a more in-depth listing of nearly every blues joint in the nation, we recommend *The Jazz and Blues Lover's Guide to the U.S.* by Christiane Bird (Addison Wesley Publishing Company). The guide includes 900 clubs in every region of the U.S., many of them featuring blues music lineups. A more up-to-date guide (although less detailed) is *Fodor's Rock & Roll Traveler USA* by Tim Perry and Ed Glinert (Fodor's). *Living Blues* magazine also publishes an inexpensive biannual national blues directory listing club addresses, blues society addresses, booking agents, and more.

Blues Festivals

You know the formula: a little sunshine, a few choice beverages, big crowds of music lovers, and loads of bands on multiple stages. That's the festival scene in a nutshell, and every host city adds its own special ingredients to the formula. It's each festival's special personality that makes the festival circuit one of our favorite performing experiences.

For a complete list of festivals, we suggest that you consult *Living Blues* magazine's May/June edition, which features festival schedules. The biannual *Living Blues Directory* also lists festivals (for information, call 601-232-5993). On the Web, the site www.bluesfestivals.com is also a great source of information.

The following festivals are the ones to watch for:

B.B. King Homecoming and Indian Bayou Festival: Indianola, MS — Scheduled for the last weekend in May or the first weekend in June in B.B. King's hometown.

Beale Street Music Festival: Memphis — Scheduled for the first weekend in May.

Chicago Blues Festival: Chicago — Scheduled for Thursday through Sunday in the first weekend in June.

Eureka Springs Blues Festival: Eureka Springs, AR — Scheduled for the weekend following Memorial Day, from Thursday through Sunday.

Kalamazoo Blues Festival: Kalamazoo, MI — Scheduled for a weekend in mid-June.

Kansas City Jazz & Blues Festival: Kansas City, MO — Scheduled for the third weekend in July.

King Biscuit Blues Festival: Helena, AR — Scheduled for the second weekend in October.

Long Beach Blues Festival: Long Beach, CA — Scheduled for Labor Day weekend.

Memphis Blues Festival: Memphis, TN — Scheduled for a weekend in August.

Mississippi Delta Blues Festival: Greenville, MS — Scheduled for the third weekend in September.

Mississippi Valley Blues Festival: Davenport, IA — Scheduled for the first full weekend in July.

Monterey Bay Blues Festival: Monterey, CA — Scheduled for the fourth weekend in June.

New Orleans Jazz and Heritage Festival: New Orleans — Scheduled for the last weekend in April through the first weekend in May.

Pocono Blues Festival: Lake Harmony, PA — Scheduled for the last weekend in July.

San Francisco Blues Festival: San Francisco — Scheduled for the third weekend in September.

Blues cruises

Put two hot trends together — blues and boat cruises — and it adds up to days of nonstop food, sunshine, and jamming 'til dawn. We recommend the Ultimate Rhythm & Blues Cruise, produced by Ultimate Cruises, Inc. and the Grand Emporium, the award-winning Kansas City, Missouri, blues club. The cruises are produced by blues lovers for blues lovers, and feature after-hours jams that go from midnight to sunup, artist workshops, and the opportunity to sun yourself poolside next to artists such as Taj Mahal, Buckwheat Zydeco, and The Radiators. Ultimate Cruises can be reached at 800-886-6132 or at their Web site: www.ultimatecruises.com.

St. Louis Blues Heritage Festival: St. Louis — Scheduled for a weekend in mid-August.

W.C. Handy Blues & Barbecue Festival: Henderson, KY — Scheduled for one full week beginning the second Sunday in June.

W.C. Handy Music Festival: Florence, Sheffield, Tuscumbia, and Muscle Shoals, AL — Scheduled for the first Sunday in August through the following Saturday.

Blues Competitions

The goal of any blues competition is to cultivate new talent and give blues fans a chance to see future stars in the making. The following are a couple of our favorite competitions.

Bluestock International Blues Talent Competition

This competition is sponsored by The Blues Foundation, the Memphis-based organization that helps to keep the blues alive. Blues organizations affiliated with the foundation stage regional competitions and send the top unsigned artists from their regions to compete in the finals held in Memphis. Winners receive a cash prize, studio time, appearances at several major blues events around the country, and the title of "Best Unsigned Blues Band." The judges also present the Albert King Award to the most-promising blues guitarist.

Legends "Best Unsigned Blues Band"

Bands can make themselves known to Chicago recording industry and broadcast professionals through this annual competition sponsored by Buddy Guy's Legends. Qualifying rounds are held once a week during the month of February, with finals scheduled for the end of the month. Prizes include studio time, a guest appearance on the blues show on WLUP-FM radio, a spot on the "Band Finder" Web page, musical equipment including a guitar, bass, snare drum, and microphones, and two opening act gigs at Legends.

Blues Music Videos

Videos are a great way to experience some of the best live blues concerts from the comfort of your living room sofa. These are some of our favorites:

- ✔ *Blues Alive* (BMG Video) — Featuring Albert Collins, Buddy Guy, Junior Wells, Charles Brown, and others.

- ✔ *Messin' With the Blues* (Rhino Home Video) — Filmed at the 1974 Montreux Jazz Festival, it includes performances by Buddy Guy, Muddy Waters, and Junior Wells.

- ✔ *Piano Players Rarely Ever Play Together* (Stevenson Productions) — A documentary featuring Cajun blues and R&B pianists "Tuts" Washington, Professor Longhair, and Allen Toussaint.

- ✔ *Pride and Joy: The Story of Alligator Records* (BMG Video) — Includes performances from the Alligator Records 1992 20th anniversary tour, featuring Koko Taylor and Her Blues Machine, the Lonnie Brooks Blues Band, Elvin Bishop, Katie Webster, and Lil' Ed and the Blues Imperials.

- ✔ *Texas Blues Guitar* (Rounder) — A collection of performances by Albert Collins, Freddie King, Lightnin' Hopkins, and Mance Lipscomb.

No TV picture, but 24-hour music

Music Choice is a cable channel that features 24-hour blues music. Although no video images are shown, the screen does display the name of the song being played, the artist, the CD title, and record label. CDs played on the channel can also be purchased through a toll-free number. For more information on this channel, contact your local cable company.

Blues Radio Shows

Where would popular music be without radio? What other medium gives you such a variety of music, for *free?* In this section of the chapter, we list some radio shows that are bringing the blues to fans across the country.

Syndicated shows

Syndicated blues programs are a solid part of radio station programming across the country. The following list is a sampling of blues programs in major radio markets nationwide. For more information on radio programs in your area, contact *Living Blues,* The Center for the Study of Southern Culture, University of Mississippi (UM-Oxford campus), University, MS 38677-9990, (601-232-5993), or search for blues Web sites, such as The Blue Highway at www.thebluehighway.com.

✔ *Beale Street Caravan:* Supported by The Blues Foundation of Memphis, this syndicated show can be heard coast to coast. The program airs on 250 public and community radio stations in the U.S. and also airs globally, via the Armed Forces Radio Network and National Public Radio Worldwide.

   Hosted by broadcasting legend Sam the Sham and by Joyce Cobb and presented in a "magazine" format, the program mixes exclusive live music recordings from blues venues and festivals with celebrity host features. Guest hosts have included record producer Jerry Wexler, musical artists John Hammond, Keb' Mo', Allen Toussaint, and Tracy Nelson, Sun Records founder Sam Phillips, record collector Richard Hite, and journalist Peter Guralnick.

✔ Other nationally syndicated shows include:

   The *House of Blues Radio Hour,* with more than 195 affiliates nation-wide. For information on radio stations in your area that carry it, point your Web browser to info@bmpaudio.com.

   Also check out *Blues Before Sunrise* with Steve Cushing, produced by station WBEZ-FM, Chicago.

Local shows

Listing every blues show on every local station in the country is all but impossible (which is actually good news — it means a lot of people are tuning in to the blues). Nevertheless, we try to give you some ideas of where to turn your radio dial.

Atlanta

WRFG 89.3 FM; 404-523-3471 — *Good Morning Blues:* Monday–Friday, 6 a.m.–10 a.m.; *Heritage Hall:* Wednesday, 11 p.m.–1 a.m.; *Route 66:* Thursday, 1 p.m.–3 p.m.; *True Blues:* Thursday, 8 p.m.–10 p.m.

WZGC 92.9 FM; 404-851-9393 — *The Blues Show:* Sunday, 9 a.m.–11 a.m.

Bloomington, IN

WTTS 92.3 FM; 812-332-3366 — *Blues Sunday:* Sunday, 8 p.m.–9 p.m.; *House of Blues Radio Hour:* Sunday, 9 p.m.–10 p.m.

Boston

WBOS 92.9 FM; 617-254-9267 — *Blues on Sunday:* Sunday, 10 p.m.–Midnight

WGBH 89.7 FM; 617-492-2777 — *Blues After Hours:* Friday and Saturday, 9 p.m.–1 a.m.

WHRB 95.3 FM; 617-495-4818 — *The Jump Hour:* Friday, 9 a.m–10 a.m.; *The Boston Blues Society:* Sunday, 7 a.m.–11 a.m.

Buffalo

WBFO 88.7 FM; 716-829-6000 — *Blues:* Saturday, 11 a.m.–5 p.m. and Saturday, 10 p.m.–Midnight*; Network blues programming:* Saturday, 4 p.m.–5 p.m., Sunday, Noon–2 p.m.

WUFO1080 AM; 716-834-1080 — *Rhythm & Blues:* Saturday, 4 p.m.–8 p.m.

Chicago

WBEZ 91.5 FM; 312-832-9150 — *Comin' Home with Niles Frantz:* Sunday, Midnight–4 a.m.

WLUP 97.9 FM; 312-591-7625 — *Chicago Blues Jam:* Sunday, 9 p.m.–11 p.m.

WXRT 93.1 FM; 773-777-1700 — *Blues Breakers:* Monday, 10 p.m.–11 p.m.

Cleveland

WCPN 90.3 FM; 216-432-3700 — *Blues with Fitz:* Friday and Saturday, 10 p.m.–2 a.m.; *Blues Before Sunrise:* Sunday, Midnight–5 a.m.

Dallas

KNON 89.3 FM; 214-828-9500 — *R&B Blues Revue:* Monday, 9 a.m.–11 a.m.; *Radio Blues Revue:* Friday, 9 a.m.–11 a.m.; *Texas Blues Show:* Monday–Friday, 6 p.m.–8 p.m.

Detroit

WDET 101.9 FM; 313-577-4146 — *Blues from the Lowlands:* Saturday, 10 a.m.–Noon; *Blues on the River:* Sunday, 8 p.m.–9 p.m.; *Blues After Hours:* Saturday, Midnight– 5 a.m.

Houston

KTSU 90.9 FM; 713-313-7591 — *Dr. Freddie Brown Blues Special,* Monday 10:30–2 a.m.; *Oldies Blues Cruise:* Friday, 2 p.m.–6 p.m.; *Zydeco Blues Connection:* Saturday, 4 p.m.–7 p.m.

Indianapolis

WFYI 90.1 FM; 317-636-2020 — *Nothin' But The Blues:* Saturday, Noon–4 p.m.; Sunday, Noon–3 p.m.; *Portraits in Blue:* Sunday, 3 p.m.–4 p.m.

WTLC 1310 AM; 317-283-1310 — *Blues with a Feeling:* Monday–Friday, 2 p.m.–6 p.m.

Las Vegas

KUNV 91.5 FM; 702-895-3877 — *Mostly Blues:* Saturday, 3 p.m.–5 p.m.; *Blues Legacy:* Sunday, 2 p.m.–4 p.m.

Los Angeles

KLON 88.1 FM; 562-985-5566 — *Nothin' But the Blues:* Saturday and Sunday, 2 p.m.–6 p.m.

KXLU 88.9 FM; 310-338-2866 — *The Bluez Hotel:* Wednesday, Midnight–3 a.m.

Milwaukee

WYMS 88.9 FM; 414-475-8362 — Blues music: Saturday, 10 p.m.–Midnight

Minneapolis

KTCZ 97.1 FM; 612-339-0000 — *Blues Hour:* Sunday, 8 p.m.–9 p.m.

New York City

WBAI 99.5 FM; 212-279-0707 — *Taste the Blues:* Monday, 9 p.m.–10 p.m.; *Gutbucket Matinee:* Saturday, 3 p.m.–6 p.m.

WFUV 90.7 FM; 718-365-8050 — *Beale Street Caravan:* Monday, Midnight–1 a.m.; *Blues Before Sunrise:* Saturday, 2 a.m.–4 a.m.

Philadelphia

WRTI 90.1 FM; 215-204-8405; *Blue Groove:* Monday, Midnight–3 a.m.

WXPN 88.5 FM; 215-898-6677 — *The Blues Show:* Monday–Wednesday, 8 p.m.–11 p.m., Saturday, 8 p.m.–1 a.m.

San Francisco

KFOG 104.5 FM; 415-817-5364 — *House of Blues Radio Hour:* Sunday, 9 p.m.–10 p.m.

KPOO 89.5 FM; 415-346-5375 — *Blues Show:* Monday, 9 a.m.–Noon; *Big Bones:* Wednesday, 9 a.m.–Noon

WALW 91.7 FM; 415-841-4134 — *Blues Power Hour:* Monday, 9 p.m.–10 p.m.; *Portraits in Blue:* Monday, 11 p.m.–Midnight; *Beale Street Caravan:* 10 p.m.– 11 p.m.

Salt Lake City

KRCL 90.9 FM; 801-363-1818 — *Illustrated Blues:* Friday, 3:30 a.m.–5:30 a.m.; *Red, White & Blues:* Monday, 8 p.m.–10:30 p.m.; *Crossroads:* Monday, 10:30 p.m.–1 a.m.

Seattle

KBCS 91.3 FM; 206-562-6194 — Blues played Monday–Friday, 3:30 p.m.– 5 p.m.; Monday–Tuesday, Midnight–6 a.m.; Wednesday, Midnight–3 a.m.; Friday, 7 p.m.–9 p.m.; Saturday, 8 p.m.–10 p.m.

KZAZ 91.7 FM; 360-738-9170 — *Nothin' But the Blues:* Sunday, Midnight–2 a.m.

Part IV
Playing the Blues

The 5th Wave   By Rich Tennant

©RICHTENNANT

Blues Revue

"Prozac may have saved his life, but it's killing his blues career."

In this part . . .

Deep inside just about every blues fan beats the heart of a blues musician. Admit it. Haven't you secretly harbored a desire to sing and play the blues yourself? We figured as much. In this part, we talk about playing the blues at the amateur as well as the professional level. (One of the great things about the blues is its community spirit. For every big-name recording artist who's touring the world, there's a little, local blues combo playing right down the street.) This part tells you about starting your own band, selecting the right instruments, and taking your act into the recording studio.

Chapter 9

Putting Together a Blues Band

• •

In This Chapter

▶ Auditioning band mates

▶ The importance of practicing

▶ Quick tips for touring

▶ A day in the life of a blues player

• •

Assembling a band — *any* type of band — and making it work can be a daunting task. Keeping a musical group together requires a delicate balance of egos, a give-and-take relationship not unlike a marriage, a dogged determination to succeed, and a disciplined routine that sometimes seems like army boot camp. But, take it from us, the end result is worth every bit of the effort.

In this chapter, we cover some of the first steps in getting a blues band up and running. And, in case you've ever had fantasies about being on the road with a band, we also give you a glimpse into the average day of a touring blues professional.

Some Up-Front Advice

The following statement may seem incredibly obvious, but we'll say it anyway: If you're going to be in a blues band, do it because you love playing the music. Most musicians who go into the blues field don't expect to make millions off their music. The art of playing and the music itself are your main — and sometimes only — rewards.

On the other hand, even if you and a few of your friends are putting together a band just for fun, you still want to avoid the cons and pitfalls that seem to plague many novice musical acts. Some common sense and basic business acumen can save you from committing some costly blunders and embarrassing yourselves down the road.

Deciding on a Musical Style

If you read the previous chapters of this book (especially the chapters in Part I), you know loads of different kinds of blues styles exist. Before you put your band together, it's a good idea to decide what type of blues you want to target and concentrate on becoming proficient in that style of playing.

The musical instruments

Depending on the kind of music you'll be playing, you also need a particular kind of instrumentalist. For instance, if you want to play acoustic blues, you may not need a bass player or even a drummer, but you may want someone who can play a dobro. If you're putting together an electric band that plays down-and-dirty Chicago blues, it's a pretty good bet you'll need to audition some harmonica players. If you want to go for that zydeco sound, you're going to need an accordionist. Or, maybe a pedal steel guitar would give your band a country-blues flavor.

The set list

Size up the style of blues you want to play, examine its component parts, and start piecing together your act from there. For instance, if B.B. King is your hero, begin building your band's repertoire around his best-known tunes. Then start investigating the more-obscure numbers he recorded and pluck tunes from that assortment. As you're doing your research, you'll discover other blues artists with similar playing styles, which means you can unearth yet more cool tunes to add to your *set list* (or *play list*).

Be aware that nearly all recorded music is protected by a copyright. If the time comes that you want to record, make an appointment with a business lawyer who can give you the basics on copyright law, permissions, and compositions that are in the public domain.

"Before you put a blues band together you have to decide what *type* of blues you want to play, then find the right instrumentation that complements it. Some blues bands can be formed with a couple of guitars, a bass, and drums. Others feature a harmonica and only carry one guitar in their lineup. But I would say if you really want to have a band that can play a little of bit of everything, you have to find yourself a good bass player, a good drummer, a good keyboard player, a good guitar player, and somebody who can sing. With those four pieces and strong vocals, you can play the blues in just about any style."

Auditioning Players

Before you can audition players, you have to find them. You can pass the word around your neighborhood, workplace, or school, but that will net you just so many candidates. Therefore, you're probably going to have to do some advertising and investigation.

Checking bulletin board postings

If you have a musical equipment store in your area, keep an eye out for postings on its bulletin board. This is a great resource for names of potential band members. (If you have multiple music stores in your area, cover them all.) These bulletin boards function as a clearinghouse for local musicians looking for work and selling equipment — two essential ingredients in putting a group together.

Posting your own notice

You can also post your own bulletin-board notice. Make it simple and to the point — for example, "Blues Musicians Wanted: Guitar player looking to form Chicago-style blues band. Need drums, bass, and harmonica players. Call Stevie at 555-0000." Include tear-off tabs with your name and phone number at the bottom of your posted notice so interested folks can get in touch with you.

Meeting potential band mates one on one

To save yourself loads of potential organizational headaches, audition players one-on-one rather than trying out the entire band at once. You have a better chance to assess each player's style, see how it fits with your vision for the band, and most important, find out whether the two of you can get along. If you're already squabbling at the audition, the situation will only get worse once you hit the bandstand.

Picking a place for the auditions

Although there's no set rule for where to hold auditions or rehearsals, a little common sense prevails in this matter. If you live in a one-room apartment, it's a pretty good bet that you'll want to find a larger place (without next-door neighbors) to rehearse a full electric blues band.

If you have some spare change, you may want to rent time in a rehearsal space. Most cities have such places available to musicians — inquire at your local musical equipment store or check the Yellow Pages under "Studio Rental."

Your basement, recreation room, or garage are other suitable locales for holding auditions or rehearsals. Just make sure the room is soundproofed (carpeted rooms with drapes will absorb more sound than a room with wood floors and no window coverings). If you're using your garage, make sure that you can keep it locked up and secured. It's no fun having your equipment (and your friends' equipment) ripped off while you're taking a break.

Screening candidates with a pre-audition interview

You don't have to audition everybody who responds to your casting call. You can usually weed out the pretenders from the real players just by asking a few simple questions over the phone. You won't need to get their Social Security number on that first call, but they should be able to provide satisfactory answers to the following questions:

- **Have you ever played in a band before?** Better to get the answer to this one right away. Lack of professional experience can make for big headaches down the road. You don't want to be constantly badgered with questions from a player who's learning the ropes while you're trying to rehearse. On the other hand, a newcomer can bring a level of enthusiasm to his or her first blues band that's refreshing and a real energy-booster for the whole ensemble.

- **Do you own your own equipment?** Take a pass on anyone who doesn't own his or her own equipment. If a candidate does own equipment, find out if it fits with what you're trying to do musically. If you're putting together a blues-rock combo that cranks up the volume, a guitar player is going to need something bigger than a little practice amp. Or, if your band will have a quieter sound and the applicant owns a gigantic amp left over from his days in a heavy-metal band, that won't do you much good either.

- **Do you have days free? Evenings free? Are you free for rehearsals? Are you free for local travel? Are you free for overnight travel?** Scheduling, scheduling, scheduling. It's what allows most bands to play beyond a ten-mile radius from their homes or, in some cases, even get off the ground. Find out what the player's schedule is and if it works with everyone else's hours.

> ✔ **Are you at least 18 years of age (to sign a contract)? Are you at least 21 years of age (to play in bars)?** Being under the age of 21 isn't a crime, but it will limit the number (and types) of places where your band can play. If you're going to be signing any kind of business agreements (including recording contracts or booking contracts), you definitely need to know who's of age (in most states, 18 years old) and who needs their parents' consent to sign a contract.

> ✔ **Do you have a driver's license?** A touring musician without a driver's license can be kind of a paperweight (unless they have their own chauffeur). Everything seems to revolve around picking up and dropping off a musician without wheels. And, sooner or later, everybody has to take a turn at the wheel of the band vehicle during those that late-night drives back from a show.

Inviting players to come on board

After you find some players you think can fill the bill, it's time to call that all-important first rehearsal. Set a date, set a time, and make sure everyone has directions to the rehearsal space and that they read them back to you over the phone (just to make sure they got them right).

Don't worry about legally binding anyone to a contract just yet. Wait until you've decided to become a band before you think about hiring a lawyer to draw up some paperwork (that is, if you even want to be bound by any contracts at all).

How Do We Get to Carnegie Hall, Again?

No matter how sharp you may think you sound the first couple of times you play together in somebody's garage or basement, you need three elements to really impress an audience: practice, practice, and more practice. Once you leave your basement for the clubs, you're going to be competing with outfits who have been together a lot longer than you have.

Polishing your sound with practice

You want to sound as *tight* as you possibly can, and standing in front of an audience is no time to forget the ending to that Albert King tune. (By the way, when we say a band sounds "tight" we mean they have a polished sound and play their instruments with precision — no one is playing too fast, too slow, or out of tune, not even slightly.)

While regular rehearsals in which you practice new tunes are the best way to build up your song list, it's always a good idea to kick off your rehearsals by playing a couple of tunes the band knows cold. This puts everybody in the musical groove, helps you to set your rehearsal volume, and gives the band a solid reference point from which to work. All the new stuff should eventually sound as good as the old standbys.

Appointing an unofficial leader

The first few times you get together to jam it's not critically important that you have a designated leader to "crack the whip." But you'll find out soon enough who *is* the take-charge person in the band and it wouldn't hurt to delegate some organizational responsibility his or her way in the beginning, even if the band has an all-for-one-and-one-for-all philosophy.

"When you're rehearsing together, you get to a point where you understand each other's playing and you know what to play to complement the other person's style. This is what makes a band really happen. A musician who plays as a member of the band rather than a star soloist is worth his or her weight in gold. If there's a certain type of style you want to master, get some records and study them. Learn the song; learn the music; go step by step until you can play it in your sleep, even if you have to learn it four bars at a time. Once you've got that first 12 bars of a blues song down, you can go on and play the whole number."

Getting Ready to Turn Pro

After some weeks of rehearsing with your band, you've probably worked up a couple sets of dynamite material. (A *set* typically consists of 45 minutes to an hour's worth of songs, with little to no dead time between each number except to say "thanks" and introduce the next tune.)

Turn it down!

Commonsense Rule of Band Practice Number One: If your rehearsal seems headed toward chaos and little in the way of creative work is being accomplished, chances are everybody's playing *too loud.* Try to rehearse a new song as quietly as possible until everybody has their parts down pat, then crank it up and gas yourselves (if you really must) just one time.

The band that can rehearse at a sensible volume will have neighbors popping their heads in, smiling, and enjoying the music. The band that plays too loud will have neighbors banging on the door and heading for the fuse box — that is, if they don't call the cops, who may show up with a noise violation notice in hand.

Now it's time to leave the safety and security of your basement and get your stuff out in front of a real, live audience — and maybe even put a couple bucks in your pocket while you're at it.

Promoting yourself

If you're just getting your feet wet, do you need a manager? (No, not really.) How about a high-powered booking agent? (Not right off the bat.) So then what *do* you need? You need a good-looking promotional (or *promo*) package that communicates the essence of your group and helps you get your foot in the door with prospective club owners and talent agents.

A promo package consists of a group shot — usually an 8- x-10-inch photo — a one-page biography of the band, a demo tape with three or four songs, and a set list of all the material a prospective client can expect to hear you play on the job.

If you have just one photo done of your band, make sure it's a glossy black-and-white shot, and if you have the spare change, have a professional shoot it. Color photos tend to look muddy when they're reproduced in newspapers, and it's the local press you want to plug your band. Make sure all the important contact information is printed at the bottom of the photo, too.

Although pulling together a promotional kit may sound like it requires a significant financial outlay, you can take a few shortcuts and still produce a good-looking promo package. Your band biography and tune list can be assembled by anyone with a computer (or even a typewriter) and run off at a copy shop. Ask a friend who's an amateur photographer to take the band's picture. Many photo shops offer deals on bulk 8 x10 prints.

Making a demo tape

Before you can promote your band, you'll need to put together a *demo tape* (a song sampler of your band's live act). Check your local Yellow Pages under "Recording Services" and start calling around to find out which studios have the best deals on recording facility services. When you call the studios, ask if they offer discount introductory sessions. If you can't afford studio time, have a friend tape you at your next rehearsal or at a friend's party.

Scouting out places to play

Find local clubs that feature an *open mike* or jam session night during which anyone is invited to play. Open mikes are usually scheduled during the "off nights" for most music clubs, such as Mondays or Tuesdays.

In an open-mike situation, you usually have to put your name on a list and wait your turn. You may be able to sit in and play on the house band's equipment; however, it's considered proper etiquette to bring your own guitars and other musical equipment with you when you show up for an open mike.

If you've set up a formal audition with a prospective "buyer" (that is, the owner or manager of a blues music venue), that audition is a service you're expected to provide for free *only once*. No reputable club owner will have you auditioning for nothing over and over again.

Looking sharp and showing up on time

If you want to be part of a blues band, you have to dress the part. A pair of blue jeans and an old T-shirt may be okay for a backyard barbecue, but if you're being paid to entertain an audience of people who forked out a cover charge at the door, make it a point to look like a group worth paying good money to see.

Punctuality is another big plus in making your blues band happen (and it makes you look like real pros). Set up a time during the day when the club owner will let you unload your gear, get it set up on stage, and test it for sound (also known as a *sound check*). Do not leave the club owner or manager guessing as to when you're going to show up.

Arrive at least an hour before you're scheduled to go on stage so that the club manager knows you're on the premises, dressed, and ready to play. If you're supposed to start playing at 9 p.m., be onstage tuning up and ready to play no later than 8:55. Rather than straggling in one by one, walk onstage as a single unit, which will make you look even more professional.

A Thumbnail Guide to Touring

The road is fraught with thrills, spills, and adventures. (Sometimes, a band's years of experience and sharply honed business sense come down to nothing more than their ability to collect a paycheck.) If you're planning to play your music away from home, make sure you adhere to the following road-touring basics:

 ✔ Buy the biggest road atlas you can find and get used to using it all the time. Always check the directions you were given against an atlas or city map and never assume that the directions you were given were absolutely correct. (Not everyone spells or pronounces street names the same way.) If you're uncertain of the address, call first.

✔ If you can afford it, carry a cell phone with you in your van or bus at all times. On a long van ride to the next gig, there's plenty of advance work and business that can be conducted on the phone (besides checking in with your boyfriend or girlfriend).

✔ Make all hotel reservations well in advance and always carry with you a complete set of brochures for various discount hotel chains, just in case the original reservations (or other overnight accommodations) fall through.

✔ If you encounter any road troubles, be sure to call the club immediately; this demonstrates a professional attitude on your part and keeps whoever is paying your freight from guessing where you are.

✔ Vehicles do break down. Have on hand a complete set of emergency equipment in case the van breaks down — a tire jack, spare tire, plenty of duct tape, road flares, distilled water, coolant, and some wrenches.

✔ Figure that every day you're on the road costs you $25 apiece in bare bones expenses, and that's not counting hotels, movies, magazines, or your bar tab. Budget yourself accordingly and you just might come home with some money to show for your travels.

A Day in the Life of a Blues Player

International blues celebrity Joe Runningwater may not get onstage to play the blues until late at night, but you can rest assured that his work day started a good 12 hours before that.

11:00 a.m. — Joe starts his day by checking out of the hotel room he stayed in the previous night. After settling up his bill at the front desk — and band members who don't are definitely *persona non grata* in the blues community — he tries to find a place that still serves breakfast (it's too late for room service).

12:00 Noon — After a quick bite to eat (the sausage was greasy and the fruit was canned), it's time for Joe and his band to start traveling. On short hops, blues bands drive rather than fly to their destinations. The rule of thumb in computing time to the next town is the total mileage divided by 50 miles an hour (even with a full set of directions, that's the average speed of a touring van or bus). You also have to factor in stuff such as rest stops, food stops, traffic jams, or accidents that could slow your trip.

3:00 p.m. — Once he reaches his destination, it's time for Joe to check into another hotel and contact the place where he'll be appearing that night.

3:30 p.m. — There's public relations work to be done that day. Joe grabs a cab and heads to a local radio station for an on-air interview (plus, he takes a moment to tape a station "plug"). He then heads back to his hotel where a music writer from the local daily newspaper is waiting to interview him. Joe's manager has also asked him to squeeze in a 15-minute interview with the local alternative weekly newspaper.

6:00 p.m. — Joe heads for the venue where his band is playing that night for a sound check, which can last for at least 45 minutes to an hour while the sound technician sets various microphone levels. (In festival situations featuring multiple bands and artists, a sound check isn't necessary. But many blues artists will hang out most of the day, catching the other acts on the bills, and be ready to go on earlier than scheduled if another act that was slated to appear is a no-show.)

7:30 p.m. — After the sound check, Joe heads back to his hotel room for a much-needed nap or some dinner before show time.

8:30 p.m. — Depending on the performance time noted on their contract, Joe's band may suit up for the show at the hotel and then head to the music venue at least an hour ahead of the scheduled performance time.

10:00 p.m. — It's now time for Joe and his band to take the stage and get down to doing their real work — playing the blues.

11:00 p.m. — The first set is over and Joe heads out into the crowd to mingle with some blues fans he knows from other tours through town. On some nights he may even conduct a newspaper or magazine interview during the break.

12:30 a.m. — The show is over. Joe makes sure the band members and crew load the equipment into the tour bus and settle up their bar tabs (if any). The band then spends a few moments with any friends or family who turned out for the show before heading back to the hotel.

2:00 a.m. — Joe and the band unwind with some TV, snacks, and a few libations (nobody goes straight to bed after a show, no matter how tired they are). Then they'll catch five or six hours of sleep before starting a brand-new day on the road.

Chapter 10

Axes, Harps, and Other Essential Instruments

*W*hether it's a wailing electric guitar solo, a hand-in-glove pairing of an acoustic guitar and blues harp, a boogie-woogie rhythm rolling out of an upright piano, or a saxophone blasting through an R&B solo, musical instruments shape and define blues music more than anything else besides the human voice.

Among all the instruments in the blues, without a doubt, the guitar is the most widely used. Therefore, we devote a healthy portion of this chapter to the most popular blues guitar models. We also tell you what makes a guitar collectable and the best amplifiers for maximum guitar sound. We also tell you how to select a quality harmonica (another important instrument in the blues) and even tell you about the best microphone for getting that signature Chicago blues harp sound. The piano, saxophone, and rhythm section (the bass guitar and drums) round out a blues band, and this chapter as well.

Dissecting a Guitar

All sorts of guitars (or *axes*, the slang term for guitars) are used to play the blues — and some very famous models are among them. We tell you about each of those popular models later in this chapter, but first, it's important to dig into the basic physical components of blues music's most important instrument.

Electric and acoustic guitars have many of the same parts, even though the two types of instruments may look very different. To help you identify what's what on a guitar, this section describes the major parts of a guitar and what each of those parts does. You can refer to Figure 10-1 as we go along. (The figure is based on the Gibson Les Paul Standard guitar, which is covered in the section "The Most Popular Blues Guitars," later in this chapter.)

Body

Whether it's a round-hole acoustic or solid-body electric, the construction of every guitar begins with the body. Guitar bodies can be made out of just about any solid material (and many a basement guitar builder sure has tried). However, the majority of guitar bodies are constructed from wood, the preferred material.

Solid-body guitars are carved out of hardwoods such as mahogany, maple, alder, and ash, while spruce is often layered over the top of quality acoustic guitars. The bodies of hollow-body electric models look somewhat like standard acoustic guitar bodies, while solid-body electrics come in a variety of shapes — from the traditional "figure eight" to shapes that are downright fantastic and wacky.

Neck

The *neck* is the main part of the guitar and in some cases, the most important. Necks are usually made out of either maple or mahogany and come in a variety of widths and shapes — from a rounded profile to a pronounced *V* shape, and from thick and club-like to very thin and sleek. When players complain that a guitar doesn't "feel right," they're usually talking about the neck and its shape interfering with their ability to play fluidly.

Headstock

Guitar strings are fastened to the *headstock,* the upper portion of the guitar neck. (Headstocks are sometimes also called *pegheads*.) Some headstocks are angled away from the rest of the neck of the guitar to exert a tighter pull on the strings, which gives the guitar sound greater *sustain*. (When played, the strings vibrate for a longer length of time which "stretches out" or "sustains" the sound.) Headstocks can be plain and purely functional, or very ornamental with inlaid designs.

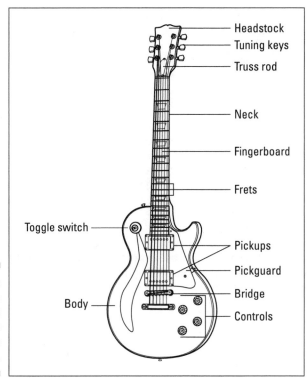

Headstock
Tuning keys
Truss rod

Neck

Fingerboard

Frets

Toggle switch

Pickups

Pickguard

Figure 10-1:
The basic
components
of an
electric
guitar.

Bridge

Body

Controls

Truss rod

Tuned guitar strings exert enormous pressure on the neck of a guitar. In addition, wood tends to warp over time, especially if it's exposed to variations in climate. The *truss rod* is the part of the neck that keeps the wood stable and playable. It typically consists of a metal rod or bar that is inserted into the top portion of the neck before the fingerboard is attached. Adjustable truss rods can be torqued to straighten the neck to adjust for any warping and to maintain the neck's proper shape.

Tuning keys

The *tuning keys* (also called *tuning pegs*) are those oval buttons that are attached to the headstock. They're used to turn the gears that tighten or loosen the guitar strings, which is how a guitarist tunes a guitar to the proper pitch. There's one tuning key for each string on a guitar. On most six-string acoustic and hollow-body electric guitars, three tuning keys are set into each side of the headstock. (Geared tuning pegs that are screwed into a headstock are also called *machine heads*.)

On most Fenders and other solid-body electric guitars, all six pegs appear on the left-hand side of the headstock. This setup makes it easy for a player whose left hand is working the guitar neck to reach over with the right hand to make quick tuning peg adjustments.

Fingerboard

The *fingerboard* is a separate piece of wood glued to the neck and inlaid with *position markers* (some of which are plain little plastic dots, while others are fancy pearl inlays). The guitar strings are strung over the length of the fingerboard, which is played by pressing the strings with the fingertips, slapping the strings with the palm of the hand, or by pressing a guitar slide over the length of the strings.

Fingerboards are made out of hardwood and, depending on the kind of wood used, the guitar produces a somewhat different sound. Rosewood and ebony tend to produce a deeper, darker sound, while maple gives a brighter and "twangier" tone to the guitar.

Frets

Frets are the horizontal metal pieces that run across the fingerboard and lie underneath the strings. When a player presses down on a string (which is called *fretting*) the hard edge of the fret alters the pitch of the notes being played. The position of the frets indicates the variations in pitch of each note in the musical scale. The spaces between each ridge are also called frets, which are numbered in chording diagrams in order to tell a guitarist which frets to play to produce a particular chord.

Pushing a string against a fret in alternating directions creates what is called a *finger vibrato,* or *trill.* Another technique, known as *string bending,* involves pushing a string against the fret to produce a higher note without having to reposition the hand on the neck.

Bridge

The bridge is the component at or near the tailpiece that the strings pass over. The strings are run through saddles built into the bridge that can be adjusted to fine-tune the guitar's *intonation* (that is, when a player wants to play in a certain octave, he or she is sure of playing exactly *in* that octave). The saddles in the bridge can be used to compensate for any warping of the wood, variations in the weight of the strings, or other variables that can affect the richness and precision of a guitar's sound. On an acoustic guitar, the entire saddle/bridge/tailpiece unit is referred to as the *bridge.*

FOR VIRTUOSOS

A pickup line that works

Essentially just bunches of thin wire wrapped around a magnet, *pickups* come in two varieties. *Single-coil* pickups, such as the kind usually found on Stratocasters and Telecasters, deliver a bright, twangy sound. The other popular type of pickup, *humbuckers,* are larger in size and are found on Les Pauls and other Gibsons. Humbuckers produce a fatter, darker sound than single-coil pickups. Humbuckers are actually two single-coil pickups wired together in order to "buck the hum" from stage lights and other electrical interference.

Pickguard

The *pickguard* is a protective piece of plastic covering the area where the guitarist strikes the strings. Some guitars, such as the Telecaster and the Stratocaster, have pickguards that cover a large part of the body, while most Gibson pickguards are smaller and more ornamental. Pickguards used to be made out of real tortoise shell and later were made of highly flammable celluloid materials. Now, pickguards are made out of plastic in as many designs and colors as you can imagine.

Pickups

Pickups (as their name suggests) "pick up" the vibrations of guitar strings and turn them into an electrical signal that's delivered to an amplifier that produces the electric guitar sound. Pickups are usually made of chrome or plastic with copper wiring and are fitted with metal screws called *pole pieces*. Pickups are typically fitted into the middle of the guitar body.

Controls

Pickups are wired to the *controls,* which usually, at a minimum, consist of a volume control and a tone control, such as you may find on a stereo receiver. If a guitar has more than one pickup, a pickup selector switch (called a *toggle switch*) is also built into the guitar. A toggle switch provides a variety of sound combinations, and the relative positioning of pickups along the length of the guitar strings also produces different tones.

Some guitars feature a volume and a tone control for each pickup. The three-pickup Stratocaster features one master volume control and two tone controls for the entire guitar.

Tailpiece

The *tailpiece* is that portion of the guitar body where the strings begin their journey toward the headstock and tuners. Some guitars, such as the Fender Telecaster, feature *ferrules* into which the strings are anchored. As a unit, the ferrules function as the tailpiece. On some hollow-body electrics, the hinged apparatus bolted to the bottom of the guitar body is called the *bail tailpiece*.

Hand vibrato

A *hand vibrato* is a special attachment on a guitar's tailpiece. It's the handle that pokes out of the bridge and tailpiece area. (See Figure 10-2.) You'll also hear it called a *vibrato bar, tremolo bar,* or *whammy bar.*

When the vibrato bar is depressed, it detunes the strings (or alters the pitch), and when it's lifted back up, it sets the strings back into tune. Wiggling the bar back and forth creates rapid oscillations on all six strings — producing everything from Duane Eddy–style low quivers to Jimi Hendrix–style outer-space sounds.

If you're a pro, you should definitely know the difference between the terms *vibrato* and *tremolo.* The two are often mistakenly interchanged when discussing guitars and amps. *Vibrato* refers to the moveable apparatus discussed in this section of the chapter. A *tremolo* is an electronic unit found in guitar amplifiers that causes the guitar signal to pulsate to different speeds set by the user. To confuse matters even further, Fender calls the tremolo on their amplifiers a vibrato and the hand vibrato on their Stratocaster model a tremolo!

The Most Popular Blues Guitars

Just about any guitar that's used to play rock, country, or jazz can be used to play the blues. For example, the Gibson Flying V model is usually seen in the hands of heavy metal rockers. But it was also Albert King's signature instrument (and no one was about to tell Albert he wasn't playing a "blues guitar").

Most blues guitars are six-string models; however, some mighty music has been made on 12-string models by blues artists including Leadbelly, Barbecue Bob, and Robert Jr. Lockwood (who favored an electric 12-string).

Some electric guitar models have stood the test of time to become music industry standards. Those are the guitars that you hear on records, in commercials, and on movie soundtracks, and see in music videos and live performances. The two biggest manufacturers of electric guitars in the world are Fender and Gibson, whereas Gibson and Martin are the best-known acoustic guitar manufacturers. The following list tells you about models that made blues guitar history and are still hard at work on the job.

Fender Stratocaster

Without a doubt, the Fender Stratocaster is the most popular electric guitar in the world today. Its sleek, curvaceous (almost tailfin-like) form was considered radical for its time. Introduced in 1954, this guitar has proven to be Fender's most popular model. It's used to play everything from blues to rock to country.

The evolution of the solid-body electric guitar

In the beginning, all guitars were acoustic guitars, and all acoustic guitars were also called *Spanish guitars*. Blues acoustic guitars fall into one of two groups: the steel-string, round-hole *flat-top* models and the f-hole, *arched-top* models. (An *f-hole* is one of two cursive f-shaped openings in the body of some acoustic or electric acoustic guitars. You'll also find f-holes on violins, cellos, and other stringed instruments.)

Some time during the late 1920s and early 1930s, guitar manufacturers started experimenting with adding *pickups* to guitars — the first baby steps in the evolution of what we now know as the electric guitar. (See the section "Pickups" in this chapter.)

Although flat-top guitars remained for the most part free of electronic gizmos, the first mass-produced electric guitars were the Gibson arched-top hollow bodies. (Meanwhile, the first solid-body *lap steel* guitars were made by the Rickenbacker Company. Lap steels were the precursors to today's steel guitar that's used mainly in country music.)

The big, hollow-bodied Gibson electrics are almost always referred to as "jazz guitars," although many of them made it into the hands of blues artists, including T-Bone Walker, B.B. King, Clarence "Gatemouth" Brown, Eddie Taylor, Lowell Fulson, Robert Nighthawk, and Memphis Minnie.

But these newfangled electric instruments were not without their problems. The hollow-body electrics sent forth screeching feedback the moment an amplifier was turned up past cocktail-lounge settings. And while solid-body lap steels were used in country and Hawaiian music circles, they hadn't made much of an impact in the blues community.

That was pretty much the state of things until the late 1940s, when separate experiments by guitar builder Paul Bigsby (the fellow who invented the Bigsby hand vibrato seen on many Gibson and Gretsch models) and radio repairman Leo Fender developed the first workable solid-body instruments that could be played like a regular six-string guitar. They were built in a modular fashion, with the necks, bodies, controls, and hardware manufactured separately and then screwed and bolted together. Fender put his model into mass production in 1950 and the state — and sound — of popular music were changed forever.

No electric model has as distinctive and readily recognizable a sound as the Stratocaster (see Figure 10-2). "Strats" are distinguished by having three pickups and, on most standard models, a hand vibrato unit that's considered by many to be the best one ever made. These features make for greater tonal and pitch variations and maximum control of the guitar's sound. The Stratocaster is so essential to a particular kind of effect that even diehard Gibson players keep one around to get that "Strat sound" when they need it.

Notable Stratocaster players: Eric Clapton, Robert Cray, Debbie Davies, Buddy Guy, Jimi Hendrix, Magic Sam, Otis Rush, Kenny Wayne Shepard, Jimmie Vaughan, and Stevie Ray Vaughan.

Suggested Stratocaster listening: Eric Clapton — *From The Cradle* (Reprise); Buddy Guy — *Buddy's Blues* (MCA-Chess); Magic Sam — *West Side Guitar* (Paula); Otis Rush — *Cobra Recordings* (Paula); Jimmie Vaughan — *Strange Pleasure* (Epic); and Stevie Ray Vaughan — *Greatest Hits* (Epic).

"My first electric guitar was a Strat. That's the guitar I learned to play on. I got mine because I saw B.B. King and Gatemouth Brown both playing one and I thought if *I* got one, I would sound more like them. The Stratocaster is a good rock 'n' roll and blues guitar that almost plays itself. It's a model with a real clear sound to it. You can always tell when somebody's playing a Stratocaster. I'd say a Stratocaster probably has the easiest guitar neck to play for a beginner. And they aren't as delicate as one of your big, hollow-body Gibsons. If your guitar strap breaks and your Strat hits the floor, you can probably pick it up and continue playing!"

Fender Telecaster

The Fender Telecaster wasn't the first solid-body electric guitar ever manufactured — that distinction going to the Rickenbacker company in California and guitar builder and hand vibrato maker Paul Bigsby. But the Telecaster (see Figure 10-2) was the first *mass-produced* model, and it completely changed the guitar industry when it debuted as the Fender Broadcaster in 1950.

With its neck bolted onto a plain-looking, plank-style body, this new guitar looked and sounded different from anything that had existed before. Suddenly, the humble Telecaster (the name change came in 1951) made the solid-body electric guitar an affordable reality for most players.

Both blues and country players quickly adapted to the "Tele." Its immediate popularity forced even stodgy Gibson — until then, the only manufacturer of hollow-body electrics — to start making their own version of the solid-body guitar. The Telecaster's distinctive, clear tone is reminiscent of trebly steel guitars. Its ability to withstand wear and tear and general abuse makes it a favorite of road musicians to this day.

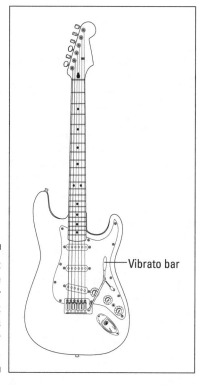

Vibrato bar

Figure 10-2:
At left is the
Fender
Stratocaster;
at right is
the Fender
Telecaster.

Notable Telecaster players: Clarence "Gatemouth" Brown (early record-ings), Albert Collins, Lightnin' Slim, Brewer Phillips with Hound Dog Taylor, and Muddy Waters.

Suggested Telecaster Listening: Clarence "Gatemouth" Brown — *The Peacock Recordings* (Rounder); Albert Collins — *Ice Pickin'* (Alligator); Lightnin' Slim — *Rooster Blues* (Excello); Hound Dog Taylor — *Beware Of The Dog!* (Alligator); and Muddy Waters — *Live At Newport — 1960* (MCA-Chess).

"A Telecaster has a rougher sound to it than a Stratocaster. It has more high-end than a Strat and has a real *bite* to it. The Telecaster is a guitar that'll really take a beating."

The Fender Book by Tony Bacon and Paul Day (Miller Freeman). This great 100-page book tells the story of all the Fender electric guitars ever made. A reference section helps to identify models by year of production, body shape, and structural changes. This book is loaded with great color photos of vintage Teles, Strats, and other classic Fender models to drool over.

Gibson ES-335

The Gibson ES-335 (the *ES* stands for *electric Spanish*) is the blues player's favorite hollow-body electric guitar. Place an asterisk next to that "hollow-body" designation however. This model is actually a thin-bodied, semi-solid/semi-hollow guitar with a solid block of wood running through the middle of it with hollow "wings" clamped to each side.

Introduced in 1958, the Gibson ES-335 essentially combined a hollow-bodied guitar with a solid-body guitar — the first of its kind. Unlike *feedback*-prone hollow-body electrics that would pick up their own sound from the loudspeakers and turn it into a horrible howling noise, the ES-335 was much less apt to produce feedback.

B.B. King immediately started using one, citing its slim body, long neck, and humbucking pickups as his favorite features (*humbuckers* are pickups that reduce background noise). More deluxe versions soon followed, including the ES-345, and the ES-355, better known as B.B. King's signature *Lucille* model (see Figure 10-3). Gibson's parent company, Epiphone, later brought out their own versions of the 335 and 355 with their Riviera and Sheraton models. These models were later played by Magic Sam, Otis Rush, and others.

Notable Gibson ES-335 players: Lonnie Brooks, Lowell Fulson, John Lee Hooker, B.B. King, Freddie King, Magic Sam, Otis Rush, and Eddie Taylor.

Suggested ES-335 Listening: B.B. King — *Live At The Regal* (MCA); Freddie King — *Just Pickin'* (Modern Blues); Magic Sam — *West Side Soul* (Delmark); Otis Rush — *So Many Roads-Live* (Delmark).

"Now, a 335 has more of a thicker sound to it than a Fender. You can play soulful at a low volume on those guitars and get exactly what you want out of them. With a solid-body, you need more volume to get your sound happening. But with a 335 or a 355, you can get a full, round sound and sustain at a low volume. The strings resonate more due to those hollow body f-holes in there."

Gibson Les Paul

After sales of Fender's Telecaster took off in the early 1950s, industry leader Gibson decided to come up with their own version of the solid-body guitar. But they didn't churn out a copycat version of the Telecaster. The Gibson solid-body featured looks and construction similar to their more ornate hollow-body instruments, with a glued-in neck mounted on a mahogany body with a carved maple top. Who better to endorse this new radical model than jazz musician-engineer-inventor and life-long Gibson player Les Paul (how's that for a hyphenate?).

Introduced in 1952, the Gibson Les Paul guitar immediately found its way into the hands of blues and country players and later became the instrument of choice for rock 'n' roll players the world over. The original models featured a gold-finished top (the "Gold Top" model) with white single-coil P-90 pickups. The late 1950s models featured dual humbucking pickups and a gorgeous sunburst finish. The design has remained virtually unchanged for more than four decades, but why mess with success?

Notable Les Paul players: Michael Bloomfield, Eric Clapton, Guitar Slim, John Lee Hooker, Freddie King, Hubert Sumlin with Howlin' Wolf, and Muddy Waters (early recordings).

Suggested Les Paul Listening: Eric Clapton — *Blues Breakers with Eric Clapton* (Mobile Fidelity); Guitar Slim — *Suffering Mind* (Specialty); Howlin' Wolf — *His Best* (MCA-Chess); Freddie King — *Hide Away: The Best Of Freddie King* (Rhino).

"Les Pauls are great for blues and rock 'n' roll. They're solid-body boxes like the Fenders, but they're heavy as all get out! They've got a nice neck on them, have a real nice, fat sound and, if you're a guitar player who likes to play loud, they'll stay right with you and won't feed back."

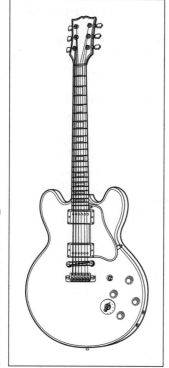

Figure 10-3:
The Gibson ES-355, better known as "Lucille," B.B. King's signature model.

Gibson Guitars: 100 Years Of An American Icon by Walter Carter (General Publishing Group). This book tells the complete story (the ups and the downs) of one of America's longest-operating guitar makers. The book covers the first mandolins and guitars made by Orville Gibson in his one-man shop in the 1880s, right up to the new instruments made by Gibson USA in their Nashville and Montana plants. Beautiful photographs of the various instruments make this book a great coffee table browser.

Acoustic models

The most widely used acoustic guitars are manufactured by the Gibson and Martin guitar companies. Several of these guitars — the Martin D-18, D-28, and OOO-28 models, and the Gibson J-200, J-50, and LG-O models — have been used by famous blues players for decades.

The Martin Company produces some of the finest flat-top guitars made anywhere. The Martin model names are actually a code of sorts. The letter stands for the size of the guitar and the number is the guitar's style (usually the higher the number, the fancier the design). The Martin HD-28 (shown in Figure 10-4) is Martin's biggest body size (the *D*, by the way, stands for *Dreadnaught,* the name of an early 20th century battleship).

The blues has also been played acoustically on a variety of budget boxes from now-defunct guitar manufacturers such as Stella, Kay, and Harmony. While the sound and structural integrity of these cheaper models don't rival that of a Gibson or a Martin, they do produce a raw tone quite suitable for blues playing, especially for finger-picking and slide-guitar playing.

Notable acoustic players: Barbecue Bob, Blind Blake, Big Bill Broonzy, Lightnin' Hopkins, Blind Lemon Jefferson, Robert Johnson, and Charlie Patton.

Suggested acoustic guitar listening: Barbecue Bob — *Chocolate To The Bone* (Yazoo); Blind Blake — *Ragtime's Foremost Picker* (Yazoo); Big Bill Broonzy — *Do That Guitar Rag* (Yazoo); Lightnin' Hopkins — *Mojo Hand: An Anthology* (Rhino); Robert Johnson — *King Of The Delta Blues* (Columbia/Legacy); and Charlie Patton — *Founder Of The Delta Blues* (Yazoo).

The Martin Book by Tony Bacon and Paul Day (Miller Freeman). No acoustic flat-top guitars are more famous than those made by the Martin Guitar Company for the past 150 years. This quick, informative book is jam-packed with photos of legendary Martin models and makes a perfect introduction to the acoustic guitar in general.

Figure 10-4:
The Martin
HD-28.

Dobros

The instruments of choice for most blues slide-guitar players in the 1920s and early 1930s were the metal-bodied National and Dobro brand guitars. In essence, *dobros* were the original amplified guitars (pre-electric division). They were loud, they had a bright sound, they could be heard in the noisiest juke joint in the world, and if a surly patron wanted to pick a fight, the dobro provided a ready weapon that could survive a knock with nary a scratch or dent.

The story of the dobro and other *resonator guitars* is a long and somewhat confusing one. (Actually, the term dobro and resonator guitar are synonymous.) In the mid-1920s, three brothers named John, Rudy, and Emil Dopyera worked for a Chicago guitar company called National. In 1926, they came up with a guitar design that involved a wooden neck mounted onto a metal body that resonated when played, owing to a perforated aluminum cone attached to the bridge of the guitar. (See Figure 10-5.) An early model — the National Tri-Plate Metal Resophonic Guitar — actually came with three six-inch cones and a T-shaped bridge support across the front of the guitar, but later models featured a single cone and biscuit-shaped bridge assembly.

Figure 10-5:
A dobro
resonator
guitar.

Tailpiece

In 1928, John, Rudy, and Emil split from National and formed their own company, Dobro, an acronym for the DOpyera BROthers. They began making wooden-body guitars with metal resonators to distinguish their models from National's brass-bodied, nickel-plated wonders. Competition became very fierce between the two companies and National switched to making wood-body resonator models while Dobro started making metal ones. The two companies merged in 1934 and manufactured National Dobro guitars through World War II.

The Dobro name was dropped in 1947 when National became National-Supro-Valco. But Dobro's designs so dominated the resonator guitar market that their name became synonymous with the instrument, not unlike Scotch Tape or Kleenex. Whether made by National, Regal, Slingerland, or an off-brand such as May Belle, all resophonic models were, and are, referred to as *dobros*.

By the early 1960s, the dobro tale takes another twist. Emil split from National and started making wood-body dobros under a variety of brand names, including Hound Dogs and Dopera (the Americanized family name) Originals. For a period of time in the mid-1960s, the Mosrite company acquired the Dobro name and manufactured the first electric version of a wood-body dobro.

In 1971, the Dopera brothers regained the right to their brand name and their Original Musical Instrument company made dobros until it was acquired by Gibson in the early 1990s. Today, Gibson makes new Dobro models and a small company in California called National makes letter-perfect reproductions of the original metal-body guitars.

Notable dobro players: Black Ace, Scrapper Blackwell, Bo Carter, Blind Boy Fuller, Corey Harris, Son House, Tampa Red, and Bukka White.

Suggested dobro listening: Black Ace — *I'm The Boss Card In Your Hand* (Arhoolie); Scrapper Blackwell — *Virtuoso Guitar, 1925–1934* (Yazoo); Bo Carter — *Greatest Hits, 1930–1940* (Yazoo); Blind Boy Fuller — *Truckin' My Blues Away* (Yazoo); Corey Harris — *Fish Ain't Bitin'* (Alligator); Son House — *Father Of The Delta Blues* (Columbia/Legacy); Tampa Red — *The Guitar Wizard* (Columbia/Legacy); and Bukka White — *The Complete Bukka White* (Columbia/Legacy).

Slide guitars

Most Chicago blues artists who moved there from the South in the first half of this century will more than likely tell you about their first musical instrument — a strand of baling wire nailed to a barn door and propped up by bottles or tin cans and played with the edge of a pocketknife. Many blues players who later played on the finest of instruments started out playing slide guitar on this sort of homemade *diddley bow*. As influential as the single-string guitar style of B.B. King is, it's really no surprise that he modeled his famous finger vibrato after local Mississippi slide players, and most especially his cousin Bukka White.

Slide guitar covers a lot of musical ground. It can sound silky smooth or harsh and edgy, and everything in between. It's the most vocal of all blues guitar styles and also the starting point for most aspiring blues guitarists.

The origin of slide guitar can be traced back to the rise in popularity of Hawaiian music. The notion of fretting a guitar string with a smooth object (such as a metal blade or a bottleneck) rather than with one's fingertips is attributed to Joseph Kekuku, a Hawaiian student who popularized the playing style in 1894. By the turn of the century, it was the hottest musical craze in the U.S. and its pop appeal lasted well into the 1940s.

The Hawaiian guitar is played with the instrument sitting in the lap of the musician who plays the notes by depressing the stings with a steel bar. (This style was later adapted to create the steel guitar found in country music.) African-American blues musicians replaced the steel bar with a bottleneck or metal tube fitted to one finger and simply played the guitar in the standard Spanish (or acoustic guitar) position.

The slide was used primarily for lead fills, or as an extension of the singer's voice, and the instrument could still be fretted for more conventional chording when the slide wasn't in use. By the time slide guitars started appearing on phonograph records in the late 1920s, the banjo's days as a popular blues instrument were almost over and the slide guitar was in.

Just as amplification forever changed the sound of the acoustic guitar, so it did with the slide guitar. Amplifiers turned up to maximum level give the slide a wild, unearthly sound that still continues to be explored.

Notable slide players: Earl Hooker, Son House, J.B. Hutto, Elmore James, Robert Johnson, Robert Nighthawk, Bonnie Raitt, Tampa Red, and Hound Dog Taylor

Suggested slide guitar listening: Earl Hooker — *Blue Guitar* (Paula); Son House (and various artists) — *Masters Of The Delta Blues* (Yazoo); J.B. Hutto — *Masters Of Modern Blues* (Testament); Elmore James — *Best Of Elmore James: Early Years* (Ace); Robert Johnson — *King Of The Delta Blues* (Columbia/Legacy); Robert Nighthawk — *Live On Maxwell Street* (Rounder); Tampa Red — *The Guitar Wizard* (Columbia/Legacy); and Hound Dog Taylor — *Natural Boogie* (Alligator).

"You know those really cheap electrics you see at the pawn shop and at yard sales sometimes? Well sometimes those cheap guitars make the best slide guitars. Also, a cheap hollow body makes a great slide guitar. Don't worry so much if the neck is a little warped because when you're playing slide, you're not concerned about bending the strings or even fretting the strings just so; it's all in the contact between your slide and the strings."

Vintage Blues Guitars: The Lowdown on Upscale Collectibles

Those old, beat-up guitars that you see in the hands of many blues players look like they have plenty miles on them for a good reason. They're all vintage guitars and each of them is probably worth a small fortune. At one time, an old Telecaster, Stratocaster, Les Paul, or ES-335, was just that, an *old* guitar. Now a whole vintage guitar market revolves around the selling, trading, and buying of vintage guitars for what non-collectors would regard as outlandish sums of money.

Used guitars can command such inflated prices because early models from the 1950s and 1960s feature superior construction and workmanship, plus they sound great, feel good, and look sensational, even the beat-up ones. If the guitar is in pristine condition, of course, then it's worth even more.

Consequently, many mint-condition vintage guitars are merely sold or traded from one collection to another, and never get played, which would diminish their value.

Blame famous rock guitarists for those astronomical prices

Folk musicians have been chasing after vintage Martin and Gibson acoustic guitars for decades (and jazz players have been more than willing to pay top dollar for arched-top vintage acoustics made by D'Angelico, Stromberg, Epiphone, and Gibson). The vintage electric guitar market started building up around the late 1960s when the first guitar superheroes came on the scene.

Blues-rocker Michael Bloomfield of the Paul Butterfield Blues Band was America's first guitar hero in the faster-louder sweepstakes. After Bloomfield was shown on the back of the first Butterfield Band album with a mid-1960s Fender Telecaster, suddenly the "Tele" — which suffered lackluster sales during the surf music era and British Invasion period — became *the* guitar for all aspiring blues players to own.

A late-1950s Gibson Les Paul model that featured twin humbucking pickups and a cherry sunburst finish became the first vintage guitar to gain widespread popularity. This was due in large part to its being the hard-rock weapon of choice for Eric Clapton, Jeff Beck, and Jimmy Page, whose work with Led Zeppelin made sure the model was popular well into the 1970s. A model that originally sold for $500 could fetch $2,000 by the mid-1970s. Today, $30,000 is not an unheard of sum to pay for one of these models, and some in mint condition have been sold for more than three times that amount.

Clapton started the next vintage guitar trend when he switched from his Les Paul to a 1950s maple-neck Stratocaster, the model seen on the back cover of the original *Layla* album. This sent the prices of old Strats soaring, although nowhere near those of the sunburst Les Paul.

Parts are more than just parts

When it comes to valuing a vintage electric, the playability and tone are considered less important than the paint color and other structural or visual details. Some collectors are not players at all; they're investors who want a vintage piece in its exact, original condition, right down to the soldering joints, if they can get it. This demand has driven up the prices for original replacement parts for vintage guitars. In fact, more money can be made by stripping a guitar for individual parts than for selling the guitar intact!

The next collecting frontier: Pawnshop and discount store wonders

Most vintage Fender and Gibson guitars are out of the price range of regular folks. A few years back, prices reached the point of absurdity. As a result, a new phenomenon occurred — the rise in popularity of the cheap pawnshop guitar.

Many collectors who desired instruments from the 1950s and 1960s could no longer afford Les Pauls, Telecasters, and Stratocasters. So why not collect guitars with the brand names Danelectro, Kay, Harmony, Supro-National, or Mosrite that provide that same 1950s or 1960s-era buzz at a fraction of the cost of Gibsons or Fenders?

These cheaper instruments, the Fords and Chevies of the American guitar world, were well-built and playable instruments, and each had a peculiar sound of its own. You can add to this list the Japanese-made Teisco models sold at discount stores in the late 1960s under a variety of brand names (Teisco Del Rey, Winston, Kingston, Kimberly, and Checkmate). Teiscos came in flashy colors and odd shapes, and sported a host of pickups and knobs (you can still occasionally find this brand of guitar at yard sales).

The story of Danelectros and leftover lipstick tubes

Perhaps the most unusual of the "ugly duckling" guitars were those made by Nathaniel Daniel in Neptune City, New Jersey, under the Danelectro logo. All Danelectro models, including those built for Sears & Roebuck under their Silvertone brand name, had bodies constructed of Masonite (yes, the same material used for kitchen counter tops), and had dual steel bars instead of an adjustable truss rod in their hardwood necks. (Hey, they were cheap!)

The quirkiest features of Danelectro instruments were their pickups, nicknamed "lipstick tubes" because their covers were actually lipstick tube caps bought in large lots, welded together, and re-chromed for the occasion. The unique twang that those pickups produced spawned numerous copycat models made by companies to attempting to build their own versions of the Danelectro.

The original Danelectro company went out of business in 1969. But, the look and sound of their instruments live on thanks to the work of Nashville luthier Jerry Jones. He builds excellent upgraded replicas of the most popular original Danelectro models (a *luthier*, by the way, is someone who builds stringed musical instruments).

The Ultimate Guitar Book by Tony Bacon (Knopf). This deluxe coffee table book features most of the famous — and not so famous — mass-produced and custom-made guitar models. This book includes everything from vintage Fenders, Gibsons, Martins, and Dobros to Danelectros, Supros, and stuff so wacky that you may have a hard time believing anyone would attempt to play them.

Now Hear This: Blues Music Amplifiers

The first guitar amplifiers produced in the mid-1930s were about the size of a cereal box and built with crude electronics. Although considered state of the art for their time, those early amps weren't always reliable, but when they worked they got the job done.

In the early 1950s, the tubes that powered amplifiers became more stable. As a result, the power ratings of amps got bigger and so did the amps themselves. Guitarists soon noticed that the amplifier their guitars were plugged into could totally change the sound of their instruments.

The modern guitar amplifier was created by radio repairman Leo Fender, the developer of the Telecaster, Stratocaster, and the Precision Bass. Fender's uncomplicated yet reliable products took the music world by storm. Nothing else came close to them for versatility and durability. In 1961, Fender debuted the first *piggy back unit* (with the amp and the speaker in separate cabinets). Those amplifiers were the prototype for the giant stacks of high-powered amps made in England by the Marshall Company. Marshall amps have been essential equipment for hard-rock bands for more than 30 years.

The five most popular blues amplifiers used in clubs, on concert stages, and in the studio are all Fender models. You can hear these amps on literally hundreds of famous blues recordings. Some of them were built 40 years ago and they're still on the job.

"The best amplifier I think anybody can get — that's really dependable — is a Fender. You can play outside or inside a club venue with them and still get the same sound. Some people think you have to spend a lot of money for a big amp. But sometimes those big amps are too loud and you can't use them in every situation. A Fender isn't that big; you can carry your amp and your guitar by yourself and always get a good sound."

Fender Bassman

The Bassman, Fender's first attempt at an amplifier for their electric bass guitar, ended up being *the* guitar amp of choice in the blues community. After guitarists plugged in and heard their sound beefed up with 45 watts of power through four 10-inch speakers, that was *it*. Popular with country, rock 'n' roll, and blues players, the Bassman was the first large-size concert stage amplifier. The Bassman also became the club amp of choice, good for anything you wanted to plug into it. Some blues bands on a tight budget have run a guitar, a bass, and a microphone into one Bassman and played just fine.

In 1961, Fender debuted the piggy-back version of the Bassman. By the end of the 1960s, the original tweed-covered 4-10 Bassmans from the 1950s had achieved legendary status. Used 4-10 models were sold for the same price (or higher) as a new amp. By 1990, the original Bassmans were selling for thousands of dollars and Fender reissued the 4-10 Bassman to great acclaim, sparking an entire amp reissue series.

Fender Champ

In 1948, Fender debuted the Champion 800, their budget-priced amp designed for guitar students. With only one power tube, one preamp tube, and one rectifier tube (a bare-bones power supply), the Champ nevertheless put out a solid four watts of power through a six-inch speaker. By 1955, it was known as the Champ, and boasted an eight-inch speaker by the following year.

The modest little Champ, the entry-level amp for players on a budget, soon found its way into the recording studio. Its minimal circuitry and compact size made it the perfect recording amp. And its single control for volume, tone, and power could dial in anything from a spanking-clean tone to the dirtiest blues sounds imaginable. A humble Champ on a folding chair was all the amplification needed by small combos working with acoustic instruments such as a piano, acoustic guitar, string bass, drums, or saxophone.

Aside from some cosmetic changes and a two-watt upgrade, the Champ stayed unchanged until 1982. At that time, changes to the power supply and speaker configuration signaled the last of the original design. Original tweed-covered Champs now command top dollar. However, many later models with the same power supply and speakers can be bought for much less, making them a great bargain right now.

Fender Deluxe and Deluxe Reverb

The Fender Deluxe was one of the three amplifiers designed by Leo Fender that were put into production in the late 1940s (the others were the smaller Princeton and the top-of-the-line Pro). The Deluxe featured a single 12-inch speaker and 20 watts of power, making it an ideal *combo amp* (combination amplifier and speaker in a single unit) for both club work and recording. The Deluxe amp was capable of delivering any sound from clean and twangy to dirty and distorted with just a twist of the volume knob.

In 1964, after numerous cosmetic changes, the Deluxe was reborn as the Deluxe Reverb. Still pumping 20 watts into a single 12-inch speaker, this new version featured tremolo and *spring reverberation* (the electronic signal passing through the springs made it sound as if the guitar were being played in a large concert hall). This model quickly became a favorite with studio musicians everywhere.

Fender Super Reverb

Debuting in 1963, the Fender Super Reverb had more in common with the old tweed Bassmans than with other more high-end amps. They featured the same power rating (45 watts) and four 10-inch speakers as the Bassmans. But the Super Reverbs also featured *tremolo* and *reverb* and put out more high-end frequencies than the original Bassmans.

This amp has become a staple on blues stages around the world. It makes just about any guitar you plug into it sound great (and it's a particularly good match with a Stratocaster — the Super Reverb's throaty tone brings out the best in the instrument). Right now, the Super Reverb is no longer produced and prices for the 1960s originals keep escalating, while many are still in regular, road-worthy use.

Fender Twin Reverb

The Twin Reverb (introduced in 1964) is the big daddy of Fender's combo amp line and *the* workhouse amp of road musicians the world over. Originally designed for big concert stages, it has the added benefit of not needing to be miked through a p.a. system. The original 1950s Twins pumped 30 to 50 watts of power into two 12-inch speakers. The Twin Reverb's wattage hit the 80 to 100 range and eventually an ear-splitting 135 watts by the late 1970s. All that extra juice meant you could crank the amp and still get a perfectly clean and clear sound that was loud enough to cut through a fully amplified band.

Twin Reverbs sound great with a variety of guitars, including the Telecaster. They're superbly mated with the Gibson ES-335 — the Twin Reverb's broad tone and power adds sustain to all hollow-body guitars. Original 1970s Twin Reverbs are still on the job at many equipment rental firms, delivering the same great tone that they did decades ago.

Fender never stopped making a version of the Twin, and reissued the 1965 Twin Reverb in 1991 using the original specifications, bringing back another classic into the company's lineup.

Fender Amps — The First Fifty Years by John Teagle and John Sprung (Hal Leonard). A deluxe, 256-page book that details every major and minor model of Fender amplifier ever made. Complete with a 30-page color insert — including a sumptuous foldout — this the best book on the subject of amps and a great read.

More than Just a Harmonica: The Blues Harp

Next to the guitar and the human voice, the most popular blues instrument is the harmonica. It's certainly the most portable of all blues instruments. Stick a harmonica in your pocket and you can play the blues anywhere at a moment's notice. The harmonica is also one of the most expressive solo instruments in the blues. Its sound ranges from a mournful wail to a guttural growl to a sax-like blast, clean as a whistle or dirty and distorted, and everything else in between.

The invention of the blues harmonica style

The harmonica wasn't always a mainstay of the blues. It became popular in the mid-1920s, replacing *pan quill pipes* as the small wind instrument of choice. The harmonica's popularity had a lot to do with volume. Like the electric guitar, the harmonica (also called a *harp* and sometimes a *Mississippi saxophone*) was loud enough to be heard over a crowd and the accompanying instruments.

Early *pan quill pipes* (or *panpipes*) were a crude affair consisting of three hollowed-out pieces of cane of various lengths tied together. Panpipes are played somewhat like a harmonica, but sound very different. The most famous panpipe player today is Zamfir, who's made a career through TV sales of his records.

By the early 1930s, harps began showing up on blues records, both as a solo and as an accompanying instrument. Early harmonica wizards (including George "Bullet" Williams, Sonny Terry, and DeFord Bailey) figured out how to hold the harmonica in such a way that they could bend and shape notes. The resulting "wah-wah" tones sounded much like the human voice.

John Lee "Sonny Boy" Williamson (for more on him, see Chapter 4) probably did more than any other blues artist to bring the harmonica into the modern age. Williamson's popular and influential 1940s recordings inspired numerous young players to pick up the blues harp.

The creation of the electric blues harp sound

The next major development in the history of the blues harmonica came in the wake of the post-War blues boom in Chicago. Newly arrived Mississippi blues artists amplified their guitars and added drums and piano to flesh out the sound. To keep up with the decibel count, harmonicas were amplified as well.

Musicians played their harps into cheap microphones plugged into tiny amplifiers turned up to the max. Players held both mike and harmonica tightly in both hands, and the resulting blast into the tinny mikes resulted in the massive distortion and broad, dirty tone that characterize the electric blues harp sound.

Several blues artists have claimed the distinction of being the first to amplify the harmonica. But no one popularized (or better exemplified) the sound of the Chicago blues harp than Little Walter (see Chapter 5). Walter had a sound the size of a pickup truck, creative ideas galore, and hit records to boot. He brought the blues harmonica uptown. By the early 1950s, blues bands may have survived without a drummer, but they had to have a harp player if they wanted to work.

The three types of harmonicas: Diatonic, chromatic, and tremelo

The most commonly used type of harmonica is the 10-hole *diatonic harmonica* (you'll also occasionally see a 14-hole bass version being played). A good 90 percent of all live or recorded blues harp music you hear is played through a 10-hole Diatonic. With the diatonic models, the harmonica reeds are tuned to produce the natural notes in a musical scale without sharps or flats, with the four middle holes providing a complete eight-note octave. The holes on either side of the four in the middle enable a musician to play chords for rhythm work.

The second type of harp used in the blues is the *chromatic harmonica*. It can play a complete 12-note octave including the sharps and flats. Each hole has four reeds — a blow reed and a draw reed for the two natural notes of the scale and two more reeds for the chromatic (sharp and flat) notes. The chromatic reeds are operated by a lever on one end of the harp. Chromatic harps are larger than the standard diatonics and the chromatics' heavier reeds make bending notes more difficult. Many blues harp players use a chromatic for minor-key effects, or when they're relying less on single notes and more on chording. Little Walter is widely credited with bringing the chromatic harp into the blues.

The third type is the *tremolo harmonica*. It features double holes, one mounted on top of the other. Each hole has two reeds that play the same note, but one is tuned slightly higher than the other which creates a tremolo (or echo) effect. Certain models are double-sided and are tuned to a different key on each side of the harmonica. All of this sounds pretty impressive but if you're planning on playing the *blues* on one of these gizmos, forget it. While fine for folk music, their multiple-reed setup makes note bending impossible and just isn't suited for playing the blues.

The top blues harmonica brands

Good quality harmonicas are manufactured by companies such as Huang, Suzuki, and Lee Oskar. (Former harmonica ace with the rock-R&B band War, Oskar is now making his own signature models with replaceable reeds.) But the Big Kahuna of harp makers is the M. Hohner Company of Germany. Matthias Hohner produced the first harmonica models in 1857 and by 1900 the company completely dominated the market. M. Hohner Company continues to manufacture millions of harmonicas every year.

Plastic — Great for bottles and bumpers but not blues harps

A word to the wise: Avoid *any* harmonicas made entirely of plastic, no matter how cute they look or how cleverly they're packaged. You can find plastic harps — and their cheap pressed-wood and even cheaper metal counterparts — displayed in bubble pack at your local discount chain store. Those are *toys*, not musical instruments. Every one of them delivers a tiny tone that sounds like an ant bugle. Save them for open mike night — at your local comedy club.

Their ten-hole Hohner Marine Band model was introduced in 1896 and sold for 50 cents. It quickly became the standard for blues harmonicas and has probably appeared on more blues recordings than any other model ever made. Other Hohner models that work well for the blues include the Special 20, Blues Harp, Pro Harp, the bargain-priced Old Standby, and the larger bass harp version of the Marine Band, the latter two both used extensively by Sonny Boy Williamson II.

Hohner also makes the best chromatic harmonicas, from the small eight-hole Chrometta 8 model all the way up to the gigantic 64 Chromonica model. The latter is the preferred choice of blues harp players looking to extend their tonal and musical vocabulary.

The Green Bullet mike — A sure shot of blues harp sound

Blowing a harp into a microphone meant for singing or speaking leaves a lot to be desired. It seriously lacks real blues "oomph." If you want to sound like Little Walter, Big Walter Horton, Junior Wells, James Cotton, or any other Chicago harp wizard (or if you even want to come *close* to sounding like these gentlemen), what you need is a Shure Green Bullet (see Figure 10-6), an Astatic JT-30, or a similarly designed microphone.

These brands are gloriously cheap, *high-impedance* (a fancy term having to do with sound pressure and volume) microphones that are shaped roughly like the pointed end of a bullet (hence, the name). They're built with an inexpensive *diaphragm* (the main working part of a mike) that captures only midrange and a few high-end frequencies, a desirable quality for an electric blues harp mike. In fact, the Green Bullet look and sound is such an integral part of the blues that almost all cheap harmonica microphones are called "green bullets," regardless of who manufactures them.

Because the diaphragms in these mikes are so cheaply built, the microphones tend to squeal (or "feed back") like crazy if they're turned up too high. Therefore, most blues harp players plug their mikes into a small amp that can be turned up to get that signature distorted sound. (The Fender Champ amplifier is a particularly good choice for this purpose.) The sound can then be miked through a p.a. system so the harp isn't drowned out by the rest of the band and the feedback problem is avoided.

Even if you've never seen a green bullet, you've heard one used if you've ever ordered fast food through a drive-through speaker. (The order-taker on the other end is probably using a green bullet.) Because of their walkie-talkie sound quality, many mikes used by radio dispatchers and ham radio operators also make excellent blues harmonica microphones.

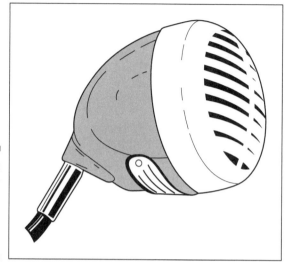

Figure 10-6:
The Shure
Green
Bullet, the
true blues
harp mike.

Notable harmonica players: William Clarke, James Cotton, Slim Harpo, Big Walter Horton, Little Walter, Jerry McCain, Snooky Pryor, Jimmy Reed, Sonny Terry, Junior Wells, John Lee "Sonny Boy" Williamson, and Sonny Boy Williamson II.

Suggested harmonica listening: Slim Harpo — *The Best Of Slim Harpo* (Hip-O/Excello); Big Walter Horton — *Mouth Harp Maestro* (Ace); Little Walter — *His Best* (MCA-Chess); Jerry McCain — *That's What They Want: The Best Of Jerry McCain* (AVI-Excello); Snooky Pryor — *Snooky Pryor* (Paula); Jimmy Reed — *Speak The Lyrics To Me, Mama Reed* (Vee-Jay); Sonny Terry — *Sonny Terry* (Capitol); Various Artists — *Sun Records Harmonica Classics* (Rounder); Various Artists — *Chicago Blues Harmonica* (Paula); Various Artists — *Harmonica Classics* (Rhino); Junior Wells — *Hoodoo Man Blues* (Delmark); John Lee "Sonny Boy" Williamson — *Throw A Boogie Woogie* (RCA); and Sonny Boy Williamson II — *His Best* (MCA-Chess).

The First Blues Instrument: The Piano

Before the guitar, the harmonica, and just about every other instrument except the human voice, the piano was *the* musical instrument of the blues. Starting around 1900 with the ragtime craze, the piano was the dominant instrument in popular music until the 1920s when the guitar took its place. Over the decades, piano players created myriad blues offshoots including boogie-woogie, New Orleans second line, barrelhouse, West Coast jazz, and Chicago blues (see Chapter 2 for more on the various styles of piano blues).

There's really no such thing as a "blues piano." A concert or baby grand, an old battered upright, or even a little spinet model (the kind found in churches and grade school music rooms) can produce boogie-woogie rhythms just as easily as they can play Sunday school hymns.

But don't expect to see a full-size piano lugged onto a nightclub stage. What you will find are electronic keyboards capable of sounding like a piano or organ and that can also produce a variety of "sampled" and synthesized sounds — which, in the end, makes the piano the most modern instrument of all.

Notable piano players: Albert Ammons, Leroy Carr, Professor Longhair, Big Maceo Merriweather, Otis Spann, Sunnyland Slim, Roosevelt Sykes, and Katie Webster.

Suggested piano listening: Leroy Carr — *Naptown Blues* (Yazoo); Big Maceo Merriweather — *The Bluebird Recordings, 1941–1942* (RCA); Professor Longhair — *Fess: Professor Longhair Anthology* (Rhino); Various Artists — *Chess Blues Piano Greats* (MCA-Chess); Various Artists — *Chicago Piano* (Paula); and Katie Webster — *Katie Webster* (Paula).

For That Big Blues Sound: Sax and Horns

Horns have always been somewhat of a peripheral element in the blues, reaching their peak in the blues during the late 1940s jump blues craze when big band sounds were emulated by small-combo lineups. Outside of a retro jump band with its full complement of wind and brass instruments (trumpets and trombones), the one horn you'll most find most often in a blues band is the tenor saxophone. (Strictly speaking, the saxophone falls somewhere between a woodwind instrument, such as a clarinet or oboe, and a military or orchestral brass instrument, such as a trumpet.)

The saxophone's breathy, broad tone works well for both expressive soloing and for honking along with the rhythm section. (Obviously, you won't find much in the way of horn playing on country blues or folk blues recordings.) The majority of horn and sax playing turns up on records made after World War II in urban music centers. In the Chicago blues style, Elmore James and J.B. Lenoir fleshed out their sound with two saxophones, both live and on record.

Notable sax and horns players: Lee Allen, Alex Atkins, J.T. Brown, Joe Houston, Illinois Jacquet, Louis Jordan, Big Jay McNeely, Red Prysock, A.C. Reed, Eddie Shaw, Sam "The Man" Taylor, and Eddie "Cleanhead" Vinson.

Suggested sax and horns listening: Wynonie Harris — *Bloodshot Eyes: The Best Of Wynonie Harris* (Rhino); Joe Houston — *Cornbread and Cabbage Greens* (Specialty); Elmore James — *The Early Recordings* (Ace); Louis Jordan — *The Best Of Louis Jordan* (MCA); B.B. King — *Live At The Regal* (MCA); J.B. Lenoir — *Natural Man* (MCA-Chess); Jimmy Liggins — *And His Drops Of Joy* (Specialty); Amos Milburn — *Down The Road Apiece: The Best Of Amos Milburn* (EMI); and Various Artists — *Blues Masters, Volume 5: Jump Blues Classics* (Rhino).

The Rhythm Section: Bass and Drums

Together, the bass guitar and drums form what's commonly called the *rhythm section* of a band. They hold down the beat while shaping and driving the rhythm of a song.

You won't find much in the way of flashy instrumental pyrotechnics in blues drumming or bass playing (no one could rightfully be called the Buddy Rich or Charles Mingus of the blues). When it comes to the rhythm section in a blues band, three words come to mind: simplify, simplify, simplify.

Which one's the bass guitar?

In the old pre-electric days of popular music, the bass guitar was known by a number of names — *string bass, upright bass, bull fiddle,* or *doghouse bass.* These four-string behemoths, which are mainstays of symphony and jazz orchestras, were a regular part of blues bands until the early 1950s.

Until the 1950s, no one was playing a bass guitar (acoustic or electric) in the same manner as a regular six-string guitar. And, if they were, no one was manufacturing a bass that was designed to be played like a lead instrument. If a blues band wanted to add a bass player, the band had to either hire someone with a big string bass or tune down the bottom strings of a six-string guitar to simulate a lower bass sound and play single-note lines bass-guitar style.

In 1951, Leo Fender unveiled a whole new instrument — the solid-body Precision Bass. The curved, fretless fingerboard of the string bass was replaced by an elongated neck that was bolted onto a solid guitar body that was larger than the standard guitar shape. The fingerboard featured frets that marked each position on the neck so that the bass could be played with "precision," hence the model name.

The new bass design was an immediate hit. Much like the dobro before it, every manufactured electric bass came to be called a "Fender bass," regardless of who made it. In the past four decades, several other electric bass models have been made by various companies.

You still see the Precision bass (called a *P-bass* by musicians) used quite regularly in blues bands, along with its more upscale cousin, the Jazz Bass. Also found in regular use (at long last) is an acoustic flat-top bass that produces a warmer "woodier" tone than standard solid body models.

If you want to tell at a glance who's playing bass in a band, it's the person with the four-string (as opposed to six-string) guitar. How can you tell from across the room how may strings a guitar has? Just count the number of tuning pegs on the head of the guitar.

Notable bass players: Willie Dixon (upright bass), Big Mojo Elem, Willie Kent, Jesse Knight, Jr., David Myers, Jack Myers, Brewer Phillips (bass played on a six-string guitar), and Mac Thompson.

The big beat: Drums

Drum sets used in the blues have come a long way from an empty cardboard box pounded with a rolled up newspaper or even the bare-bones snare drum, bass drum, and lone cymbal setup. (And — just for the record — for you drum solo enthusiasts out there, no equivalent of "Wipe Out" exists in the blues.)

The standard *drum kit* includes a *snare drum* (which makes a snappy sound, owing to the strings stretched across its lower head), a *bass drum* (it's the largest in the kit with the deepest sound), two or three tom-toms, a ride cymbal, a crash cymbal, and a hi-hat. *Tom-toms* (which are longer and narrower than the other drums in the kit) are usually mounted on the bass drum, except for the floor tom-tom that stands separately on its own legs, usually to the right of the bass drum.

The *ride cymbal* is usually the biggest one in the set, used for keeping the beat, while the *crash cymbal* is used for accents — it produces a high-pitched "crashing" sound that cuts through the rest of the percussion. *Hi-hats* are pairs of smaller cymbals set on a stand — usually to the left of the bass drum — and operated by a foot pedal that opens and closes them to produce various effects. (If a drummer isn't playing the ride cymbal, then he's usually marking time on a hi-hat.)

When the volume needs to be softened a bit, wire brushes are used in place of standard drum sticks. Because 99.9 percent of all blues is played in 4/4 time (counted out as 1-2-3-4, 2-2-3-4, and so on), the snare drum accents are generally placed on the back beat, stressing the 2 and 4 of a 4-bar measure.

"Drummers each have a different way of playing. You can go to other parts of the country and the drummers will be playing a different beat to the blues. A Louisiana drummer has a different beat than a Texas drummer, and a West Coast drummer plays differently than a drummer from Chicago. That's what helps gives blues music its regional flavor."

Notable drummers: Fred Below, Francis Clay, Elgin Evans, Sam Lay, S.P. Leary, Odie Payne, and Earl Phillips.

Suggested rhythm section listening: Big Mojo Elem — *Mojo Boogie* (St. George); Howlin' Wolf — *His Best* (MCA-Chess); Little Walter — *His Best* (MCA-Chess); Jimmy Reed — *Speak The Lyrics To Me*; *Mama Reed* (Vee-Jay); Hound Dog Taylor — *Beware Of The Dog!* (Alligator); Muddy Waters — *Live At Newport–1960* (MCA-Chess); Sonny Boy Williamson — *His Best* (MCA-Chess); and Hop Wilson — *Steel Guitar Flash Plus* (Ace).

Chapter 11

Making a Blues Record

Recording technology has come a long way from when Thomas Edison cut his rendition of "Mary Had a Little Lamb" into a foil cylinder. (Edison's record made the history books, but to our knowledge, didn't hit the charts.) In today's high-tech recording studio, audio signals are digitally scanned and then edited, copied, altered, cut, and pasted into a finished commercial product. An artist doesn't even have to be in the same room when a record is being made to contribute to the end product, and doesn't even have to compose the whole thing — it's now accepted practice to *sample* the works of other artists and then add them to the final mix.

Blues recordings (especially the early ones) have usually been relatively simple affairs that concentrate more on capturing a certain feeling than showing off any studio wizardry. In this chapter, we examine some studio basics to show you a little of how a musical group's sound is captured and then turned into a recording.

First, Some Recording Studio History

In the 1920s, when the first blues records appeared, the recording process was fairly rudimentary. The artist and the musical accompanists all sang and played simultaneously into a large wooden horn that picked up the vibrations of the singing and playing.

The sound waves were then transferred to a steel needle that etched a single, continuous groove into a flat wax disk, starting from the outside edge of the platter and continuing in to the center of the disk — a basic recording method that remained largely unchanged for decades.

One goof and you start all over

The wax disk that was pressed at a recording session was called a *master*, and all copies of that finished 78 rpm recording were made off that one very fragile original (hence the expressions "waxing a record" and "cutting sides"). This process often resulted in inconsistent sound quality. In addition, each performance had to be recorded in a single take, with everyone there, with no mistakes of any kind from any of the performers. One slip-up and the master was junked and the process started all over again.

Time-saving modern advances

The invention of the microphone in the late 1920s and the use of electricity in making records were the first big advances into the modern age of recording. By the end of World War II, the use of magnetic tape made it possible to rearrange recorded segments in order to perfect the sound of the finished product (and cut out the stuff that didn't work). The necessity of a wax master to make final recordings became a thing of the past.

Capturing Early Blues Recordings

The early blues recordings were made anywhere and everywhere blues artists happened to perform. Beginning in the 1930s, record companies sent *field recording* scouts to record blues artists in everyday surroundings. Makeshift "studios" included radio station broadcast booths, hotel rooms, or warehouses — places that had good acoustics or that were quiet enough that the performance could be preserved with a minimum of ambient noise. (Robert Johnson, among other blues legends, made a number of records this way.)

Alan Lomax and the song collectors

The first "portable" recording machines (some of them weighing more than 300 pounds!) came into use by the early 1940s. At the time, musicologists were hired to research and record American music for the Library of Congress. Probably the most famous person working in that field was folk song collector and biographer Alan Lomax. When he recorded Muddy Waters at Stovall's Plantation in 1941, Lomax captured an honest and unvarnished blues sound that was in sharp contrast to the cold precision of the major-label studio recordings of the time.

The sound may not have been the cleanest, but there was so much genuine feeling in the records that this "recording on the fly" technique became *de rigueur* among certain blues and folk music producers for the next decade.

For example, Howlin' Wolf was recorded at a West Memphis, Arkansas, radio station; B.B. King recorded his "3 O'Clock Blues" at a Memphis YMCA; and Elmore James was recorded off the p.a. system at a Canton, Mississippi, juke joint.

The '60s folk-blues recordings

Records made during the folk-blues revival of the 1960s were also pressed using bare-bones portable equipment. An album-format market really didn't exist for blues during the 1950s and early 1960s, and very few blues albums were recorded in stereo. But by the late 1960s, the renewed interest in the blues among music aficionados and new interest from the major record labels resulted in more professional-quality blues recordings. By that time, the majority of blues artists were working in real (and not makeshift) studios.

"Back in the 1950s, when I first started cutting records for Goldband Records in Lake Charles, Louisiana, we had a real small little studio with only one or two tape tracks to record on, maybe one microphone to sing into, and one or two other mikes to pick up the rest of the band and my guitar. It was real crude compared to all the stuff they have nowadays, but you learned to work with what you had and get the best sound you could. But, if you listen to those old records and you can still hear still some serious blues playing going on!"

Exploring a Recording Studio

In the rest of this chapter, we provide you with a quick tour of some of the gizmos found in modern recording studios, plus an explanation of a few common recording techniques.

The studio space and the control booth

If you've ever visited a recording studio (or even seen pictures of one) you probably noticed the two-room layout. One room of a recording studio is miked for sound — that's where the musicians and singers set up and where the numbers are performed. There's no set size for a studio space, nevertheless, most professional facilities can accommodate a full orchestra with a string section.

The other half of the studio is the control room. Sound is picked up by the microphones and fed directly to equipment in this room. The sound is then recorded, played backed, analyzed, and tweaked by the studio engineer, record producer, and sometimes the artists themselves.

Overdubbing: Hey, why not?

Generally speaking, an *overdub* is any recorded material added to the original session material. An added harmonica part, for example, is an overdub. Going back to fix some of your mistakes is overdubbing. Taking another swipe at your guitar solo (which can be recorded over the original or recorded separately onto another track) or "doubling" your vocal (singing along right on top of the vocal you just recorded) is also overdubbing. Bottom line: If it wasn't recorded live at the original session, it's an overdub. Overdubbing is used quite frequently on many blues recordings, but that wasn't always the case.

Blues music sessions from the late 1940s through the 1950s were rarely recorded in stereo, even when a full band was backing up the artists. No need (or desire) existed for most musicians to overdub their parts (with the exception of a few, including John Lee Hooker, who was experimenting with overdubbing in

the early 1950s). The truth is, many of the artists lacked the technical ability to play along with themselves and stay right on the money.

By the late 1960s, some blues artists began using studio tools more extensively. When B.B. King started fixing his flubbed guitar or vocal lines with a quick overdub patch, blues recording entered the modern age. Suddenly it was okay for the bass player or piano player to go back in and overdub a mistake, with no one the wiser.

While the all-live-and-no-overdubs versus the use-every-studio-tool-available debate still rages on between blues purists and fans who just want a good quality blues record, most professionals will tell you if you can get it all down live in one take, great! But, if you need to fix it a little, you can do so and still not loose any of the spontaneity that's a hallmark of the blues.

The mixing board

The centerpiece of any control room is the *mixing board* (or *mixer*) — a table-sized apparatus used to make electronic adjustments to sound values. It's here where the recording engineer and record producer manipulate various knobs and *faders* (slider buttons such as you'd see on a home stereo system) that adjust the volume of each microphone and control every aspect of the sound before it is permanently recorded.

Each fader controls a separate *channel* on the mixing board, and each channel usually has a single microphone assigned to it. The other knobs (besides the volume fader) on a mixing board channel are used to brighten or deepen the sound. This sort of adjustment is called *equalization,* or *eq,* for short. (Other effects such as reverberation or echo can also be added to the mix.) The recording engineer then determines where each element of the recorded sound will be placed in the final *mixdown* in which all the instrumentals and vocals are grouped together in a single arrangement.

Instruments that use multiple microphones are often mixed down to a predetermined number of tracks on the recording device. For example, a drum set that requires eight microphones to capture its sound may be mixed down to four tracks with individual tracks assigned to just the snare drum and bass drum and a stereo pre-mix on the rest of the set. This gives the engineer 20 remaining tracks on a 24-track recorder for the other instruments and vocals in the mix.

Sometimes mixdowns are done to achieve a certain effect (and not because of a shortage of tracks or microphones). For example, the massive drum sound on Led Zeppelin's version of "When The Levee Breaks," was created by miking John Bonham's drum kit with only two microphones placed at each end of a long hallway where his drums were set up. Another way of achieving a big sound is to place multiple microphones on an instrument or amplifier and then mix the mike tracks together, which produces a bigger sonic blast than if they were separated in the stereo mix.

Multitrack recorders

Once all the microphones are set into position and the miked sound is routed into the mixing board, the channel assignments are then sent to a *multitrack recorder*. Every tape recorder has its own channel or channels upon which the audio signal is recorded. These channels are called *tracks*. The two-track, reel-to-reel tape recorder of the 1950s has evolved over the decades into a massive 24-track unit that requires two-inch-wide audio tape.

In most pop-rock recordings, a song's *band track* is prearranged with the session musicians or the band and recorded first, and then the vocals are added later. This allows the musicians to record the instrumentals over and over again until the performance is perfect. Then the rehearsed-to-perfection vocals can be recorded onto the perfect instrumental band track making — ultimately — a flawless pop-rock record.

Blues artists in general dispense with trying to achieve perfection. Blues performances are most powerful (and visceral) when captured in their raw state without loads of piecemeal multitracking. Even after the invention of the microphone and magnetic tape, the greatest blues performances were recorded live with every member of the band playing all at once. Repeated attempts to capture a particular sound weren't needed. Once those blues players were in the studio, the message was: Make it "hot" or make it not.

Baffles

After the session musicians are set up in place and properly miked, a studio assistant rolls out partitions the size of car doors that are covered with carpeting and other padded material. These cushioned walls are called *baffles.* They provide moveable soundproofing that helps the engineer muffle any errant sound waves. Baffles are positioned in front of amplifiers, drums, or anything else that can produce a lot of noise.

Microphones are extremely sensitive, and the more you turn them up to capture some vocals or a particular instrument, the more of *everything* being played in the studio is picked up. A snare drum with its own mike and another microphone that happens to be nearby will overpower whatever sound it is you're trying to isolate. With no baffling between instruments and amplifiers, and between amplifiers and singers, miked sounds tend to "bleed" into each other, turning a professional recording into a total racket that sounds like a roofing job in progress.

This bleeding of sound is also called *leakage,* the dreaded nightmare of modern recording. Many of the old mono recordings from the 1940s and 1950s are filled with microphone leakage galore, which blurred the audio mix. Baffling eliminates as much bleeding as possible so that each instrument can be heard clearly on its own, and adjusted to the proper level in the final mixdown.

The isolation booth and the headphone mix

Singers (or singer-guitarists, as the case may be) who work live "on the floor" with the rest of the band usually do their vocals inside a vocal booth, separate from the other musicians, with their instrument amplifiers in another part of the studio. If a singer plays acoustic guitar, the guitar is miked separately to allow for a certain amount of vocal bleed in order to achieve a more "authentic" sound.

Isolating a particular instrument or amplifier in a separate room that has strong acoustics of its own (the room may possess a distinctive echo or ambient quality) can achieve some interesting results. Although reverberation and echo can be added later electronically, placing an amplifier in a heavily tiled space, such as a bathroom (where the hard porcelain surfaces and metal fixtures deflect and bounce the sound around the room), creates an effect that can't be duplicated any other way.

After every instrument and amp is in place and the lead singer is isolated in the vocal booth, band members can monitor how they sound through headphones that feed into the engineer's sound mix. Depending on how fancy the studio facilities are, each player will have a separate mix or the players will hear a mix of the overall combined sound.

Now it's up to the artists in the studio to deliver the goods. When that red light goes on, ladies and gentlemen, it's blues time!

Part V
The Blues Community

The 5th Wave   By Rich Tennant

"That's the third time tonight that's happened. They start out playing the blues, but by the end, everyone's playing a polka. I blame the new bass player from Milwaukee."

In this part . . .

*I*n this part of the book, we welcome you to the ever-expanding blues community — from the organizations, foundations, and societies that are doing loads of good work for the blues, to the best blues Web sites and places on the Internet where you can chat with other blues fans. We even give you ideas for throwing a party with a blues music theme.

Chapter 12

Blues Organizations Worth Checking Out

*B*lues foundations and societies are part of the glue that holds the blues community together. These groups are at the front lines in the effort to keep the blues alive and bring it to a growing audience. In this chapter, we supply you with some information on blues organizations that are dedicated to getting the word out about the blues.

Foundations: Lending a Helping Hand

Blues foundations offer help to artists in financial need. (Even today, many hard-working blues musicians are just scraping by.) These groups also promote music award programs and are active in educational efforts. In this chapter, we list some of the larger blues foundations you may want to contact if you're interested in becoming part of the effort to support the blues.

The Blues Foundation

This nonprofit organization is the largest and best-known blues foundation. Founded in 1980, its mission is to promote and preserve blues music around the world. The foundation's impressive list of sponsored programs includes the annual W.C. Handy Blues Awards, the Keeping the Blues Alive Awards, the Blues Hall of Fame, The International Blues Talent Competition, the Lifetime Achievement Award, and the nationally syndicated weekly blues radio program *Beale Street Caravan*.

The Blues Foundation encourages and recognizes the achievements of artists, writers, music promoters, and other supporters of the blues. You can contact the foundation at 49 Union Avenue, Memphis, TN 38103; 901-527-2583; or on the Web at www.blues.org.

Blues Heaven Foundation

This nonprofit organization was founded in 1981 by legendary blues performer Willie Dixon (1915–1992), who campaigned during his lifetime to ensure that the blues remains a cornerstone of popular music. Dixon established the Blues Heaven Foundation to gain recognition for blues artists and wider acknowledgment of the blues as an influential musical form.

The foundation sponsors the Muddy Waters college scholarship, a musical instrument donation program, and supports the Educational Blues Center located at the former home of Chess Records in Chicago. You can reach Blues Heaven at 2120 S. Michigan Avenue, Chicago, IL 60616; 312-808-1286; or at 249 N. Brand Blvd., #590, Glendale, CA 91203; 818-507-8944.

The International House of Blues Foundation

Created by the House of Blues chain of music clubs, this foundation joins socially conscious groups in an effort to encourage the instruction of art and music in public schools. The foundation was created in January 1993 when a group of Boston-area educators, civic leaders, and House of Blues representatives gathered at the Center for the Study of Southern Culture at the University of Mississippi. Today, the Foundation supports the House of Blues School Room, Resident Artist Program, and Blues Ambassador Scholarships. For more information, call the House of Blues at 617-491-2583.

MusiCares

MusiCares is an important resource for blues musicians in need of help. This foundation was established in 1989 by the National Academy of Recording Arts & Sciences, Inc. to ensure that music people have a place to go for emergency care. MusiCares directs its efforts to issues that directly impact the health and welfare of those in the music community.

MusiCares provides a wide range of health and human services, including a Financial Assistance Grant Program for emergency shelter, utilities, and other basic necessities; medical assistance; and treatment for HIV or substance abuse. You can reach MusiCares at 3402 Pico Boulevard, Santa Monica, CA 90405; 310-392-3777.

Other key blues foundations include:

The Blues Community Foundation: P.O. Box 607698, Chicago, IL 60660. This charitable organization helps blues artists in need and promotes blues education. It was founded by Bruce Iglauer, president of Alligator Records.

Foundation for the Advancement of the Blues: P.O. Box 578486, Chicago, IL 60657-8486; 773-278-1352 (contact executive director Mike Beck).

Rhythm and Blues Foundation: 1555 Connecticut Ave., N.W., Suite 401, Washington, DC 20036; 202-588-5566.

Societies: Bringing Together Blues Fans

Blues societies sponsor festivals, concerts, and radio shows, publish newsletters, and generally work to unite the blues community. More can be done to strengthen the network of blues societies in the U.S. In the mean-time, societies are keeping up the good work by fostering appreciation of an original American art form.

To find a blues society in your area, consult the *Living Blues Directory* published biannually by The Center for the Study of Southern Culture, University of Mississippi, University, MS 38677-9990.

Several excellent Web sites offer information on blues societies. The Blue Highway (www.thebluehighway.com) features tributes to blues greats, radio listings, a chat room, blues news, and links to other blues-related Web sites. BluesWEB (www.island.net/~blues/soc.html) includes loads of blues news, lists of e-zines, audio files with snippets of blues classics, and an exhaustive list of blues organizations (just click on the link Blues Societies & Foundations). For a list of just about every blues society in the U.S., head to (http://afl.angelfire.com/ca/kwiksilver/index.html), the page for American Blues Societies.

The following is a list of the more active blues societies in the U.S. and Canada. *Note:* Addresses and phone numbers are subject to change as society presidents change, but we did our best to provide as accurate a list as possible.

Blues Society of Indiana: P.O. Box 2263, Indianapolis, IN 46206; 317-470-8795

Central Iowa Blues Society: P.O. Box 13016, Des Moines, IA 50310; 515-276-0677

Detroit Blues Society: P.O. Box 3703, Troy, MI 48007; 810-262-6890

Hawaiian Blues Society: #75-5680 Kuakini Highway, Suite 308, Kailua-Kona, HI, 96740; 808-329-5825

Houston Blues Society: P.O. Box 7809, Houston, TX 77270-7809; 713-942-9427

Kalamazoo Valley Blues Society: P.O. Box 50507, Kalamazoo, MI 49005

Kansas City Blues Society: P.O. Box 32131, Kansas City, MO 64111; 913-341-1202

Lima Blues Society: 318 Boyd Ave., Van Wert, OH 45861

Linn County Blues Society: P.O. Box 2672, Cedar Rapids, IA 52406

Maui Blues Association: P.O. Box 1211, Puunene, Maui, HI 96784-1211; 808-242-7318

Mississippi Valley Blues Society: 318 Brady Street, Davenport, IA 52801; 319-32-BLUES

Oklahoma Blues Society: P.O. Box 76176, Oklahoma City, OK 73147-2176; 405-791-0110

Ozark Blues Museum: P.O. Box 691, Eureka Springs, AR 72632; 501-253-9344

Phoenix Blues Society: P.O. Box 36874, Phoenix, AZ 85067-6874; 602-252-0599

Piedmont Blues Society: P.O. Box 9737, Greensboro, NC; 910-275-4944

River City Blues Society: P.O. Box 463, Peoria, IL 61651

Sacramento Blues Society: P.O. Box 60580, Sacramento, CA 95860-0580; 916-556-5007

San Antonio Blues Society: P.O. Box 33952, San Antonio, TX 78265; 210-641-8192

San Luis Obispo Blues Society: P.O. Box 14041, San Luis Obispo, CA 93406; 805-772-4924

Shasta Blues Society: P.O. Box 964693, Redding, CA, 96099; 916-245-2117

Sonny Boy Blues Society: P.O. Box 237, Helena, AR 72342; 501-338-3501

South Skunk Blues Society: P.O. Box 607, Grinnell, IA 50112; 515-236-7268

Southern Maine Blues Society: P.O. Box 4703, Portland, ME 04112-4703; 207-627-7284

St. Louis Blues Society: P.O. Box 78894, St. Louis, MO 63178; 314-241-2583

The Pittsburgh Blues Society: 5850 Centre Avenue, Suite 606, Pittsburgh, PA 15206-3780; 412-362-1328

Tucson Blues Society: P.O. Box 30672, Tucson, AZ 85751; 520-570-7955

Washington Blues Society: P.O. Box 12215, Seattle, WA 98102; 206-632-3741

West Michigan Blues Society: 20 Division Avenue South, Grand Rapids, MI 49503; 616-458-1787

Wisconsin Blues Society: 2613 S. 51st Street, Milwaukee, WI 53219; 414-321-0188

Chapter 13

A Blues Event: Throwing a Theme Party

In This Chapter

▶ Picking the party music

▶ Dishing up a mouth-watering menu

▶ Planning a party for a large gathering

*T*he tradition of great blues get-togethers began decades back, when blues musicians and their friends and families threw weekend fish fries and other parties as a way to relax after a hard work week. These gatherings were a way of life for folks who later became famous blues legends. But no matter what you do for a living, you can get down to some serious jukin' and boogie-woogie your woes away by throwing your very own blues-themed party.

You don't need to be Martha Stewart to turn a simple gathering into a blues bash. No expensive delicacies or vintage wines are required. All you need for a good time is a selection of classic blues music from your own collection of CDs and records, or if you have some spare change and enough space, the music can be supplied by a DJ or live band. Add some soul food and a gathering of friends who enjoy the blues as much as you do, and the magic of the music will take care of the rest.

First and Foremost: Choosing the Music

Just like the best weddings, your music selection should include something old, something new, something borrowed, and the "something blue" is already taken care of. Try mixing blues music classics with new CDs from younger blues musicians. Ask guests to bring their favorite blues CD (don't forget to label each CD case with the name of the owner).

Make sure you have some blues standards on hand that everyone is sure to recognize, such as the following tunes that have been covered by a number of artists:

- "Got My Mojo Working"
- "Wang Dang Doodle"
- "The Blues Is All Right"
- "Sweet Home Chicago"

We asked Jim Feeney, resident blues expert at the Jazz Record Mart in Chicago for his recommendations. First, get yourself some of the classics that feature the main ingredients of the blues — harmonica, guitar, and red-hot vocals:

- Junior Wells, *HooDoo Man Blues* (Delmark Records)
- Magic Sam, *West Side Soul* (Delmark Records)
- Koko Taylor, *Live in Chicago in Audience with the Queen* (Alligator Records)
- James Cotton, Junior Wells, Carey Bell, and Billy Branch, *Harp Attack* (Alligator)
- Hound Dog Taylor and The House Rockers, *Natural Boogie* (Alligator Records)
- Room Full of Blues, *Turn It Up, Turn It On* (Bullseye Records)
- Clifton Chenier, *King of Zydeco* (Arhoolie Records)
- Stevie Ray Vaughan, *Live at Carnegie Hall* (Epic Records)

Next (and, this is especially important if you don't want to be your own DJ and change CDs every five minutes), buy some compilation CDs. That way, you get a variety of blues-playing styles performed by a number of artists. The following are some recent compilation releases:

- Various artists, *Roadhouse Blues "Living in the House of the Blues"* (House of Blues)
- Various female artists, *Red Hot Mamas* (Blue Chicago)
- Various male artists, *Clark Street Ramblers* (Blue Chicago)
- Various artists, *The Alligator Records 25th Anniversary Collection* (Alligator)

Dishing Out a Key Party Ingredient: The Food!

Potluck was the only way to cater the original blues parties, but you may have more options for putting out a spread. But, make sure you have plenty for everyone — you can't appreciate the blues on an empty stomach.

Figure 13-1 lists suggestions for an all-out blues party feast. For your party, you can pick and choose a couple items from each category to serve. To assemble the meal, ask your guests to bring their own dish (which would be the truly authentic way to create a menu), strap on an apron and prepare all the fixings yourself, or just head for the deli section of your local super-market (but we won't tell).

We've found some of our favorite soul food recipes in *Cookin' Up the Blues* by Tabasco Brand Pepper Sauce (McIlnenny Co.) out of Avery Island, Louisiana.

We recommend a buffet-style meal, so everyone can help themselves — and go back for seconds and thirds. Part of the fun of a blues party is the laid-back atmosphere. So don't work too hard on fancy table settings and centerpieces.

Make sure that if you're using disposable plates they're super-sturdy so they can hold all those ribs and gravies (and sweet potato pie) without collapsing.

B.B. King throws a blues bash

"My idea of a good blues party would be to invite over John Lee Hooker, Robert Cray, and Lonnie and Wayne Brooks, along with a bunch of other good friends. We'd serve up fried and smoked fish and some dip and carrots. We'd have beer but not too much hard liquor be-cause I'd want people to play music, dance, and then drive away safely. The first tune on the CD player would be my favorite, 'You're Always on My Mind' by Willie Nelson. Then we'd play lots of music from Jimmy Reed, T-Bone Walker, Buddy Guy, Bobby Bland, Koko Taylor, Bonnie Raitt — and let's not forget Etta James!"

Main Dishes

Barbecued ribs

Beef brisket

Chicken pot pie

Fried chicken

Meat loaf

Seafood gumbo

Shrimp creole

Spaghetti with meat sauce

Side Dishes

Cheese grits

Collard or mustard greens

Corn bread

Lettuce salad

Mashed potatoes and gravy

Potato salad

Red beans and rice

Figure 13-1:
This list is a
veritable
banquet,
so you'll
probably
want to
choose just
two or
three items
in each
category.
Ask guests
to bring a
potluck dish
. . . that'll
make the
spread all
the more
authentic.

Desserts

Brownies

Coconut cake

Sweet potato pie

Drinks

Beer

Iced tea

Lemonade

Soda pop

Mixed drinks

John Lee Hooker remembers "house rent" parties

John Lee Hooker says his favorite blues gatherings were the "house rent" parties he and his friends threw in Detroit in the late 1940s. Back in those lean years, making the rent required resourcefulness — and resulted in some raucous parties. "My friends would buy beer and make soul food — fried chicken, fish, cornbread. We made a little money by charging for the food and drinks," he remembers. "With the cash I got from my friends, I was able to pay my own rent, too." The entertainment? Why, John Lee himself.

Hosting Parties on a Larger Scale

Assuming that you're very ambitious and have some spare change for entertaining (or are in charge of your company's annual party), you may be thinking about throwing a large blues-themed bash — for 50 people or more at a venue such as a blues club or other rented party space. Now, what do you do?

We recommend that you hire a professional party planner. (Try looking in your local Yellow Pages under "Party Planning" or "Event Planning.") A professional can provide you with cost estimates, find a place to hold the party, work with a booking agency to hire the DJ or band, and hire a caterer. If you decide to go this way, here are a few tips:

- Be ready for significant costs in hiring a professional blues band (amateurs or novice professionals may charge much less, but we'll stick to what we know the professionals charge). Depending on their experience and how much they're in demand, bands may charge from $1,000 to $50,000 per night. Depending on the size of both the band and the venue, sound equipment and lighting can add another $1,500 to $3,500 per show.

- Hiring a DJ (disk jockey) costs less than hiring a band, but you still have contracts to sign, power to supply, and sophisticated equipment that has to be either rented or supplied by the DJ.

- Plan well ahead of the time you need the entertainment. The most popular bands are booked three to four months in advance.

- Keep the decor simple. As we said earlier, blues is not about the most expensive food or the fanciest atmosphere.

- Or, you can go all out with more elaborate decor. We know of one party planner who can turn a plain convention hall into a "blues club" — neon sign and all.

- Consider one other form of entertainment in addition to the band or the DJ. Your party planner may be familiar with actors and other entertainers who can bring additional life to the party. Why not hire actors to dress up like Jake and Elwood Blues and circulate among your guests?

Robert Cray describes his dream blues party

"My ideal blues party would be held in Memphis, where the blues scene is hopping on world-famous Beale Street every night of the week. I would make it a small gathering. My dream invitation list? It would include John Lee Hooker, B.B. King, Buddy Guy, Taj Mahal, Koko Taylor, Bonnie Raitt, Jimmie Vaughan, and the Brooks family. Not a bad crowd to hang with!

"Of course, I would cook everything myself that morning. To get in the mood, I'd put some Muddy Waters tunes on the stereo. Then, I'd get the black-eyed peas boiling in the pot and cornbread baking in the oven. When the guests arrived, they'd smell the most delicious aroma, which would lead them outside to the backyard, where there would be a fish fry and barbecue. On one side of the yard, I would have catfish and perch frying in a pan on the grill (served up later with hot sauce on the side, of course).

"On the other side of the yard, there would be a barbecue pit dug in the ground with ribs and chicken cooking in it.

"When my guests had eaten their fill, I would play some Howlin' Wolf CDs and then bring out my guitars and harmonicas and we'd all have a mini-jam. When the hour got late, I would put on the last tune of the night — Elmore James' 'Mean, Mistreating Mama Blues' and then lead everyone down to B.B. King's Beale Street club for an all-night jam."

Chapter 14

The Blues Online

● ●

In This Chapter

▶ Cruising to the best blues Web sites

▶ Checking out our favorite blues chat room

▶ Seeking out the best blues newsgroups

● ●

"Surfin' for Dem Blues" probably sounds like some super-session between Muddy Waters and the Beach Boys that never quite jelled. But, the fact is, blues lovers worldwide have staked out their claim on the Internet.

Numerous blues Web pages are yours for the browsing, from unofficial fan sites created on a shoestring to professionally designed multimedia presentations. The blues world is definitely jacked into cyberspace.

We've spent some time filtering through some of the best stuff on the blues on the Internet. In this chapter, we list our personal favorites of the bunch (but as you browse around you may find other destinations worth bookmarking).

The Best Blues Web Sites

The following sites are top-quality in terms of both content and presentation, plus they're just plain fun to bop through.

B.B. King

B.B. King's site at MCA records is outstanding. It includes sample stories from "On the Road with B.B. King" — an interactive biography on CD. Head over to

`www.bbking.mca.com`

Blues Access

Billed as "The Distinctive Blues Magazine," it has loads of information on blues festivals and blues labels, plus a message board and links to other sites. Point your browser to

```
www.bluesaccess.com/ba_home.html
```

BluesWEB

You'll find plenty of blues information and news, plus loads of audio snippets of blues classics, from the people behind the King Biscuit Time radio show. You can find BluesWeb at

```
www.island.net/~blues
```

Blues-Link

"If it's about the Blues . . . you can get there from here." That's what the page says and that's what it means. You can find links to Web pages about blues music and the people who make it at

```
www.blues-link.com
```

Blues World

Discover links to sites for magazines and radio stations, record labels, information on festivals and concerts, and more. Browse over to

```
www.bluesworld.com
```

Memphis Mojo

Even if you've never been to Memphis, you'll have a blast with this outstanding guide to the city that's home to Beale Street. You can find the site at

```
www.memphismojo.com
```

That Blues Music Page

Here, you'll find information on blues bands, blues societies, blues labels, and a guided tour of the Chicago Electric Blues. Tap in the following URL:

```
www.fred.net/turtle/blues.html
```

The Blue Highway

This site boasts tributes to blues greats, chat rooms, radio listings, merchandise links, blues news, and a guide to the best blues music on the Net. You can find it at

```
www.thebluehighway.com
```

House of Blues Online

Experience a fun and flashy site from the nationwide string of music clubs. Point your browser to

```
www.hob.com
```

Tri-State Blues

If you're looking for blues news and features, radio stations, clubs, festivals, and more for the New York, New Jersey, and Connecticut area, then head to

```
www.tristateblues.com
```

Lonnie Brooks Band

Head to the following Web site for pictures and biographies of Lonnie, Ronnie, Wayne, and the rest of the band, plus information on their tour schedule:

```
www.LonnieBrooks.com
```

Our Favorite Blues Chat Room

Most major blues sites also have a chat room. Our favorite is the Howell Productions, Inc. (HPI) Blues Chat Site, which won a "Keeping the Blues Alive" W.C. Handy Award in the category of "Blues on the Internet." (The W.C. Handy Awards, covered in Chapter 13, honor people whose efforts help to keep the blues a dynamic cultural and artistic force in the U.S. and beyond). You can find the HPI Blues Chat site at:

```
www.blueschat.com
```

The site hosts an impressive number of chats with artists who have in-cluded Kim Wilson, James Solberg, Jonny Lang, Magic Slim, and Syl Johnson, and on-location chats from clubs and festivals. HPI has also designed sites for many artists, and you can link to them from the Blues Chat site.

Designed like a house, each "room" in the site features something different (the library has all the archived interviews, the kitchen has recipes from great blues artists, the bathroom has a "graffiti message board," and the hot tub out back . . . well, that's where you're always welcome to join the chat).

Blues Chat features interviews from 10 p.m. to midnight every night, Blues Trivia at 10 p.m. on Mondays, and Chicago Blues Chat at 10 p.m. on Tues-days (Eastern Time on all).

Blues News Groups of Note

Newsgroups exist on just about every topic of interest, including the blues. Usenet newsgroups worth checking out include:

```
alt.music.blues
```

```
alt.music.blues.delta
```

```
bit.listserv.blues-l
```

```
rec.music.bluenote.blues
```

Part VI
The Part of Tens

"Well, you fooled us kid — that was one scorching blues solo you took on that triangle of yours. Especially when you went down on your knees and started playin' it behind your head."

In this part . . .

This is the part of the book where we test our mathematical skills. Each chapter contains ten tidbits for your blues-reading pleasure — ten ways the blues is reaching a wider audience and ten of the most sought-after blues records.

Chapter 15

Ten Reasons Why the Blues Just Keep on Growing

- -

In This Chapter

▶ Teaching the blues in the schools

▶ Recognizing artistic achievements in the blues

▶ Sending the blues around the world

- -

*O*ne of the main reasons we wrote this book was to educate everybody out there about the blues and the people who play it. The more recognition and exposure that blues music gets, the more people will appreciate the sound, style, and art that defines the blues. In this chapter, we list ten (or so) indications that the blues is not just staying alive but growing more popular all the time.

Blues Musicians Taking Their Acts into the Classroom

In 1978, the City of Chicago public schools introduced the "Blues in the Schools" program which is still going strong after two decades. Professional blues musicians are invited into grade schools, high schools, and community colleges to conduct classes on the history of the blues, famous blues musicians, the different style of blues, and how to write, sing, and perform the blues.

Musicians including Fruteland Jackson, Billy Branch, and *Blues For Dummies* author Wayne Baker Brooks have taught courses in which they cover topics ranging from *field hollers* (a centuries-old form of work song with musical shouts and call-and-response singing) to the guitar stylings of B.B. King.

Class members are also treated to live demonstrations of various kinds of blues, including music from the Mississippi Delta, the Piedmont region, and the East Texas Coast, plus minstrel, classic female, songster, and Chicago-style blues. (We talk about these various flavors of the blues in Chapter 2.)

The Blues in the Schools program has spread to other cities, including Boston, Los Angeles, and Seattle. For more information on how the schools in your area may offer a similar program, contact your local public school system or your state's arts council. Or you can call Blues Island productions toll-free at 1-888-912-5837.

The Blues Symposium

The Blues Symposium is the primary educational program of The Blues Foundation (for more on the foundation, see Chapter 13). The organization sponsors symposiums twice a year during the W.C. Handy Foundation weekend and at the International Blues Talent Competition in Memphis.

Panel members participating in the symposium include movers and shakers from all parts of the music world who address the important issues facing the music industry and blues artists. The symposium also includes musical performances and video presentations. For more information, call the Blues Foundation at 901-527-2583.

The Blues Educational Center

The former home of the legendary Chess Records label (2120 S. Michigan Avenue in Chicago) is now the home of the Educational Blues Center, the education arm of the Blues Heaven Foundation. (For more on the foundation, see Chapter 13.) The foundation now has plans to refurbish the historic building by creating a studio, gallery, and general headquarters for the foundation's programs. This effort is spearheaded by Marie Dixon, the widow of Willie Dixon, who founded the Blues Heaven group.

The Grammy Awards

Grammy awards are presented annually by The Recording Academy, whose voting membership (artists and technical professionals) honor excellence in the recording arts and sciences. Grammys are awarded in two blues categories — Best Traditional Blues Album and Best Contemporary Blues Album.

The 1998 blues music winners (for the 40th annual Grammy awards) included John Lee Hooker for Traditional Blues Album (for *Don't Look Back*) and Taj Mahal for Contemporary Blues album (for *Señor Blues*).

"We were happy to see the Grammy award producers give much more attention to the blues in 1998. But we'd still like to see at least one of the blues category awards televised. Also, we hope that some day the American Music Awards people consider creating a separate 'blues music' category (right now, soul/rhythm and blues are grouped together)."

The W.C. Handy Awards

The W.C. Handy Awards are among the most prestigious honors in the music industry. Awards are given out in 23 categories and the ceremonies take place annually in Memphis. Winners are selected by the voting membership of the Blues Foundation and by readers of *Blues Access, Blueprint,* and *Blues Revue* magazines.

Nominees for the 19th annual Handy awards included Luther Allison, Ruth Brown, B.B. King, Rod Piazza, Bobby Rush, Charlie Musselwhite, Joe Louis Walker, Smokey Wilson, Marcia Ball, Deborah Coleman, Debbie Davies, Sista Monica, Koko Taylor, and Toni Lynn Washington, and many other group and individual performers. (See Chapter 6 for more information on some of these folks.)

The Handys give a nod to some of the best records (blues or otherwise) released in any given year. If you're looking for a great reissue album, try the Handy reissue nominees for 1998: R.L. Burnside, *Acoustic Stories* (MC Records); James Harman, *Extra Napkins* (Cannonball Records); Jessie Mae Hemphill, *Feelin Good* (High Water); Mississippi Fred McDowell, *The First Recordings* (Rounder); and Jimmy Rogers, *The Complete Chess Recordings* (MCA/Chess).

Keeping the Blues Alive Awards

The Blues Foundation also sponsors the Keeping the Blues Alive awards, which are presented to individuals and organizations who have made significant contributions to the blues industry. For the past three years, the foundation has also presented a Lifetime Achievement Award that spotlights the recipient's career and features performances by musicians who were influenced by the honoree. Recipients have included John Lee Hooker, B.B. King, and record producer Jerry Wexler. The award ceremony is held annually in Los Angeles.

The Living Blues Awards

The Living Blues Awards have been awarded annually since 1993 through readers' and critics' polls conducted by *Living Blues* magazine. The results of both the readers' top choices and the critics picks are published in the magazine. The readers' perennial favorites are B.B. King, Buddy Guy, Luther Allison, and Koko Taylor, while the critics have tapped regular favorites Otis Rush, bassist Willie Kent, and drummer Sam Carr.

Critics vote for the year's best guitarist, pianist, singer, bassist, drummer, harpist, overall top blues artist, blues album of the year (in contemporary blues, traditional blues, soul-blues, and debut album), artist most deserving of wider recognition, comeback artist of the year, song of the year, and zydeco album of the year.

The Rock and Roll Hall of Fame and Museum

As the song goes, "the blues had a baby and named it rock and roll." So, it only stands to reason that a number of inductees in Cleveland's Rock and Roll Hall of Fame and Museum are artists from the blues music firmament.

The Hall of Fame inductees from the world of blues make for an impressive list. Among them are the following people we feature in this book: Bobby "Blue" Bland, John Lee Hooker, Howlin' Wolf, Elmore James, Etta James, Jimi Hendrix, Robert Johnson, Janis Joplin, B.B. King, Leadbelly, Elvis Presley, Ma Rainey, Jimmy Reed, Bessie Smith, Muddy Waters, and record label owners Leonard Chess and Sam Phillips. Plus, this list doesn't include the many artists in the Hall of Fame who are rhythm-and-blues performers or blues-rockers. In fact, without the blues, there probably would never have been a rock 'n' roll museum at all. (For more information on the museum, call 1-800-493-ROLL or visit it on the Web at www.rockhall.com.)

International Blues Music Festivals

The blues is one of America's great cultural exports. Take Europe, for instance, where they've enjoyed a lively blues scene and strongly supported blues musicians since the 1970s. The huge demand for live blues music overseas convinced a number of American blues musicians including Memphis Slim, Luther Allison, Champion Jack Dupree, and Eddie Boyd to make their homes in Europe at one time or another.

If you're planning the ultimate blues vacation, you can hook up with the concert scene in Europe (and Canada) during the summer music festival season (or at numerous blues concerts scheduled year-round). Here, we list some of the major festivals and when they're usually scheduled.

Belgium R&B Festival: Peer, Belgium — July

Bagnols Blues Festival: Bagnols, France — July

Montreal Jazz Festival: Montreal, Quebec — July

Montreux Jazz Festival: Montreux, Switzerland — July

North Sea Jazz Festival: La Hague, The Netherlands — July

Notodden Blues Festival: Notodden, Norway — August

Pistoria Blues Festival: Pistoria, Italy — July

Utrecht Blues Festival: Utrecht, Germany — April

Vienne Jazz Festival: Vienne, France — July

Blues Periodicals

For the most up-to-date information on the blues music scene and your favorite blues artists, check out the following magazines that are dedicated to writing about the blues. You should be able to find the following periodicals, which are published in the U.S., on the shelves of any large bookstore or music-and-books emporium.

- ✔ *Blues Access*
- ✔ *Blues Revue*
- ✔ *Bluespeak*
- ✔ *King Biscuit Times*
- ✔ *Living Blues*

A number of fine blues periodicals are published outside of the U.S. Ask about these titles at your local bookstore, or keep an eye out for them when you're taking that dream trip to foreign blues music capitals.

- *Back to the Roots* (Belgium)
- *Block and Lick* (UK)
- *Blueprint* (UK)
- *Blues & Rhythm* (UK)
- *The Dutch Ones* (UK)
- *Jefferson* (Sweden)
- *Juke Blues* (UK)
- *Real Blues* (Canada)
- *Soul Bag* (France)

Chapter 16

Ten Collectible Blues Records You Wish You Could Afford

. . . .

In This Chapter

▶ Pricing rare 78 rpm blues records

▶ Pricing even-rarer 45 rpm issues

▶ Finding out where to order these platters (if you have the dough)

. . . .

*L*ong before the advent of digital recordings and compact discs, and before "albums" became "CDs," records were pressed on vinyl (and, before that, on acetate). Because records made of vinyl and acetate tend to warp, scratch, and fracture like nobody's business, few old records exist that are in decent shape. This is especially true of some of the oldest blues recordings, which weren't pressed in big numbers.

If you add the rarity factor to the playable-condition factor, and throw in the legendary-artist-performing-a-blues-classic factor, you have the formula for a *really* expensive record.

How Record Prices Are Determined

The prices listed in this chapter are for original first pressings in pristine, mint condition. That beat-to-death copy you found at your neighbor's yard sale isn't worth a fraction of a gem-condition platter.

All of the following recordings were released as singles (the album format really hadn't been invented yet when these records were released). Although the prices listed in this chapter are *approximate* value, they'll undoubtedly climb higher and higher as times goes by and as the demand continues to exceed the supply.

Some Rare 78s and What They Cost

Open up your wallet and dig in deep for these collectibles. These prices aren't for the fainthearted (the record label is noted in parentheses).

- ✔ "Love In Vain" by Robert Johnson (Vocalion) — $10,000
- ✔ "I Believe I'll Dust My Broom" by Robert Johnson (Vocalion) — $2,500
- ✔ "Ora-Nelle Blues" by Little Walter J. (Ora-Nelle) — $500
- ✔ "Down Home Child" by Sunnyland Slim (J.O.B.) — $500
- ✔ "Broke Down Engine Blues" by Blind Willie McTell (Atlantic) — $400
- ✔ "Dust My Broom" Elmore James (Trumpet) — $150

Some Rare 45s and What They Cost

In the early days of the recording business, record labels were loathe to press certain titles (which weren't going to sell that many copies in the first place) in both 45 rpm and 78 rpm formats. This was especially true of blues records. Therefore, early blues records in the 45 rpm format are much rarer than their 78 rpm counterparts and thus command a higher price. For a record pressed in both formats, the more common 78 pressing sells for a mere fraction of the price of the rarer 45 version.

The following 45 pressings are not reissues — they were released at the same time as the 78s of the same title. Bootleg reproductions do exist and buyers should be careful when plunking down hard cash for a rarity.

- ✔ "Wolf Call Boogie" by Hot Shot Love (Sun) — $2,500
- ✔ "Combination Boogie" by J.B. Hutto & His Hawks (Chance) — $750
- ✔ "The Boogie Disease" by Doctor Ross (Sun) — $500
- ✔ "Tough Times" by John Brim (Parrot) — $450

Where to Find Them

For those of you with deep pockets looking to purchase the records mentioned in this chapter (and others like them), a good place to shop for vinyl rarities is Good Rockin' Tonight, P.O. Box 6180, Newport Beach, CA 92658. In addition to regularly publishing an updated price list, they also hold frequent auctions of rare vinyl records. Most of the prices listed here are from the Good Rockin' Tonight auction list and reflect either the minimum-bid asking price or the actual selling price of the record.

Appendix
CD Liner Notes

The *Blues For Dummies* compact disc is loaded with classic song titles by some of the greatest names in blues history. Fire up the disc to hear a dozen timeless blues tunes by the original artists.

(I'm Your) Hoochie Coochie Man

Artist: Muddy Waters. **Writer:** Willie Dixon. **Song publisher:** Hoochie Coochie Music (BMI) adm. By Bug. **Track time:** 2:28

Who better to kick off this CD than Muddy Waters singing a Willie Dixon song (that literally screams "Chicago blues") and backed by the first great electric blues band? The riff that begins this track and runs all the way through it is now commonplace in the blues, but when this record was released in 1954 it was as cutting edge as recorded music ever gets.

Juke

Artist: Little Walter. **Writer:** Walter Jacobs. **Song publisher:** Arc Music Corp. (BMI). **Track time:** 2:43

Little Walter was the modern genius of amplified blues harmonica and "Juke" was the tune that changed the whole scene for harp players nationwide. Cut at the tail end of a Muddy Waters session, this was the band's "break tune" — a number they'd play on the bandstand just before intermission. Originally titled "Your Cat Will Play" (and based on Snooky Pryor's earlier recording, "Boogie"), this became a Top 10 R&B hit in 1952 and launched Walter's successful solo career.

Sweet Little Angel (live version)

Artist: B.B. King. **Writers:** B.B. King and Jules Taub. **Song publisher:** Careers-BMG Music Publishing Inc. / Modern Music Pub. Co. (BMI). **Track time:** 5:07

B.B. King scored a hit with a studio version of this number back in 1956 (which was itself an adaptation of an old Tampa Red tune). But this is probably the most famous version of "Sweet Little Angel," recorded live before an energetic audience at Chicago's Regal Theater in November 1964. This track is off the album *Live At The Regal,* arguably one of the most influential blues albums of all time.

Killing Floor

Artist: Howlin' Wolf. **Writer:** Chester Burnett. **Song Publisher:** Arc Music Corp. (BMI). **Track Time:** 2:49

No one ever sang the blues more ferociously than Chester Arthur Burnett, known to blues fans worldwide as Howlin' Wolf. His sandpapery growl of a voice was inimitable and his backing band could drive the beat home like nobody's business. Wolf made blues records that were not just enormously influential but also highly adaptable by rock 'n' roll groups, including the Rolling Stones and Led Zeppelin, who borrowed a riff from this number to use in "The Lemon Song" on the album *Led Zeppelin II.*

First Time I Met the Blues

Artist: Buddy Guy. **Writer:** Eurreal Montgomery. **Song publisher:** Flomont Music (BMI). **Track time:** 2:16

These days, Buddy Guy is an internationally known blues artist with Grammy awards, hit records, and a Chicago nightclub with his name on the door. This track dates from early in Buddy's career. Recorded in 1960, it was his first hit, and a better introduction to his bracing vocal style and stinging guitar licks would be mighty hard to find.

Frosty

Artist: Albert Collins. **Writer:** Albert Collins. **Song Publisher:** Songs of PolyGram International, Inc. (BMI). **Track Time:** 3:02

The Master of the Telecaster began his career with a set of influential instrumentals that explored the cool 'n' icy side of his guitar stylings. Cut in Texas in the early 1960s, "Frosty" became a national hit. Featuring his signature staccato guitar licks, this record served as the calling card that brought Collins international acclaim and a raft of guitar disciples who continue to carry on his musical legacy.

I Pity the Fool

Artist: Bobby Bland. **Writer:** Deadric Malone. **Song Publisher:** MCA-Duchess Music Corp. (BMI). **Track Time:** 2:40

With a voice full of warm, honeyed tones one minute, and roof-raising, gospel-style intensity the next, Bobby "Blue" Bland single-handedly defined the genre of soul-blues. He has produced a steady stream of fine recordings since the early 1950s. "I Pity the Fool" was one of his biggest hits, featuring a super-charged, horn-laden chart from bandleader Joe Scott.

Okie Dokie Stomp

Artist: Clarence "Gatemouth" Brown. **Writer:** Plummer Davis. **Song Publisher:** MCA-Duchess Music Corp. (BMI). **Track Time:** 2:32

This number has "Texas blues" stamped all over it. Clarence "Gatemouth" Brown stormed out of the Houston area in the early 1950s playing a heady mix of blues, country, jazz, and Cajun music. "Okie Dokie Stomp" is a shuffle speeded up to a breakneck tempo, with stops and starts he negotiates with consummate ease. Guitar players across the country trying to learn Gatemouth's licks wore this one out right down to the turntable.

Rooster Blues

Artist: Lightnin' Slim. **Writer:** Jerry West. **Song Publisher:** Embassy Music Corp. (BMI). **Track Time:** 2:40

Louisiana blues man Lightnin' Slim sang the blues so mournfully it sounded like bad luck took up permanent residence right outside his door. But Lightnin' also had his joyous side. Witness "Rooster Blues," his biggest hit, a playful bit of up-tempo boogie bordering on the whimsical that made the national R&B charts in 1959. ***Note to parents:*** Because the lyrics of "Rooster Blues" sound almost like nursery rhymes, this song makes a wonderful introductory blues tune for young children.

Walkin' the Boogie (alternate take)

Artist: John Lee Hooker. **Writer:** John Lee Hooker. **Song Publisher:** Arc Music Corp. (BMI). **Track Time:** 3:00

Mississippi born and bred, John Lee Hooker moved to Detroit in the late 1940s. He promptly set the blues world on its ear with a collection of solo recordings that earned him the nickname "King of the Boogie," beginning with his first hit, the highly influential "Boogie Chillen." "Walking The Boogie" is a thinly veiled rewrite of that first big hit and was originally issued with overdubbed, speeded-up guitar tracks and a double-tracked vocal. Here we give you the basic track without any electronic gimmickry — just straight, natural boogie from the master himself.

I'm Wild About You Baby

Artist: Lightnin' Hopkins. **Writer:** Bob Shad. **Song Publisher:** MCA-Northern Music Co. (ASCAP). **Track Time:** 2:52

Lightnin' Hopkins was virtually a one-man institution of Texas blues and a multifaceted performer (he adroitly cast himself as both a solo folk singer and electric blues player). "Wild About You Baby," from 1953, captures him playing a blazing up-tempo boogie-woogie, tearing off spitfire licks that he played against his laid-back vocals.

Let the Good Times Roll

Artist: Louis Jordan & His Tympany Five. **Writers:** Fleecie Moore and Sam Theard. **Song Publisher:** Rytvoc, Inc. (ASCAP). **Track Time:** 2:46

Louis Jordan was the number-one purveyor of jump blues, a rollicking combination of party-time lyrics and horn-based boogie-woogie music that enabled him to cross over to the pop charts a number of times. "Let the Good Times Roll" makes for a marvelous closer to our compact disc compilation — the perfect invitation to a blues party.

Note: If the CD is damaged or defective upon receipt, you can exchange it by contacting us at (800) 762-2974 and press option 2 when prompted, or you can contact us by e-mail at techsupdum@idgbooks.com. Please note that phone service is limited to Monday–Friday, 8:30 a.m.–5 p.m. EST.

Note: This is an *audio-only* CD that can be played on any CD player.

Afterword

· ·

*B*lues music is America's music, and young people especially should know about the artists who helped to create the blues and make it such a popular and powerful musical form.

I'm glad to see individuals such as Robert Cray, Kenny Wayne Shepherd, Deborah Coleman, and other young talents playing the blues and carrying on the tradition of this music. My personal dream is to see more high schools and colleges teaching about Muddy Waters, Howlin' Wolf, and Bessie Smith, as well as Bach, Beethoven, and Brahms. To teach more people what blues music is all about — that would definitely be taking the blues to new heights.

B.B. King

Index

(continued)

IDG BOOKS WORLDWIDE BOOK REGISTRATION

Register This Book and Win!

We want to hear from you!

Visit **http://my2cents.dummies.com** to register this book and tell us how you liked it!

- ✔ Get entered in our monthly prize giveaway.

- ✔ Give us feedback about this book — tell us what you like best, what you like least, or maybe what you'd like to ask the author and us to change!

- ✔ Let us know any other *...For Dummies*® topics that interest you.

Your feedback helps us determine what books to publish, tells us what coverage to add as we revise our books, and lets us know whether we're meeting your needs as a *...For Dummies* reader. You're our most valuable resource, and what you have to say is important to us!

Not on the Web yet? It's easy to get started with *Dummies 101*®: *The Internet For Windows*® *95* or *The Internet For Dummies*,® 5th Edition, at local retailers everywhere.

Or let us know what you think by sending us a letter at the following address:

...For Dummies Book Registration
Dummies Press
7260 Shadeland Station, Suite 100
Indianapolis, IN 46256-3945
Fax 317-596-5498

BUSINESS AND GENERAL REFERENCE BOOK SERIES FROM IDG

COMPUTER BOOK SERIES FROM IDG